Visualiz... for Cha...

2nd Edition

PATRICK FANNING

NEW HARBINGER PUBLICATIONS, INC.

Publisher's Note

This publication is designed to provide accurate and authoritative information in regard to the subject matter covered. It is sold with the understanding that the publisher is not engaged in rendering psychological, financial, legal, or other professional services. If expert assistance or counseling is needed, the services of a competent professional should be sought.

Copyright © 1994 by Patrick Fanning
New Harbinger Publications, Inc.
5674 Shattuck Avenue
Oakland, CA 94609

All rights reserved
Edited by Kirk Johnson
Cover design by SHELBY DESIGNS & ILLUSTRATES

Library of Congress Catalog Card Number 94-067044
ISBN 1-879237-85-7 Hardcover
ISBN 1-879237-84-9 Softcover

Distributed in the U.S.A. primarily by Publishers Group West; in Canada by Raincoast Books; in Great Britain by Airlift Book Company, Ltd.; in South Africa by Real Books, Ltd.; in Australia by Boobook; and in New Zealand by Tandem Press.

Printed in the United States of America on recycled paper

First Edition
First printing July 1988, 10,250 copies
Second printing February 1989, 5,000 copies
Third printing July 1989, 5,000 copies
Fourth printing August 1990, 3,000 copies
Fifth printing March 1991, 5,000 copies
Sixth printing April 1992, 5,000 copies
Second Edition
First printing, 1994, 10,000 copies

For Nancy—
again, still, and always

Contents

Acknowledgments

My heartfelt thanks go out to all those who have helped me in the creation of this book: Matthew McKay for his encouragement and insistence on getting it right; to Kirk Johnson for his tireless editing; to Diane Eardley for guiding me through the thickets of the immune system; to Judith Kaufman for sharing her story; and to John Argue for his opinions and advice.

Introduction

Dear Friend,

Thank you for picking up my book. This is the second edition of a book I wrote originally in 1987, and I'd like to tell you about it.

Back in 1987 I was having a busy, stressful, but wonderful time. My best friend and business partner Matthew McKay and I had published our first five self-help books, and our company, New Harbinger Publications, was starting to make enough money to actually support us.

My wife, Nancy, had spent six months of the year before in bed, pregnant and in constant danger of miscarriage. But our son, Michael, had been born big and healthy, with no complications. Nancy was fully recovered and had gone back to work half-time as a nurse. We were living in an old house in Berkeley, California, and fixing it up as time and money allowed. Our life was full and happy.

I had written three books with Matt and other collaborators, but I'd never done one all on my own. I wanted to do a book on visualization, all by myself. I converted a corner of the attic of our old house to an office space, replaced my trusty Kaypro CPM machine with one of those new-fangled IBM clones from Taiwan, and I was ready to write.

At that time, Shakti Gawain's *Creative Visualization* had been a steady best-seller for eight or nine years. First published by a tiny company in northern California, it had been picked up by a big New York publishing house as a mass market paperback. It had sold well over a million copies by then.

Shakti's book was far and away the most popular book on visualization, and deservedly so. It was short, simple, warm, personal, positive, and inspiring. The "New Age" was in full swing, and *Creative Visualization* was one of its sacred texts.

Nevertheless, I had my own ideas about visualization as a very powerful tool for personal growth, healing, and positive change. But was there room for another book on visualization, published by yet another tiny company in northern California? I figured that I would "position" my book as the scientific, rational, thinking person's guide to visualization. I'd put in lots of historical background, cite lots of scientific studies, and back up everything I said with facts and real-life examples. My book would be a toolbox, chock full of useful exercises and practical tips. It would be a lot less mystical and "New Age" than Shakti's book. I wouldn't try to explain the universe—just cover the more down-to-earth applications of visualization for therapy, healing, and self-improvement. I'd sell a million copies and get rich.

Well, *Visualization for Change* got written, and I was very proud of it. I worked hard, did my homework, and produced the best book I could. But it didn't sell millions. It sold about 50,000 copies—a successful, profitable book, but not a best-seller.

Now it's seven years later. I've reread my book and I've reread Shakti's book. I see why hers sold millions and mine sold thousands. She was writing from her heart and I was writing from my head. Her book explained the universe and mine was a toolbox. Hers inspired its readers, while mine merely informed them.

Faced with updating *Visualization for Change*, I first thought I would just bring the literature citations and the history section up to date, add a couple of new techniques I had worked out, and let it go at that. But when I reread the book, I realized how much I had changed in seven short years.

Since the first edition of this book, I have moved to the country. I now work only half-time at book writing and publishing. The rest of the time I spend with my friends and family. We had a barn raising. We have a big garden and chickens and sheep. Nancy and I have time to spend together. Life is still full and busy, but less frantic. I'm not trying to sell millions of books and get rich now.

I have returned to painting watercolors, a love of my youth. I have learned to fly a plane. Both enterprises have given me a broader, looser concept of visualization than I had seven years ago when this book first came out.

I formed a men's group when I moved to the country, and Matt McKay and I wrote a book called *Being a Man* that shifted how I think about men in particular and people in general. Spiritual questions occupy me more now. I pay more attention to my dreams. I am more interested in understanding and accepting what is, and less interested in changing things for change's sake.

My son, Michael, is eight now. When I tuck him in most nights I make up a "stupid ghost story" to tell him. I've been doing this for four or five years now. It's taught me a lot about how creativity waxes and wanes, how imagination can surprise and delight.

When I reread the first edition of *Visualization for Change,* I realized that I no longer feel that I have to prove how good a scientist I am. These days I don't have such a compulsion to be objective and to keep my personal opinions and stories out of the text. I no longer have to prove that I can write a real, adult book, all by myself. I don't worry about not having a Ph.D. any more. I'm more secure in my self.

These changes in me have found their way into this second edition in the form of more personal examples, more opinions, more enthusiasm, and a greater trust in the scope and power of visualization. I'm especially pleased with the new chapter on visualization for pleasure, because in this brief life it's important to take time to have fun.

And yet, it's still a toolbox. All the practical, step-by-step instructions remain. I still believe that change is important and that visualization is a skill that anyone can learn to perform better.

I hope you like this incarnation of my visualization book. I hope you find it practical, helpful, and inspiring. I wish you success in making the changes you want in your life.

Most of all, enjoy yourself.

Patrick Fanning
Graton, California, 1994

I

Visualization Primer

1

What Is Visualization for Change?

"The greatest discovery of my generation is that human beings, by changing the inner attitudes of their minds, can change the outer aspects of their lives."

—William James

Visualization is a powerful tool for changing your life. Five minutes of visualization can cancel out hours, days, even weeks of negative thinking or acting. Three five-minute sessions a day can change a habit that took years to form and reinforce.

Everybody visualizes. You visualize whenever you daydream, remember a past experience, or think of someone you know. It's a natural, largely automatic activity like breathing or walking. This book teaches you how to improve your existing powers of visualization so that you can harness this automatic activity and use it consciously to help keep yourself sane, fit, healthy, and happy.

You probably have a lot of questions about visualization: What is it exactly? Is it like dreaming or meditation or hypnosis? Is it a mystical or religious kind of experience? How do you do it? Is it difficult? What can it be used for?

This chapter will answer the most common questions about visualization, and explain how to get the most out of this book.

A Definition

In this book, visualization is defined as *the conscious, volitional creation of mental sense impressions for the purpose of changing yourself.*

Almost every word in this definition is important for understanding exactly what I mean, and don't mean, by visualization.

The word "conscious" sets visualization apart from dreams, which occur in an unconscious state. Many people who study visualization are also interested in dreams and dream interpretation, and indeed there do seem to be some real connections between visualization and dreaming. But since this book focuses on the really important *skills* that you can learn, I've omitted any in-depth discussion of dreams.

"Volitional" means that you choose the time, place, purpose, and general content of your visualization. This aspect distinguishes visualization from hallucinations or visions. The visualization skills you will learn in this book work without having to take drugs or believe in any particular religious or mystical system.

"Creation" means that the process is creative. Your visualizations will often be fantastic or impossible. This sets visualization apart from normal perception or cognition, which is, hopefully, based in reality. Work on a problem using visualization is very different from just thinking about it.

"Mental sense impressions" reminds you that visualization is not all visual. Besides mental pictures, you will also create mental sounds, tastes, smells, sensations of temperature, texture, and so on. The visual component is usually the strongest, but all the senses must be brought into play to get the most from visualization. It's unfortunate that terms such as "visualization " and "imagery" and "imagination" stress the visual aspects of the process. But no other satisfactory term seems to exist in English, so you just have to keep in mind that "visualization" includes the use of all the senses.

"For the purpose of changing" is included because this book is about visualization *for change.* It doesn't deal with visualization used solely for entertainment, for relieving boredom, for generating pure insight, for exploring past lives, for communicating with the dead, for recovering lost memories and objects, for enhancing mystical experiences, or as part of the study of psychic phenomena. These endeavors are omitted not because they are unworthy of consideration, but because they are usually not concerned with the kind of changes covered in this book: self-improvement, therapy, healing, and pain control.

"Yourself" means that this book doesn't have much to say about using visualization to change *others.* Many people have pointed out the similarities between visualization and some of the techniques employed by shamans or witch doctors in primitive societies. These healers often visualize an imaginary journey for the purpose of healing their patients. The subject of the shamanistic healing of others is interesting, but beyond the scope of this book. You will learn to "change" others only by changing yourself and how you interact with people.

Types of Visualization for Change

Receptive Visualization

Receptive visualization is listening to your unconscious. In its purest form, you just close your eyes, relax, and wait to see what comes into your mind. You might set a minimal scene first, or ask a question and wait for the answer.

This kind of visualization is good for exploring your resistance to some change in your life, for uncovering your true feelings when you're ambivalent, for unearthing your personal images or symbols of change, or for clarifying what you really want to do when faced with several confusing alternatives. The information that comes up during receptive visualization is sometimes vague, like dream images. It often requires some interpretation before the meaning becomes clear.

Jennifer was a pediatrician just finished with her residency. She didn't know whether to look for a secure job on the staff of a big hospital or to join a private practice being started by someone she knew in school. Jennifer lay down on the couch one day and closed her eyes, with the intention of just clearing her mind and letting her true desires surface. She saw herself in a fog, and heard twittering noises like birds. She drifted forward and two buildings came into sight: a gray concrete structure and a cute little cottage. The cottage seemed welcoming and the concrete building seemed cold. At this point she opened her eyes and realized that the warmer, more personal environment of the private practice was more important to her than the security and excitement of a big hospital.

Programmed Visualization

If receptive visualization is listening to your unconscious, programmed visualization is talking to it. You create what you want to see and hear and feel in great detail and manipulate it according to a predetermined script. You stay in conscious control.

Programmed visualization is good for achieving goals, improving athletic performance, speeding up the healing of injuries, and intensifying images in general.

Bill was a carpenter who broke his leg on the job. While he was laid up, he used visualization to speed the healing of his leg. He would spend several minutes each day visualizing his leg bone as a splintered piece of wood. He saw himself straightening out the wood, pressing the jagged edges into place, spreading glue on the break, and clamping splints around it. He would make himself very small and go inside the bone, plastering over microscopic cracks as though he were fixing an old plaster wall. He saw the cells of his leg bone knitting together like the frame of a house being built. In this way he used very detailed, familiar images of construction and repair to enhance the natural healing process.

Bill was back on the job a full two weeks before his doctor had predicted he might be.

Guided Visualization

Guided visualization is actually a combination of receptive and programmed visualization. You set a scene in detail, with certain crucial elements left out, and then let your subconscious fill them in.

Most visualization is of the guided variety. In fact, it's nearly impossible to create a visualization that is purely receptive or totally programmed. Your rational mind is likely to add conscious detail to the former, while your unconscious mind tends to toss unexpected images into the latter.

Marilyn's visualization about weight loss is a good example of how planned and unplanned elements make up a guided visualization. As part of her campaign to lose forty pounds, Marilyn practiced seeing herself having fun in the future in her slim new body. One time she was visualizing herself dancing at her older sister's wedding, which was coming up in six months. She concentrated on hearing the music, feeling her handsome partner's arms around her, seeing the swirling lights, and feeling happy and attractive—all as planned. Then she "zoomed back" from the scene to get a look at her slimmer self, and was surprised to find that she was not only slimmer, but shorter. She looked like a midget. This surprised her and she snapped out of the scene.

Later she decided to explore the scene by re-creating it in detail. She asked her shorter self what had happened and received the reply, "I've lost so much weight, I'm disappearing." This unplanned, unsought-for information made Marilyn realize that one reason she had been overweight for so long was that it made her feel "substantial" in the world. Her weight made people notice her. Marilyn used this realization to reprogram her vision of the future to include a full-sized, substantial, noticeable Marilyn who happened to be thinner. She did start losing weight, and danced at her sister's wedding in a two-sizes-smaller dress.

The Possible Changes

Visualization as taught in this book is good for self-improvement, therapy, healing, and pain control.

Self-improvement covers a lot of ground. On the one hand, it involves getting control of or getting rid of negative aspects of your life such as smoking and overeating. On the other hand, self-improvement means acquiring or increasing positive aspects of your life by fostering creativity, solving problems, achieving goals, improving study habits, and excelling at sports.

Therapeutic change runs the gamut from reducing stress, bolstering self-esteem, and conquering insomnia to relieving painful emotions such as depression, anxiety, anger, and shyness.

Visualization techniques for healing and pain control work for a wide range of injuries, diseases, infections, and immune system disorders.

How To Use This Book

Read the next chapter on rules for effective visualization carefully. It contains the information you need to get started. You should refer back to the rules from time to time to refresh your memory and get ideas for improving your visualizations.

Do the exercises in chapters three, four, five, and six. They contain the basic skills that you must practice to become skilled at visualization.

Remember, this is a skills book. The whole purpose is to teach the skill of visualization for change. If you just read through without doing any of the exercises, you're wasting your time. You might as well toss this book into the garbage right now.

If you have trouble doing the exercises, but sincerely want to learn visualization, try using this book with someone else—a therapist, doctor, advisor, friend, or with those in a support group. Get the help you need to stick with the exercises. Set up agreements or contracts for how many times you will practice each day or week.

Once you have mastered the fundamental skills in chapters three, four, five, and six, skim ahead to the applications that interest you. But don't skip all the other chapters entirely. Each application chapter contains examples and insights that may apply to the topic of another chapter. You may find that a method of intensifying images used for controlling asthma is just what you need to sharpen your vision of the perfect tennis game.

The last section of the book begins with a chapter on the history and theory of visualization. You don't need to study history and theory to use visualization effectively—it's a largely intuitive, "right-brain" activity that you learn by doing. But reading about history and theory is interesting, and it can give your rational, "left-brain" side something to chew on while your more creative "right brain" is busy learning how to visualize.

See the last chapter if you want to try prerecorded or homemade cassette tapes, video tapes, visualizing while listening to music, visualizing with a partner, and so on. There you'll also find suggestions for further reading in the bibliography.

Putting Visualization in Perspective

Visualization for change is a powerful skill that works in harmony with other agents for change in your life. It augments and enhances everything you do, but it doesn't *replace* anything. Having bought this book, you cannot now fire your doctor, stop therapy, quit your job, drop out of school, and stop eating a balanced diet, confident that you will henceforth prosper by mind power alone.

It doesn't work that way. Visualization can ease the pain of a serious sinus infection and maximize your body's natural defenses—but antibiotics are still the treatment of choice. Likewise, you can imagine yourself breezing through a job interview, and it will probably help relax you—but success is more likely if you also practice your self-presentation with a friend, bone up on relevant facts you'll need to know, and talk about your fears with a professional counselor.

If you feel seriously sick, see your doctor. If you feel seriously disturbed, see a therapist. You owe it to yourself to muster all the help available.

2

Guidelines for Effective Visualization

"Everything should be made as simple as possible, but not simpler."

—*Albert Einstein*

The guidelines in this chapter are drawn from many sources: from the history of visualization as practiced throughout the world for hundreds of years, from various theories of how and why visualization works, from my own experience of visualization, and from discussions with many people who use visualization for different purposes.

These guidelines are a consensus, a distillation of the really important facts about visualization that most "experts" accept, regardless of their point of view. For example, the importance of employing positive as opposed to negative images is stressed by scientists studying pain control, by gurus teaching meditation, by therapists helping disturbed children, and by career consultants training executives in how to conduct a job interview.

In terms of changing your life and healing what ails you, the guidelines are listed in order of importance. If you just lie down, close your eyes, and relax a little bit three times a day, without doing any formal "visualization," you'll go a long way toward reducing stress and getting a refreshed outlook on life. Follow the next three guidelines—creating, manipulating, and intensifying positive sense impressions—and you will have mastered the basics of visualization. Following the remaining guidelines should come naturally after that, and you will become really adept.

For easy reference, the guidelines are summarized immediately below, followed by detailed explanations of each guideline.

1. Lie down

2. Close your eyes

3. Relax

4. Create and manipulate sense impressions

5. Deepen and intensify

6. Accentuate the positive

7. Suspend judgment

8. Explore resistance

9. Use affirmations

10. Assume responsibility

11. Practice often

12. Be patient

13. Use aids if they help

1. Lie Down

Lying down is best for visualization because it is the most relaxing position. Lie flat on your back on a bed, couch, or carpeted floor. Keep your hands and feet uncrossed. Try to tilt your pelvis a little to flatten the small of your back against the floor. Putting a pillow under your knees can help to take the strain off your back. The goal is a lying position that lets you release tension in all your muscles. None of your muscles should be working to hold you in a particular position. Your arms can be at your side, or your hands can be resting lightly on your chest or stomach. Wiggle around and experiment until you find the most comfortable position for you.

If you notice that your belt or collar is too tight, loosen it. If it crosses your mind that you should have gone to the bathroom or brushed your teeth or unplugged the phone, get up and do those things so you won't be distracted. Make sure it's warm enough. The object is to get as comfortable as you can.

It's possible to do visualization sitting or even standing up, especially after you've had some practice. But an upright position is not the preferred way. Some people find that visualizations done while sitting up seem dull and unimaginative, somehow contrived. Perhaps this is because they associate sitting with desk work, a very rational, linear, left-brain function.

2. Close Your Eyes

Let your eyes slide shut gently. Don't clamp them down with clenched eyelids. You might try rotating your eyeballs upward slightly and inward, looking toward the center of your forehead. This rotation of the eyes is recommended in several methods of meditation. Schultz and Luthe also used this upward and inward rotation as part of their Autogenics instructions. In 1959 they performed an experiment that showed an increase of alpha brain waves when the eyes were rotated in this manner.

But nothing is gospel. Some people find that the muscular effort required to keep looking upward interferes with their efforts to relax. So try several positions and do what feels best. You may even want to try looking downward. This method is recommended by some Yoga teachers, who use it as a way of getting in touch with the heart chakra. Do whatever works for you.

The obvious reason for closing your eyes is to shut out the real world, with all its myriad objects to look at. Shutting your eyes is also a signal to your mind that it's time to look inward. The mind makes automatic association with night, relaxation, sleep, and dreams.

You can't close your ears as well, but you should make sure you're in a quiet place where you won't be disturbed by noises like ringing phones, doorbells, and so on. Tell the people you live with that this is your quiet time, and ask them not to disturb you. Earplugs or headphones may help to shut out distracting noises.

3. Relax

This is the single most important guideline. More than half of the benefits of visualization come from simple relaxation. Relaxation by itself has been shown to be an effective way to reduce anxiety, depression, anger, fear, and obsessive thinking. Relaxation training is the obvious prescription for muscular tension and muscle spasms, but it is also highly effective in the treatment of headaches, ulcers, chronic fatigue, insomnia, obesity, and many other physical disorders.

When you relax, your brain produces alpha waves, which are associated with feelings of well-being, heightened awareness, creativity, and openness to positive suggestions. In a relaxed state, your conscious images will be sharper and easier to retain and manipulate. Spontaneous images will tend to come from deeper, more basic and authentic levels of your unconscious. There is a synergistic relationship between visualization and relaxation—they depend on and augment each other. You need to be relaxed to visualize, and visualization is very relaxing.

You are naturally most relaxed just before you fall asleep at night and immediately upon awakening, so those are good times to do visualization. If your goal is to visualize three times a day, you can get two of your sessions accomplished in bed, leaving only one to fit into a busy schedule.

You will be given extensive training and practice in relaxation in the next chapter, and later chapters will continue to remind you of the importance of relaxation. If you plan to use visualization to reduce stress in your life, there is a special chapter just for that purpose.

4. Create and Manipulate Sense Impressions

Involve All Your Senses

Vision is the predominant sense in humans, so most people find that visual images are the easiest to imagine. When I say, "Think of an apple," you probably get a visual picture of an apple. A few people will get a sound first, such as the crunch of biting into an apple, the wind in an apple tree, or some other sound they associate with apples. Such people are rare, and not at all to be pitied. They have much in common with great composers like Mozart and Beethoven, both of whom reported having a primarily auditory experience of the world.

It doesn't matter whether you are predominantly visual or auditory. You just take what you do naturally and build on it. Practice improves both the intensity of images in one modality and your ability to get impressions in other modalities. So if the word "apple" creates only a dim visual image in your mind, you can sharpen the image and add details to it with practice. After you have worked on the visual image for a while, you'll find that elements of sound or taste or smell or touch will be easier to add.

When you start to create images in your mind, they may seem to float in space in front of your eyes. They may also seem to be in the back of your head, the front of your head, on a movie screen, or even arising from your solar plexus or some other part of your body. There is no single "right" way to experience images.

Chapter four will give you extensive practice in using all your senses in visualization.

Transform Abstractions and Language Into Images

In general, it's best to find a distinct, concrete image or sound to represent sent words and ideas in a visualization. This can be very challenging. For example, it's possible to explore an abstract idea like "justice" by translating the concept into sense impressions: Try seeing "JUSTICE" written on a sign or a blackboard. Hear a voice say it. Associate a color like the black of a judicial robe, or visualize a symbol like the scales of justice. Make up a story and run it in your mind like a movie. Play around with your associations until you get some concrete images that you can manipulate. Be sure to pay attention to the emotional overtones of your images.

Sometimes seeing or hearing words in a visualization can evoke strong sense impressions. When this happens, language is functioning on an early, primitive level, at which a word stands for a real thing and calls that real thing clearly to mind. For example, I once made a harpsichord from a kit. It took a long time and I really got involved in the details of authentic keyboard instrument construction. I came to know every inch of that harpsichord, until I could just sound one chord and know its state of tune and adjustment. Now if I see or hear the word "harpsichord" in a visualization, it evokes a rich stew of images and full body sensations of making and playing my harpsichord.

On the other hand, nonmusical people may hear "harpsichord" and get no image at all. For them, the word is operating at a later, more "advanced" level, at which language is a set of abstractions or labels for conveniently categorizing objects and experiences. This kind of language is essential for getting by day-to-day, but it's pretty useless in visualization. You have to transform it into detailed images.

Trust Your Intuition

In deciding how to structure a visualization—figuring out what techniques to use, images to select, or sequences to follow—nothing is so important as following your heart. Choose the techniques and images to which you feel drawn. I may suggest that images in full color are best for vivid visualization, but you may find that the dramatic black and white tones of an old movie are sometimes just right. Or always right for you. You are an individual and have your own individual best style of visualization.

You will return to this principle again and again as you develop your skills. Particularly in the chapters on creating your special place and finding your inner guide, you will be given ample practice in evoking your personal, intuitive images.

5. Deepen and Intensify

Deepen Relaxation

This happens naturally, as you get more and more involved with your images. But you can be distracted, or tense up due to negative images. So take a moment to deepen relaxation by throwing in some deepening images: going down staircases or elevators, sinking deeper through water, melting, lying in the sun, or whatever fits in with the rest of your visualization.

Hypnotists know that the trance state should be deepened in stages. You get relaxed, let the trance stabilize, then relax some more, stabilize, go deeper, and so on. Visualization works the same way.

Intensify Sense Impressions

Add details. Vividness comes from realistic details. If you are visualizing a steam locomotive, you might start with a vague cylinder for the boiler, and several big steel wheels, and some sort of cab at the back where the engineer rides. To intensify the image of your locomotive, add a big headlight, a funnel-shaped smokestack with a red band around the top, lots of shiny nickel-plated knobs and levers and handles, the sound of the steam chuffing and hissing, the blast of the whistle, the clang of the big brass bell. Sprinkle coal dust inside the cab, and include the engineer's lunch pail and the fireman's shovel. Really see the gauges and dials with their quivering needles inching toward the red danger zone as the train pounds on through the night. You add details for realism the same way a novelist or a movie director does.

Add movement. Your real eye and your mind's eye are both attracted to movement. Move both the object you're looking at and also your imaginary point of view. To make your dream car come alive, see it from several angles, as if you were walking around it in the showroom or it is rotating on a pedestal. Then see it zooming down the highway or climbing a mountain road, with you in a helicopter above. Move your point of view into the car and see the road streaming toward you. Glance at the instruments and watch your hands move over the gearshift and steering wheel. Creating a vivid scene in your mind is like creative writing: verbs and action words have more impact than nouns.

Add depth. As in normal perception, nearer details are seen first in visualization. Many people visualize images on one plane, as if each scene were displayed on a movie screen at a set distance in front of their eyes. Add depth by deliberately creating a foreground, a middle ground, and a background. Your eyes, even though shut, will change focus as you imagine images at different distances, giving you a much more vivid sense of reality. It's like the difference between a snapshot and a stereopticon view, or a regular movie and a 3-D movie.

Add style. Visit art galleries or look at books, magazines, billboards, and other graphics to see the many possible styles that vision can take. Your visualization can be realistic, cubistic, cartoonish, surrealistic, impressionistic, and so on. It can look like your favorite movies, magazines, or album covers.

Increase contrast. In normal perception, your eye is drawn toward sharp contrasts and the edges of things, as opposed to dull contrasts and the middle of things. When you're trying to visualize a particular object with great clarity, take advantage of this fact. First picture a black outline on a white background, and let your mind's eye roam over the boundary. Then fill in the middle and add natural color, but keep the shape against a background that provides sharp contrasts.

Switch among different senses. In real perception, all your senses work together. You often hear of the "five senses," but for visualization, it helps to think of over a dozen senses or kinds of sensing:

1. Sight

2. Hearing sounds

3. Hearing the *direction* of sounds

4. Taste

5. Smell

6. Touching hard versus soft

7. Touching rough versus smooth

8. Touching hot versus cold

9. Touching wet versus dry

10. Touching yourself versus anything else

11. Feeling pain of various types

12. Kinesthesia—sensing your body's movement and position in space (including your sense of balance and the feeling of dizziness)

13. Internal sensations—nausea, hunger, fatigue, and the distinct bodily sensations associated with emotions such as fear, anger, depression, or excitement

Take advantage of the fact that all your senses work together to confirm and round out impressions. In the chapter on warmup exercises, you'll get a lot of practice starting with a visual image, adding sound, touch, taste, smell, and so on.

Include appropriate emotions. Don't just see yourself as president of the club. Feel in your body the pride, the excitement, the sense of power and accomplishment. Furthermore, create the outward signs of the emotions you expect to feel: images of yourself smiling, receiving congratulations and compliments, giving advice to grateful members—make the experience real and concrete by translating the abstraction "pride" or "success" into observable actions.

If contradictory or negative emotions come up while visualizing, allow yourself time to experience and explore them for a while. These feelings may be a form of resistance, or a message about your conscious goal—that it may not be what you really want or need at this point in your life. For example, if you see yourself receiving a long-awaited diploma, but feel sad or anxious during the visualization, explore the feeling. Give your sadness or fear a shape and a color. Make an imaginary character the spokesperson for your feeling and ask this character about it. You may find that graduation means more than simple success to you. It may mean sadness at leaving your school friends or fear of having to look for a job.

If negative emotions get very strong, pull back from the scene and visualize something else. If painful images persist, terminate the session.

Create metaphors. This technique is at the heart of visualization. Effective visualization does not progress rationally like a syllogism or a doctor's logical prognosis:

A. I have a tumor.

B. Some tumors grow smaller.

C. Therefore, my tumor may grow smaller.

This is a bleak statement. The only thing it has going for it is that it is positive (after all, proposition B could state that "some tumors grow larger"). This sort of verbal, linear thinking inspires few images and has no power. To make such a truism into a powerful visualization, you must use your imagination to make a metaphor.

The verb "grow" can inspire you to make an organic metaphor: a tumor is like a plant in that it grows. That's all a metaphor is—an example of the likeness between one thing and another. The better-known thing teaches you about the lesser-known thing. In this case, you probably know a lot more about plants than you do about tumors. So you use what you know about plants to make a series of comparisons, or metaphors, between plants and your tumor.

For example, plants need sun and water and fertilizer to grow. They are green when healthy, yellow when dying, and brown when dead. You cultivate the plants you want, and pull the weeds you don't want. From this simple knowledge of plants you can construct a very effective metaphorical visualization:

> My tumor is like a plant. I am shading it out, shutting off the sunshine of my worry and the water of my tears. I am shutting off the faucet of its blood supply, starving it. My tumor is turning yellow. It's dying. I chop at its roots with a hoe, dig it out like a weed. It shrivels up and turns brown. It dries up and blows away. Healthy, normal tissue like vibrant bean plants grows in its place.

Metaphors elaborate. They turn abstractions into visual and auditory footage you can screen in your mind and spend substantial amounts of time viewing, editing, and reviewing. Metaphors give you firm handles on otherwise slippery concepts.

Metaphor dressed up to go out is symbol. Goethe said that "symbols are the visible standing in for the invisible to reveal the unknowable." Gone are "like" and "as." The tumor *is* a weed, your blood is life-giving water, you really *are* chopping with a hoe.

This is the rich *patois* of the unconscious, the language of dreams. If you are skilled, you can master a conscious facility at simulating this language. You can come to speak a pidgin dialect of symbols in which you can couch many fruitful suggestions to your unconscious self.

6. Accentuate the Positive

In the Present

Approach each visualization session with a positive attitude. Expect success and expect to have a good time. If you don't see or sense something that you're seeking, assume it's there anyway. If you're looking for a way to solve a tough problem, and receptive visualization is not presenting any inspiring images, assume that the answer is there. Now just isn't the right time for it to come clear.

When you visualize yourself, *see yourself as basically OK and lovable in the present*, right now. Sure, maybe you smoke, maybe you're too anxious, or maybe you're unemployed at the moment. But none of that takes away from your intrinsic human value. See yourself as having high self-esteem in the present, before you even begin work on any of your problems.

During an ongoing visualization, negative thoughts may pop up: "This won't work.... This is stupid.... This'll never happen," and so on. Put these thoughts aside and keep your positive images before you. If negative statements persist, visualize them written on a blackboard, and erase them. Keep visualizing the blackboard and erasing the negative thoughts until they fade away.

In the Future

Include the positive consequences of attaining your goals. See yourself enjoying favorite activities in your new-found leisure, running, dancing, swimming, or whatever you would like to do. See yourself surrounded by loved ones and friends, popular and relaxed, having a good time. See yourself out of the hospital, enjoying a healthy, normal life. See yourself wearing new, stylish clothes, driving a new car, playing with a new tennis racket or skiing on new skis.

The Global View

It helps greatly to see the universe as a benevolent system in which there are plenty of material, emotional, spiritual, professional, and intellectual goodies for all. See humankind as perfectible. Assume that right can win over might, that you can always get what you need. In *Creative Visualization*, Shakti Gawain says, "Unless you can create a context that the world is a good place to be that can potentially work for everyone, you will experience difficulty in creating what you want in your personal life."

What if you just don't believe in a benevolent universe? What if you think it's a dog-eat-dog world, that only the fittest survive, or that the human race is basically greedy, petty, or weak? Visualization will still work for you. Maybe not as well, maybe not as fast, but it will work. Your mind is wired to your body in such a way that visualized changes tend to come to pass, regardless of your rationalized beliefs.

Many "New Age" teachers of visualization take the view that visualization taps some creative, universal force for good and growth in the universe. They say that it cannot be used for evil, ignoble, or selfish ends. I think this isn't so. You can use visualization to help you accomplish evil, and it will work just fine. It's a tool, not a virtue, and like any other tool it can be used for creation or destruction.

Thus visualization is a double-edged sword. It not only gives you the power to heal yourself, but also gives you the power to make yourself sicker. All the more reason to accentuate the positive. For example, don't create visualizations involving negative feelings about your body. Bernie Segal, author of *Love, Medicine, and Miracles,* tried to eat less by imagining seasickness before meals. He actually started to experience severe nausea and vomiting.

7. Suspend Judgment

Expect the Unexpected

Visualization is a right-brain activity—nonrational, nonlinear, intuitive, and so on. You can expect the unexpected. You try to visualize a red square and you keep getting a green Oldsmobile. You try a receptive visualization to uncover your deepest feelings about yourself, and you get nothing but old *Roadrunner* cartoons. Funny images make you cry and tragic images give you a chuckle.

Your rational, logical, left-brain self will get in the way all the time, with doubts and intellectual interpretations that throw you off the track. You will tend to want to censor images that put you in a bad light or seem too violent, too weak, too sexual, too crazy, or whatever.

Through all this, you must remember to expect the unexpected, and go with the flow of spontaneous images. When you begin to tap your intuition, it will push you toward areas that seem foreign to you. If you are a shy, retiring, contemplative type, your visualizations may well be full of action and conflict. If you are a competitive go-getter, your unconscious might serve up images of contemplation and acceptance.

Not only should you expect the unexpected, you should suspect the *expected.* Kenneth Pelletier, author of *Mind as Healer, Mind as Slayer,* says that during a receptive visualization, if you first come up with an image that is exactly what you expected, it's wrong. It's probably a coverup. Look deeper.

Time is simultaneous in the imagination, not sequential. For example, in sexual fantasies the mind keeps jumping ahead toward the climax, then flashing back to fill in the arousing details. When you're visualizing, don't worry if the sequence of events or cause and effect get mixed up. Your imagination is not linear, not sequential, not causal. Even if you are doing a carefully programmed visualization with a plot and dialog and everything, don't worry if you keep skipping ahead in the story or flashing back to earlier parts of the script. In fact, rejoice when this happens. It means that your intuitive side is getting into the action and making its timeless connections.

Take What You Get

Everything you get in a visualization comes from some part of you. It's all genuine, all you. Some parts are probably more important or interesting than others, but none of it is bad or wrong.

There is no right way or wrong way to do it. Only your way. Take what you get in an interested, nonjudgmental way. If you continually pass judgment and censor what goes on in a visualization, your imagination will dry up. Your creative, intuitive side will be laboring under a heavy load of critical static from your logical, judging side. This is especially important in receptive visualization, where you want to open clear channels to your unconscious.

Trust Yourself

All the experts give examples of images to use for various purposes, just like I do. Then we all say the same thing: Your image is the best. The best image for curing colitis is the patient's image. The best image for increasing sales is the salesperson's image. The best image for countering a phobia is the client's image. Even if these images don't make sense to a doctor, a sales manager, a therapist, or anyone else.

Trust yourself. Your mind is connected intimately with your body and your history. You know in every cell of your body, in every chemical and electrical shift in your brain, exactly what images to generate to perfectly represent and foster change.

8. Explore Resistance

Each time you use visualization to answer a question or solve a problem, ask yourself whether you really want the answer or really want to solve the problem. Do you feel you really deserve what you're seeking? Are you willing to take whatever comes up, even if it doesn't look like what you expected? If you have resistance to these questions, explore and resolve the resistance first. You need to be positive and single-minded to get the best results.

If you feel reluctant or ambivalent about visualizing a particular goal or other change, you may be afraid of confronting pain, finding a hard answer, or having to pay too high a price for what you want.

During visualization, you may "wince" inside or sense a voice saying no to something you want. Explore the no. Find out why you are conflicted. Finding out exactly what you want and if you really want it are the first steps to getting what you want.

9. Use Affirmations

To affirm something means to make it firm, to give it shape and substance and permanence. An affirmation is a *strong, positive, feeling-rich statement that something is already so.*

Strong means simple, short, and unqualified. *Positive* means that it contains no negative words for your unconscious to misconstrue. *Feeling-rich* means that the affirmation is couched in emotional language, as opposed to theoretical or intellectual terms. It is a *statement* in the form of a simple, active, declarative sentence. It is in the present tense to show that the desired result is *already so,* reflecting the timelessness of your imagination.

Here is an example of a very poor affirmation:

Except insofar as it is necessary to maintain a baseline of ethical conduct, I will not be self-critical, will not harm myself by staying up too late and working too hard, and will not dwell on my past mistakes.

This breaks all the rules. First, it's weak. It needs to be simpler, shorter, without qualifiers. Eliminating the qualifying first phrase would help a lot:

I will not be self-critical, will not harm myself by staying up too late and working too hard, and will not dwell on my past mistakes.

This is better, but it's negative. A positive version would go something like this:

I will be self-accepting, will take care of myself by going to bed early and working reasonable hours, and will let go of past mistakes.

We're getting there, but the affirmation still lacks feeling and it's still too long. One solution is to break it up into three affirmations, getting rid of the mention of bedtime and work hours, which are just examples of taking care of yourself:

I will accept myself.
I will take care of myself.
I will forgive myself.

We're almost home free. All that remains is to switch to the present tense, to show that the change is already so:

I accept myself.
I take care of myself.
I forgive myself.

Can this be improved even further? That depends on your personal, internal vocabulary—the way you habitually talk to yourself. You might prefer to make the obvious conceptual leap and reduce these three affirmations to an underlying truth:

I love myself.

On the other hand, maybe not. You may prefer to be more specific and stick with three affirmations that spell out what it means to love yourself.

How Affirmations Work

Affirmations reprogram or replace the negative self-statements that float around in your mind. They also function as reminders to suspend your judgments and set doubt aside.

During visualization, affirmations can be made silently, spoken out loud, written down in imagination or on actual paper, or even chanted.

Here are some affirmations that have worked for others. Pick out several that you like and rephrase them in your own internal language.

Every day in every way I'm getting better and better.

I have everything I need within me.

I accept and love myself.

The more I love myself, the more I can love others.

I am right here, just now, doing exactly what I'm doing.

My relationship with _____ is more and more satisfying. I can close my eyes and relax at will.

I accept my feelings as a natural part of myself.

I am getting stronger and healthier every day.

If you believe in Christ, God, Buddha, Universal Love, a Higher Power, or whatever, use them in your affirmations. Mention of spiritual matters can strengthen affirmations. Here are some examples:

Christ is manifest in my actions.

I am following God's plan for me.

I am in harmony with the Higher Power.

Divine love is guiding me.

Shakti Gawain makes much of affirmations. She says that they have three elements: *desire* (you must truly want change), *belief* (you must believe change is possible), and *acceptance* (you must be willing to have the change take place). All three add up to intention. She summarizes this notion in the affirmation:

I now have total intention to create this here and now.

Affirmations are especially important at the end of a visualization, where they function like posthypnotic suggestions. Shakti Gawain likes to end a session with:

This, or something better, now manifests for me in totally satisfying and harmonious ways for the highest good of all concerned.

This affirmation allows for an unforeseen, better change to come about. It eliminates the chance of "devil's deals," where you get what you ask for but aren't satified. And it purifies your motive, eliminating selfishness.

You should remember and repeat your affirmations throughout the day, when you aren't actively visualizing. Repeating affirmations during the day is like visualizing all day long. It keeps your unconscious focused on the change you are making. It reminds you to notice images in your everyday life that can become part of your visualizations. For example, when you're washing the car, you can think of washing all your tiredness away. When you put out the trash, you are setting aside your troubles and limitations so they can be picked up and hauled away.

10. Assume Responsibility

Visualization is a way of building up a sense of control in your life. A sense of control is an essential part of mental and physical health. Visualization works best when you assume that you are responsible for everything that happens in your life, even the parts that seem accidental or beyond your control. You are the cause of your life. You are in control, even of your autonomic nervous system and all the vagaries of everyday existence.

You should take responsibility for what you accomplish with visualization. Some theorists such as Shakti Gawain say that visualization functions automatically for the good of all—that it won't work for revenge, for instance. Actually, this isn't so. Visualization can accomplish harm as well as good, and it is your ethical responsibility to choose the good.

11. Practice Often

Visualization is tool for change that sharpens with use. You should use it daily and for many kinds of change.

Your early images may seem dull and lifeless, like mere verbal descriptions running through your mind. You'll feel like you're "making it all up." Later, with practice, your images will get more vivid, more like real seeing and hearing and touching.

Likewise, your first attempts to relax and shut out the outside world will probably be only partially successful. You'll only achieve a shallow relaxation and you'll be easily distracted. With practice, you will go deeper, faster. Soon you will be able to drop into an altered state of consciousness, with its profound relaxation and focusing of attention, almost at will.

Part of your practice should include fading out and turning off images, in case negative or unpleasant images arrive and need to be banished. For example, suppose you are creating a Garden of Eden setting as a special place in which to relax, and an unwanted snake slithers into view. You can have the snake fade out like a scene in a movie, or "beam" it someplace else, like an unwelcome visitor to the Starship Enterprise. Or you can delete it like a line in a word processor, or paint it out like an image in an acrylic painting. Or freeze it into immobility and turn it into a stuffed snake. Use your imagination. Practice changing and erasing images and you'll be ready for the rare unpleasant image that turns up.

12. Be Patient

Visualization is a skill that takes time to learn. It's like learning to ice skate. The first time out on the ice, you wobble and fall. The second time you have a little bit more control, and by the third or fourth time you can actually get around without falling so much. Then, if you get some coaching, you can refine your technique and start looking graceful and going faster. With further practice and coaching, you can begin cutting figures, racing, or playing hockey.

All this inevitably takes time, and proceeds in a series of steps, not in a straight-line progression. Athletes frequently find that they reach a "plateau," a level of skill at which they must perform for a while before they begin to improve further. Sometimes the plateau becomes a slump, and skill actually seems to decline for a while. The same applies to visualization. You have natural abilities that will improve with practice to a point where you "plateau out." Then books like this one or a teacher can be your coach. Over time, with coaching and practice, you become an expert.

However, there is a danger in approaching visualization in the same way you would learn to ice skate. Learning to visualize effectively is a matter of letting go of something, not forcing it to happen. This is when patience becomes of paramount importance—when you have to sit back and patiently take what you get, even when it's not what you expect or want, even when your internal critic is whispering to you, "This is dumb.... You'll never get it.... Give it up."

Patience must also be exercised *during* a visualization session. Often the first image that comes to your mind in a receptive visualization is an easy, "cover-up" image, hiding your real, less acceptable feelings about a person, place, or event. Keep open, be patient, and see what else comes up.

Like any growth process, visualization makes changes happen over time. A strong visualization experience needs to be integrated and resolved just like a strong waking experience. Your reaction to this morning's visualization may change by the end of the day or next week. Often, the answer you seek in a visualization may not come during the session, but surface spontaneously hours or days later.

13. Use Aids If They Help

There are many aids that can enhance visualization while it is going on: music, tape-recorded instructions, sounds of nature like surf or birdsong, sleep masks, ear plugs, rhythmic rattling or drumming, focusing on a yantra image, or chanting a mantra. In addition, you can enrich your visualizations by incorporating images or stories gleaned from reading fairy tales, primitive folklore, psychology, sociology, mythology, archeology, comparative religion, inspiring literature, and so on. You can use literature as a guided imagery exercise, living out parts of your favorite stories or changing the plots to suit yourself. You can also attend consciousness-raising events and discuss your visualizations with like-minded friends, steeping yourself in the life of the mind.

There is a long tradition of having a teacher, counselor, guru, or fellow student help you master a mental discipline. Whatever you call them, such guides and fellow travelers can be invaluable. It helps to have someone to talk to, to share difficulties, to keep you practicing, and to help you reach depths of understanding and heights of inspiration that might be out of reach for you on your own.

Another powerful aid is keeping a journal of your visualizations. You can record your experience and your thoughts and feelings about them while they are still fresh in your mind. Later you can go over your journal to glean ideas for future visualizations. Even if you don't go back over your entries, the mere act of writing in a journal is powerful. It will increase your ability to visualize in detail, develop your powers of introspection, and help you remember your visualizations. If you don't write your images down or tell them to someone, they can fade quickly from conscious memory.

It's important to mention one traditional aid that is not recommended: drugs. Some primitive societies and some holdovers from the late 60s and early 70s use drugs to loosen the imagination and provide extremely vivid or surreal visions. It's my conviction that in the long run, everyday drugs like alcohol, coffee, tobacco, tranquilizers, and marijuana only dull the intuition. Stronger drugs like LSD can indeed induce strange and vivid images, but these images are more properly classed as hallucinations. They are not volitional and not oriented toward change, and therefore not visualization as it is practiced in this book. So lay off drugs if you want to really get the most out of visualization for change.

There are so many possible aids that an entire chapter is devoted to them at the end of the book. Look there for full details on how to choose and use aids.

Contraindications

Visualization is one of the most natural, gentle, and safe self-help disciplines. There's not much that can go wrong. However, there are people for whom visualization is not recommended, and situations in which it won't work well.

For example, if you have persistent visions of blood, death, violence, or hurting people, you have a problem. See a therapist right away.

You have a problem if you spend so much time daydreaming that you have trouble getting along in the real world. If your fantasies keep you from getting places on time, keeping commitments, getting schoolwork done, making simple plans for the future, and so on, then visualization may not be for you. You must be able to confine your visualization sessions to a reasonable amount of leisure time.

You have a problem if you put all your energy into visualizing impossible goals that you can never reach. The goals you set should be a stretch for you, but not entirely out of reach. Measure what you want against what is possible for someone in your situation to get. If you're not sure about a goal, talk to someone about it.

You have a problem if you find yourself investing a lot of energy in unrealistic fantasies in which you find the perfect lover or the ideal romantic relationship, get even for ancient injuries, or perform incredible feats of strength, daring, or invention that you don't possess. Visualization cannot help you attain the unattainable.

If your self-esteem is low and you don't believe you deserve good things, then you will have trouble visualizing them into becoming real. Work first on your self-esteem by using the self-esteem chapter in this book or by reading *Self-Esteem*, a book I wrote with my psychologist friend Matthew McKay.

Review the Basics From Time to Time

I've covered a lot of ground in this chapter. You won't retain it all. So each time you begin a new visualization adventure, return to this chapter and review these guidelines. Suggestions that don't seem important to you now may make more sense on a second or third or tenth reading. A guideline that you have just skimmed over may later prove to be exactly what you need to open new vistas or solve a problem that has you stuck.

II

Fundamental Practices

3

Relaxation

"A quiet mind cureth all."

—*Robert Burton*

"Close your eyes and relax."

This is how every visualization in this book starts, with instructions to close off the outside world by shutting your eyes and to open up the inside world by relaxing your body.

Relaxation is the single most important part of visualization for change. It's important for two reasons.

First, relaxation by itself has great healing, calming powers. Relaxing your muscles makes your breathing slow down, your heart beat slower, and your skin perspire less. If you relax deeply enough, often enough, it will lower your blood pressure. While you're completely relaxed, it's impossible to feel negative emotions such as fear, anxiety, depression, or anger—they all depend on a minimum level of physical arousal before they can be felt. This is the basis of relaxation's great healing power. It returns you to a natural balance, a centered, calm state of homeostasis in which your body heals itself and your mind is at peace.

Relaxation is most often recommended for the treatment of muscular tension, anxiety, insomnia, depression, fatigue, irritable bowel, muscle spasms, neck and back pain, and high blood pressure. Actually, it will aid healing in any part of your body. Add visualization to relaxation, and its power and scope are increased enormously.

The second reason relaxation is important is that it is an absolute prerequisite to effective visualization. Effective visualization takes place when your brain is emitting alpha waves. These waves can only occur when your body is very relaxed.

By "effective" visualizing, I mean creating rich, varied sights, sounds, smells, and so on, using all your senses. When you're under stress, your muscles tense up, your focus centers on problems and dangers, and you "keep a sharp eye out" for trouble. Literally—under stress, most people pay attention only to visual information and they don't hear or smell or feel much. Hence the expression, "You've got to stop and smell the roses along the way." When you relax, you can recall all the sensory components of a scene, increasing the vividness of your visualizations immensely.

Effective visualizing also means that unconscious memories, assumptions, and feelings are accessible. What you are aware of as you go around on the average day is only the tip of a very large iceberg. Unconsciously, you perceive and file away a lot more than you have time to notice. In a relaxed state, you can call up this unconscious information and use it to heal, to solve problems, and to change your life. It's as if your senses were a radio receiver. When you relax, you open up the width of your receiver band. Where before you only got AM, now you get AM, FM, short wave, police calls, the coast guard, foreign stations, alien spacecraft, Jack Benny, the Shadow—broadcasts from all other places and times.

Actually, it's somewhat artificial to separate relaxation and visualization—to talk about one coming before the other, or one existing independently from the other. They go together. They're two sides of the same coin, halves of the same unitary experience. Whenever you consciously try to relax your body, you do it by calling up images and other sense impressions, whether you're aware of them or call this process "visualization" or not. And when you daydream, creating pleasant scenes in your mind, your body automatically relaxes, just as if you were actually experiencing the pleasant scene.

Progressive Muscle Relaxation

In 1929 a Chicago physician named Edmund Jacobson published *Progressive Relaxation,* a book describing a simple procedure of deliberately tensing and releasing major muscle groups in sequence to achieve total body relaxation. Sixty years later, Jacobson's methods are still the basis of nearly all relaxation training.

The procedure is easy. You start with your arms, tensing the various muscles, noticing what that feels like, then relaxing the muscles and noticing what relaxation feels like. You go on to do the same thing with the muscles associated with your head, then your torso, and finally your legs. You do each muscle group at least twice, with more repetitions for especially tense areas.

Fifteen minutes, twice a day is the recommended schedule. In one or two weeks you should be able to reach deep levels of relaxation fairly quickly. You will know which muscles need more relaxation and you'll be very sensitive to the buildup of tension in your body. After you've mastered the basic procedure, you'll probably want to try the shorthand procedures and develop your own routine for quick relaxation prior to visualization.

Basic Procedure

Lie down in a comfortable position with your arms and legs uncrossed. You can put a pillow under your knees to take strain off your lower back. Close your eyes gently. Now clench your right fist, tighter and tighter, studying the tension as you do so. Keep it clenched and notice the tension in your fist, hand, and forearm. Clench the muscles for about five seconds. Now relax. Feel the looseness in your right hand, and notice the contrast with the tension. Concentrate on the feeling of relaxation for about fifteen seconds. Repeat this procedure with your right fist again, always noticing as you relax that this is the opposite of tension. Repeat the entire procedure with your left fist, then both fists at once.

Now bend your elbows and tense your biceps. Tense them as hard as you can and observe the feeling of tautness. Relax. Straighten out your arms. Let the relaxation develop and feel that difference. Repeat this, and all the following steps at least once. Hold tension for about five seconds and concentrate on relaxation for about fifteen seconds.

Turn your attention to your head. Wrinkle your forehead as tight as you can. Now relax and smooth it out. Let yourself imagine your entire forehead and scalp becoming smooth and at rest. Now frown and notice the strain spreading throughout your forehead. Let go again. Allow your brow to become smooth again. Squint your eyes shut tightly. Look for the tension. Relax your eyes until they're just lightly closed. Now clench your jaw. Bite hard and notice the tension throughout your jaw. (A lot of tension can build up in your jaw muscles.) Now relax your jaw. When it's relaxed your lips will be slightly parted. Let yourself really appreciate the contrast between tension and relaxation. Now press your tongue against the roof of your mouth. Feel the ache in the back of your mouth and down into your throat. Relax. Press your lips forward now, purse them into an "O." Relax your lips. Notice now that your forehead, scalp, eyes, jaw, tongue and lips are all relaxed.

Press your head back as far as it can comfortably go and observe the tension in your neck. (A lot of people carry tension around in their tight neck muscles.) Roll your head to the right and feel the changing locus of stress. Roll it to the left. Straighten your head and bring it forward, pressing your chin against your chest. Feel the tension in your throat and the back of your neck. Relax, allowing your head to return to a comfortable position. Let the relaxation deepen. Now shrug your shoulders. Keep the tension as you hunch your head down between your shoulders. Relax your shoulders. Drop them back and feel the relaxation spreading through your neck, throat, and shoulders—pure relaxation, deeper and deeper.

Give your entire body a chance to relax. Feel the comfort and the heaviness. Now breath in and fill your lungs completely. Hold your breath. Notice the tension. Now exhale, letting your chest become loose. Let the air hiss out. Continue relaxing, letting your breath come freely and gently. Repeat this several times, noticing the tension draining from your body as you exhale. Next, tighten your stomach and hold it tight. Note the tension, then relax. Now place your hand on your stomach. Breathe deeply into your stomach, pushing your hand up. Hold, and relax. Feel the contrast of relaxation as the air rushes out.

Now arch your back, without straining. (If you have back trouble, skip this part. Don't tense your back muscles, but just concentrate on letting tension drain from them.) Keep the rest of your body as relaxed as possible. Focus on the tension in your lower back. Now relax, deeper and deeper.

Tighten your buttocks and thighs. Flex your thighs by pressing your heels downward as hard as you can. Relax and feel the difference. Now curl your toes downward to make your calves tense. Do this gradually, since in some people this procedure can cause cramps in the sole of the foot. Study the tension. Relax. Now bend your toes back toward your face, creating tension in your shins. Relax again.

Feel the heaviness throughout your lower body as the relaxation deepens. Relax your feet, ankles, calves, shins, knees, thighs, and buttocks. Now let the relaxation spread to your stomach, lower back, and chest. Let go more and more. Experience the relaxation deepening in your shoulders, arms, and hands—deeper and deeper. Notice the feeling of looseness and relaxation in your neck, jaws, and all your facial muscles.

As you scan through your body, you may still feel tense in some area. Go back to that area and repeat the procedure of tensing and relaxing.

At any point in Progressive Muscle Relaxation, it helps to silently affirm to yourself:

> *I'm letting go of the tension.*
> *I'm throwing the tension away.*
> *I feel calm and rested.*
> *Let the tension melt away.*

Shorthand Procedures

After you've mastered the basic procedure, you won't have to spend so much time getting relaxed. You can develop your own shorthand procedure. One way is to tense and relax several muscle groups at once. Jacobson divided the body into four major areas for this method:

1. Curl both fists, tightening biceps and forearms, in a "Charles Atlas" pose. Relax.

2. Wrinkle up your forehead. At the same time, press your head as far back as possible, roll it clockwise in a complete circle, and reverse it. Now wrinkle up the muscles of your face like a walnut: frowning, eyes squinted, lips pursed, tongue pressing the roof of your mouth, and shoulders hunched. Relax.

3. Arch back as you take a deep breath into your chest. Hold. Relax. Take a deep breath, pressing out your stomach. Hold. Relax.

4. Pull your feet and toes back toward your face, tightening your shins. Hold. Relax. Curl your toes, simultaneously tightening your calves, thighs, and buttocks. Hold. Relax.

There are other possibilities for altering the basic procedure to suit yourself. For example, I like to start at my feet, working upward, while timing the tensing and relaxing with my breathing: breathe in and tense, breathe out and relax. There's nothing sacred about Jacobson's sequence or timing. You may find that a different sequence works best for you. Also, as you grow more proficient, you'll probably find that it takes a little less than five seconds to tense your muscles and much less than fifteen seconds to experience full relaxation.

When you become an expert at noticing stress in your body, the deliberate tensing of muscle groups will be less important. You may want to switch to a "body awareness" method, in which you systematically scan your body for tension and release it from your muscles without first tensing them. This method is not only faster, but it is sometimes the only way to go if you have sore or injured muscles that you don't want to aggravate by extra tension.

Again, the right way is the way that works for you. Give all the suggested methods a fair trial, and stick with the ones that give you the best results.

Breathing

If your breathing is shallow, with short breaths in a choppy or lazy rhythm, you may not get enough oxygen. Your complexion will be poor because your blood is dark and bluish instead of bright red. Your digestion will be bad, you'll get tired easily, you'll have trouble coping with stress, and you'll tend to fall more easily into states of anxiety and depression. Full, deep, slow breathing corrects these tendencies by relaxing your body, oxygenating your blood, and removing waste from your circulatory system.

Full, Natural Breathing

This exercise makes you aware of how you breathe and teaches you to breathe fully and deeply. If your nasal passages aren't clear enough for you to breathe through your nose, don't worry about it—you can just breathe through your mouth.

1. Lie down on your back on the floor with your legs spread slightly and your arms at your sides, not touching your body, palms turned up. Put a cushion under your knees if your lower back feels tight.

2. Close your eyes and bring your attention to your breathing. Place your hand on the spot that rises and falls the most as you breathe. If this spot is on

your chest, you're not using your full lung capacity. You're breathing mostly in the top of your lungs.

3. If your hand is on your stomach, that's good. It shows you are breathing more deeply, into the bottom of your lungs. Put your hand on your stomach if it's not already there. Notice how your stomach rises with each inhalation and falls with each exhalation.

4. How does your chest move in relation to your stomach? Does it start to move first, move exactly at the same time, or lag behind your stomach? The full, natural cycle is for your stomach to rise first, as the lower part of your lungs fills. Then your chest starts to rise as the tops of your lungs are inflated. As your chest rises, your stomach sinks a little bit to compensate. On the exhale, your stomach should sink first, followed by your chest, emptying your lungs in the reverse order.

5. Try this full, natural breathing, taking long, slow, deep breaths and exaggerating the movements start to inhale into your stomach, pushing it up. Halfway through the inhalation, let your chest start to rise. Your stomach will sink slightly to compensate. Hold your breath for a couple of seconds, then exhale slowly. Let your stomach fall first, then halfway through the exhalation, let your chest fall. Hold your breath for a couple of seconds with your lungs empty. Repeat this in a steady rhythm, concentrating on smoothness and coordination. Keep it up until this sequence becomes automatic.

Cleansing Breath

This is an adaptation of a Yoga exercise. Although westerners have only recently learned about the importance of breathing, eastern cultures have over centuries devised breathing exercises to aid in physical, mental, and spiritual development.

1. Lie down on the floor and close your eyes, as in the preceding exercise. Begin breathing in the same way as before, with full, deep, natural breaths.

2. As you inhale, imagine that your nostrils are located in your heels. See your breath as a white cloud of steam or fog, very pure and cleansing. It comes in at your heels and sweeps up the back of your body, reaching your head as your lungs become full. The cloud picks up all impurities, tension, distractions, and fatigue as it passes through you. You can visualize these things as darkness, grit, dust, or cloudiness.

3. On the exhale, imagine this white cloud swirling around, down the front of your body, picking up more impurities, and exiting through your toes. As your lungs are emptied, the cloud leaves your body completely and is dissipated in space. It carries with it all the dark impurities, all the gritty tension, all the dusty fatigue, all the annoying aches and pains.

4. Continue to breathe slowly and deeply. Imagine the white cloud coming in at your heels, swirling around to fill every limb and digit, and carrying all the darkness out your toes. Your body gets brighter, cleaner, lighter with each breath.

If you're uncomfortable with the traditional heel and toe imagery, change the entry and exit points to suit yourself. You could have your breath coming in your head and going out your feet, or in your nose and out your mouth, or whatever. Find the arrangement that feels the most logical and cleansing to you.

Energizing Breath

This is similar to the cleansing breath exercise, but the central image is one of accumulating energy rather than flushing out impurities.

1. Lie down and close your eyes as before. Breathe deeply and fully.

2. As you inhale, imagine that the air is energy in the form of white light, flowing in through your nose and centering in your chest.

3. As you exhale, see the white light expanding to fill your entire body with revitalizing energy.

4. With each breath, draw more energy into your chest and disperse it throughout your body. Think of the lifegiving rays of the sun or a fire growing as more oxygen feeds it.

5. Experiment with changing the color and intensity of the light. Try making it pulsate. Find an image of energy that best fills you with a sense of power, vibrant health, and enthusiasm.

Relaxation Images

As you learn visualization for change, you will develop a personal repertoire of relaxation images. These are imaginary objects, places, activities, or events that convey the essence of relaxation to you. You'll incorporate these images into all visualization sessions to get relaxed and to deepen relaxation as you go along. To get you started, here are some images that many people find relaxing:

Twisted ropes, untwisting and going slack

Ice or butter melting

Harsh red light changing to soft blue or white light

Musical discords changing to harmonious chords

Peaceful forest glade or meadow

Blankets being piled on to make you warm and heavy

Warm sunlight

Beach scene with warm sand, surf noise, soaring gulls

Your limbs being gently covered with warm, heavy sand

Rocking in a hammock or cradle

Crumpled paper being smoothed out

Waves subsiding to ripples, ripples to glassy smoothness

A warm bath

A gentle massage

Again, you need to find your own unique images of relaxation. These may be unusual or incomprehensible to anyone else. For example, few people would find a roaring, bucking, snorting rototiller a relaxing image, but one gardener found that that was just right for him. He liked to think of his tight muscles as compacted soil and to see relaxation as a rototiller breaking up the hardpan and making the soil loose and soft.

A skindiver had another unusual image for relaxation. She thought of her tense muscles as abalone tissue. When it comes fresh from the shell, this large shellfish is like a softball-sized chunk of hard rubber or shoe leather. You have to slice it thin and pound it with a big wooden mallet to tenderize it. Despite the violent images of slicing and pounding, the skindiver found the thought of making her muscles like a tender, succulent abalone cutlet very relaxing. What can I say? It takes all kinds.

Special Considerations

If you find that you're straining to create and hold images, quit and try something else. Effective visualization is nearly effortless. If you have to strain, you won't get relaxed. Instead, take a warm bath, go for a walk, sit quietly and read, listen to music for a while, or take a nap.

Sometimes you may have trouble finishing a visualization session because as soon as you get relaxed, you fall asleep. This usually means that you're over-tired, and sleep is just what you need. It's no problem if the purpose of your visualization is relaxation—falling asleep means that you have accomplished your goal. But sometimes you may not want to fall asleep. When this is the case, try raising one arm up into the air a few inches and holding it there while you do your visualization. Tell yourself that if you start to doze, your falling arm will wake you gently and you will continue your visualizing without interruption.

If stress is a major problem for you, you should spend plenty of time mastering the basic techniques in this chapter and in the next two chapters. Then go on to the stress reduction chapter. There you will find details on refining your visualization techniques, coping with stress in your life, and achieving lifestyle modifications to avoid stress.

4

Warmup Exercises

"Every event in the visible world is the effect of an image, that is, of an idea in the unseen world."

—*I Ching*

You should read this chapter and do the exercises in it after mastering the material in the relaxation chapter. If you can't "close your eyes and relax" at will, you should go back to the previous chapter and practice relaxation some more.

You may find that you can breeze right through this chapter. Or you may have trouble with one or two exercises and have to spend a little more time mastering them. Take your time. A few extra minutes spent on the material here can save you a lot of frustration later.

The purpose of this chapter is to train you in the basics of forming, holding, and intensifying sense impressions, using all your senses. At the same time you will begin to see the great variety of possible visualization experiences.

Be sure to do the first five exercises, and do them in the order given. They proceed logically: (1) exploring single senses, (2) putting it all together, (3) strengthening your recall, (4) altering your point of view, and (5) field trip.

The last five exercises are optional explorations that you can try for fun or if you need extra practice.

For the exercises with long, detailed steps, you might want to tape record the instructions and play them back. This will allow you to concentrate on the visualization without having to remember all the steps or repeatedly open your eyes to read the next instruction.

Exploring Single Senses

In this first exercise, you'll focus on one sense at a time. This is similar to the way Yogis, Moslem mystics, and Sufis learn to meditate.

Sight

Lie down and close your eyes. Use your relaxation routine to get very relaxed. If distracting thoughts pop into your mind, let them drift away and refocus your mind on your planned visualization.

Start with a simple visual image: imagine a black circle on a white background. Make the circle perfectly round, perfectly black. Make the background a pure, brilliant white. Let your interior eye move around the boundary between black and white, outlining the perfectly circular shape.

Now change the color of the circle to red. Make it a bright, primary red. Keep the background a brilliant white.

Let the circle fade out until it's barely a pink stain. Good. Now let it fade out entirely. Replace it with a green triangle. Make the sides of equal length, with one side on the bottom and a point at the top. It can be any shade of green you want. Experiment until you get a color you like: grass green, kelly green, forest green, pine green, or whatever.

Next erase the green triangle and make an orange rectangle. Keep the sides straight and the angles a perfect 90 degrees. Make the rectangle narrower and longer. Keep thinning it out until you have a long, thin orange line. Change the color to black. Make it like a very thin black thread, stretched tight. Let the thread break in the middle and fly apart.

Now let your imagination create, alter, and erase many different shapes in many different colors. See how vivid and exact you can make a shape, then change it as fast as you can. Work on building speed and accuracy.

Sound

For this part of the exercise, let your mind's eye close. Make the shapes and colors go away. See a formless expanse of gray fog, or darkness, or whatever seems easiest to sustain. In this fog or darkness you can see nothing. You can only hear.

First, imagine you hear your phone ringing. Concentrate on hearing the exact tone, the exact duration of the ring, and the exact interval of silence between rings. Let it ring ten times, then stop.

Next, hear a car horn in the distance, honking irritably in short bursts. Add another horn. Then add several horns honking at once, like an exuberant wedding party rolling down the road.

Hear a dog barking in the distance, with the sound traveling through the air of a lazy summer day. Add the sound of construction: an electric saw and hammering. Hear traffic going by on a distant highway.

Now hear one note on a piano. Hear it struck loudly and sustained until it gradually fades away. Now hear the scale: do, re, mi, fa, sol, la, ti, do. Run the notes up and down the scale. Now hear a simple melody—Twinkle Twinkle Little Star, Three Blind Mice, or something similar. Finally, imagine hearing a full, lush arrangement of a favorite piece.

Next, hear your mother saying your name in a loving tone. Then hear your father, brothers or sisters, friends, and other loved ones.

Go on to create your own favorite sounds—birdcalls, surf, wind chimes, violins, wind in the trees, and so on.

By now, you're probably ready for a break. Open your eyes and sit up and stretch for a while. You can continue with the exercise right away, or come back to it later.

Touch

Lie down, close your eyes, and relax.

You cannot see or hear. You are in a visual and auditory fog, cutting off and deadening all sight and sound. You can only feel.

Imagine that you are sitting in a wooden chair. Feel the firm support and the hardness of the chair back. It's smooth and slightly cool against your buttocks, legs, and back.

Reach out your imaginary hands and feel a smooth wooden tabletop in front of you. On it, find a small marble and pick it up. Roll it around in your fingers and feel how hard and perfectly spherical it is. Notice that it's cool when you first pick it up, and then warms in your hands.

Put the marble down and find an emery board on the table. Notice that it's thin and flexible. Rub your finger over the sandpaper surface and feel how gritty and rough it is. File one of your fingernails with it.

Put the emery board in your right hand and with your left hand pick up a small piece of thick velvet, about six inches square. Really feel the contrast between the sandpaper and the velvet. Rub them gently against your cheeks and study the textural differences.

Now put the emery board and the velvet down and pick up a rubber band. Stretch it and feel the resistance. Wrap it around your fingers. Flip it off into space.

Now for a real challenge. Reach out and pick up a little kitten. Feel the softness, the warmth, the gentle movement in your hands. Pet her and scratch her behind the ears. Feel the vibration as the kitten starts to purr. (If you don't like cats, try a puppy or a hamster.)

Let your animal go and imagine that you are sitting on a park bench. See how quickly you can change locale. Feel the sun on your face and arms. Notice that the wind is blowing and the air feels just a little chilly. Reach out and feel the slats of the bench. Feel the painted wood, smooth with wear and warmed by the sun.

It's getting colder. It's starting to rain. Feel the first few drops on your face, cold and wet. Reach out and grab your umbrella. Open it, concentrating on the feel of where you put your hands and how the mechanism feels as you work it.

Turn off the rain, the sun, the park bench, and get ready for the next exercise.

Taste

Now you'll concentrate on your sense of taste. Close off all your other senses and imagine that you have just put a few grains of salt on your tongue. Taste the intense saltiness that makes your mouth water.

Next imagine the taste of a lemon—sharp, tart, sour. You can feel your whole mouth pucker up.

Now taste some sugar: gritty and sweet, melting in your mouth.

And now imagine that you have touched your tongue to a hot chili pepper. Let the spicy, intense sensation burn in your mouth.

Cool your tastebuds with some ice cream, your favorite flavor. Feel how cool and refreshing it is. Taste the rich flavor.

Finish up by imagining that you're eating some of your favorite foods. Concentrate on the taste, smell, temperature, and texture of each course on your menu.

Smell

Now turn off every sense except your sense of smell. Try to recapture some of the smells of your childhood: roast turkey in your mother's kitchen, chalk on the blackboard erasers at school, chlorine in swimming pools, Christmas trees, freshly baked bread, birthday candles after they've been blown out, shoe polish, paint.

Explore the world of smells, imagining your favorite scents like rose, violet, vanilla, or your first lover's perfume or aftershave. Include some of your non-favorites, like roofing tar, skunk, locker room sweat, or mildew.

When you're ready, remind yourself of where you are and open your eyes.

Analysis

Analyze your experience. Some senses probably came easier than others. Most people find visual images easiest to form, with sound coming second. But it doesn't matter which is your strong point. You can start by using the sense that comes easiest for you, and soon all your senses will come more fully into play.

You may have found it hard to concentrate on one image at a time. For example, the words "forest green, pine green" may have inspired a brief glimpse of trees. This is natural and good. It means that you are already visualizing metaphorically, in terms of the likenesses of things.

You may have found that your impressions of taste or smell were rather flat. That's because you seldom experience a pure taste unrelated to vision, smell, or touch. When you bite into an apple, the experience is made up of the sight of the shiny, round fruit, its heft in your hand, the sound of your teeth crunching through the skin, the smell of the apple, the cool spurt of juice into your mouth, the tactile sensation of chewing, and lastly, the actual taste of the apple.

In the next exercise, you will put impressions from all your senses together to form a much more convincing imaginary experience.

Putting It All Together

In this exercise you are going to peel and eat an orange, creating as full and accurate an experience as you can. If you don't like oranges, do the exercise with an imaginary banana or apple or other simple food you like.

Lie down, close your eyes, and relax completely. As you get more and more relaxed, let your mind clear. If distracting thoughts come up, notice them but let them drift away.

First form a visual image of an orange. See the round orange shape sitting on a familiar plate. See the little pits in the orange skin, the shiny highlights near the top, the shadows on the bottom. See the indented navel at one end and the buttonlike little stem at the other end.

Now bring your sense of hearing into play. Rub your imaginary thumb across the orange and hear the slight squeak. Pick it up and let it drop a couple of inches onto the plate. Hear the thump as it lands and the clatter of the plate.

Now hold the orange up and feel its weight in your hand. Turn it around and sense the three-dimensional roundness. Rub it and feel the smooth, slick, slightly bumpy skin. Dig your thumb in at the stem end and start to peel the orange. Feel the resistance, the tearing sensation.

Smell the orange, that first, sharp, oily, tangy smell as you start peeling. See the tiny spray of oil droplets from the skin as you compress and tear it. See the white membrane and the orange flesh under the skin.

Finish peeling the orange, dropping the peel onto the plate with a slight sound. Keep looking, hearing, smelling and feeling it. Divide the orange into segments. When you have a segment free, touch your tongue to it and taste the first hint of orange. Bite the segment in half and taste the juice as it floods your mouth. Feel the tang on your lips and feel your mouth watering.

Continue until you have eaten the entire orange. Switch constantly back and forth from the sights to the smells to the sounds to the tastes, to the sensations of touch. Notice how the look and smell of an orange are a big part of how it tastes. Notice how imagining the heft and feel of the orange in your hand makes the experience more real, more three-dimensional. Tell yourself at this point, "I'll remember this experience and compare it with the real thing the next time I eat an orange."

When you're finished, imagine wiping your fingers off on a paper napkin or rinsing them at the sink and drying them.

Now reorient yourself to your surroundings. Remember where you are, open your eyes, and end the session.

Strengthening Your Recall

This is a simple exercise you can do sitting or standing in front of a drawer full of miscellaneous items. You know the drawer—the one in your kitchen or desk or room into which you toss all the junk.

Open the drawer and really study it for about ten seconds, noticing each object and its position in relation to the rest of the things.

Close your eyes and visualize the drawer, placing all the objects you re-member in their correct place. You'll probably find that there are several "blank" spots that your memory can't fill in.

Open your eyes and "fill in the blanks." Notice what you left out of your visualization.

Close your eyes and visualize the drawer again, re-creating everything.

Open your eyes and check your accuracy. Keep closing and opening your eyes another three or four times, building up a complete, complex picture of the drawer in your mind.

Here's a hint for organizing this task: with eyes open, start at one corner of the drawer and sweep your eyes around in a clockwise circle, noting the con-tents in sequence: push pins, scissors, 3 x 5 cards, rubber bands, scotch tape, pen, pencil, note pad, stapler, extra keys, and so on. Close your eyes and start in the same corner, moving your mind's eye around in the same direction, filling in items. Open your eyes and look in the same pattern, close them and try again, and so on. Most people can recall objects in a linear sequence more easily than objects as part of a total array.

Any way you approach it, this exercise will strengthen your ability to re-member what you see. It will also teach you two facts: that most of what you "see" you don't really see, since it's forgotten immediately; and that continually adding details to a visualization is the way to make it seem more and more real.

You can do this exercise any time you have a few moments to kill: looking at a landscape, a magazine page, a doctor's waiting room, or a street scene.

You can also do an auditory variant of this exercise. Just close your eyes wherever you are and listen to the ambient sounds around you. Even in a "quiet" room you will notice sounds going on that you were not aware of: traffic, wind in the trees, dogs barking, birds chirping, saws sawing, refrigerators humming, music playing, people shouting or laughing. True silence is very rare. If the room is quiet enough, you can hear your own heartbeat pulsing in your ears.

Altering Your Point of View

When you visualize, you're the director of a mental movie. This exercise will show you some of the many different "camera angles" and special effects that are available to you. It's like being the director of a movie with an unlimited budget.

Lie down, close your eyes, and relax. Visualize a house or other building you know very well. See it from the front, as if you are walking up to the door. Get closer to some detail like a door or a window. Try different ways of getting closer: you can move your imaginary body and walk up to the building, or you can float toward it as if gravity doesn't exist and your eye was a camera on a boom. Or you can see the whole building moving toward you as your point of view remains stationary.

Look at the side of the building by walking around it. Now look at another side by just flashing on it, like a quick scene change in a movie. Now look at another side by rotating the building as if it were on a giant turntable. Practice moving around in these different ways.

Zoom in and out like a camera lens. Notice that there is no limit to how close you can get. You can zoom in until you have a microscopic view of a tiny area. You can even get down to the molecular or atomic level. You can enter into the wall itself, slipping between spinning electrons. You can scan the wall with X-ray vision and see the wires and pipes inside. You can lift the building off the ground and raise it up to see the bottom. You can send it out into space until it's a tiny speck. Or you can ride into space on top of the roof and visit the moon. You can make your body and your point of view insubstantial and walk through the walls. You can melt the walls down like candle wax, burn the building up, or remodel the whole place at your whim.

Try all these tricks and any others you can think of. This kind of playful exercise loosens your imagination and gives you good practice at getting control over your images.

Reorient yourself now to the room and your surroundings. When you're ready, open your eyes and end the session.

Field Trip

This exercise is designed to introduce you to different styles of vision.

Go to an art museum, a big gallery, or a library with a collection of art books. Look at as many different styles of painting and sculpture as you can: medieval religious triptyches, Roman statues, photo-realism, cubism, surrealism, art deco, Romantic portraits, abstracts, impressionistic landscapes, pop, op, and comic book art.

Notice how many ways there are to depict a man, a woman, a child, a dog, a house, a tree, a garden, a flower. The next time you do a visualization, cast it in a style that appeals to you: take a stroll through a Monet garden, try to wind a limp Dali watch, pet the sharp corners of a cubistic cat, or dance with Disney cartoon characters in a fantasia of your own.

Optional Exercises

If you have trouble forming vivid images, or if you just want to have fun sharpening your skills, try some of these optional exercises:

Projecting a Triangle

Do this one if you have trouble forming and retaining sharp images, or if you find the open drawer exercise too confusing.

Look at the illustration of a white triangle on the next page. Notice that it's a white, equal-sided triangle on a gray background. Now close your eyes and see it in your mind, as if it were about eighteen inches in front of your eyes. Projecting the triangle outward in space like this will make it easier to run your mind's eye over the image and see every part of it. If the image fades, open your eyes and look at the illustration again to reinforce it in your mind.

Try this exercise with other simple objects—an apple, a ball, a stone. Project them in front of you instead of trying to "see" them inside your head.

Your Favorite Things

This is a good exercise if you get easily distracted. Choose an object or a sensation that you like very much: a photo of a loved one, a gold ring, the taste of chocolate, the feel of a favorite silk scarf.

Actually go and get the photo, the ring, a box of chocolates, or your silk scarf. Experience the favorite thing directly: look at the photo, eat a chocolate, put the ring on, or drape the scarf around your neck.

Next, close your eyes while you continue to hold the photo in your hands, move the actual ring around your finger, taste the real chocolate, and touch the real scarf. Get the sensation firmly in you mind with eyes closed.

Now put the photo down, swallow the chocolate, remove the ring or the scarf. Imagine that you can still see your loved one, taste your chocolate, feel the ring or the scarf. If your attention wanders, open your eyes and reinforce your imagination with another look or taste or touch.

Keep alternating the real and the imaginary sensations until the imaginary ones become more vivid and easier to hold onto.

Brainstorm Recording

You may feel that your imagination is sluggish and dull, that you can't think of any images, or that the ones you do think of come hard and aren't interesting. This exercise will show you that your images come faster and are more fantastic than you think.

Set a tape recorder running next to you while you're lying down to visualize. Let anything come into you mind, and as it does, describe it out loud. For instance, if you just get an image of yourself lying on the bed, say, "Lying on the bed."

Perhaps you think you look asleep, so just say, "Asleep." At first this process will feel stupid, and associations will come slowly. But as you relax and let your mind freely associate, you will be talking more: "Asleep . . . Sleeping Beauty . . . cartoon . . . dwarfs . . . deer . . . turkey . . . Thanksgiving . . . mother . . . witch . . ."

If you do this exercise a few times, you will find that you can't talk fast enough to even briefly label each image that flashes into your mind. When you play the tape back, you'll be surprised at how quickly images come and go, and how varied they really are.

You Oughta Be in Pictures

This is an exercise in point of view that can be a lot of fun and very revealing. Visualize a scene from your favorite movie. See it as if you were in a movie theater watching it normally.

Next, pretend that you are living the movie. Take the role of the character with whom you identify most, and live out a favorite scene. Add all the details from the movie, the camera shots and the soundtrack. Add your own "sense track" of tactile sensations, tastes, smells, hot and cold, wet and dry. Try to transcend the camera angles used in the movie so that you're seeing each scene exclusively from your character's point of view.

Now really stretch your imagination and become a character you don't identify with. Try being the villain. If you're a woman, try being the leading man. If you're a man, try being the leading woman. Make your role as real as possible. Actually try to feel the emotions you've seen portrayed on the screen so many times.

5

Creating Your Special Place

"Chance favors only the prepared mind."

—Louis Pasteur

In later chapters you will find the instruction, "Go to your special place." A special place is an imaginary setting to which you can return again and again in your visualizations.

In this chapter you will be guided through the creation of two of these special places, one outdoors and one indoors. The places you create will be exactly the way you want them, tailored to your unique personality, preferences, and expectations.

Uses of Your Special Place

Your special place has several uses. First of all, its creation is a good exercise in controlling mental images. It will give you essential practice in creating and revising scenes to get them exactly the way you want them.

Second, and most importantly, your special place will be used for relaxation. It's a safe, secure retreat where you can let go of all tension. You can let your guard down and relax totally. You will automatically associate your special place with deep levels of relaxation and peace, so that even a brief thought about it will begin to relax you.

Your special place can provide a quick release from anxiety. For example, June was a clerk at a title company. She often had to deal with people who were tense and angry with her because they were borrowing large amounts of money and didn't understand something about the loan fees or other expenses. When June felt very anxious after such a confrontation, she would go to the ladies room, lie down, and spend a minute visualizing her special place to calm herself. She would see herself lying on the beach in front of her grandfather's house at the lake. She hadn't actually been to the lake for years, but it represented peace and contentment for her. A minute on the beach eased June's anxiety and made her ready to go on with her job.

Your special place is also where you go to meditate, to mull things over, and to solve problems. In your special place you are a deep and clear thinker. You can penetrate to the core of a problem. You can enter into and understand complexities of feelings and motivations that are opaque to you elsewhere. You are in touch with your own unconscious, able to remember and know things that in ordinary places are hidden from you.

You'll go to your special place to do receptive visualizations. Once you have found your inner guide (discussed in the next chapter) you may invite him or her to join you in your special place to answer important questions you have about your life. For example, Richard agreed to help his mother run a flea market for her church group, even though he would rather have done something else that weekend. He was irritable and got very angry with his mother on the phone Friday night, for no apparent reason. Before going to sleep that night, he went to his special place—a meadow by a mountain stream. He reviewed his phone conversation with his mother, then invited his inner guide to join him and explain what had gone wrong. Richard's inner guide—a bearded old man named Oscar— stepped out from behind a tree. Oscar had a roll of stickers like kids buy at the candy store. Each sticker was printed with a big "YES" in bold letters. Oscar was pasting these stickers all over Richard's face. It was very uncomfortable and annoying. Richard said, "Stop it! Stop it! No!" At once the stickers disappeared and Oscar smiled. He held up one last sticker that read "NO" and said, "*No* is your magic word," and walked away behind the tree. Richard realized then the source of his conflict with his mother. He should have told her no, he couldn't help with the flea market that weekend. It was too late to back out, but at least he understood the source of his resentment and could cope with it. He would remember it the next time he felt uncomfortable with one of her requests.

Characteristics of Your Special Place

Most often a special place is a nature scene: a beach, forest, mountain, desert, meadow, or other pleasant outdoors area. It can also be indoors: a study, den, library, castle, dream house, teepee, cabin, cave, or some other enclosed area, either man-made, natural, or some combination of the two. In this chapter you'll make up an outdoor and an indoor place that you can visit as the mood strikes you.

A special place can be based on a real place you've visited, such as a national park where you went on vacation or someplace you spent a lot of time in as a child. Or your special place can be entirely made up, a pure work of imagination. It's likely that it will have elements of both reality and imagination.

Your special place can be based on a fictional, historical, or legendary locale. You can go to Alice's Wonderland, Marie Antoinette's palace at Versailles, or the Hanging Gardens of Babylon.

There are certain characteristics that you should be sure to incorporate into your special place. First of all, it should be quiet. Avoid crashing surf if you choose a beach scene, and don't include a roaring waterfall as part of your stream setting. Likewise, your place should be comfortable: not too hot, cold, windy, bright, dark, and so on. If you choose a desert scene, make it warm but not hot. If you want to be on the top of a mountain, go easy on the snow and wind. Since you're making it all up, you can do away with the sunburn and mosquitoes that you usually can't escape in a real natural setting.

Your place should be safe, secure, and relaxing. If it's in the woods, there needn't be any bears or mountain lions. However rugged and picturesque, it should have a place for you to sit comfortably and a place to lie down.

Include some means for another person or animal or object to appear. This can be a rock or tree to hide behind, a path down which somebody could walk, a door that can be opened and shut, or a treasure chest that you can open and find something in. These are all mechanisms by which your unconscious can send messages.

To make your special place more realistic, it should have perspective and be stocked with many details. Make sure there's a foreground, a middle distance, and a background. Include flowers, plants, rocks, furniture—whatever seems appropriate. Especially include any favorite things of your own or that you'd like to have. There aren't any logical limits, so you can have a color TV in the Middle Ages or a big, four-poster bed in a redwood grove.

Some handy things to have in your special place are a mirror or reflecting pool for looking at yourself, paints and canvas, paper and pencil, musical instruments, clay for making statues, and any other aids you can think of for self-expression or discovery. For imagining the future or visualizing goals within your special place, include a natural stage area, a TV, movie screen, or a crystal ball.

Nature Scene Exercise

Lie down, close your eyes, and relax. You are going to gradually create a special place for yourself in nature. The instructions will be necessarily somewhat vague, since you have to fill in details with special meaning to you.

Imagine a path. It can be in the woods, at the seashore, in the desert, or in the mountains. It can be a place you know or would like to know. Imagine that you are standing on the path, looking down it. Notice the surface of the path:

the dirt or sand, the rocks, the color and texture. Begin walking on the path and notice how it feels against your feet. You can be barefoot or wearing comfortable shoes, boots, or sandals.

As you stroll down the path, look up and notice the countryside. See the colors and shapes of the trees, rocks, mountains, or whatever. Listen and hear the birds, the sound of water, of wind, and of your own steps. Notice how quiet and peaceful it is here in this special place. Take a deep breath and smell the fresh air. Take in the smells of earth, water, and green growing things. Feel the sun shining and a gentle breeze blowing against your face.

Continue down the path until you come to some sort of enclosed area. This will be your special place. If it doesn't seem inviting, change the aspects you don't like, or go a little further down the path until you come to a spot you like more.

Take a look around this special spot. It can be a meadow, a clearing, a cove, a glade, a hollow, a peak—whatever feels right to you. Notice its shape and general layout. Take in the sights, sounds, and smells. Notice the ground, rocks, grass, bushes, and so on. Are there any little animals like birds or squirrels? Is there water nearby that you can see or hear?

This is your place, special for you alone. You can come here any time you want. No one else can come unless you invite them. It's safe and secure, a quiet place of relaxation and peace.

Walk around your special place and notice the quality of light. Make it comfortable, not too bright or too dim. You are in control. You can make the temperature warmer or cooler, make the wind stronger or cause it to die away entirely. Notice what you are wearing—the colors and style and how it feels against your skin. Change to something else if you want. You can dress any way you choose here.

Find a comfortable place to lie down. It could be a bed of dry moss, a patch of sun-warmed sand, or even a real bed with sheets and blankets and everything. You can have it just the way you want it. Lie down and try it out. Make sure it's a good place to rest. What do you see when you look up?

Get up and go to the center of your special place. Turn in a circle and notice what you see, first right in front of you. Then raise your eyes and fill in the middle distance. Then look out as far as you can see. Make sure that there are near and far things to look at.

Look around and find a place where someone else could be, nearby yet hidden from you. This is where you will have your inner guide and other visitors appear. It can be a rock outcropping, a big tree, a bend in the path, or even a cave or hole in the ground.

Next make a place in which you can store things: a hollow tree, a cupboard, a hole under a rock, a treasure chest, a niche in a cliff face. Into this space, place some paper and a pen or pencil. Make it the kind of art paper you loved as a child, and your favorite kind of pencil or pen. Include some paints and some modeling clay. If you play or would like to play a musical instrument, put that in too. If your instrument is a grand piano or something else that won't fit in the storage space, put it in a convenient corner of your special place. Remember, you can do anything in your special place, including playing an instrument on which you have had no training.

Look around and find a reflecting surface where you can see your face. Create a mirror or a reflecting pool. Also make some provision for a place to watch imaginary scenes: a spot in the middle distance that seems like a stage, or a crystal ball on a pedestal, or even a TV monitor. Perhaps your reflecting pool can double as a viewing screen.

Go around your special place experiencing and refining all the things you have created. Look at them, smell them, touch them, even taste them. Fill in details. Change colors or textures. Make your special place just as perfect as you can. Remind yourself that this is your place, to come to any time you want. It is peaceful and serene, a safe refuge from the cares of the world.

Take a last look around, then walk out of your special place, down the path the way you came. Entering and leaving your special place by the same path is a way to heighten its reality for you.

Stop walking on the path and begin to remember your actual surroundings at this moment. When you are ready, open your eyes, get up, and stretch. During the day, think back on your special place. It's your place. You can go there any time.

Indoor Scene Exercise

Once again, lie down, close your eyes, and relax. You are going to create another special place, this time indoors. This can be based on a real room you know, a setting from a favorite book or movie, or a totally imaginary room of your dreams. You are the architect, and you can design your room any way you want.

Start by imagining that you are in your *outdoor* special place. Leave it and walk down a path. Take a moment to notice the sights, sounds, smells, and temperature of your surroundings. What kind of vegetation and terrain do you see? What is the weather like? What are you wearing?

Come around a bend in the path and encounter a building. What kind of building is it? It can be a modern house with lots of natural wood and glass, a Victorian mansion, a hide yurt, a stone cottage with a thatched roof, a circus tent, a crystal palace, a teepee, or a pyramid—whatever you want to contain your indoor special place.

Enter the building and find your special place inside. Notice what the door is made of. Make sure it has a lock if you want one, and a peephole to look through. Close the door and go into the center of the space.

Look around you and see the doors, walls, and windows (or whatever kind of surface and openings your space has). If things are unclear, take some time to experiment with wall coverings and window positions. You can alter things until they seem right. Try changing the floor plan around, so that you have interesting nooks and crannies to give scale and comfort.

What kind of flooring do you like? Carpet, rugs, hardwood, tile, earth, even growing grass? Make up a good floor. Then look up and see how high you want the ceiling. Maybe you want it low in some places and high in others.

Put in some furniture. Make sure you have a comfortable chair, a table or desk to work on, a bed or couch of some kind to lie down on, bookcases and other places to store your art supplies or musical instruments, and so on. The furnishings should be exactly what you've always wanted, precisely to your taste. Don't forget purely decorative items like plants, flowers, sculpture, paintings, photographs, or wall hangings. If you like small pets, throw in a tank of fish or a parrot in a cage. Make this the room you always wanted.

If a view is important to you, go around to each window and look out. Create what you want to see: an ocean, a forest, the city at night, fields of grain, or whatever.

Pay some attention to the means of lighting—overhead, table lamps, track lighting, indirect, skylights, and so on. Notice where the switches are.

Make a closet with a door or a niche with a curtain where you can "discover" messages from your unconscious. Also, you should have a TV, mirror, movie screen, stage, or some other means of viewing imaginary scenes.

Look around you and coordinate the visual style of your special place. It can be as plain and ascetic as a monk's cell, or as barbarically splendid as a sultan's throne room. Just make sure the colors, shapes, and textures all work together visually in a way that pleases and excites you.

Now add some sound. Create a stereo system to play your favorite music. Consider warbling birds, a tinkling fountain, wind chimes, wind or water sounds from outside.

This is your special place. It belongs to you alone. You can do anything in this room, and no one will care. No problem or other person can bother you in this special place. Here you are relaxed, content, creative, and fully alive. This is a room where you can come any time you want to rest or think.

Walk around and touch the things in your space. Feel the unique textures of fine wood, fabric, paper, brass, and glass. Switch the lights on and off. Open and shut doors and windows, get the tactile feel of the place as you sit in different chairs and flop on the bed.

Smell the scent of your cut flowers, or create a bowl of exquisite fruit and sample the taste.

Continue looking and walking around your special place, changing and refining details until you're satisfied with it. You will come back to this space many times to solve problems, answer questions, or just escape daily stresses and relax.

When you're ready, recall your immediate surroundings and open your eyes. Get up and go about your usual routine, remembering from time to time that you now have a special place you can enter whenever you like.

Examples of Special Places

My outdoor special place is a beach scene, very similar to a beach in northern California where I have gone camping, fishing, and skin diving.

It's a small cove, with rocks to the north and south and a sandy beach just about fifty yards long. The water is clearer and warmer than is actually the case on the north coast, and the surf is very gentle. I usually sit on the sand near the water and lean my back against a big driftwood log that is warm and bleached white in the sun. The sun is usually shining, hot but with a breeze off the water to keep it pleasant. A steep path goes up a rocky cliff to a bluff above the beach. And at low tide you can walk around the point to the north without getting wet.

There's a boathouse at the base of the cliff. In it I store my paper and pen, water colors, a flute, a recorder, some diving and fishing gear, clothes, and whatever else I want from time to time. The idea is that whatever I'd like to have, I can find it in the boathouse. There's a futuristic phone there that includes a TV screen and a computer keyboard. I can talk to anybody in the world and see them face to face. I can visualize the future or make up little plays on the screen. I can write poems or music on the keyboard.

When I want someone else to appear in my special place, I usually have them climb down the cliff path. Sometimes they arrive in a boat or walk around the point at low tide, or I just call them up on the TV phone.

My *indoor* special place is on the bluff above the cove. Set in a grassy meadow with eucalyptus trees, the building is an octagonal structure of redwood and glass. The outside shape has always been a little unclear, since it's the inside that is important to me.

I enter my special place by going down three steps. It's dug into the ground a little. The door is thick oak with art nouveau iron hinges, battens, and a big iron ring for a handle. Inside, my special place has floor-to-ceiling walnut bookcases taking up almost all the available wall space. The bookcases are filled with leatherbound classics, worn storybooks from my childhood, and some favorite magazines and how-to books on woodwork, musical instruments, airplanes, and automobile restoration.

The floors are red tile near the entrance and dark oak elsewhere. The walls are white plaster, the ceiling beamed redwood, very high. In the center of the room is a huge refectory table with turned wooden legs and a thick top. There's a big oak chair with a maroon velvet cushion. Another chair is an old leather armchair just like one I have at home. There's a daybed with a Navajo blanket over it, brass bowls filled with cut yellow roses, and some Tiffany table lamps scattered around on end tables. I've tried several times to put oriental carpets on the floor, but they disappear as soon as I stop concentrating on them, so I've given up on carpeting.

Everything is a little old and well-worn, but very clean. My special place reminds me of a very old Spanish house I once knew in Santa Barbara, California.

I have a violin hanging on the wall, and I play it sometimes when I'm feeling musical. Of course, in reality I can't play the violin at all.

At one end of the room is a small raised platform like a stage, with a curtain I can raise and lower just by thinking about it. This is where I have people appear sometimes. I also have imaginary visitors just knock on the door, and I look through a peephole to see if I want to let them in.

On the central table is a complicated machine made of wood and brass and lots of little ceramic knobs and glass dials. It has a dial I can turn to change the time and date in a little window, and a screen for viewing the past and future. It's like a combination time machine and television, done up in a nineteenth-century, Jules Verne sort of style. If I want a "big screen" effect, there's a movie screen on a roller that I can pull down from the ceiling like a window shade. If I want to look at myself, there's a full-length mirror on a closet door.

I like to keep an easel with a blank canvas set up in one corner, and a big pile of clay on a table in another corner, in case I feel inspired. When I was remodeling my house, I put in a drafting table so that I could fiddle around with floor plans in my special place.

The room is warmed by a fireplace. I often make it foggy outside and sit in the quiet room with a little classical music playing in the background and a fire crackling on the hearth. Sometimes I have a glass of wine from a bottle in a little cupboard. The bottle is never empty. The wine tastes wonderful and doesn't give me a hangover.

Looking out of the four windows, I can see a rocky coastline, Monterey bay, a meadow with wildflowers, and a heavily forested range of hills. The views are actually four different places I have seen in real life, brought together here.

I could go on and on. Both of my special places change and grow as I do. I am constantly adding and changing details as I feel like it. Since the first edition of this book, I have learned to fly in real life. So my special place now has a landing strip and a 1955 Piper Tripacer in mint condition. This is a place I can come to in an instant when I need to feel relaxed and refreshed. Sometimes when I'm stuck in traffic or struggling with a difficult task, I close my eyes for just a second, take a long, slow breath, and imagine sitting at ease in my big leather chair, leaning against my driftwood log, or flying my airplane. It relaxes me instantly, and I can open my eyes and go on with a bit more patience.

6

Finding Your Inner Guide

"It is easier to go to Mars or to the moon than it is to penetrate one's own being."

— Carl Jung

This is the last of the "must read, must do" chapters. When you have completed this chapter, you will have all the basic skills you need to practice visualization for change. You'll know the rules, know how to relax, and know how to form, hold, and manipulate sense impressions in your imagination. You'll have two special places in which to relax or stage a visualization, and you'll have an inner guide to serve you in many ways.

Your inner guide is an imaginary person, animal, or other being that you create to help you solve problems or answer questions. Your inner guide is the personification of your inner wisdom. It's your unconscious, all-knowing mind given a form and a voice.

Inner guides can take many forms: wizard, priestess, old woman, circus ringleader, angel, Greek goddess, stag, space alien, grandfather, old childhood friend, movie star, and so on.

Your inner guide answers questions and gives you advice. He or she or it can be of great help in resolving dilemmas—when you are stuck between two or more mutually exclusive choices. Your inner guide helps by being a channel for messages from your unconscious. Consulting your inner guide is really a matter of uncovering feelings you may not be fully aware of and clarifying what you really need or want.

Characteristics of Your Inner Guide

An inner guide can be someone you know or have met, someone who is now dead, a character in a book, play, or movie, someone out of myth and legend, or an entirely imaginary being who just feels right to you. It doesn't matter whether your inner guide is of the same or opposite sex.

The most important characteristic is that your inner guide is wiser and smarter than your conscious mind. Your inner guide knows everything you have ever experienced or thought, even things you didn't consciously notice at the time. Your inner guide isn't confused by emotions or complexity. Your inner guide can arrive at correct conclusions and decisions directly by intuition, without having to go through a long chain of logical reasoning and rationalizations.

You can communicate verbally or nonverbally with your inner guide. When you ask a question, your guide may say yes or nod or smile as an answer. If your guide is an animal, it may purr, smile, lick your hand, or whatever—you decide the meaning and the means of communication. Sometimes your inner guide may show you visions—little visualizations within a visualization—that provide you with insightful answers. Or your guide may give you something, a symbolic gift that represents the answer you seek. For example, you may be considering whether to go back to school and finish your degree, and your guide gives you an academic robe or a pencil box like you had on your first day of school. Or your guide may give you a tool or some other item that means, "Better keep working at what you're doing."

Like the ancient Greek oracle at Delphi, your guide may sometimes be cryptic or silent. This might mean that the information you are seeking is just not available to you at this time. For instance, you may be trying to clarify your true feelings about another person, but it's actually too early to tell how you feel. A cryptic answer might also mean that the information you're seeking is something you really don't want to know, some truth that you're not yet ready to face. For example, an art student was considering dropping out of school. She asked her guide, "Is my art any good? Am I really an artist, or just pretending?" Her guide, an incredibly old Indian chief who resembled Picasso, just looked confused and gave a Gallic shrug. Months later she decided that she wasn't really committed to art, but at the earlier time, she wasn't ready to face that evaluation.

Your inner guide can show up anywhere in your visualizations. You can call your guide into your special place for a consultation, or take your guide along on any kind of imaginary exploration, or encounter your guide somewhere along the way, either by plan or unexpectedly.

Treat your inner guide like a trusted friend. Your guide has your best interests at heart. Don't make a commitment to your guide unless you mean it. Be honest in what you say to your guide. Remember, your guide is your wiser self. If you try to fool your guide, you're fooling yourself.

Treating your inner guide like your best friend is a way to build your self-confidence and self-esteem.

Since he or she is really you, your inner guide reflects your personality. Your guide's timidity reflects your own fear. Sarcasm reflects your own cynicism. Dire warnings reflect your own negativity.

Your inner guide will change over time as you change. He or she may get older or larger or more outgoing, reflecting changes in your own life. Your original inner guide may disappear and be replaced by a different one that better suits your current circumstances and feelings. If you notice changes in your inner guide, ask about them. It may give you some valuable information about how you're changing.

You may choose to have more than one inner guide. For example, it makes sense to have a child guide, a man guide, and a woman guide. This is recommended by David Bresler, a pain control expert. He reasons that you have all three elements in your personality—the child, the male, and the female. Having three guides provides all three elements of your personality a clear channel of expression.

Or you may have a guide that has many moods. For example, you could create a Zen monk who can be very serious, very funny, very earthy, or very mysterious, depending on what you need from him at different times.

By the way, humor is very important. Consulting your unconscious self sounds like a very serious and formal enterprise, but the results are often funny. Your inner guide may even take the form of a clown or a comedian. Humor often has its roots in unconscious desires that are too powerful or threatening to be allowed any other kind of expression. Along these lines, you may find that your inner guide communicates to you by using puns or riddles. This is just another way you protect yourself by expressing unconscious desires in a coded or disguised form. Figuring out what your guide is really saying is often like interpreting a goofy dream.

Finally, you must pay attention to the rule of visualization that says, "Take what you get." Your inner guide may not live up to your expectations. You may start the exercises below expecting to find a beautiful Indian maiden or Gandalf the Wise, only to end up with the nerd who broke your bike in fifth grade or a dwarf smoking a cigar. Your unconscious will be doing the choosing in the next exercise, and it's not predictable, reasonable, or literal in its creations. So don't be surprised, and take what you get.

Inner Guide Exercise

Before you begin this exercise in discovering an inner guide, prepare a question to ask. For this first experience, the best question is, "Are you my guide?"

This is simple, with no negatives to confuse your unconscious. The rules for making up good questions for your guide are the same as the rules for making up good affirmations: Keep them short, simple, positive, rich in feeling, and in the present tense whenever possible.

Begin the exercise by lying down, closing your eyes, and relaxing. Go to your outdoor special place and settle in. Notice all the details of sight and sound, touch and taste and smell that define your place and make it real to you.

From your special place, look off into the distance. See a tiny figure there. It's so far away that you can only see a speck moving in the haze. Imagine that this figure is your inner guide, approaching very slowly, getting larger very slowly. Soon you will be able to make out some details.

By now you can see the general shape of the figure. Is it a person or an animal? Wait until you can see this. Then try to tell if it's a man or a woman, or what kind of animal it is.

As the figure gets closer, see more and more details. How is this figure dressed? In regular clothes, in robes, not dressed at all? Any hats, staffs, bags? What colors and textures do you see?

You can see small details now: the color of the eyes, the texture of skin, the shape of nose and chin and brow. You can hear the figure's steps. Let this being, this possible guide, get closer, right up to the edge of your special place, then stop.

Does this figure look friendly? This is an important question. If the figure you've called up looks angry or dangerous, there's no need to invite it into your special place. Turn it around and have it walk away into the distance and disappear.

If you're confronting an animal figure, it may be hard to tell what "friendly" means. If you feel afraid of the animal, send it away. If you are in doubt, offer it some food and see if the feelings warm up.

In Shamanistic teachings, there are stern warnings about dealing with figures in the shape of snakes, lizards, fish, dragons, or beings who have the features of these scaly, cold-blooded creatures. So if you have conjured up some kind of reptilian figure, you might want to send it away and try again. On the other hand, maybe you have warm memories and a strong identification with Puff the Magic Dragon or Cecil the Seasick Sea Serpent, and a scaled, friendly guide is just right for you, however cold-blooded and serpent-like. In the final analysis, choose what feels right.

You can have several figures in turn approach from the distance and keep sending away the unfriendlies until you find a friendly one that you like. But don't send away a possible guide just because he or she doesn't meet your expectations. You may find that the same weird figure returns over and over. This is an indication that you have the right figure, even though it seems odd to your conscious, critical mind.

When you're satisfied that your guide is friendly, invite it into your special place. You can speak out loud and say, "Come in," or gesture, or use mental telepathy to communicate your desire. Greet your guide in an appropriate way: say hello or shake hands or embrace.

Grasp hands or look deep into the figure's eyes and ask your prepared question: "Are you my guide?" Your guide should say yes or nod or indicate in some other way that he or she is indeed your guide. If the answer is ambiguous, ask again until you get a clear answer.

If no clear answer comes or the answer is no, send the figure away with the instruction, "Please send me my guide." Then try again with another figure approaching from the distance.

Once you are satisfied that you are in the presence of your authentic guide, take a walk together and notice what you see. Hold hands during the walk, if that feels right. Return to your special place and show your guide around, as if you were showing off a new apartment or garden.

If your guide is an animal, pet or groom it. Ask for a gift or give something to your guide. If a simple question pops into your mind, ask it. Tell your guide that you trust him or her, and are glad to have your guide in your special place.

Finally, say goodbye. Promise to keep in touch. Have your guide promise to visit you whenever he or she is invited into your visualizations. Suggest to your guide that he or she should "drop in" on you whenever there is something important for you to know.

Rest for a moment alone in your special place. Know that you have an inner guide that you can trust. Your guide comes to you whenever you need it. Your guide is wise, all-knowing, and has only your best interests at heart.

When you are ready, remind yourself of your actual surroundings. Open your eyes and end the session.

In the next day or two, do this exercise again. This time, have your inner guide visit you in your indoor special place. Your guide can come to the door or appear in one of the places you have prepared for such visits. Repeat the question, "Are you my guide?" and interact in the same way you did outdoors.

When you're exploring particularly complicated or confusing issues, try meeting your inner guide deep within a cave or maze. Imagine finding the end of a thread at the mouth of a cave. Pick up the thread and follow it into the cave. Go deeper and deeper into the cave, following the thread as it leads down different tunnels, through tight spots, across great open chambers, and so on. Gradually come to a small, dark chamber deep within the cave. Your inner guide is there, holding a small light. In this special setting, ask for enlightenment. The cave imagery symbolizes the descent into your unconscious and a delving beneath the superficial surface of your situation. If the idea of going into a cave makes you nervous, imagine walking into a maze of hedges or a building with many corridors and doors.

Examples

Sarah had an unusual guide. It was a black panther. She could look into its eyes and communicate telepathically. As time went on, the panther got larger and larger. Finally it turned into a cat woman who could talk. Sarah liked the cat woman better because she was more human and easier to communicate with.

Jean had three guides. The first was a little girl who looked like Dorothy in *The Wizard of Oz*. In fact, Jean called her Dorothy. She was very plucky, showed good common sense, and was Jean's clearest guide to what she really wanted out of life. Jean's woman guide was quite old. She wore a blue robe and a circlet of golden laurel leaves in her hair. This guide was very compassionate, and often counseled Jean not to feel so guilty and self-condemning about her failings. Jean's male guide was young, strong, and dressed like a lifeguard. He was good for cheering her up when she was depressed and encouraging her to get a little fun out of life.

Larry's guide was an old, wise man. He looked like a cross between Buddha and Willie Nelson. He always dressed in dusty coveralls and a Mets baseball cap. He had a deep voice, glittering eyes, and a sarcastic chuckle. His answers to Larry's questions tended to be brief and harsh, but Larry liked him a lot. Larry had a couple of other guides—a young woman named Mazda and a boy who looked like Larry at age six—but they didn't show up very often.

III

Applications for Self-Improvement

7

Pleasure

This is a new chapter for the second edition. When I first wrote this book, I was determined to be serious. I wanted to cover only major, important kinds of change such as controlling pain or treating cancer. I didn't realize that visualization "for change" should include visualization for pleasure. Getting more pleasure in your life is one of the most important changes you can make.

Sometimes you can get so obsessed with improving the factual circumstances of your life that you completely disregard the subjective quality of your life. You may be able to visualize and achieve major goals but remain unhappy.

Take my friend Phyllis, for example. In the last five years she has received her M.D. degree, joined a thriving pediatrics practice, and given birth to a beautiful baby girl. To achieve these major life goals, she had to overcome parents who thought she should become a nurse instead of a doctor. She struggled for years with limited finances. She and her husband had serious infertility problems that made conception difficult. You'd think she'd be happy now, but her life is still miserable. She remains a negative, complaining person. She takes almost no pleasure from her academic accomplishments, her new profession, or her pretty new child.

On the other hand, there are people whose circumstances are daunting, but they go through life with a smile and a song. My cousin Jane is a single mom with a bad back and a seven-year-old son with a learning disability. But they have great times together. The simplest things give them pleasure: a walk in the rain, a kitten and a piece of string, a caterpillar crawling across the path.

It's a cliché, but what they say about the glass being half full or half empty is true: happiness is a matter of perception, a matter of how you visualize your circumstances. Good luck and hard work are important, but they are secondary to your attitude, to how you see your life. If you see your life as an interesting adventure and focus on the positive, you will enjoy yourself. If you see your life as one long dental appointment, you will suffer.

Pleasure depends on visualization in a more direct way as well. Visualization is an essential component of pleasure. You can't read a novel and enjoy it without visualizing the characters and the setting. A key part of the pleasure of dinner out at a fine restaurant is the anticipation—visualizing what it will be like. Sexual desire and its fulfillment are about ninety percent visualization and only about ten percent biology. The pleasure of listening to music is enhanced by the mental images it inspires. Even looking at a beautiful painting induces collateral images and feelings that are not actually present in the pigment on the canvas.

In one sense, you can't feel any pleasure at all without visualizing—without bringing your awareness to the object of pleasure. A gorgeous sunset might bring you no pleasure if you have a headache and are too preoccupied with your pain to notice the sky.

This chapter will address all the ways in which pleasure and visualization are connected. There are four skills to learn:

1. How to visualize for pure pleasure.

2. How to identify and expand the list of things that bring you pleasure.

3. How to create visualizations that can give you short bursts of pleasure anywhere and anytime.

4. How to see the glass as half full.

Unguided Fantasy

In the other chapters of this book you perform receptive visualizations in order to explore your resistance to change, to gain insight into a problem, or to generate images that will be used later in a programmed visualization. In this chapter, the receptive visualization exercise is a completely unguided fantasy. There is no purpose beyond the visualization itself. The only rule is to have the intention of experiencing pleasant mental images. Just close your eyes and daydream.

I have a confession to make. This kind of unguided fantasy is what I do when I'm supposed to be "meditating." Occasionally on a Monday night when my men's group isn't meeting, I drive down to the Spirit Rock Center in Marin

County. Spirit Rock is a Buddhist meditation center run by Jack Kornfield, a wise and compassionate teacher to whom I love to listen. Part of the Monday night teaching is a forty-five-minute sitting meditation.

Now I know how to meditate the "right" way—focusing on the breath or a mantra, trying to stay in the moment, returning my awareness to the object of meditation, and so on. And I have on occasion actually meditated that way. But more often than not I visualize instead. I enjoy an unguided fantasy. I embark on a visualization adventure.

My body is sitting cross-legged on the floor, but my mind is flying off in Galaxy X, taking a technicolor ride with special effects that make Hollywood's productions seem like grammar school skits.

Since I learned how to fly a plane, I seem to do a lot of flying in my fantasies. But I'm usually a bird or superbeing, not a pilot of a plane. On good nights there are lots of bright colors and interesting scenery. I often fly through caves or out into space.

Sometimes the lurid comic-book images soften and I have a more lyrical, impressionistic vision of flowers or gems, with string music in waltz time. Bits of movies or past dreams sometimes weave themselves into the fantasy.

Often I'm alone. When others join me, they are likely to be my wife or my father or my son, but sometimes changed or combined, the way it is in dreams where people's identities are unclear or keep changing. Strangers rarely figure in, although last Monday I was sitting next to a beautiful blond woman who showed up in a decidedly pornographic fantasy. When that happens, relax and enjoy it. Remember that visualization is not fornication. Your fantasy life is your own business, and you don't have to feel guilty about purely mental behavior.

Change is the only constant. One sense impression leads to another, often at high speed. A sequence like this: *flower opens with egg inside, egg turns to obsidian skull, heats up, explodes into hot lava from volcano, lava becomes warm mud bath, feels like massage, smells like hand lotion, see Ginny's face in the mirror when she was crying, salt tears on the tongue, lemon juice on spinach salad reminds me I've got to plant the lettuce bed in the garden . . .* flashes by in half the time it takes to read it.

You may find that you experience rapid changes of point of view. You can switch from one point of view to another so fast that it's almost like your awareness is split or multiplied. You'll be caught up in each image, then notice yourself watching the show, then think "This is neat," and then start analyzing the connections and meanings of some of the images.

This free association of images often happens spontaneously just before you fall asleep. In fact, you may fall asleep when you try this exercise. That's OK. Don't worry about it. Take a little nap and try again when you're not so tired.

The actual instructions are simple: in the next few days, set some time aside to sit or lie comfortably alone. Close your eyes and relax. Entertain whatever images arise, with the intention of enjoying yourself. Keep a passive, curious, nonjudgmental attitude. Accept whatever images come up for you, even if they don't seem "right" or particularly enjoyable. Keep practicing until you can look forward to these visualizations as a pleasant interlude.

My Favorite Things

You've heard the song from *The Sound of Music*:

> *Raindrops on roses and whiskers on kittens,*
> *Bright copper kettles and warm woolen mittens,*
> *Brown paper packages tied up with strings,*
> *These are a few of my favorite things.*

You may not agree with Rogers and Hammerstein's sentimental list, but you undoubtedly have your own list of things that bring a smile to your heart when you see or think of them.

Get a piece of paper and make a list of things you like. Include big things and little things. Try to list something that appeals to each of your senses of sight, hearing, touch, taste, smell, and so on. Avoid abstractions like truth, justice, or prestige.

If you have trouble making this list, try a short receptive visualization. Close your eyes and think back to the last time you remember enjoying yourself. Imagine you are back in that scene. Then pick out little details of the experience that you remember as particularly appealing.

For instance, if you like horseback riding, remember the last time you went riding. Focus on the details: how soft the horse's nose felt, how his hot breath snuffed into your hand as you fed him a sugar lump, the creak and smell of the leather tack, the feel of wrapping your legs around your mount and working your feet into the stirrups, how your legs move slightly outward as the horse inhales, the way the world looks from the vantage of horseback, the feel of control over a strong animal, the first pleasure as the horse starts walking, the sun on your head and shoulders, the sound of the horse whinnying.

From this little visualization you can pick three or four items that you really enjoy and add them to your list. As you make your list, consider these possibilities:

Music	Clothes
Food	Nature
Sex	Favorite possessions
Sports	Places
Hobbies	Scents
Friends	Sounds
Family	

For the next few days, notice the simple things you do and see and hear that give you pleasure. Carry a small notebook or an index card in your purse or pocket and jot down pleasant items as you encounter them. This will sharpen your eye for the pleasurable opportunities in your daily life. If you have a tendency toward chronic anxiety and constant vigilance, it may make the universe seem a friendlier, safer place.

Programmed Visualizations

Use your list of favorite things and your experience with unguided fantasies to create short programmed visualizations that give you intense pleasure. You can use these intense fantasies to cheer yourself up when you're feeling blue, to while away a long, boring wait at the building permit office, or to distract yourself while sitting in the dentist's chair.

Throw in some affirmations such as:

I deserve to have fun.

Pleasure is good for me.

This is my time to enjoy myself.

It's OK to have fun.

God wants me to enjoy the good things of life.

I take joy in the wonders of the world.

I trust myself and love myself.

I allow myself pleasure.

Here are some further suggestions for pleasant visualizations.

Visualize activities you enjoy but can't actually participate in at the moment such as skiing in the summer, playing tennis in the winter, gardening in the rain, sailing your boat while at work, hiking while you have a broken leg, playing the piano while driving, and so on.

Work on your ultimate sexual fantasies. They're normal and healthy, everybody has them, so you might as well get really good at sexual fantasies and enjoy them fully. However, back off on sexual fantasies if they begin to replace real sex with your regular partner or make you more likely to perform some indiscretion or infidelity that you want to avoid.

In your imagination, you can visit with dead or distant friends and relatives. You can have a discussion with Socrates, play catch with Babe Ruth, or watch your great-grandmother's vaudeville act.

You can visualize places and times past: roam through the house you grew up in, drive your grandpa's Packard, float down the Nile in the time of the Pharaohs.

Try living through a favorite movie or book, taking the point of view of your favorite character.

Visualize doing things you probably won't ever do: climbing Mount Everest, winning Olympic track events, performing at the Met, flying like a bird, operating a steam locomotive, traveling around the world, or meeting real aliens from another planet.

You can also just hang out in your special place and have fun. Listen to music or dance or make love. Invite your inner guide to join you and suggest ways for you to get more pleasure out of life.

Visualize your spiritual or religious life. If you believe in an afterlife, pretend you're there. See and hear and feel every detail. Travel back in time and visit with Jesus or Moses or Mohammed. Meet angels and saints. Witness the miracles of sacred scripture.

Visualizing the Glass as Half Full

I'd like to conclude this chapter with some ideas that are perhaps a step removed from visualizing for pleasure. But they're related and they're important.

Nearly everything Norman Vincent Peale wrote years ago in *The Power of Positive Thinking* was true. All the other motivational speakers and writers since then have just elaborated on his key idea: It's better to think positively than negatively. Your life will be happier if you see the glass as half full instead of half empty.

Cognitive psychologists such as my friend Matt McKay have developed exhaustive lists of the logical fallacies and irrational beliefs that lead you to view your life negatively. And they have come up with some genuinely effective ways to refute your negative self-talk and achieve a more positive outlook.

I think there's a special kind of visualization that offers a third path. It's a way that is not as greedy or success-oriented as positive thinking. It's not as intellectual or pathology-oriented as cognitive therapy. What I have in mind is similar to Buddhist ideas of acceptance, learning from difficulties, and letting go of desire.

This special kind of visualization is called the "Can't Lose" point of view. It's incredibly simple: whenever you're in a painful or confusing situation and you're not sure of the outcome, visualize each possible outcome in turn. In each scenario, find some positive benefit. Then sum up the situation for yourself as an "I Can't Lose" statement.

For example, I have a white 1949 Chevy truck sitting in pieces in a shed. Sometimes it bothers me that I haven't gotten around to putting the truck back together. Sometimes my friends or family kid me about it. When that happens, I tell myself, "I can't lose: if I let it sit there, it is growing in value and I have an interesting project to look forward to. If I put it back together, I'll get some good use out of it. If I sell it as-is, I'll have some extra storage space and money."

Here's another example: My friend George was very unhappy about the way his gardener took care of his lawn. It was full of dandelions that the gardener said would eventually be crowded out by healthy turf. But George wanted the dandelions weeded out by hand. He dreaded a confrontation with his gardener. I pointed out that he couldn't lose: either he would clear the air and the gardener would weed the lawn, or the gardener would get mad and quit, or George would get mad and fire the gardener. In the last two cases, George would be free to hire a new gardener whom he could train from the beginning to do the yard his way.

My wife, Nancy, tells me this isn't visualization. She says it's nothing more than the old-fashioned Methodist practices of seeing a silver lining in every cloud and counting your blessings. I say that may be so, but then all those old-time Methodists back in Ohio are practicing creative visualization and don't even know it.

Whether you call it the "Can't Lose" point of view or the "Silver Lining" method or "Blessing Counting," it amounts to the same thing. It's a matter of visualizing an unfortunate situation in terms of its positive aspects. Rather than positive thinking, it's positive imagining.

Don't let the apparent simplicity of this technique put you off. Try it. The next time you are looking forward to a job interview or a weekend with a sullen teenager, go into the situation with a "Can't Lose" attitude. Tell yourself that you'll either get the job and have money or not get the job and have more free time. Tell yourself that you'll either make meaningful contact with the teenager and grow closer or remain distant and pursue your separate interests in peace.

This doesn't mean that you shouldn't try to achieve your desired outcome. Of course you should. You should do your best in the job interview and make sincere overtures to the teenager. The Can't Lose point of view means that you should be prepared to accept any outcome and make the best of it. It allows you to let go of attachment to a rigid view of black-and-white results. It allows you to be more open, more relaxed, more flexible.

Ultimately, taking the Can't Lose point of view means that you will tend to visualize the whole universe as a positive, expanding, welcoming place, full of energy and potential. You'll tend to see people as basically good, not evil. You'll live your life in a way that supports and celebrates others, rather than putting down and competing with others. And you'll make lots of room for pleasure in your life. Because in a universe that is inherently good, pleasure is a form of worship.

8

Weight Control

"All the things I really like to do are immoral, illegal, or fattening."

—*Alexander Woollcott*

Chances are better than fifty-fifty that you bought this book hoping to use visualization to lose weight. More diet books are sold than all other kinds of self-help books.

And yet, research in the last fifteen years has repeatedly turned up physiological evidence proving what you may have suspected all along: that diets don't work. You count calories, eat weird food you don't really like, resist incredible cravings, and generally suffer for weeks to lose a few pounds. Then, when you go off your diet and eat "normally," you gain all the weight back again.

The 1980s and 90s have seen the emergence of the "anti-diet" approach. This approach is based on the *set point* theory of weight control, which states that your body has a *set point* weight that it prefers. Each person has an amount of body fat that is optimum for him or her to maintain. Some people are naturally very skinny, others are naturally very fat, and most of us are naturally somewhere in the middle.

The goal of modern weight control experts, and of this chapter, is to help you reach and live at your set point happily, without any more dieting or obsessing about your weight.

Your Set Point Weight

Your set point is a relatively narrow weight range that is predetermined by your heredity and your basal metabolism. In your younger years, and as long as you get a good amount of exercise, you'll tend to stay at the lower range of your set point. As you become older or more sedentary, you'll drift to the higher end of the range. But nothing, not even exercise, will change your set point—nothing will shift the entire range higher or lower. You can starve yourself and be miserable constantly to maintain a weight lower than your set point—but you can't change your set point. The minute you go off your diet and eat what you crave, you will bounce right back to your set point. This is why so many diet plans fail.

Your body defends its set point tenaciously. Have you ever gone on a diet and lost five pounds right away, then had trouble losing any more, even though you stuck religiously to your plan? When you drop below your optimum, set point weight, your body gets more and more efficient, making the utmost use of every calorie to keep weight on. The longer you starve yourself, the less you lose.

The news gets worse for dieters. When you give up on a diet and begin to eat what you crave, you will probably return to a weight *higher* than your set point, as your body tries to compensate for the time you spent in a starved condition. Many scientists now think that this yo-yoing of weight is the cause of much of the heart disease, high blood pressure, and premature death formerly blamed on obesity. It now seems that weight fluctuation is much worse for you than merely staying at a higher weight.

How can you determine your set point? By digging out any old medical records you can find that show your weight at different ages. Look for a time when you had reached your adult height and were eating without being conscious of any weight problem. What you weighed then was your set point weight for the level of exercise you were getting.

If you have been diet- and weight-conscious since your teens, you may not be able to accurately determine your set point weight. In that case, you'll just have to start eating normally and rid yourself of your habitual preoccupation with weight. In time you will settle at your set point.

So what do you do? The new generation of "anti-diet" experts have these suggestions:

Stop weighing yourself and counting calories.

Get rid of your too-tight clothes and wear only what's comfortable and attractive on you as you are now.

If you're always checking your body in mirrors and store windows, stop doing it. (If you habitually avoid seeing your reflection, start cultivating the habit of looking at yourself and noticing those features you like about your body.)

Concentrate on nutrition and balance in your diet, not calories or what's fattening and nonfattening. Move gradually toward less fat, less sugar, less salt. Add more whole grains and raw fruits and vegetables. Go for health, not slenderness.

This is the hard part: don't worry about what will happen when you go off your succession of diets. You may fear that you will start to binge and eat everything in sight. In fact, you probably will have some strong cravings for the foods you have been denying yourself. That's OK, go right ahead and eat them.

"But," you say, "I'll gain weight like crazy." Unfortunately, this is possible. You will probably gain some weight. How much depends on your set point weight, how much you weighed when you gave up dieting, and how long you have been on the weight loss roller coaster. But few people will gain more than ten pounds. And consider the alternative—if you try to resist your cravings, you will be plunging yourself right back into diet madness. You will gain and lose those ten pounds several times over, with the resultant wear and tear on your body and mind.

Now here's the good news: those ten pounds aren't necessarily here to stay. As time passes and you don't institute any new reigns of terror in the form of starvation diets, your body will calm down and be more reasonable in its demands. The cravings will subside and you'll find it easier to eat a balanced, healthy diet. Any weight you've gained over and above your set point will gradually come off.

How gradually does this process work? Very gradually. You should allow at least a year for your weight control program to work. If you've been dieting for years, it might even take two years for your body to reach a normal balance.

One to two years is a long time to sustain any kind of self-improvement program, so you should expect some setbacks. You may decide to try some intriguing new diet or go on a fast. When that happens, and the diet or the fast doesn't work, remember this paragraph. Forgive yourself for being human and go back to trusting your body and focusing on eating all you want of a healthy, balanced diet. You spent years developing your old ideas about weight, so it's going to take a long time to make permanent changes in your attitudes and behavior.

You can speed up your journey toward your set point by getting more exercise. Regular exercise tones your body, reduces cravings, relieves boredom and depression, and allows you to reach your set point quicker. Choose some form of exercise you really enjoy and make it part of your life.

To stay comfortably at your set point weight, you need to clean up any serious addictions you might have to drugs that can interfere with a normal appetite: alcohol, caffeine, nicotine, uppers, tranquilizers, and so on. Alcohol stimulates your appetite and adds a lot of worthless calories to your daily diet. It can push you to the high end of your set point range and keep you there. If you drink to great excess, alcohol can kill your appetite entirely. Your appetite can also be suppressed by caffeine, nicotine, stimulants, or appetite suppressants sold as diet pills, or tranquilizers. If you can't get off these drugs on your own, get help.

Work on attitude changes: notice your own attractive points that have nothing to do with weight. Stop assessing other people automatically as fat or thin. Reflect on the fact that in the past, thin people were considered ugly and fat people beautiful—preferring slenderness is a matter of *fashion*, not a matter of health or absolute universal truth. Have compassion for heavy people and for yourself. Learn to recognize the essential humanity in everyone, including yourself, regardless of shape.

Resist the "fattist" messages of the media. TV and magazines will continue to present skinny adolescent models, made up to look like grown women and men, as the ideals for all adults to emulate. You should consider this as vicious, dehumanizing propaganda that can undermine your attempts to form a more healthy, humane attitude toward weight. You will have to be eternally vigilant to resist media brainwashing.

Why You Eat and Overeat

There are some psychological factors that can interfere with your attempts to reach and maintain your optimum weight. These are tendencies that make you feel hungry when in fact your body doesn't need food.

Your Body

On the purely biological level, you eat to sustain life, fuel activity, and preserve health. You eat because you're hungry. Hunger is your body's signal to you that it's time to seek food. Hunger is a strong feeling because getting food is a major part of surviving as an animal in the wild state. Your body is built to a prehistoric design, to cope with prehistoric conditions. In the wild state, food is scarce and you eat what you can get.

Your body is also designed so that eating is pleasurable, and the pleasure continues even for a little while after you're "full." This allows you to eat a little more than you actually need at any given moment to sustain life, activity, and health. If an animal happens upon a little extra food, its body can make use of it to store up some fat against future lean times.

The problem is that you don't live in prehistoric times. There's plenty of food around now. And it's not all roots and berries, either. The current "food environment" is not only more plentiful, it also has higher proportions of fats and sugars than the prehistoric menu had to offer.

Perhaps in a few more million years, the human race will evolve a hunger drive more suited to civilized conditions. But you can't wait. You're stuck now, trying to control a prehistoric appetite with a modern conscious mind.

Your Mind

If your mind was in perfect working order, all the time, it could just tell your body, "Here, eat these sprouts, they're good for you. . . . That's enough now, stop eating."

Unfortunately, your mind can have its own reasons for overeating, and they are just as compelling as any prehistoric appetite. And because your mind is mostly unconscious, it can be hard to uncover your many reasons for overeating.

Receptive Visualization

Visualization is an excellent way to uncover, refute, and change your reasons for overeating, putting you in more conscious charge of your appetite. To get started, do this receptive visualization:

Lie down, close your eyes, and relax.

Drift back to the last time you overate. What did you have to eat? What time of the day was it? Imagine that you are eating the same food. Really taste and smell it. Is it delicious? Does it give you lots of pleasure?

Move back a little bit in time to just before you started eating. What is going on? How are you feeling? Are you anxious or scared about something? Are you just bored? Have you had a fight with somebody? Are you feeling depressed? Do you feel lonely? Have you been under a lot of stress? Are you celebrating some success or consoling yourself for a failure? When you think about eating, do you get a rush of pleasure at the prospect?

When you imagine yourself getting ready to eat and eating, is somebody else around? Is that person suffering because of your weight problem? Is it like a punishment for that person? Or do you get sympathy from someone because of your weight? Do the people around you expect you to clean your plate? Does your overeating please them in some way?

If these scenes of overeating don't inspire you, try consulting your inner guide. Take a walk down an imaginary path, or go to your special place. Encounter your inner guide and ask about your weight. Ask, "Why do I overeat?" and "Why do I stay heavy?" See what answers you get.

When you're ready, end this visualization and go on to the checklist below.

Checklist

Examine these common reasons for overeating and the payoffs for remaining overweight. Allow yourself to consider them honestly and check off those that might apply to you:

- ☐ 1. I eat when I feel anxious or afraid of something.
- ☐ 2. I eat when I'm bored.
- ☐ 3. I eat when I'm angry, especially if I can't or don't want to express my anger.
- ☐ 4. I often eat when I'm depressed.

☐   5. When I feel lonely, I eat too much.

☐   6. I always eat a lot when I'm under stress.

☐   7. I just feel empty inside, and eating fills that emptiness.

☐   8. I eat to celebrate success.

☐   9. I eat to console myself for failure.

☐   10. I just plain love food. It's my greatest pleasure in life.

☐   11. Eating well allows me to reexperience my mother's love. She always rewarded and comforted me with food.

☐   12. I hate to waste food. I want to get my money's worth.

☐   13. I eat for social reasons: it's polite, it's expected of me.

☐   14. I eat to punish myself or someone else.

☐   15. Being overweight means I'm big instead of skinny and weak.

☐   16. Being big protects me. It's like armor. Others are kept at bay by my wide boundaries.

☐   17. My weight problem gets me sympathy.

☐   18. If I solved my weight problem, then I'd have to do something about my job, my family, my smoking, or some other problem.

☐   19. My weight problem keeps me busy. If I didn't have to think about food and dieting, I might feel bored or empty.

☐   20. Since I'm so overweight, I don't have to worry about sex. If I lost weight, I might receive unwanted sexual advances.

☐   21. Being overweight means I don't have to compete in sports, for pop-popularity, or in the sexual arena.

☐   22. I'm too big to be seen in public, so I can avoid all sorts of scary social engagements.

If you can think of any other reasons for overeating or staying overweight that are not listed here, add them to the list.

Look over the reasons you have checked. You may see a pattern. Perhaps most of your reasons have to do with easing painful emotions, or with your early childhood experiences with food, or with your fear of social situations.

On the other hand, maybe none of these psychological reasons seems really compelling. Maybe you have been dieting for years without permanent weight loss, and overeating is a direct result of your interference with your natural appetite and your optimum set point weight. Perhaps you overeat because of powerful cravings that your body develops in an attempt to get the food it needs to defend your set point weight.

Your visualizations for weight control will be designed to counter your typical reasons for overeating with new, saner, more powerful reasons for good eating habits. It will remind you that your goal is no longer a super-slender body, but rather a stable, healthy weight maintained by good nutrition and exercise. The first step is to make up a set of four or five affirmations about food and weight that apply specifically to you.

Review your reasons for overeating or staying overweight, and the material on set point theory. Pick out four or five themes that seem strongest in your preoccupation with weight. Make up an affirmation to counter each reason for overeating or reinforce each idea about healthy eating habits.

Remember, an affirmation is a strong, positive, feeling-rich statement that some desired change is already so. Here are some sample affirmations that have worked well for others:

1. *When I'm anxious, I'd rather do relaxation exercises than eat.*

2. *When I'm bored, I'd rather go for a walk than eat.*

3. *When I'm angry, I'd rather talk to someone about it than eat.*

4. *When I'm depressed, I'd rather go jogging or swimming than eat.*

5. *When I'm lonely, I'd rather call up a friend than eat.*

6. *When I'm under stress, I'd rather do deep breathing than eat.*

7. *I am a worthwhile person.*
   I am full of love.

8. *When I do something good, I congratulate myself.*

9. *When I make a mistake, I forgive myself.*

10. *Food is only one of many pleasures I enjoy.*
    I enjoy food, but it is only moderately important to me.
    When I'm full, I put down my fork and clear the table.
    I eat just enough to stay healthy, active, and feeling good.

11. *I am a grownup person now.*
    I am intelligent and sensitive.
    I seldom think about food between meals.

12. *At restaurants I eat until I'm full and leave the rest.*
    I always know the instant I'm full.
    I choose quality over quantity when I cook.

13. *When I visit friends, I'd rather talk than eat.*

14. *I can forgive myself and others.*
    Only I am responsible for my life.

15. *I can weigh less and still be strong.*

16. *I can protect myself.*
    I can be safe without my fat armor.

17. *I now have respect instead of pity.*

18. *I am in control of my life. I solve my problems step by step.*

19. *I'm too busy sewing to think about food.*
    I have many interesting things to do.

20. *I'm self-confident when I'm thinner.*
    I can learn to be assertive.
    I can handle sexual advances.
    I accept my own sexuality.

21. *I choose when and where I want to compete.*
    I weigh what I have chosen to weigh.
    I can choose to weigh more or less.

22. *Being slender gives me confidence.*
    I can be slimmer and still stay at home if I want.

And here are some "set point" affirmations:

I'm happy at my set point weight.

I'd rather be healthy than too skinny.

I trust my body.

My body knows what I need.

Food is my friend.

I eat what I want.

I count on good nutrition, not calories.

In mirrors I see my nice _____ and _____
    (insert the things you like about your body).

I never weigh myself.

I look fine just as I am.

TV is make-believe.

Fashion magazines are fairy tales.

Models are skinny adolescents.

People come in many beautiful shapes.

I love full figures as well as slender ones.

Weight Loss Visualization

The following visualization takes you through an ideal day, with many images of sane eating and a positive attitude about weight. You should pick out and elaborate on the images and experiences that apply to you and skip over the rest. Use this description as an inspiration to form short visualizations tailored to your needs. For instance, you could use the first part about getting up in the morning as your visualization while falling asleep at night. You could use the restaurant sequence before going out to eat, or the dinner sequence before shopping for clothes. You might want to tape record this visualization to make it easier to follow the steps.

Lie down and get comfortable. Close your eyes and relax. Imagine that you are waking up in the morning. Drift from vague dreams to an awareness that it's morning and time to get up. Feel the weight and warmth of the covers. Rub your eyes and imagine opening them and seeing your bedroom. Look at the clock and see what time it is. Stretch and yawn. Get out of bed. Go into the bathroom to take a shower or bath. You feel rested, wide awake, light, and healthy. You're glad to be alive and feel good in your body.

In the bath or shower, run your hands over your body as you wash. Notice that your skin is smooth and healthy-looking. Note that your body seems firmer and leaner than usual. If any negative thoughts about your body come to mind, say to yourself, "Stop! I love my body just the way it is." Get out of the bath and look at yourself in the steamy bathroom mirror. Write with your finger on the mirror: "I love you." Really feel the slick, cool mirror and the muscles of your arm and hand moving as you write. See your face becoming clearer as you wipe the condensation away.

Now get dressed. Put on some new, attractive clothes that are exactly the right size for your body just as it is—not the size you wish you could wear. Feel how soft and luxurious the fabric feels on your clean, firm skin. Smell the faint hint of sizing—that "department store" smell that new clothes have. Look at yourself in a full-length mirror and notice how good you look in clothes that are the right size and don't pinch and squeeze you. Really enjoy the loose, free feel of clothes that fit.

Go into the kitchen and prepare some breakfast. Have some fruit, some cereal, whole grain toast, juice, or some other light, nutritious food. Take your time and enjoy. Savor your food and be sure to eat enough. Tell yourself, "I love food. Food is my friend. I eat just enough to stay healthy, active, and feeling good."

Walk out your front door with a spring in your step. Feel rested, satisfied, full of pep. Swing your arms and shoulders and hips a little more than usual, enjoying the sheer pleasure of moving in your healthy, well nourished body.

Go to work, to school, or somewhere else where you have something to do that involves other people. Look at the other people and notice that they are all human beings, whether fat or skinny or "just right." All have needs and desires and dignity. Expand your standards until everybody looks "just right," just human.

Imagine you are doing your work or going to classes. Allow yourself to feel different emotions. First, feel bored. Imagine that you have no interest in anything, that you are at loose ends. Allow the thought to enter your mind: "I could get something to eat." But instead, see yourself get up and go for a walk. Get some exercise and fresh air. Feel a renewed interest in your job or studies. Tell yourself, "I have many interesting things to do. I'm actually much too busy to think about food."

Now feel anxious. Feel like someone is going to judge you or test you on something you don't know well. Allow yourself to think about food as a way to quell the anxiety. But instead of heading for the cafeteria or the refrigerator, see yourself going into a quiet place and doing a relaxation exercise: deep breathing and visualizing your special place. Feel your anxiety level decreasing. Tell yourself, "I'm a worthwhile person. I always do my best. If I make a mistake, I forgive myself. If I do well, I congratulate myself."

Next feel depressed. Let yourself slide way down. Nothing is worth bothering with. There is no hope. As the thought of food enters your mind, shout, "No! Eating will just make things worse. I can go jogging or swimming. I can take a brisk walk or do some aerobics. After all, I'm in control of my life. I can solve my problems step by step."

Feel angry. Imagine some insult or slight or unfairness. But pretend that it seems too dangerous to show your anger. Stifle it. Think of some way to smother your anger or console yourself, like eating some ice cream. But instead of heading for the freezer, dial the phone and call up a friend or relative. Tell that person about your anger. Say, "I just had to talk to somebody about this. I'm so angry." Feel your anger, and your false hunger, fading away as you tell your story. Think to yourself, "I alone am responsible for my life and my feelings. I can express my anger. I can forgive others and myself."

Finally, feel stressed out. Imagine that there are a million deadlines and demands on your time. Let the pressure build. Feel the intense craving to take a break for some coffee and a donut. But instead, see yourself taking a deep breath and letting it out slowly. Watch your eyes close. Feel the deep, slow breathing as it calms your body and washes away the feeling of pressure. Feel your muscles unclench as you relax. See yourself opening your eyes and calmly beginning to organize your time, all thoughts of a donut break vanished. Say the affirmations, "I am a grown-up person, intelligent and sensitive. I seldom think about food between meals."

Next, you notice that it's time to go to lunch. Walk to a favorite restaurant. On the way, look at your reflection in the shop windows. Just for fun, imagine that you have suddenly become skinny as a rail. See yourself as a "ninety-pound weakling." Does it scare you? Do you feel suddenly unprotected, like you've lost your armor against the world? Repeat to yourself, "I can weigh less and still be strong. I can protect myself. I can be safe without my fat armor."

Resume your normal shape and go on to the restaurant. Go inside and notice the sights, sounds, and smells. Take a moment to intensify the scene and deepen your relaxation.

Open the menu. As you scan the choices, look for what you really want to eat. Tell yourself, "I trust my body. It knows what I need." See yourself ordering exactly what you want, not what you think is low-calorie or proper. If you want fries and a milkshake, go ahead. If you want the pasta instead of the salad, go ahead. If you want a cocktail, some wine or beer, or some coffee, go ahead and order it. If you have a problem moderating your intake of these things, see yourself declining them or having just one serving.

When your lunch comes, enjoy it. Taste and smell your food. Feel its temperature and texture in your mouth. Gradually feel fuller and fuller, less and less hungry. When you're full, put your fork down and push your plate away. Talk to your companion if you have one, or imagine reading a good book until the check comes. Tell yourself, "I always know the instant I'm full. I'd rather leave food on the plate than eat too much and feel stuffed.

On the way out of the restaurant with some change in your hand, pass a pay scale. Put your change in your pocket or purse and pass the scale by. Tell yourself that you're not interested in how much you weigh. How you feel is more important.

Take a walk toward your home. Enjoy your full but not stuffed feeling. Notice the weather, the traffic, the buildings. Pass by a theater that is showing an R-rated movie. Look at the poster and think about sex. If it makes you nervous, tell yourself, "I accept my own sexuality. I can handle sexual advances. As I get firmer and more attractive, I also get more confident. I'm becoming more assertive daily."

Walk past a park with tennis courts. Pause and watch some good players volleying. As you think about sports and competition, tell yourself, "I choose when and where I want to compete. I weigh what I have chosen to weigh. I can choose to weigh more or less. I am in control of my life."

Go home and hang out for a while. Spend some time by yourself, until you start to feel a little lonely. Nobody's around, you're all by yourself, and beginning to feel a little sorry for yourself. Maybe you should go get a little treat to make yourself feel better. But no. Instead, you call up a friend. Imagine that your friend cheers you up and invites you to come over after dinner.

Go out for a while and get some exercise. Take a walk, go jogging or cycling, go to the gym or go swimming, take an aerobics class, or whatever. See yourself as enjoying the exercise for its own sake, not because it's part of a weight-loss program. Tell yourself, "I exercise regularly because I love it."

Turn on the TV or page through a magazine, looking at the skinny people in the ads. Shake your head in disbelief and amusement. Tell yourself, "Those are just teenagers, dressed up to look like adults. The older ones either have unusually low set point weights or they must suffer constantly to be that slim."

Fix a light, well-balanced dinner, something you really like. Or if someone else usually fixes dinner, suggest a light, balanced menu. Take your time and enjoy it. The moment you feel full, get up and start clearing the table. Tell yourself, "I take care of myself. I eat plenty of good food and I'm happy at my set point weight."

Go over to your friend's house. Meet several of your friends there for an impromptu party. Have just one or two drinks, and maybe just a little of the abundant party food. Tell yourself, "At parties, I'd rather talk or dance than eat. I can have a good time without eating constantly."

See yourself as a little fitter, slightly lighter, moving gracefully, and smiling. Feel comfortable in your well-fitting clothes. Enjoy the feeling of health and vitality in your body. Love your body just the way it is. See your friends laughing and smiling while talking to you.

Look forward in time and see yourself at the same healthy set point weight year after year, feeling good, enjoying food, and not even thinking about weight control or dieting.

End this visualization by repeating the four or five affirmations that you have composed especially for yourself.

Changes To Expect

Use your expanded adaptations of this visualization three times a day, especially before meals or parties and just when awakening or going to sleep. You can expect a heightened awareness of food and weight at first, as your usual dieting mind-set rebels against these new ideas and images of unrestrained eating.

Some of your affirmations will lose power and have to be replaced by new ones. Some of your scenes will fade in intensity and you'll have to add new locales and details to spice them up. Review the chapter on rules for effective visualization for hints on keeping your weight control visualizations vivid and powerful.

As time goes by, your cravings should diminish and you should begin to eat a more balanced diet. If you have been starving yourself to stay excessively slim, you will gain weight. You will probably reach a weight higher than your set point, then sink back down to your set point. If you were heavier than your set point to start with, you may gain a little, but you'll soon settle down at your set point.

Increasing your exercise level will help you reach your set point weight faster, and ensure that you stabilize at a lower weight within your set point range. But beware of embarking on a vigorous exercise program for the sole purpose of losing weight. This is just part of the old dieting mind-set, and you won't be able to keep it up. Pick some activity you really like and try to do it two or three times a week. Having a relaxed, unhassled attitude about your exercise is more important than getting a certain amount of exercise every week.

Your attitude about eating and weight will change slowly. Eventually you will be able to enjoy food, stay at your set point weight, and not have to even think about calories and fat. But along the way there are bound to be setbacks and relapses. You'll feel that the "anti-diet" approach doesn't work, that it is just keeping you fat, that you're just being weak and lazy. This is normal. You've been brainwashed all your life by our "fattist" society to think that way. It's going to take time to change your attitude.

Keep reading books like this one, anti-diet books like Susan Kano's *Making Peace With Food* or *My Lifetime Weight Control,* and books and articles on good nutrition. Keep doing your visualizations, updating your images and affirmations as your situation and concerns change.

Example

Mary Ellen was five feet, six inches tall and weighed 150 pounds. Her mother was also heavy, although her two older sisters were not. She had worried about her weight and tried many diets since her teens. By the time she got fed up with diets and weight obsessions, she was 32, divorced, and working as a clerk in a hardware store. She was depressed, and the only social contact she had was a monthly meeting of a folk music club.

Mary Ellen began her campaign to stop dieting by doing some receptive visualizations. When she imagined overeating, she felt depressed, and could hear her sisters' voices in the background, talking to boys on the phone. This brought back memories of her high school days, when her older sisters would go out on dates and she would stay home, eating ice cream in front of the TV. She felt she could never compete with her sisters. If she remained fat, she wouldn't have to compete for attention and boyfriends—her weight gave her a reasonable explanation of why she was always the stay-at-home, always the wallflower.

Three affirmations were at the core of Mary Ellen's plan for visualization:

When I'm feeling blue, I'd rather play the guitar than eat.

This was intended to replace food with music as a solace when she was depressed.

I'm not Beth or Jane—I am my own person, with many worthwhile qualities.

This affirmation countered her feelings of inadequacy when she compared her sisters' lives with her own.

I eat sensibly and I weigh whatever I weigh.

This reinforced her acceptance of her set point weight, whatever it was. Because she had been dieting and obsessing about her weight since age twelve, she didn't really know what her set point range was.

Mary Ellen did her visualizations when she woke up in the morning, as soon as she got home from work, and before falling asleep at night. In the morning she would visualize herself healthy and happy, unaware of her weight. She would see herself at work, talking with the other employees or playing her recorder alone during coffee breaks instead of going to the cafe for a piece of pie. At work before lunch and coffee breaks she would find some shelf-stocking to do in a quiet corner of the store, and just close her eyes for a moment to repeat her affirmations.

When she got home, Mary Ellen would relax by doing her visualization exercise. Sometimes she forgot, or was feeling so miserable that she consciously skipped it and went straight to the refrigerator instead. But at least half the time she did her evening visualization. She would concentrate on seeing herself having fun with her folk music, going to movies with her best friend, or working on craft projects. She began using the affirmations: "I have lots of interesting things to do" and "I'm too busy to be depressed."

Before falling asleep, Mary Ellen would visualize herself as in the peak of health, a little heavy but happy. She would say to herself, "I weigh what I weigh and I accept it." She would remind herself in the visualization not to weigh herself in the morning, her usual time for fretting about her weight.

Mary Ellen had lots of relapses. Before Christmas and after the New Year she briefly relapsed and tried a couple of diets she read about in *Reader's Digest* and *Family Circle*. Both times she lost several pounds, stopped following the diet, and gained the weight right back. But she kept coming back to her visualizations and the anti-diet approach.

Gradually, Mary Ellen lost her weight obsessions. She bought a juicer and made nutritious drinks. She asked for vegetarian cookbooks for her birthday and started trying some recipes. She found that sometimes she actually preferred to order salad instead of french fries, or herbal tea instead of pie *a la mode* for dessert. She began walking home from work instead of taking the bus. She took an ornithology class at the junior college and spent several weekends tramping around a marsh identifying birds. She even met an interesting man in class and went out with him on a picnic. Nothing became of it, but it was quite an accomplishment for Mary Ellen to risk involvement with a stranger.

Mary Ellen is remarried now, to a banjo player from the folk music club. They have a five-year-old daughter named Caitlin. Mary Ellen is still plump, but less so than she used to be. If you ask her what she weighs, she says, "I don't know—around one hundred thirty-five, one hundred fory—somewhere in there."

9

Nonsmoking

"The wretcheder one is, the more one smokes; and the more one smokes, the wretcheder one gets."

— *George du Maurier*

It's hard to stop smoking even when you know intellectually that you should. That's because the habit of smoking is not maintained by an intellectual decision. Smoking is a habit and an addiction. As a habit, it fills needs that may be totally out of your awareness. As an addiction to nicotine, smoking is self-perpetuating— your body craves the powerful stimulant to which it has become accustomed.

Visualization can help you stop smoking in four ways: (1) by helping you discover the unconscious needs that smoking fills for you, (2) by reinforcing alternative means of meeting those needs, (3) by creating a strong image of yourself as a nonsmoker, and (4) by serving as a means of relaxation during the jitters of nicotine withdrawal.

Why You Smoke

Nurturance.   You may smoke as a way of nurturing yourself. The first cigarette in the morning can be a solace as you look forward to another day of the same old grind. A cigarette on the way to work makes you feel less sorry for yourself. Smoking can help when you're lonely or bored. A smoke can be a reward for a job well done or an unpleasant task accomplished. Having a pack of cigarettes in your pocket or purse can feel like having a friend along with you. It's a twenty-member support group that fits in the palm of your hand, promising instant companionship at the flick of your lighter. Smokers who point out the similarities between sucking on a Marlboro and nursing at your mother's breast are not so far off the mark.

Social lubricant.   At a party or in a group of strange people, a cigarette gives you something to do with your hands. It is also a common bond between you and other smokers, offering something safe to do and talk about in those first awkward moments of meeting someone new. In areas where smoking is not allowed, stepping outside for a smoke is a legitimate way to escape from the crowd for a few minutes.

Smoking may make you feel more confident, more a man or woman of the world. You may admire someone in your life who smokes, and the shared habit is a way of being more like that person.

Stress relief.   Lighting up a cigarette can be a relaxing ritual (even though the nicotine in the tobacco is actually a stimulant). First, the familiar sensations are reassuring: the look and feel of the cigarette and the flame, the taste and smell, the sight of the smoke drifting out and up, the automatic shaking of the match or putting the lighter back into your pocket. You are in complete control, you know just what is going to happen, and there's no way you can fail.

As you take that first drag, the deep inhalation and long, slow exhalation are natural relaxers. If it's been a while since your last smoke and your body has been craving nicotine, the first few puffs relieves that little edge of anxiety caused by nicotine withdrawal.

While you're lighting up, you can't be doing anything else, so there's a welcome break from whatever you were doing. And no matter how depressed or tired you are, lighting the cigarette puts you in an anticipatory frame of mind— something pleasant is coming.

Weight control. Smoking depresses the appetite. You may continue smoking because you want to curb a normal appetite or keep the brakes on your overeating. You might be afraid that if you quit smoking you will end up weighing a ton.

Complement to other pleasures. Cigarettes go great with coffee, with booze, after sex, in a friendly bar, during conversations between friends, and so on. It probably seems impossible to enjoy some pleasures without smoking at the same time.

Self-destruction. Some people smoke partly *because* it's bad for them. They feel that they don't deserve to be healthy nonsmokers. Their self-esteem is so low they feel that it's appropriate that they should have a self-destructive habit like smoking.

With the exception of self-destructive impulses, these common reasons for smoking make sense. They are not stupid or evil or silly. They have positive functions. It's good to want to nurture and take care of yourself. It's reasonable that you should want to feel comfortable at a party or want to imitate someone you admire. It's smart to seek relief from stress and maintain a healthy weight. It's perfectly natural that you seek pleasure and avoid pain.

The trick is to recognize, accept, and find ways to keep the positive benefits of smoking—without smoking.

Receptive Visualization

The first step is to uncover all your reasons for smoking by means of a receptive visualization. You might want to tape the following instructions.

Begin by lying down, closing your eyes, and relaxing. Imagine that you are getting up in the morning. See and hear and feel all the details. Light the first cigarette of the day and notice what it feels like. Do you feel nurtured? Relaxed? Get a cup of coffee or tea and have another smoke. Notice how much you enjoy smoking with a hot drink.

Leave the house and travel to work or school, or to visit a friend. Smoke on the way and notice whether it relieves boredom, gives you a lift, or reassures you in some way. Imagine that you are working on an involved, demanding task and take a cigarette break. Notice how you relax while smoking.

Now shift the scene to a favorite restaurant. Imagine that you're with a friend who smokes, waiting for your order. You light up together and talk, laughing and smiling. Notice how smoking is a part of this pleasant experience. After your meal, glance at the desserts on the menu and decide to just have coffee and a cigarette instead. Let all your usual concerns about weight and calories and smoking come into your mind.

Go back to school or work or your home. It's a long, slow afternoon and you're bored. Have a smoke and see if that relieves the boredom. Notice that it's your last cigarette and go to the store for more. At the store, notice how secure you feel once you have a full pack on your person. You've got your cigarettes, your matches, your lighter. You're all set.

Now it's early evening. In a bar or your home, fix yourself a drink—beer, wine, a cocktail, coffee, or whatever you usually have. Light a cigarette, read your book, turn on the TV, talk to someone—go through whatever evening relaxation ritual you like that involves smoking. Notice how familiar and reassuring it is.

Now imagine that you're going to a party, make sure you have plenty of cigarettes. At the party, notice how smoking serves you. Does it give you something to do with your hands? Do you gravitate toward the smokers in the room? Do you offer or ask for a smoke as a way of breaking the ice? Look around the room. Is there a smoker whom you particularly admire? Notice whether you equate smoking with being confident, worldly, and grown-up. Notice if smoking reminds you of anyone you admire.

Let your mind wander for a while. Go to any time of day or night in which you particularly like to smoke. Where are you? What are you doing? Who is there? What are they doing? How do you feel? What is the particular pleasure you feel or pain you avoid that makes it especially important to smoke at this time?

Back at home, late at night or in the wee small hours of the morning, have the last cigarette of the day. Go into the bathroom and watch yourself smoke in the mirror. If you ever feel dissatisfaction with yourself, let it surface in your mind now. If you worry about lung cancer or emphysema, deliberately entertain those worries now. Look in the mirror and see if you look like someone who deserves to be a nonsmoker. Do you look hopeless or hopeful? Honestly ask yourself if you are punishing yourself in some way by smoking.

You can also go to your special place and ask your inner guide why you smoke. If the answer is unclear or not forthcoming, try simpler yes or no questions: do I smoke for nurturance? to relieve boredom? as a social lubricant? to control weight? to relax? to appear confident?

When you're ready, orient yourself to your surroundings and slowly open your eyes. Before getting up, think back over the visualization you have just done. Pick out the three or four most important needs that smoking fills for you. Resolve right now to find alternative ways to meet these needs.

Affirmations

You need three kinds of affirmations:

Aversive. Compose something like "Smoking is a filthy, disgusting, deadly habit." You will pair this with images of soggy cigarettes floating in cold coffee dregs, the early morning taste of stale smoke after late night smoking, dingy yellow teeth, blackened lungs, and so on.

Positive self-image. You'll need one good affirmation that says, "I am a healthy nonsmoker." This will help you develop an image of your future self as a *non*smoker, not an *ex*-smoker. As a nonsmoker, you *choose* not to smoke, you *prefer* not to smoke. Ex-smokers have to *force* themselves not to smoke. Phrase this affirmation in a way that reinforces this distinction for you. Here are some examples:

I am a healthy, energetic nonsmoker.

I seldom even think about smoking.

I choose to be healthy and strong.

I am full of clean, vital energy.

Alternatives. Finally, your most important affirmations will be several that reinforce alternative means of getting your needs met without smoking. These will require creativity to compose, and you'll have to keep changing them as you find new and better ways to get your needs met. For each of the needs that smoking fills for you, figure out some alternative ways of meeting that need. Make up affirmations that briefly describe the situation, the need, and how you intend to fill it. Here are some examples to get you started.

When I'm lonely, I phone a friend.

I write letters when I feel isolated.

When I feel ignored at a party, I start asking questions.

When I'm unhappy, I go for a walk.

I take deep breaths whenever I feel stressed out.

I can write about it in my diary when I feel insecure.

Feeling awkward is OK. I can handle it.

If I feel uncomfortable, I can go into the bathroom for a minute.

In the car I listen to tapes instead of smoking.

I do crocheting instead of smoking while watching TV.

I can read or make lists while waiting for my food.

After eating I concentrate on the conversation.

Instead of smoking after meals I help clear the table.

At my desk I suck on lemon drops, not cigarettes.

In the lunch room I sit at the nonsmoking table.

In bars, I ask for peanuts with my beer.

At parties, I stand or sit on the floor, away from smokers and ashtrays.

For companionship, I have my dog and my music.

At work I walk around the block for my break.

If I need comforting, I'll hug someone or make myself some tea.

If I start gaining weight, I'll read the weight control chapter.

It's all right to look unoccupied.

I can keep my hands busy with knitting, manicuring my nails, cleaning my glasses, munching carrot sticks.

When I'm bored I do situps or read a book.

When I need a break, I switch to a different kind of activity.

Nonsmoking Visualizations

When you're changing a strong habit like smoking, it's important to do short, frequent visualizations. Each session should include three elements: an example of successfully getting your needs met without smoking, an image of yourself as a healthy nonsmoker, and an aversive image of smoking as unpleasant. Some of these little visualizations can be very brief—just five seconds with your eyes closed whenever you feel a strong craving for a smoke.

Three times a day you should set aside enough time for a longer visualization. At these times, include two or three scenes of meeting your needs without smoking and spend more time on images of your nonsmoking self. You should probably record the following instructions and listen to different segments of the tape each time you visualize.

Lie down, close your eyes, and relax.

Imagine that you are waking up in the morning. The first thing you notice is how clean your mouth feels. Then you realize that your lungs are clear—no hacking and coughing. You get out of bed feeling rested, refreshed, and fit.

Imagine having a wonderful breakfast. Fill in the details of bright sunlight, cheerful colors, a clean tablecloth with no ashtrays or smudges. Take some deep breaths and feel the clean, cool morning air deep into your lungs. Start eating and notice how good the food tastes and smells. Have a cup of coffee or tea or juice. Watch yourself enjoying the meal fully, without a cigarette in sight. Say to yourself, "I can be nice to myself without smoking," or use one of your prepared affirmations.

Now shift to work. See yourself working under pressure, trying to get a report finished or some products arranged or a machine fixed. Feel the tension building in your body until you just have to take a quick break. Get up and stretch. Take three deep breaths and touch your toes or do a duck squat. Walk around the room or go get a snack or chat with a co-worker for a minute.

Now you're eating your lunch. It tastes great. You're enjoying the people around you. After you finish eating, you linger to talk with the other people. Some of them light up, but you have no craving for an after-lunch smoke. In fact, the smell of cigarette smoke makes you queasy. Somebody stubs out a cigarette in a plate of mashed potatoes and it's so disgusting you have to look away.

This is enough for one session. End the visualization when you are ready.

This visualization concentrated on the needs for nurturance, stress relief, and enjoying special food and drink without smoking. Pick two or three of your most important needs to concentrate on at first. Practice visualizing different scenes in which you feel these needs, and see yourself successfully meeting your needs without smoking. Remember to work in the positive health and self-esteem benefits of nonsmoking, plus the aversive, negative images of smoking. Reinforce your images with appropriate affirmations—both during the visualizations and at intervals throughout the day.

As you learn to meet your strongest needs without smoking, branch out into other areas. For example, you can see yourself going for some exercise. Notice how much wind and endurance you have now that you're a nonsmoker. You feel light and strong, like you could go on forever. You can imagine looking into a mirror and noticing that your teeth are now shiny white. Your breath is sweet and you breathe easily.

Visualize yourself at parties and in other social situations. See how you can converse and enjoy yourself without the prop of a cigarette. Practice seeing images of people you admire and notice what you can emulate besides their smoking habits. Put yourself in boring or uncomfortable scenes and watch yourself coping without smoking.

Special Considerations

Smoking is an addiction that involves strong physical cravings as well as the psychological complications we have discussed. Many people quit smoking and start up again several times before finally quitting for good. Some find that before they can quit they have to taper off—smoking fewer and fewer cigarettes a day, or smoking brands progressively lower in tars and nicotine, or both.

Don't be discouraged if you have relapses. Keep doing your visualizations, including your relapses in your imagined scenes. See yourself eventually quitting for good. If you are trying to taper off, visualize yourself smoking fewer and fewer cigarettes. See yourself smoking low tar brands, then fewer of them. Keep up the images of yourself as a nonsmoker, projecting them into the future.

In the face of strong physical cravings, you're going to need all the help you can get. Ask your family and friends to support you in your resolution. Let them know that you will probably be twitchy and grumpy for a while, so that they can make allowances. If you have relatives or friends who still smoke and don't support your efforts to quit, avoid them as much as you can. Quitting with someone can be a great source of mutual support, especially if that someone is your spouse, intimate friend, or roommate. On the other hand, if you're quitting and your spouse isn't, that makes it harder.

If you have a strong, negative image of yourself as a smoker and you constantly berate yourself for your "weakness," see the chapter on self-esteem for additional help.

If you are overweight or fear becoming overweight if you stop smoking, see the chapter on weight control.

Example

Oscar was a thirty-five-year-old editor for a textbook publisher who had been smoking since his teens. He had about a pack and a half of Camels every day. He decided to stop smoking after trying to go running with Karen, his new wife. His wind was bad and he had a terrible pain in his chest after just a quarter mile. Oscar had tried to quit a couple of times, usually on the spur of the moment. His longest success previously was five days without a cigarette.

This time Oscar was more serious. He knew it would be tough, so he lined up a lot of support. His wife was an occasional smoker, but she wanted to quit too, so they made a pact that they wouldn't let each other smoke. Oscar got rid of all his cigarettes, ashtrays, and matches both at home and at work, and told his co-workers that he was quitting. He asked them not to smoke in his office and not to offer him smokes.

In the three days before he decided to quit, Oscar did some receptive visualizations. He found that he used cigarettes mostly to relax on breaks from editing and to unwind at home in the evenings with a glass of brandy and the news on TV. He also found out later that he really missed having a smoke with coffee in the morning. Karen tried visualization too, and found what she expected: that she smoked in social situations to relieve anxiety or be part of the crowd.

Oscar's affirmations were:

Smoking was killing me.

I can be a healthy, creative nonsmoker.

When I need a break, I get up and stretch.

I can unwind with deep breathing.

I love air more than smoke.

Karen's affirmations were:

Smoking is a silly, sickening habit.

I am a confirmed nonsmoker.

I keep my body pure and clean.

I can watch others smoke without wanting to join in.

Both of them did their longer nonsmoking visualizations in bed at night before falling asleep, in the morning after breakfast, and at work during lunch. Oscar would concentrate on seeing himself working on a manuscript, moving surely and quickly through it, getting up occasionally to stretch and yawn, then going back to work refreshed. He would also see himself going for a run in the evening instead of pouring his usual brandy and lighting up. He imagined running fast and free, with plenty of wind and a springy stride. Karen's longer visualization always included an aversive image of a lung x-ray with big, white, moldy blotches on it. She would go to her special place and run a movie of a friend's birthday party at which she had smoked a lot. But in her revised version, she didn't smoke, told a lot of funny anecdotes, and had others hanging on her every word.

Often during the day Oscar and Karen would briefly close their eyes and do a "quickie": a brief mental glimpse of a soggy cigarette butt, immediately replaced by a romantic picture of them running toward each other in a meadow of wildflowers. It became their own in-joke: Oscar would say, "Hey, Karen," and when she looked at him, close his eyes and take a deep, melodramatic breath. It became their code for "Boy, would I like a cigarette right now." Sometimes Karen would sidle up to Oscar and say, "How 'bout a quickie, big boy?" and Oscar would look offended and say, "No thanks, ma'am, I don't smoke." It didn't make much sense, but they needed something to laugh at. Oscar was feeling the pain of nicotine withdrawal. He got edgy, depressed, sarcastic, hypercritical, and with-drawn by turns.

Everything went fine for two weeks, and then it was New Year's Eve. They went to a party where the champagne flowed freely. By midnight they were both smoking, having agreed that "life's too short to deprive yourself—what the hell." The next day they nursed their hangovers with coffee and cigarettes. They felt mostly defiant, with a little guilt around the edges.

By January 3rd, Karen quit smoking for good. Oscar changed his tactics to a "switch down and quit" program he had read about. He switched to Marlboros for two weeks, then to Mores, and so on, tapering off on brands with less nicotine and tar. He kept up his visualizations, seeing himself as eventually a nonsmoker. In May he quit for good.

10

Creativity and
Problem Solving

*"Few people think more than two or three times a year. I've
made an international reputation for myself by thinking once
or twice a week."*

—*George Bernard Shaw*

Creativity and problem solving go together because creativity lies at the heart of
successful problem resolution. There are several systems that have been proposed
to systematically solve all sorts of problems. All of them require creativity in analyzing the problem and coming up with a list of possible solutions.

What is creativity? Is it something that only geniuses have? Is it the exclusive province of the *avant garde,* of outlandish types who frequent art gallery
openings and obscure foreign films? Is it applicable to anything besides works of
art?

Creativity is not the same as genius. It's not merely intelligence. Many smart people aren't creative, and many creative people are only of average intelligence. A certain basic intelligence is a necessary but not sufficient criterion for creativity.

Nor is creativity just being eccentric or unusual. A creative work or solution must be novel, at least to the creator, and it must also be appropriate in some way. It must be seen as useful or meaningful or satisfying by other people.

Nor is creativity confined to artistic endeavors like paintings and sculpture. The famous psychologist Abraham Maslow said that a first rate soup is better than a second rate painting. He meant that anything you do can be creative, from writing a poem to cooking dinner, from playing the piano to shining your shoes.

For the purpose of creating positive changes in your life, the definition of creativity is easy: it's your ability to produce ideas and insights that are new and valuable to you. This ability arises out of your uniqueness, regardless of your score on an IQ test or any special talent or training. Your artwork or solutions are creative as long as they are new and valuable to you. It doesn't matter if somebody else has already thought of your ideas or if others don't like your approach.

How Creativity Works

Examining how creativity works can give you hints on how to become more creative. Teresa Amabile, an associate professor of psychology at Brandeis University, has studied creativity in both children and adults. She has found that the degree of creativity that people bring to any task is influenced by three basic ingredients:

1. Expertise. This means talent, information, and technical or artistic ability.

2. Mental skills. Among these are concentration, persistence, flexibility, and the ability to see new possibilities.

3. Intrinsic task motivation. This is the sheer delight in doing something for its own sake. It is more important than the first two ingredients. Both adults and children do more creative work when they do it for sheer pleasure, compared to doing it for money, attention, prestige, or competitive success.

What does this mean in terms of how to develop more creativity in your life? First of all, you can increase your expertise in the area in which you want to be more creative: take a class, practice, read up, collect information, pick the brains of others in the field, and so on. This will give you more tools to work with, a larger vocabulary to draw on, and a wider range of techniques to put into action.

Second, you can use visualization to increase your powers of concentration, become more sensitive to the sights and sounds around you, sharpen your powers of observation, and open yourself up to your unconscious storehouse of creative alternatives.

Finally, you should have fun. Do what pleases you. When a task becomes drudgery or a matter of life and death, creativity flies out the window.

Applications

When you first think of creativity, you probably think of a painter, poet, or composer creating a masterpiece in a kind of a trance—what Shakespeare called "the spell in which imagination bodies forth the forms of things unknown." Indeed, many artists have described their creativity in just this way. William Blake literally saw visions, which he later drew, engraved, painted, or used to inspire poetry. Coleridge reported writing Kublai Khan while in an opium daze in which he effortlessly saw two or three hundred lines all at once. Only the intrusion of the "person from Porlock" kept him from transcribing all three hundred lines upon awakening. Wagner and Beethoven both got musical ideas from dreams. Mozart and Tchaikovsky both said that their most creative sequences emerged as spontaneous, nonthinking passages—auditory visualizations.

Scientists also know this kind of sudden, creative visualization. In the nineteenth century, Kekule discovered the benzene ring and the schematic method for portraying the carbon chain after intense visualization experiences. Darwin and Einstein said that their most creative ideas emerged spontaneously, in the form of mental images as opposed to words.

What works in art and science can work in daily life. You can create a way not to be lonely, a way to increase your income, a way to cope with your fears, a way to reorganize your files, a way to get more rest, a way to get a better job, a way to revitalize your relationship, a way to move to the country—whatever everyday problems you have, you can find more creative solutions for them.

It might be hard at first. By the time you finish high school, you've spent 11,000 hours in the classroom, mostly developing the rational, logical powers of your left brain. Add to that any time you've spent in college or working at a traditional job in which creativity is not encouraged. Then there are all the predigested images you have absorbed through TV and other media. Plus the inertia of your habitual, uncreative ways of solving chronic problems. And don't forget the fear of trying something new, or the fear of criticism for being different. No wonder people aren't more creative!

This chapter will concentrate on using visualization to overcome your obstacles to creativity and to generate creative solutions to your problems.

Basic Steps

Analyze Your Problem

This is the first step whether you're seeking to solve an artistic, practical, or emotional problem: writing a song, getting your son to clean up his room, or feeling closer to your mate. The idea is to write down or compose in your mind a statement of the problem. For example:

I want to write a song.

Michael should help clean up his room.

Rebecca and I are drifting apart.

Analyze your problem by asking yourself who, what, when, where, and why? Who is involved besides you? What exactly is it that bothers you? When and where does the problem typically occur? A good way to explore these questions is to do a receptive visualization like this:

Lie down, close your eyes, and relax. Go to your special place and settle in. Turn on the TV or pull down your movie screen. See an image of yourself and whoever else is involved with your problem. Set the figures in motion. Start to hear voices. What are you saying? What are the others saying? What are you doing that makes it a problem? How are you trying to solve the problem?

Now go into the screen and take your place in the problem. Take a moment to intensify your sensations of sight, hearing, touch, taste, and smell. Go through your problem behavior and notice how it makes you feel: depressed? angry? anxious? bored? Notice what you're thinking. Are you thinking nonproductive or blaming thoughts? Are you making assumptions about the negative motives and feelings of the others who are involved?

If you can, switch to a scene in which the problem is solved. See yourself on the other side of the problem, having got what you wanted or accomplished what you set out to do. Notice the details and what appeals to you most about success. Notice whether the vision of success really has a direct connection to your problem as you have stated it.

Act out as many scenes as it takes to fully explore all the instances of your problem. Make a note of any insights or possible solutions that crop up at this point. Watch and listen for hints that will help you analyze the problem. When you're ready, end the visualization.

If you were doing a visualization about song writing, you might see yourself sitting in your room with your guitar and some blank staff paper. You watch yourself tune the guitar and strum through different chord progressions. As you move into the scene, you might hum and try out a few phrases, or play and sing a song you admire to get you in the mood or inspire you. Then when nothing seems to gel, you get discouraged and put the guitar down. Then you switch to your success scene and see yourself playing your new song for your boyfriend. You see the love and admiration in his eyes. Tell yourself, "This will happen for me."

If you visualize your son playing in his room, you see him gradually pulling all his toys out of the toy box and leaving them on the floor. He climbs up on the box and pulls his books down from the shelves. He opens the Lego drawer and scatters them all over. Then you come in and say, "Oh no, look at this mess. You've got to help me clean it up." He starts whining, you keep scolding, and in the end you clean it all up yourself, with your son just getting in the way and making more mess. When you switch to your success scene, you see the room all neat and tidy, with everything up on the shelves and tucked away in the drawers. Tell yourself, "The answer is in me." You notice that the room really has too many toys. You also notice that you have no real way of securing your son's cooperation, other than yelling.

If you visualize an evening at home with your wife, you see her cooking dinner while you watch the news or play with your daughter. At dinner it's bedlam, with no chance to really talk. After dinner you have to retire to the study to do some important work, then put your daughter to bed. Your wife does the dishes and some vacuuming, and before you know it, it's time for bed and you haven't really said two words to each other. You merge into the scene and feel the frustration, the isolation. You remember the first years of your marriage when you felt so close, and think that those days are gone forever. Then you do a success scene, and see the two of you cuddled up on the couch, eating popcorn and watching TV. Use and affirmation like, "I can create this and more."

In addition to thinking about and visualizing your problem, gather together all the information, materials, supplies, and so on that you might need. All this preparation will saturate your left brain with the problem and all the possible solutions you can think of now.

Before going on to the next step, rephrase your problem. Your analysis and visualizations should allow you to be more specific. You may even have realized that the problem is something else entirely. Here's how the songwriting, room cleaning, and intimacy problems might be rephrased:

I want to write a love song for Jim in the key of D.

I need to weed out Michael's stuff so his room is easier to clean.

I want more relaxing time alone with Rebecca.

Brainstorming

When you "brainstorm," you list every idea about solving your problem that you can think of, as fast as you can. In 1963, A. F. Osborn brought out the third edition of his classic *Applied Imagination: Principles and Procedures of Creative Problem Solving*. In it he laid down the rules of brainstorming:

No criticism. While you're listing ideas, you must not judge them to be good or bad, practical or stupid. When the judging, critical part of your mind is working, the creative part shuts down. It's like trying to drive a car by stomping on the brake and the accelerator simultaneously. Judgment comes later, after you have a long list of all kinds of alternative ideas.

Be crazy. Freewheeling is encouraged. The crazier and wilder an idea is, the better. By opening yourself up to crazy ideas, you may break out of a mental rut. You may see your problem, and thus its solution, in an entirely different light. Or a crazy idea might have a grain of pure sanity in it that later leads you to an elegant solution.

Go for quantity. The more ideas you generate, the better your ultimate solution. Quality comes from quantity. Edison said that he created and tested three thousand ideas in order to invent the electric light bulb. Don't stop brainstorming until you have a long list—if Edison could come up with three thousand ideas, you can come up with at least a dozen.

When it comes time to brainstorm, you will probably have several ideas for solutions that you thought of while stating and analyzing your problem. Those are the start of your brainstorming list. Write them down.

Then use visualization to put yourself in touch with your unconscious and open your mind to the flow of creative ideas. A good way to use visualization to brainstorm is to have a pencil and paper next to you. Do a short visualization, then open your eyes and write down the ideas that came to you. Close your eyes again and try another kind of visualization, open them and write down the new ideas, and so on.

There are many ways you can structure brainstorming visualizations, depending on the nature of your problem and what usually works for you. Here are some suggestions:

Special place. Your special place should have some little curtained niche or treasure box in which you can "discover" things. Imagine that a solution to your problem is inside, then open the curtain or box and see what's there. You can also take your problem into your special place with you. For example, if you want your son's room to be neater, invite your son into your special place and see what he does. You might see that he talks with you about what is in the special place, and doesn't mess things up as long as you are talking. Then you could become invisible and observe him by himself in your special place. If he immediately begins to throw things around, you could take this to mean that your son makes messes to get your attention, and that if you spent more time talking with him, he would be neater.

Inner guide. Ask your inner guide to suggest ideas. Try to phrase questions that can be answered yes or no. If you ask open-ended questions like "What should I do to be closer to Rebecca?" be prepared for ambiguous answers. Your guide might reply, "Be still." You could interpret this as a nonresponsive reply, or as a suggestion to do less, to spend more quiet time with your mate at home. Keep asking the same question for several days in a row and see if the answer changes. It may take a few days for your creative mind to come up with solutions to a problem you have been working on with your conscious, logical mind.

Create within your visualization. Do your art inside the visualization. On a path or in your special place, come to a blank canvas or a stone with sculptor's tools, a guitar, or whatever. Imagine yourself painting a picture, carving a statue, playing a song. Imagine that you are a great artist, at the height of your powers. Watch yourself create stunning art effortlessly. Play around with the materials and have fun. See what you come up with.

Use affirmations. Compose an affirmation to use with each visualization technique. Keep them simple and accepting: "I am creative," "Good ideas come spontaneously to me," "The solution is within me."

Ask your child. Become a kid again in your visualization. Regain that un-critical, ruleless state before you went to school and learned the "right" way to do things. This is a good way to get those wild and crazy ideas that turn out to be not so crazy after all. Sink yourself into a strong memory of a time when you were under six years old. Take a look at your problem from that perspective. For example, how would you as a child sing a love song? A child might just repeat the loved one's name over and over to a simple melody, or drop the loved one's name into another song like singing "Jim had a little lamb" instead of "Mary had a little lamb."

Architect Donald Kenneth Busch employs an interesting variation on this technique. He helps interior designers and their clients go beyond their conven-tional tastes—what they *think* they should like—to discover what they *really* like. He has you visualize your childhood home. Take a leisurely tour through the home you remember best from your childhood. Notice the colors, textures, the light, the proportions, the furniture and spaces that seem cozy and comfortable. The likes and dislikes you created as a child in your earliest surroundings are the basis of your personal taste.

You can use this technique literally too. Ask a real child what to do about your problem. I once asked my son, two-years' old at the time, what we could do about getting a toy airplane off a high roof. He said, "Buy another one." And he was right—there was no way to get the original airplane off the roof, so the best course of action was to give up on it and go buy a new airplane.

Reverse roles. If your problem involves another person, reverse roles in your visualization. Imagine a problem scene between you and the other person in which you first take your part, then take the other's part. Really see, hear, and especially feel what it's like to be on the other side of your problem. For example, if you're trying to get closer to your mate, imagine a typical breakfast table in-terchange. But take your mate's part instead of your own. What do you sound like to your mate's ears? What needs does you mate have that are not getting met? What does your mate see as the real problem?

Deus ex machina. Imagine that you are in an elevator. You are descending deeper and deeper into understanding your problem. The elevator stops and the doors open upon a solution to your problem. You can get out and explore that solution, or you can let the doors close again and descend to another level and see other solutions.

Another *deus ex machina* technique is to imagine opening a bunch of fortune cookies, each of which contains a suggestion about your problem instead of a fortune. Or you could imagine that you are pulling the string on one of those talking toys that have a large repertoire of recorded messages. One pull might yield, "Take more rest," and another might produce, "Trust yourself." Keep open-ing cookies or pulling strings until you get all the messages available.

Change one aspect at a time. This is a graphic design technique in which the various parts of a design are altered, one at a time, to spark creative ideas.

You can reverse the field and the ground—have white letters on a black background instead of black letters on a white background. Another trick is to make each element in turn bigger or smaller. You can also add or stop motion. Make the color brighter or darker, hotter or colder. Change colors.

A subset of this trick is to add yourself to your composition. Visualize a design that you're working on as if it were a three-dimensional landscape. Shrink yourself down and walk around in it. If it's an abstract design, just imagine yourself rolling around among the shapes and colors. Try to find a sound and a taste and a smell to associate with your design.

You can use this technique to explore non-graphic problems. You can give any problem a shape, a color, a sound, and see what happens. For example, writing a song can be given the color green, the sound of water bubbling out of a jug, and the taste of a grass stem chewed on a hot summer day. These almost random associations can spark further memories and images that will find their way into the song.

Changing one element at a time is also a good strategy for shedding light on practical, real-world problems. Let's say you are trying to understand why your son won't help clean up his room. You can imagine a quarrel with your son in which you change sizes—your son is big and you are small. This could teach you something about the power issues involved. You could change the toys into piles of money or garbage and see what that tells you about your attitude toward his possessions. You could change the scene from bedtime to morning and perhaps learn that the conflict has a lot to do with your daily energy levels.

When you're stuck. For shedding light on poorly defined or very abstract problems, imagine that you are literally "boxed in." See yourself as shut up in a box that represents your problem. What do you do? Notice whether you break out, sit back and enjoy the peace and quiet, call for help, give up in despair, carefully dismantle the box, or whatever. How does the symbolism of the box apply to your problem? You can do this with images of being in a closed room, being painted into a corner, coming to a dead end, and so on. Many cliches about problems can be mined for useful images.

Make up a metaphor. Make an extended metaphor comparison between your problem and something that seems to have nothing to do with it. For instance, close your eyes and get an image of a cardboard box. How is an argument with your mate like a cardboard box? Well, it puts you in a dull brown mood. You feel boxed into a corner. You fill up an argument with all sorts of unrelated issues, like tossing junk into a box. There's an obvious outside, and a darker, more mysterious inside. Arguments are tacky, cheap. One argument is much like another, as indistinguishable as cardboard boxes. An argument could make you put your things in a box and leave. Boxes *have* flaps, arguments *are* flaps. And so on.

How is your problem like an apple, a chair, a wheel, a cloud? Turn your problem into a car or a bike and drive it around for a while. Where does the metaphorical journey take you?

Da Vinci's trick. When Leonardo was stale or stuck, he would look at a wall with lots of cracks and stains, or at cloud formations, and see different shapes and objects. This can give you the shape or juxtaposition you are looking for. It also trains the visual imagination. You can use this technique with sounds too: Close your eyes and listen to a stream, rainfall, a vacuum cleaner, or traffic. Let your mind drift and sometimes you can hear melodies or human voices.

Consult your male and female selves. Shakti Gawain often has her clients use visualization to get an image of both their male and female selves. The images can be persons, animals, colors, shapes, or whatever. You can see your male self as a bull, a tree, a cowboy, a tramp, the color red, three notes played on an oboe, and so on. You can see your female self as a goddess, cat, triangle, stone, taste of apple, dark cloud, the sound of harps, and so on. Your male and female selves may have something to say to you about your problem. Visualize them engaging in some way with your problem, first separately, then together, then merged into an image of your complete self. Notice what they say or do together that sheds some light on your problem, your creative process, and your personality.

The following are examples of brainstorming lists, showing the ideas listed after analyzing the problem and the ideas listed after brainstorming with visualization.

I want to write a song.

Analysis:	Too vague—what kind of song?
	A love song for Jim
	Folksy, upbeat sound
Restate problem:	*I want to write a love song for Jim in the key of D.*
Brainstorming ideas:	Humorous
	Play on his name: Slim Jim
	Jug-band rhythms
	Slap guitar body for emphasis
	Many feminine rhymes for comic effect
	Make it a riddle song
	Kazoo break in middle
	But tender, loving message
	Discords at punchlines
	Play on words "love" and "like"
	Two parts: jiglike funny part and waltz time for loving refrain
	Enough for two songs here

Michael should help clean up his room.

Analysis:	Big part of problem is too much stuff
Restate problem:	*I need to weed out Michael's stuff so his room is easier to clean.*
Brainstorming ideas:	Throw out all toys left on floor
	Give away toys he no longer plays with
	Put away half of toys for a while
	Talk to him more
	Give him attention, not toys
	New shelves
	Clothes pegs for coats
	Put one set of toys away before bringing out another set
	Play together more
	Don't be so critical
	Just leave the mess on grouchy evenings
	Tell him about my feelings
	Ask Michael how he wants his room
	Corkboard for drawings
	Organize and supervise his play more

Rebecca and I are drifting apart.

Analysis:	Too many routine chores
	Wasted opportunities for intimacy
	Daughter takes all our attention
Restate problem:	*I want more relaxing time alone with Rebecca*
Brainstorming ideas:	Quit work
	Don't bring work home
	Get a babysitter and go out more
	Don't hide behind a book at breakfast
	Share feelings—tell her I want more of her time
	Hire a full-time housekeeper
	Take a class together

Watch videos instead of working
Bring home little presents
Take a vacation
Encourage daughter to go away on
    more overnights
Eliminate and simplify chores
Lower household standards

Combine, Improve, Discard

This is the fourth of Osborn's rules for brainstorming. Now you can put your critical faculty back into gear. After you have your list of at least a dozen ideas, look them over to see which you can improve and/or combine together. Often two fair ideas can be combined to produce one excellent idea. Discard the unworkable ideas.

In the song writing example, you might combine and improve on six of the ideas and write a song titled "Slim Jim": a humorous love song in the key of D, with jugband rhythms, percussive guitar-slapping effects, cute feminine (multi-syllable) rhymes, and a kazoo break in the middle. You would then discard the ideas of using discords and having two parts in different tempos as inconsistent with a folk-style song. You might save the ideas about a riddle song, playing on the words "like" and "love," and a tender message. Those could lead to a second, more serious love song some other day.

In the example about Michael's room, most of the practical ideas are obviously good ones and can be put into action: giving away unused toys, hiding some toys away for a while, putting one set of toys away before getting out a new set, and installing new shelves, clothes pegs, and a corkboard. The idea about throwing away toys that are left out is too vindictive and should be discarded. Then there is a whole category of ideas that have nothing to do directly with the clean-up project.

What has happened here is fairly common in creative problem solving. You start by wanting to change someone else's behavior (*Michael should help clean up his room*). Then analysis shows you that it would be easier to change the environment in some way (*I need to weed out Michael's stuff so his room is easier to clean*). And when you use visualization to brainstorm ideas, you find out that your behavior is part—perhaps the most important part—of the environment. To change someone else's behavior, you have to change your own behavior: *talk to him, give him attention, play together, don't be so critical, tell him about feelings,* and so on.

The ideas about getting more relaxing time alone with Rebecca can be improved by combining some of them. For example, getting a babysitter and going out more is a little vague, and the idea of taking a class isn't too good because it gives you more time commitments instead of fewer. But you can combine the idea of a class on a regular schedule with the occasional babysitter idea: get a babysitter lined up for every Wednesday night and go out and do different things together. The ideas about a full-time housekeeper and quitting your job should be discarded as financially disastrous, but not bringing work home is a good plan. In fact, to be safe, you should make Friday your regular babysitter night, so that in case you do have to bring work home, you'll have the weekend to do it and not miss out on being with Rebecca. And maybe the full-time housekeeper could be changed to someone to help out four hours a week. That, combined with simplifying chores and lowering standards would go a long way toward solving the "too many routine chores" part of the problem. And sharing feelings is always a good idea—the first and maybe most effective thing to do.

Visualize the Future

After you have combined, improved, and discarded ideas, you will have a list of good, creative ideas. Put these ideas into a logical sequence and you will have a plan of action. To make sure you put your plan into action effectively, visualize it first.

Lie down, close your eyes, and relax. See yourself later today or tomorrow—as soon as possible. See, hear, and feel yourself taking the first step in your plan to solve your problem. Include the setting, the people, the conversations, the things, the events—whatever will be there. Listen to yourself playing the first few bars on the guitar. Hear yourself explaining to Michael how you feel and what you are going to do in his room. Watch Rebecca's eyes as you tell her that you have been feeling distant and want to spend more time alone with her.

This is a good place to use an accepting, open-ended affirmation like "This or something equally positive will come to pass for the good of all concerned."

Most importantly, see the positive consequences of putting your plan into action right away. See the smile on Jim's face when he hears that you're writing a song about him. Notice how Michael starts helping you as you spend more time with him organizing his room. See you and Rebecca holding hands in a candle-lit restaurant.

Continue this way, visualizing each step of your plan, including the positive consequences at each step. This visualization will do three things for you: (1) Fix the sequence of events in your mind. (2) Encourage you to make the first step. (3) Give you a rehearsal so that you will be less anxious and more polished when you go on to solve your problem in real life.

Include some expected problems and roadblocks in your visualization: getting stuck for a rhyme, your son throwing a tantrum, or showing up late for a Friday night dinner with your wife. But see yourself overcoming the inevitable difficulties and eventually succeeding.

What To Expect

You may be asking yourself whether being creative is worth the trouble. It's too much to do every time there's a problem to be solved—writing everything down, lying down to do a visualization, popping up to write more stuff, flopping down to visualize and brainstorm, making a plan, and so on.

Don't worry. You only have to go through this whole routine the first few times. With practice, much of this process becomes automatic. When confronted with a problem requiring a creative response, you will automatically analyze the problem to see if it can be restated more accurately. You'll gather together the resources you need by mulling it over for a while, saturating your left brain with the details. In the meantime, your right brain, the creative, unconscious part, will be brainstorming. You might just close your eyes for a few moments and let the creative ideas rise to the surface. Most of the time you'll keep your list of ideas in your head. Combining and improving on the good ones and forming a plan of action will also be largely automatic. Visualizing the future will be something you usually do as a kind of daydream, looking forward to solving your problem.

You will save the full, formal, creative problem-solving process for those big, important problems that you want to give your best shot.

Example

Irving was an architecture student who got a chance to design his parent's new kitchen. They wanted to remodel their small, old-fashioned kitchen to make it more efficient and pleasant. They didn't have much money to spend.

The existing kitchen was dark, with painted wood cabinets, a space-wasting corner sink, a chipped tile drainboard, no dishwasher, and a diagonal island that jutted into the room and made it cramped. The island divided the tiny kitchen from a tiny breakfast nook.

Irving talked to his parents and initially stated the problem like this:

Things wanted

More storage room

Places to put blender, food processor, toaster oven

More counter space

More light

New sink, not in corner

New dishwasher

Better ventilation

Easy maintenance

Things not wanted

High expense

Cramped feeling

Plasticky countertops

Irving saturated his conscious mind with the problem by talking to his mom, drawing a scale plan of the kitchen as it was, and by looking through many magazine articles and books on remodeling.

Then he lay down, closed his eyes, and imagined walking into his parents' house: in the entry, down the hall, through the dining room, and into the old, cramped kitchen. He saw his mom stacking pots and bowls all over, fighting to find enough counter space to cook a big meal at holiday time. He saw her chase his dad out of the kitchen because he was in the way in the tiny space. He saw her squinting at the roast in the oven, trying to read the thermometer in the dark. He watched her wash dishes by hand.

Then he imagined entering the house again, this time walking into a new, perfect kitchen. It was filled with light and seemed much bigger. The predominant colors were white on the cabinets and the warm glow of natural wood on the countertops. The island was gone. Light streamed in from a skylight. His mom and dad cooked together in it in perfect harmony. "I can create this beauty and harmony," he affirmed.

After this visualization, Irving tried to sketch the "perfect" kitchen arrangement with the outlines of the old kitchen walls. He saw that more space was needed. Perhaps he could knock out the east wall and build outward ten feet into the backyard. He called a contractor friend for a quote. He also called for prices on countertops, skylights, and cabinets. While waiting for replies, he started his brainstorming list with:

Skylight

Natural wood counters

More square feet

White modern cabinets

Irving did another visualization, this time pulling out all the stops and letting the wild ideas fly:

Giant copper range hood

All new resilient flooring

Two separate kitchens—for formal and for informal cooking

Break through ceiling and have breakfast nook in loft

Make new wall out of glass

Include greenhouse window with a fountain built in

Bright brass hardware

Indirect lighting in domed ceiling

Appliance hutches on back of all countertops, with cantilevered doors

Handmade Italian tiles

Cabinets all the way to ceiling

Irving tried to restrain himself from being critical until he had a long list. Then he looked it over and began improving, combining, and discarding ideas. He saw that the ideas of using copper, tile, and brass would warm up the cold feeling created by expanses of smooth white cabinets. But he would have to be careful with the available money.

About this time, some price quotes came in and Irving found out to his disappointment that he couldn't afford skylights or moving any walls. He also found out that using natural wood for a countertop around a sink was a bad idea—the wood would inevitably stain.

Money also ruled out a lot of his more fanciful ideas: new flooring, two separate kitchens, breaking through the ceiling, a glass wall, a greenhouse window, and so on. But he examined each of his ideas before discarding it. He found that several grandiose ideas had parts he could inexpensively incorporate into his design. For example, he couldn't build two separate kitchens, but he could separate the functions of cooking and cleanup. To do that, he would have to remove the island and eliminate the breakfast nook. But that was OK—it would give him the added floor space he needed and allow him to put the new sink and dishwasher under the breakfast nook window. And although he couldn't afford a glass wall, he could enlarge the sink window to let in more natural light. And since the sink was now separate from the stove area, he could still have natural wood counters in half of the kitchen. He would resort to plastic laminate around the sink, warmed up with a backsplash of Italian tile running just under the window. The appliance hutches would add too much to the cost, but he could make the cooking area counter extra deep to leave room for small appliances in the back and food preparation in the front.

Irving was off and running. He drew up final plans in one long evening's work. That night, before going to sleep, he visualized the next few weeks: making the materials lists, getting prices on appliances, cabinets, and fittings, getting bids from subcontractors on the plumbing, wiring, and finish carpentry, making up a construction schedule, and supervising the work. He visualized himself and his dad doing the demolition and the final painting together. He saw the new kitchen, fresh and gleaming. He saw his mom beaming with pleasure and pride.

As the weeks went by and he was caught up in the excitement and confusion of remodeling, he used visualization to check the work done and the decisions to be made against his mental image of what the kitchen should be. He also used visualization for stress reduction when coping with subcontractors. His favorite affirmations were, "Step by step I get the job done" and "I concentrate on one thing at a time."

The kitchen remodel went smoothly and the results were beautiful. His parents were very grateful and proud of him. They told him he could show off their kitchen to his prospective clients when he opened his own architectural office.

11

Setting and Achieving Goals

"Whatever you can do, or dream you can, begin it."
—*Goethe*

A goal is a visualization of the future. Your mind is set up to seek goals. You do it automatically. Visualization is part of the automatic mechanism by which your mind presents goals to itself, compares them to reality, and decides what to do. This chapter will show you how to take more conscious control of this process.

Your mind works toward goals in a zig-zag fashion, like a sailboat tacking first northeast and then northwest in order to arrive at a destination due north. That's why it sometimes seems that you are going at a tangent to the direction you really want to pursue, and why it's sometimes hard to get back on course—your mind is actually following the straightest possible path available to you at the moment.

In *Psycho-Cybernetics*, Maxwell Maltz says that the mind acts like a servo-mechanism in going after goals. A servomechanism mimics human movement by moving a little, receiving feedback about the results, moving a little differently, observing results, altering movement in response, checking the feedback, and so on until the movement is successfully completed. Putting on your socks is a complex movement made up of hundreds of these feedback loops. Successfully completing medical school or a prize-winning quilt are also movements of this kind—movements toward a goal in which your progress is measured and guided by constant comparisons with visualized goals.

If you have no goal, your mind will seek to fulfill the whim of the moment. If your goal is vague and unclear, the zigs and zags of your path toward it will be large—you'll wander into dead ends and long-way-around detours and your journey will be long. If you have conflicting goals, you will get nowhere. If you have negative goals expressed in the form of pessimism, catastrophic predictions, and cynicism, your mind will seek those goals and your negative expectations will come true.

But if you have positive, clearly defined goals that don't conflict with each other, your mind will seek them with a minimum of zigging and zagging. All of the many micro-decisions you encounter daily will be made in ways that give you little shoves toward your goals. Some day others may say that everything you touch turns to gold.

Rules of Goal-Setting

Following these simple, common-sense rules will help you set reasonable goals and achieve them with the least effort.

Be Specific

The part of your mind that seeks goals can't fasten onto abstract concepts like health, prosperity, or contentment. You have to be specific. Spell out what these mean in terms of observable objects, actions, sense impressions, and bodily feelings.

For example, health could translate into a slim, strong body that can lift 100-pound bags of fertilizer easily. Health could be visualized as a cholesterol count of 101 and a blood pressure of 120 over 75. Or health could be seen as rosy cheeks and the feel of taking a deep breath without coughing. You have to spell out what health means to you in positive, observable terms.

Likewise, prosperity could be visualized as buying a particular townhouse, lounging in an art deco armchair, seeing a $50,000 balance in your bankbook, driving your new Jag, the feel of a new Halston dress, the sound of a new stereo system, and so on—whatever you would buy, use, wear, and enjoy if you were prosperous. Contentment might be represented by a smiling face, a gentle smile, taking a nap, harmonica music, an old dog on the hearth, reading mysteries in a hammock under a tree, bundling up in an old sweater—whatever you would do and see and hear and feel if you were content.

Once you decide on the details of a goal, don't change them unnecessarily. If you want a pink 1959 Cadillac convertible with white leather seats, don't change it whimsically to a red one or a sedan. Changing the details needlessly ruins your focus. Stick with your initial vision and don't change it unless you genuinely change your mind about what you really want.

Set Short-, Medium-, and Long-Range Goals

Long-range goals are the biggies—the major accomplishments or acquisitions you hope to make five or ten or twenty years from now. They give your life overall direction and meaning. Medium-range goals can be accomplished in the more foreseeable future, say six months to five years from now. They are more specific and there are more concrete things you can do right now to accomplish them. Short-range goals are the things you want to get done tomorrow, next week, next month, or in six months. They are the goals that keep you going from day to day. Every time you make a list of things to get at the store you are setting short-range goals.

You need all three kinds. If you have only short-range goals, you will be caught up in petty details and lack direction in your life. If you have only long-range goals, you will never reach them because you can't take the first step, which is to set and achieve a short-range goal today.

That's the secret: every long-range goal implies a whole series of shorter-range goals stretching from the distant future back to this very moment. Being a doctor in ten years implies doing your algebra homework tonight, sending for college catalogs next week, cutting back on the time you spend windsurfing next summer, enrolling in the right premed courses in two years, and so on until you walk into the hospital on your first day as an intern. Having a loving son and daughter who will honor and care for you in your old age begins right now, with how you talk to your children while you're changing their diapers and giving them baths.

Set Different Types of Goals

Material things. These are the most obvious kinds of goals. You may feel slightly guilty about the idea of setting material goals, or it may seem self-centered and greedy to visualize how much money you will earn, the kind of house or car you want, or some other possession. But it's natural and forgivable to want things. I like the way Shakti Gawain puts it in *Living in the Light:* "Money is a symbol of our creative energy.... Because the creative energy of the universe in all of us is limitless and readily available, so, potentially, is money. The more willing and able we are to open to the universe, the more money we will have in our lives." And not just money—also love, professional success, good health, enjoyable leisure, creative accomplishments and spiritual growth.

Family and friends. You should set goals for your love life: the kind of relationship you want with the most important man or woman in your life. If you have kids or want them, you should have goals about your relationship with them, what you will do with them and the kind of family atmosphere you want.

How many and what kinds of friends do you want? What will you do with them that shows your friendship?

Educational, intellectual, professional goals. What classes do you want to take, what degrees do you want to acquire? How would you like to expand your knowledge or your intellectual powers? What job do you want in ten years? How could your chosen profession be more rewarding to you?

Health goals. Are there any chronic problems like high blood pressure, obesity, lack of fitness, or allergies that you want to have under control? What level of activity do you aspire to? What changes would you like to make in your diet?

Leisure goals. What hobbies and interests would you like to take up or find more time for in the future? Do you want to learn how to dance, fly a plane, sing, play golf, or knit?

Spiritual or creative goals. What about your spiritual development? Have you always wanted to meditate or keep a dream diary? Do you have creative urges to paint or write poetry? Don't forget your spiritual, creative, "impractical" goals. They can be among the most important and most rewarding to achieve.

Explore, Uncover, and Remove Internal Obstacles

In the receptive visualization that follows, you will look for possible internal obstacles to achieving your goals, and symbolically cast them aside. Common obstacles are fear of change, fear of success, low self-esteem, procrastination, negativity, pessimism, and conflicting goals.

The more positive you are about a goal, the more easily you can achieve it. To get what you want with visualization, you must *really want* it. If some small part of you feels scared or undeserving or lazy or pessimistic, it will weaken your visualization and lower your chances of achieving your goals.

When you prepare a list of your goals later in this chapter, you will examine it for conflicting goals. When one goal is in conflict with another, something has to give or neither goal will be achieved. For example, it is very nearly impossible to be a vice president in a large corporation and live a relaxed life in the country. One rules out the other. If you have both goals, you'll have to choose one over the other or postpone one in order to have any chance of success.

Get Support

Tell your goals to the people who really care about you and will be willing to support you in reaching your goals. Actually ask for their help in accomplishing what you set out to do. For instance, Sophie was a college sophomore who had to get a B in her statistics class in order to go on to the upper division program she had chosen. She asked her roommate, her boyfriend, and her father to support her in various ways. Her roommate agreed to keep things quiet around the apartment for the rest of the semester. Her boyfriend agreed not to go out with her on Sundays until her weekly workbook assignments were done. Her father agreed to help her out with the rent for an extra month if necessary so she wouldn't have to look for a summer job until after her statistics final. With so many people invested in her goal, Sophie felt both supported and "on the spot." She studied hard and got the B.

Sometimes your goals will have to be kept secret, at least from some people. If you have resolved to get away from an abusive husband, you can't confide in your husband or any of his friends. If you want to convert to Judaism, it's probably a waste of time to try to drum up support from your Episcopal minister. Look for support from those likely to give it, and keep your own counsel among others.

Review and Revise Goals

Save the lists of goals you create. Bring them out from time to time to see how you're doing and to change any goals that are no longer appropriate. The annual self-appraisal that most people make around New Year's is a good opportunity to revise goals. A combination of receptive and programmed visualization is good for this review. In your imagination, visit your future self, just as you did when setting your goals. Look around and notice what's different from your last trip to the future. See how your vision of utopia has changed.

As you grow, you get smarter. You learn that certain goals aren't what you once thought them to be. You find out new things about yourself and develop new interests. For example, when I was six I wanted to be a deep sea diver, when I was twelve I wanted to be a writer, when I was twenty I wanted to be a psychologist, when I was thirty I wanted to be a publisher, and now that I'm forty-eight I want to be a little of all those things but mostly to build an airplane and paint watercolors.

Set Goals for Yourself, Not for Others

When I say that you should set goals for your family life, I mean that you should describe the kind of person *you* want to be within your family. I don't mean that you should decide you want your son to be a lawyer and your daughter to be a doctor. Or that you should set the goal that your kids should be obedient and respectful at all times. Setting goals for your kids can lead to resentment, rebellion, and disappointment.

Likewise, if you set a goal such as "I want to be closer to my husband," you could be in trouble. You need to spell out what you mean by that in terms of what *you* are going to do, not in terms of what you wish your husband would do. There is no way you can meet these kinds of expectations:

Next year my husband will be more considerate.

He'll volunteer to help clean the house.

He'll tell me what's on his mind.

He won't drink so much beer and smoke so much dope.

Put like this, these aren't goals. They're wishes that probably won't come true. Here are some real goals about being closer to your husband:

Next year I'll let him know when I feel isolated from him, instead of brooding and feeling sorry for myself.

I'll ask him to keep all his papers and books in the den.

I'll tell him what's on my mind and ask his opinion more.

I'll go to an Alanon meeting with Jackie.

Receptive Visualization

In this visualization you'll visit yourself in the future—ten years, five years, and one year from now. In each of these future settings you'll look around and notice your material possessions, family life, accomplishments, use of leisure time, and so on. After the visualization you'll write down some of the things you saw and turn them into workable goals.

Anything goes here. You are not making a detailed plan or committing yourself to a particular vision of the future. This is more like brainstorming a solution to a complex problem—you want to open yourself up to the flow of spontaneous images from your unconscious. Drop your self-critical reins and let yourself run. If you feel like censoring or judging yourself during the visualization, remember that you will have an opportunity to edit your goals later.

It's a good idea to make yourself a tape of these instructions: Lie down, close your eyes, and relax. As you are relaxing your muscles and slowing your breathing, let go of all you don't want or don't need. Let each breath carry away a little bit of your old limitations. With each breath you create more space within you for something new.

Go to your outdoor special place. Settle in and then pick a direction that represents the future to you. Start walking in that direction along a pleasant path. Come to a log across the path and step over it. Think of the log as representing procrastination. Come to a rushing stream and cross it carefully, stepping on stones to keep your feet dry. Think of the stream as representing fear of change. Continue on until you come to a steep hill, representing self-doubt. Trudge up that hill until you successfully reach the top. Now the path winds down into a valley. For a while the path is rutted and full of rocks. These represent pessimism and negativity.

Continue on down into a dark forest. Tree branches droop down into the path and you have to push them aside. Think of the branches as fear of success and the feeling of not being worthy of good things.

You push past the thick trees and into a more open, pleasant part of the forest. Soon you come to where people are living. You see that the path leads to a home in the distance. This is your home, ten years in the future.

Walk around the home and look in the windows. Try the doors. They are all locked but one. Open the unlocked door and enter. Look around the rooms.

How many are there? How are they decorated? How big are they? What things do you own in this place? Take your time and make a complete survey. Go to a desk and look in the drawer. Find your bankbook and checkbook and see how much money you have. Look in the closets, the garage, the refrigerator. What do you wear, drive, eat?

Imagine you are invisible, a fly on the wall, a floating, ghostly presence that the inhabitants of this future time can't see or hear or sense. Watch yourself, ten years older, come into the home. How do you look? Are you healthy, happy looking? How much do you weigh? Watch your family come in. How do they act toward each other? What are they doing? Are you married? Do you have kids? Do you live alone?

Listen in while your ten-year-older self makes a couple of phone calls to friends. What do you talk about? What do you plan to do?

Follow yourself to work or school. What is your job? How much do you earn? What are you learning? How do you use your intelligence? What skills have you developed? What degrees or professional honors have you attained? What is your work environment like?

Watch yourself at leisure. Do you read, play tennis, watch TV, skydive, sing songs, or what?

Now let your invisible self meld together with your older self, like fitting a hand into a glove. When you are one, just ask yourself how you feel. Fit and healthy? At peace? Creative? Spiritually complete? Look back over your life so far. What are you proud of? What are you especially glad you had a chance to experience?

When you have finished exploring your existence ten years from now, let it fade away and return to the here and now. Open your eyes, get up, and make a brief list while the images are fresh in your mind. Pick one or two major goals for each of these areas and jot down the details:

Ten-Year Goals

Material goods _____

Family and friends _____

Educational, Intellectual, Professional _____

Health _____

Leisure _____

Spiritual/Creative _____

Other _____

Look over this list and fix any obvious conflicts, like wanting to be a millionaire and wanting to be a monk in a cave in Tibet. Or wanting to be a mother of a big family and also a Pulitzer prize-winning investigative reporter. Or wanting a restored Victorian mansion with a helicopter pad on top. Or wanting an open household with friends dropping in unannounced and also wanting plenty of private time.

Now prepare for the second part of this visualization. Lie down, close your eyes, and relax. As you breathe, open up more room for new things and let go of your limitations.

Go to your special place and set out on your journey as before. This time your trip will be shorter—to your home five years from now. It can be the same home or a different one. There may be fewer obstacles.

Enter your home and look specifically for the things that relate to the major goals on your list. If you saw $100,000 in the bank last time, this time look again in the desk and see how much money you need to have five years from now in order to have $100,000 ten years from now. If you saw a lovely wife and two school-age children, see what they look like at this time. If you weighed one hundred and forty pounds in your ten-year home, and this represents a significant weight loss for you, then be sure to notice what you weigh in the five-year home—maybe one hundred and fifty or one hundred and sixty pounds. Recall the other areas on your list and see where you are five years from now in relation to your career, educational, sports, creative, or health goals.

Finally, take a look around and notice anything that surprises you, anything that wasn't here last time. Perhaps there is a new goal that has sprung from your unconscious since you did the ten-year part of this exercise.

When you are ready, leave the visualization and prepare another list, noting the details of your major goals for five years from now:

Five-Year Goals

Material goods _____

Family and friends _____

Educational, Intellectual, Professional _____

Health _____

Leisure _____

Spiritual/Creative _____

Other _____

Now do the last part of the visualization. Lie down, close your eyes, and relax as before. This time go to your special place and take a short stroll to your home as it will be one year from today.

Again, look for the details that relate to your major goals. How much money have you saved? Have you met your future wife or husband yet? How did you meet? How much do you weigh? How is your health? Are you in school preparing for your later degree? What job do you have and what are you doing to make your professional aspirations come true?

Look around again for any surprises that have snuck up on you. When you've seen and heard all you came for, end the visualization and write down your one-year goals:

One-Year Goals

Material goods _____

Family and friends _____

Educational, Intellectual, Professional _____

Health _____

Leisure _____

Spiritual/Creative _____

Other _____

Programmed Visualization

Now comes the hardest part of all, making your "to do" lists. These are what you need to do today, tomorrow, next week, and next month to make your goals a reality. For example, if you want $100,000 in ten years, you need to open a savings account next payday and make a first deposit, however small. If you want to marry the woman of your dreams and raise a family, you have to go to the singles club party next Saturday. If you want to lose fifty pounds over the next ten years, you need to read the chapter on weight control tonight. If you want to get your blood pressure under control so you'll be around in ten years, you need to shop for food for dinner tomorrow so you won't end up at the Steak and Brew shoveling down the prime rib. If you want a grant to study the prevention of child abuse, you'd better start working on the proposal now.

Visualization can help. For each of your major goals, write down one small first step to take in the next week. Also compose an affirmation for each of your major goals, plus an affirmation about overcoming obstacles and about the future in general. Keep them in the present tense even though they refer to the future. Here are some suggestions:

I can set and reach my goals.

The future is within my grasp.

I have all the things I need.

I am safe in the bosom of my family.

I'm doing fine in school.

I am at the top of my trade.

I feel healthy.

I eat right.

I know how to relax and how to have fun.

I deserve to reach my goals.

I can organize my time to get things done.

I am in harmony with the energy of the universe.

Creative energy flows through me at all times.

Lie down and close your eyes. Relax and concentrate on one area of your life—your health, for instance. Let's say you want to learn to practice yoga to become stronger, more flexible, and more relaxed. Visualize yourself making the first step tomorrow: looking in the Yellow Pages or the local shopping news for places offering yoga classes. Really concentrate on the details: the color and feel of the paper, the smell of the ink, scanning for the words "yoga" and "classes," the sound of turning a page. The more vivid your visualization, the easier it will be to take the first step. Tell yourself, "I take one step at a time."

Now go forward a couple of days. See yourself dialing the phone and hear yourself asking a yoga instructor about types of yoga, size of classes, times, what to wear, and so on. Tell yourself, "I can find out what I need to know."

Now visualize a shopping and information-gathering expedition. First see yourself in the library. Imagine looking in the subject catalog under "yoga," writing down the numbers and titles, and going into the stacks to find a good book about yoga for beginners. Follow yourself through the checkout procedure. From the library, go to a sporting goods store and watch yourself trying on sweatpants, leotards, shorts, or whatever you imagine wearing while doing yoga. Tell yourself, "I'm well prepared. I look good."

Then go to your first class. Allow yourself to feel nervous and unsure as you approach the building. Tell yourself, "I'm doing something nice for myself." See yourself walking into the exercise room and taking your place among the other students. You're feeling calmer now. Imagine what your instructor and the other students might look like. Tell yourself, "I'm in the right place."

See yourself a year from now, getting up early to do your yoga exercises. Step outside onto a balcony, into the warm sun. Stretch and gently twist into the first postures. Feel your body becoming warm and limber as you do a "greeting the sun" sequence. Tell yourself, "I'm relaxed and at ease in my body."

Go on to the five-year point and see your body better than ever, your skin clear and healthy, and your eyes shining. See yourself still doing yoga every morning as part of a deeply satisfying personal ritual.

End your visualization with a flashback to the first step, looking up the phone numbers for classes. Make a final affirmation: "I'm taking the first step tomorrow."

Do your goal-oriented visualizations before getting out of bed in the morning or last thing before sleep at night. You may want to alternate among your various goal areas by doing a love-life visualization on Monday, a health visualization on Tuesday, a creative arts visualization on Wednesday, and so on.

As you accomplish the first steps in your various goals, the second step will emerge out of your daily visualizations. Also, don't forget to occasionally go back to your written lists to review and revise your goals. You might, for example, find through research and experience that you prefer tai chi or some other discipline to yoga. Or the meditative aspects of yoga may come to be more important to you than the physical benefits.

Special Considerations

Many thinkers have noted a paradox about how you accomplish important goals—you have to let go of your goals before you can grasp them. When you learn to "be here now," enjoying what you've currently got, that's when you really start making progress on your goals. Intense desire, extreme sacrifice, constant striving, and a "do or die" attitude don't get the job done as well as an acceptance of the now, with gradual steps toward your objective.

It's important to have specific goals, but it's best to hold them lightly. A heavy emotional attachment to a goal makes you too self-conscious, too afraid of not reaching it. You freeze up in the clutch like a rookie baseball player. Your fear of failure somehow makes failure more likely.

Shakti Gawain says that life is made up of being, doing, and having. All are necessary and legitimate, none is better or worse than the others. But there is a natural order to these processes: first you *be* who you are, and out of that identity you *do* what you do, and that behavior allows you to *have* the people and things you want in your life. Sometimes in goal-setting you focus too strongly on the having. The trick is to use your visualizations to focus on the kind of person you are and want to be, then to see yourself doing the kinds of things such a person would do. Then the having will almost take care of itself.

Context Map

Some people find it very difficult to visualize detailed goals. They just don't know what they want, or can't make up their minds. A context map can help. A context map is a drawing of your life done as a landscape, with the past on the left, the present in the middle, and the future on the right. You should draw a context map if you have trouble with the receptive visualization in this chapter.

The context map works because drawing is a more creative, right-brain process than writing down goals or talking about them. Drawing can reveal unconscious desires and assumptions that you can't uncover any other way.

To make a context map, get a *big* sheet of paper, at least two feet square. A five-foot sheet of butcher paper taped to a wall is best. Get a set of colored felt tip markers too.

Copy the simple line drawing on the next page, including the captions.

The past area on the left is the sea. The present area in the middle is a meadow. The future area on the right is a range of hills or mountains. These are

PAST

PRESENT

FUTURE

The future

archetypal images that parallel human evolution and development. It is a layout that is almost universally understood.

The idea is to draw objects, places, and experiences from your life, and extend them logically and intuitively into the future. This doesn't have to be great art, or even recognizable to anyone else. Only you have to know what your drawings represent. If you're stuck for an image of something, write a word. People can be just stick figures. Draw the way you did in kindergarten. You can even be abstract, using a cloud of red scribbles to represent a turbulent adolescence, for example.

Start in the ocean at the left and draw a picture of yourself as an unborn baby safe in your mother's womb. Near the surface of the water, draw something to represent your birth. Draw important toys or people from your childhood in the air over the water. Move toward the present and draw things you liked to do in your school days and adolescence. Move gradually into the present, drawing symbols or writing words that represent what you like, what happened to you, what was important or fun or educational.

If you suddenly think of something you'd like to put in the future, draw it. Your unconscious mind is timeless. It doesn't assign memories and desires to rigid past/present/future categories. What you wanted and liked in the past you still want and like in some form now, and will want and like in some form in the future. Draw lines from the positive images in the past and present and extend them into the future. Draw circles around the negative images or cross them out to prevent them from extending into the future.

Only you can draw your context map, but here are some examples of what others have included in theirs:

Sun and clouds to represent good times and bad times

Lightning bolts to mark important events

Circles with names in them to represent people

Certain colors to represent themes—e.g., love and sex always in blue

Lines and arrows running left to right to represent continuing interests—
e.g., a green line representing playing the piano

Houses you have lived in, cars you have owned

Trips you have taken

Sport and hobby equipment

Churches or halos or auras to denote spirituality Hearts to indicate love

Musical notes and feet to denote music and dancing

Diplomas, mortarboards, or schoolhouses to represent academic achievement

You can also use the context map to explore barriers to your achievement of goals. On a new sheet of paper, draw two parallel curving lines to represent a road. Have it lead to "Success" or "The Future" at the far right end. Draw road blocks, pits, broken bridges, and so on to represent low self-esteem, fear of failure, procrastination, and so on. Draw alternate routes, repair crews, hot air balloons—whatever you need to get around or over the obstacles.

Example

Mary Jane was a history major who had always vaguely thought that she would teach school and live in a quiet university town. But she was six months away from her getting her B.A. and hadn't made any plans for graduate school. Since the thought of two or three more years of school had begun to feel sickening to her, she decided that she had better set some goals.

In her receptive visualization, she went ten years into the future. She found herself living in a fancy condominium, not the comfy, old brown shingle house she had always thought of for herself. She was thinner, wearing very stylish clothes, and had many social engagements. She was single, not married with kids as she thought she would be. She had a steady boyfriend named Ken, who looked embarrassingly like the Ken doll that goes with Barbie.

In her ten-year future, Mary Jane made her living selling textbooks for a big publishing company. It involved a lot of travel and mixing with professors in many disciplines, not just history. This made some sense to her because she had worked part time keeping books for a publishing company while going to school, and she seemed to have a flair for the business. In the future she had her master's degree, but wasn't "using it" in the usual sense.

In the little leisure time she had, she went skiing or to movies set in interesting historical periods. Her creative energies were channeled into helping professors develop textbooks for publication with her company.

Mary Jane settled on these as her major goals:

Ten-Year Goals

Material goods: *Two-bedroom condo with view*

Family and friends: *Active social life, one close relationship*

Educational, Intellectual, Professional: *M.A., successful in sales and manuscript acquisition*

Health: *size eight, fit for skiing*

Leisure: *skiing, historical films*

Creative: *good at developing manuscripts in several disciplines*

In the next stage of her visualization, Mary Jane visited herself five years into the future. She found herself living in a two-bedroom flat, not too fancy, but tastefully decorated. There was no current boyfriend on the scene. However, she was very close to her old college roommate, who lived just a couple of blocks away. She had finished her course work for her master's degree, but hadn't completed her thesis on early California Indians or taken her orals. She was active in a skiing club and a running club. She had just started adding manuscript acquisition to her sales job. She was in good shape, but a little chubby and prone to colds. This is how she outlined her five-year goals after this part of the visualization:

Five-Year Goals

Material goods: *few but good pieces of furniture and clothes*

Family and friends: *still close to Jenny*

Educational, Intellectual, Professional: *On top of sales, challenged by manuscript acquisition*

Health: *fit, size nine*

Leisure: *skiing clubs and running*

Creative: *whipping thesis into shape*

Next, Mary Jane visualized her life one year from today. She found that she was still rooming with Jenny and planned to enroll in a graduate program.

She was seeing a lot of Jack, her current boyfriend, but they weren't making any marriage plans. She was skiing two or three times a season, and running in the summer. She was still a size nine, but a little lighter than her current sedentary student weight. She was working full time at the small publishing company, keeping the books and training in sales. She was surprised herself in the creative department by finding an interest in interpretive dance. Here is how she distilled these images into one-year goals:

One-Year Goals

Material goods: *redecorate apartment, buy new bedroom set*

Family and friends: *Close to Jenny and other friends, break up with Jack*

Educational, Intellectual, Professional: *apply to grad school, ask to train in sales department*

Health: *lose ten pounds*

Leisure: *start running*

Creative: *take interpretative dance class*

Over the next month, Mary Jane devised "to do" lists and affirmations to put her plans for the future into action. Each morning as soon as she woke up she visualized what she planned to do for her future that day. Here are some examples of what she planned to do and say to herself:

Area/To Do	Affirmations
Material	
Buy and frame a new print for the living room.	*I care about my surroundings.*
	I keep my home looking nice.
Call the landlord and ask about painting the kitchen.	
Price bedroom sets next month.	
Family and friends	
Make Jenny a birthday dinner.	*I'm friendly and outgoing.*
Invite Randy and Isetta to go skiing in January.	*I am a good friend.*
Educational, Intellectual, Professional	
Send memo to boss asking for more hours and sales training after graduation.	*I know what I want and I go after it.*
Go to publishers' network meetings and talk to text book sales reps.	

Throw away current grad
school applications and
ask to be put on the mail-
ing list for next year.

Health

Buy some running shoes.   *I take care of myself.*
Have popcorn without butter
instead of chocolate chip
cookies late at night.

Creative

Ask in Theater Arts depart-   *I bring creative approach to all*
ment about interpretive   *tasks.*
dance classes for ama-
teurs.
Look in bookshelf at work for
any reference material
about editing textbooks.

Mary Jane saved all her lists and notes. Every ten or twelve months she
would pull them out of her drawer and look them over. As it turned out, she
regained her interest in scholarship and got her master's degree faster than she
expected. In the running club she met a wonderful guy who didn't look at all
like a Ken doll. They got married and he was very supportive about her sales
work. She did sell a lot of textbooks and live in a beautiful condo for a while,
but in another state. She still skis and and runs in her stylish size eight sports
outfits, but her interest in dance faded. She regularly visits and writes to her old
roommate Jenny.

12

Improved Learning and Sports Performance

"To be what we are, and to become what we're capable of becoming is the only end of life."

—*Robert Louis Stevenson*

Learning and sports are covered in the same chapter because excellence in both is a matter of mental attitude. Understanding molecular chemistry requires a certain basic intelligence, and hitting a baseball requires a certain strength and coordination, but true ease and mastery of both require a relaxed, confident, prepared mind. Similar visualization techniques can help you learn faster, remember longer, play better, and score higher.

IMPROVED LEARNING

The learning covered in this chapter is the kind that gives people the most trouble: studying written material that you must remember in order to pass a test, make a sales pitch, give a presentation, answer questions in an oral exam, and so on.

The obstacles to learning covered in detail in this chapter are poor study habits, poor memory, lack of motivation, drugs, and anxiety.

Other chapters in this book can help in this area, especially the ones on self-esteem and goal-setting. Low self-esteem can undermine your confidence and raise your anxiety level so that you can't recall material that you actually know. Lack of clearly defined goals can keep you from persevering in a course of study because you're not really sure you want to complete it. If you suspect that poor self-esteem and unclear goals are obstacles to your effective learning, work through those chapters also.

Identify Obstacles to Learning

Poor Study Habits

Do you have trouble setting aside time for studying? Do you feel overwhelmed by the size of the learning tasks before you? Do you feel you have to study every moment of the day, wherever you are, and whatever distractions are going on?

The first step in developing good study habits is to schedule your time. Plan to study for one- or two-hour periods, at a set time of day—for example, after dinner from eight to ten. Keep this time inviolate. Nothing else can be scheduled then.

The second step is to break down the overwhelming mountain of material into small, discrete chunks. An entire American History textbook is too daunting. It's best to think of it as a chapter today, a chapter Sunday, and a chapter Tuesday.

The third step is to stop trying to study in front of the TV, in the cafeteria, while riding the bus, and so on. Pick one place in which to study, someplace where there aren't any other distractions or things to do. For example, decide to go to the library, to a particular table in a quiet corner. Resolve that the only thing you will do there is study. If you find that you can't study—your mind keeps wandering or you're too sleepy—then get up and leave. Don't hang around in your studying place without studying.

Take time right now to list the time, subject, and place for your next study session. For example:

Time: *Saturday morning, 10 to 12.*

Subject: *Andrew Jackson's presidency*

Place: *In the dining room, radio off, and all doors shut*

Prepare some affirmations such as:

I schedule my study time.

I study one thing at a time.

I can put distractions out of my mind.

I study for my allotted time and then stop.

Poor Memory

It's relatively easy to remember sense impressions like the smell of a rose or the feel of satin. And it's also easy to remember motor experiences, like how to ride a bicycle. The hardest thing to remember is words. Verbal memory is the weakest kind. Fortunately, scientists have studied how you remember and come up with techniques for studying that ensure maximum retention.

Test yourself immediately. As soon as you read the six signs of alcoholism, or the four types of quadratic equations, or the distinctions between Italian and German opera, close your eyes and recite them back to yourself. Open your eyes and check for accuracy. If you missed any, keep testing yourself until you've got them all. Don't tell yourself that you'll get back to it later—you won't. Test yourself right now.

Review frequently. Every couple of pages, look up and paraphrase what you have read to yourself. Skim back over the last two pages and see what you missed. Then go on.

Take breaks between subjects. After reading your sociology assignment, clean your room or walk to the corner store and back before starting in on your English term paper. Wait a while before going on to the next subject or the next block of information. This gives the material you've just studied some time to "settle," or "jell," in your mind before you dump in another load.

Sleep on it. If at all possible, study for a test the night before and get some sleep before taking the exam. The integration of new material will be completed while you sleep. When you wake you'll remember more than you would have remembered immediately after studying.

Make it logical and meaningful. The hardest thing to remember is a long list of meaningless words or numbers. You remember best what you understand best. It's a waste of time to skim over complex material you don't fully understand. Take the time to reread and think about what you've read. If you can see how the material makes sense, if you can make it truly meaningful for yourself, you'll remember it.

For example, suppose you're studying for your real estate license and you can't keep track of how the variables in amortized mortgages interact. Stop and start over from square one. Imagine that you're buying a house and need to borrow $60,000. Get out your calculator and amortization tables and figure out how much you would have to pay per month at ten percent over a term of twenty years. Then change the amount and see what that does to the monthly payment. Keep changing percents and terms and amounts and figuring the interest and principal payments until you fully understand how changing one variable affects the others. If you do this once, you'll remember it forever.

Prepare some affirmations to remind yourself of how you can bolster your memory. Here are some examples:

I test myself and review often.

I take breaks between subjects.

I get my studying done by midnight and sleep on it.

I take the time to understand what I read.

Lack of Motivation

Rewards motivate. It's hard to feel motivated to study if you can't see any reward for your work.

Think about the rewards for studying: the degree you'll receive, the job you'll be qualified for, the power you'll have, the opportunity to help people, the money you'll make, the respect others will have for you, how pleased your parents or others will be if you get good grades, the feeling of accomplishment, your pride in finishing a difficult task, and so on. Focusing on the future rewards will help you bear down and study today.

Sometimes you can't make contact with a far off, future reward. Or there really isn't a direct reward—you're just stuck studying something you hate as a prerequisite for studying something you love. In that case, make up a reward for studying and passing tests: plan to go to the movies, have a special dinner or ice cream treat, buy yourself some clothes or records or sports equipment, take a trip, go for a walk or a workout at the gym. Find something that you'd like to do, and promise yourself you'll get to do it when you finish studying or after finals. And then don't cheat. If you don't study or don't pass, don't give yourself the reward. Conversely, if you've promised yourself a milkshake after cramming for the physics final, be sure to go and get the milkshake after your study session.

Drugs

Drugs and learning don't mix. Alcohol, marijuana, antihistamines, tranquilizers, and lots of other licit and illicit drugs dull the senses and hurt your learning abilities. Uppers like coffee, caffeine pills or diet pills may help you stay awake to study, but they make you jittery. The anxiety makes you forget what you stayed up to learn. Psychologists have discovered a phenomenon called "state dependent learning." It turns out that things you learn under the influence of drugs are very hard to remember when you're "straight." To maximize learning, stay off drugs.

Anxiety

When you're anxious, your mind is in a fight or flight mode. Your priority is survival, not remembering the major political parties of the antebellum period or how to tie off the ground wire in a 100 amp. junction box. One of the biggest contributions that visualization can make to improving your learning is to help you relax, so that you can concentrate on what you're studying and remember what you know.

Review your affirmations for relaxation and consider making up some new ones for test anxiety. Here are some suggestions:

Breathe deeply and read the question again.

I've got plenty of time.

I can relax at will and get back to work.

When my mind becomes calm, the answer becomes clear.

Improved Learning Visualization

It will help if you make a tape of these instructions for yourself. Lie down, close your eyes, and relax. Look forward to your next study session. See all the details of the place you have chosen to study. Notice that all distractions have been avoided or cleared away. Glance at your watch or a clock and note that it is time to start studying. Tell yourself, "I budget my time wisely."

Sit down and lay out your books and notes. Get everything you need before you in logical order. Tell yourself, "I have everything I need."

Before you start studying, watch yourself close your eyes and take several deep breaths. You are relaxing and clearing your mind so that you can focus your attention. Tell yourself, "I can concentrate completely on the job at hand."

Imagine that you are reading your notes. After each important point, you stop and quiz yourself. Every couple of pages you pause and paraphrase the material to review it in your mind. Tell yourself, "I review until I get it right."

Imagine working steadily, with keen interest and good concentration. Then imagine yourself getting bogged down. You feel confused or discouraged, anxious or distracted. Imagine stopping the study session and getting up for a walk around the room. Look out a window or do a couple of deep knee bends. Close your eyes again and breathe deeply to relax and clear your mind. Then see yourself resuming work with renewed energy and confidence. Tell yourself, "When I get bogged down, I stop and recharge my batteries."

Imagine stopping at the end of your allotted time. Repeat to yourself, "I budget my time wisely." If you have planned a special reward for studying, see yourself enjoying the ice cream or the movie or whatever.

Now you will create a memory-boosting image to help you during tests. Go to your special place and look around. Somewhere you will see a white sheet of paper. This is a magic "crib sheet" that you can summon into your mind at any time. Imagine the paper floating up into the air and drifting in front of your eyes. Grab it and look at it. Neatly typed on the white paper are succinct notes outlining all you need to know on a given subject.

During a test, when you're stumped for an answer, close your eyes and take a look at the magic crib sheet. If you don't see the answer on the page, turn it over and look on the back. Each time you turn the paper over, the contents change. But usually the answer you seek will be on the first page. Tell yourself, "I can look within for the answer."

Now you will visualize an exam. Imagine getting up on the morning of the exam. You've studied the night before and you feel rested and well prepared. As you go into the test, you notice that you are feeling calm. You've got a calculator and all the pens, papers, blue books, or whatever you need for the test. Find your seat and look around. Fix the details of the room in your mind.

As you wait to begin the test, let yourself feel a little fear. Feel the butterflies in your stomach, the racing heart, the sweaty palms, and so on. Then imagine closing your eyes and taking a long, slow, deep breath. Tell yourself, "As I breathe out, the nervousness flows away. I remain calm and relaxed."

Start the test feeling calm. Work steadily through the test, making good progress and not worrying about the time or about questions you're doubtful about. When you get stumped, imagine the white paper in your mind and see the answer typed there. Tell yourself, "I avoid panic. I easily recall what I've studied."

If you don't know an answer, you take a deep breath and go on to the next question. You relax and remind yourself that you don't have to be perfect to do well.

Finish the test on time. Leave the room feeling relieved and confident. If you promised yourself a reward, imagine enjoying it with a light heart. Tell yourself, "I did well. I'm going to pass easily. I deserve a treat."

Finally, visualize the long-term positive benefits of your improved learning skills. Imagine wearing your cap and gown, reaching out for your diploma. Bask in the admiring, proud gaze of your family and friends. Imagine reporting for the first day's work in your exciting new job. Drive the cars and wear the clothes and eat at the restaurants you will be able to afford. See your bank account balance and feel the heft of your wallet. Imagine how fulfilled and proud you'll feel after accomplishing your goal. Look on the wall of your tasteful new home and see the framed real estate license, private pilot license, certificate of proficiency, union membership card, contractor's license, M.A. degree, or whatever. Hear people call you "doctor" or "sir" or "nurse" and defer to your expertise. Tell yourself, "I'm working a little every day to make my dream come true."

End the visualization when you're ready. This is just a guideline. Expand the parts that apply to you, filling in details and refining the scenes until they match your personality and situation exactly.

In an actual test situation, practice the coping and memory techniques you have rehearsed in visualization: deep breathing for relaxation, taking a break when you get muddled, looking inside for the answer on the magic crib sheet, using affirmations, and rewarding yourself for success.

Example

Jorge was a student in a paramedic training course who was failing his anatomy and physiology (A&P) course. It was a fast-moving course with lots of material to cover and exams every two weeks. He had to pass it with a "C" in order to go on to become a paramedic.

Jorge decided to set aside Tuesday and Thursday afternoons for studying A&P. His roommate worked those days, so he could have the apartment to himself for four hours. Jorge was on a local rowing team that sometimes had practice on Thursdays before a Friday meet. But he told his coach that he just wouldn't be able to practice Thursdays until the school year ended. If it meant being bumped from the team, so be it.

Breaking the material down into pieces was easy, since the instructor was following a rigid one-chapter-a-week schedule. Jorge just planned to work on the first half of a given chapter on Tuesday and the second half on Thursday.

In his visualizations, Jorge saw himself clear away the lunch mess from the kitchen table at one o'clock. He set out his A&P notes, textbook, and photocopies of medical illustrations with the captions blanked out. He watched himself set the phone machine to "record" and sit down to work. His affirmation was, "I set up and get right to work."

He imagined reading about the muscles of the arm, studying the illustration, then closing the book. On his blank copy of the illustration, he filled in all the muscle names that he could remember. Then he looked in the book for the ones he missed. Only when he could score one hundred percent on his self-testing would he go on to the next muscle group. He said to himself, "I stop and review at each step."

About every hour Jorge saw himself get up and stretch, drink a soda, or make out a list of things to do the next day. He timed these breaks to separate major topics in the material he was studying. He purposefully included an image of the coffee maker, cold and empty, because he had a bad habit of getting wired on caffeine during study sessions, and often ended up talking a mile a minute on the phone or playing the stereo loud and dribbling a basketball around the apartment instead of studying. He told himself, "I can stay cool two afternoons a week."

He visualized the kitchen clock reading exactly five o'clock when he stopped studying. He saw himself turn down the corner of the page, put his notes away, and go out for a run as a reward.

Next, Jorge went in his imagination to his special place, which was the cabin of a thirty-foot yacht that he had once crewed on. There on the galley counter he saw a magic crib sheet. When he picked it up, he saw the illustrations from his A&P book. Each time he turned the sheet over, a new illustration or a page from his notes would appear. He told himself, "I can view these pages any time I want."

He saw himself wake up from a good night's sleep on the morning of his next test. He went into the test whistling, feeling fine. He was able to calm his nervousness by closing his eyes and reviewing his imaginary notes. When he started the test, the fill-in-the-blank illustrations and the essay questions looked like old friends. When he was unsure for a moment, he closed his eyes and looked at his mental notes. He saw himself finish the test five minutes early and sit back with his arms behind his head, totally at ease.

Jorge always ended his visualizations with an image of himself dressed in a white coat, swinging out of an ambulance or a fire truck with a stethoscope looped around his neck and a portable EKG machine dangling from his hand. He looked cool and purposeful in his movements. Frightened people made way for him as he approached an accident victim. He saw himself as a professional, a lifesaver. "This is my reward," he said to himself.

In real life, Jorge managed to keep to his study schedule most of the time. Most important, he was more relaxed during tests. His scores began creeping up along with his confidence. He went into the final with a "C + " and clinched it by getting a solid "B" on the test.

SPORTS PERFORMANCE

Coaches and athletes are pragmatic. If something will help athletes run faster, jump higher, lift more, throw farther, or move with greater precision and grace, coaches and athletes will search it out and use it. They don't worry about whether a technique is too "New Age" or whether an acceptable authority condones it. They just try everything and adopt what works.

For this reason, coaches and athletes have been using visualization to improve sports performance for years. And psychologists have been studying their use of visualization, since sports performance provides easily quantified results.

The classic study was done by Australian psychologist Alan Richardson. He picked three random groups of basketball players with no previous experience of visualization techniques. Each group made a series of free throws on the first and the twentieth days. In the meantime, the first group practiced making free throws daily for the whole twenty days, and improved twenty-four percent. The second group had no practice between the first and twentieth days, and they made no improvement. The third group didn't touch a basketball between the first and twentieth days, but they visualized making free throws daily. They used all their senses in the visualizations and were told to correct their aim when they saw themselves miss. On the twentieth day they shot real free throws and had improved twenty-three percent—only one percentage point lower than the group who practiced daily with real balls and hoops.

The results of this study have been duplicated in other sports. With gymnasts, Richardson confirmed that the most powerful use of imagery was to combine it with basic instruction and daily practice. Jean-Claude Killy, a three-time winner of Olympic gold medals in skiing, was once injured and unable to practice for a major race. He skied it mentally as his only preparation, and it turned out to be one of his best races. Commenting on his outstanding performance in football, O. J. Simpson said, "I've run that play so many times in my mind, I just knew it. All the runs I have made a million times in my mind."

Peter Karns, coach of the U.S. biathalon team in the 1976 Winter Olympics taught his team members to use deep relaxation and visualization of the course to prepare. Similar techniques were used by Karen Korfanta and Hank Taubler, coaches of the slalom racing team. East European athletes often listen to the largo (slow) movements of baroque music to relax them. Their heart rates become synchronized to the sixty beats-per-minute rhythm of the bass notes.

Guidelines for Sports Visualizations

All this research and anecdotal information makes it possible to draw up fairly specific guidelines for using visualization to improve your sports performance:

Master the basics first. Visualization won't replace basic training. You need to practice the fundamentals of your sport until you have mastered them. For example, in tennis you need to learn how to hold your racket, make the basic ground shots and volleys, and serve. Then visualization will help you refine your game. In baseball you need to know the rules, strategy, how to hit, field, throw, and run bases. Then you can work on the fine points with visualization. Each sport has a baseline of knowledge and skills that you must acquire before you can really say that you engage in the sport, and before visualization will help you significantly.

Visualization shouldn't replace practice, either. Research has shown repeatedly that the most effective strategy is to start with a firm grounding in the basics, then combine frequent practice with visualization.

Compose affirmations. You should have affirmations about the basic moves and about sports in general. The language of sports abounds in ready-made affirmations. For example:

Keep your eye on the ball.

Head down, left arm straight.

Swing level.

Bend your knees.

Control is most important. In your visualizations, concentrate on seeing yourself or feeling yourself in complete control. This is more important than vividness or clever symbolism. The best way to experience control is to break your performance down into incremental steps and observe each one closely. Include as many details of correct form as you can.

Use slow motion. In order to see yourself in control of all those tiny details, slow the action down to a crawl. Make your visualization like an extreme slow motion sequence in a movie.

Include errors, then correct them. Studies have shown that cognitive rehearsal works best when you see yourself having trouble, making mistakes at first, and then succeeding. So if you're visualizing the high jump, see yourself take off too soon or drag an elbow over the bar. Then watch yourself correct the mistake and make a successful jump. If you're a runner, see yourself stumble and falter, then regain a smooth rhythm.

Use symbolic visualization during performance. When you're actually doing your sport, have a symbolic aid in mind. For instance, runners can imagine a skyhook pulling them up and forward, or a giant hand on their back, pushing them on to greater speed. Skiers can imagine that they're birds, wheeling and skimming through the sky. Shot putters can imagine that the shot is made of balsa wood instead of metal. Pool players can imagine that the balls are strung on wires or rolling in grooves that lead straight to the pockets.

Forget the details in competition. When you're competing in an important game or event, forget about the fine points of technique. You should have used your visualization and practice sessions to go over and over the details, so that during actual competition you can just go with the flow. Researchers have concluded that the best performance comes when responses are almost automatic, when the details of technique and strategy are hardly present in your conscious mind. Psychologist Mihalyi Csikszentmihalyi, studying rock climbers, surgeons, and gymnasts, called these performances "flow experiences": being in complete unity with the activity in which they were involved. The same will be true for your best days as an athlete.

In *The Inner Game of Tennis*, Timothy Gallwey says, "The theory of the inner game is that your performance is dependent on the state of your mind. The real game is to learn how to reach that state of mind and stay in that state of mind in which your performance is best and your perception is at its clearest."

Sports Performance Visualization

For best results, tape record these instructions and listen to the tape instead of trying to remember all the steps. Lie down, close your eyes, and relax. Imagine that you are watching yourself playing your sport. What are you wearing? What do the equipment and the surroundings look like? Concentrate on the normal sights and sounds to make the scene real.

Focus on a particular aspect of your sport that you have been working on—your tennis serve, your soccer kick, your drive off the tee, or whatever. Watch yourself go through the motions the way you usually do, including your usual mistakes. Watch yourself grimace or shrug or do whatever you do to express dissatisfaction with your performance.

Now wind the action down to extreme slow motion. Observe each tiny component of the action. Keep breaking the moves down into smaller and smaller parts. Figure out where each hand and foot goes, how and when each joint moves, where your weight and center of gravity are at each stage. See where you go wrong.

Keep the scene in slow motion and repeat it. This time, watch yourself improve. Gradually, let your moves approach perfection. Feel in control, confident. Tell yourself, "I'm getting smoother, more coordinated, more graceful. "

Now speed up the film to normal speed. Watch yourself succeeding at your sport. Include the positive benefits: the applause, the sense of accomplishment, receiving a prize, being notified of a chance to compete on a higher level, the feeling of fitness in your body. Tell yourself, "I'm at the top of my form."

Now "step into" your observed body. Actually feel yourself doing your sport. First run through the correct moves in slow motion. Imagine how each tiny increment feels, how you should position your feet and hands, how it feels to shift your weight perfectly, the way it feels to move with your muscles and mind in skillful coordination. Tell yourself, "I'm concentrating on the basics."

Then speed things up to a normal pace. Imagine that you're preparing to do your sport. Allow yourself to feel some of the excitement and anxiety that you usually experience. Then breath deeply and calm yourself. Now start doing your sport at normal speed. Perform each step perfectly, with all the parts flowing smoothly together. Run this sequence over and over in your mind, adding more and more details. If you feel your breathing and heart rate speed up a little during this part, you'll know it's working well. Tell yourself, "I'm strong, I'm ready."

If there is a particular course or situation in which you will be competing, visualize it in full detail. Imagine proceeding through an upcoming competition, seeing what you will see, hearing what you will hear, feeling what you will feel. Tell yourself, "I'm flowing through the event."

Do this visualization night and morning. When you are actually practicing your sport, use your affirmations to remind yourself of the basics that you're working on. Also try various symbolic images. See some outside help pulling you along or insuring your accuracy. Imagine that you are filled with helium to make you light on your feet, or that your muscles are made of steel, or that a gyroscope in your chest keeps you balanced. Use whatever images work best for you to represent speed, precision, balance, rhythm, or some other important aspect of your sport.

During actual competition, when you're through practicing and the game is for real, clear your mind of all but the most essential affirmations and images. Concentrate on staying relaxed, calm, and centered. Allow your mind and body to get into the *flow* of your sport. Don't just do or play your sport—*become* it.

If there is some form of conditioning or training important to your sport that you tend to skimp on, spend a minute visualizing yourself doing that training regularly and enthusiastically. For example, you may need to do more weight lifting, study the playbook, or do wind sprints that are taxing and boring. Plan when you will next perform this training and tell yourself, "I'm willing to pay the price. I keep to my training schedule."

Example

Janice was an amateur runner. She did it "for the fun and the exercise," but she secretly took it more seriously than that. She wanted to try running a marathon—over twenty-six miles of sustained running. She had done well in shorter races, but she was worried about her endurance over the long haul.

Each morning before she got out of bed to go for her training run, she visualized her marathon. First she saw herself passing the twelve-mile point—the longest distance she had regularly run before. She saw her stride shorten, her footfalls become heavy and jarring, and her push-offs become weak and mushy.

She slowed the action down until she could see every fault of her running style when tired.

Gradually, Janice changed her slow motion images. She lengthened the stride, added shock absorbing resilience to her knees, and snap to her push-offs. She told herself, "Mind over muscles. I can *will* my form."

Speeding up her images, Janice saw herself run easily through the twentieth mile. The marathon course included a stiff uphill grade at mile twenty—the point where many runners drop out. She saw herself slow down and breathe harder, but maintain a smooth, even stride to the top of the hill. She used the affirmation, "I've trained for this. I can make it one step after another."

Then Janice stopped merely observing herself and imagined actually running in the marathon. She concentrated on the mile twenty "wall" that stops so many runners. She would feel her legs get heavier and her breathing turn to panting as the road rose up in front of her. The top of the hill seemed miles away. She felt a "What does it all matter?" attitude and the desire to stop creep into her mind. But she concentrated on her three basics: keeping a long, even stride, cushioning with the knees, pushing off smartly with the toes. When she had her stride right, she focused on her breathing affirmation: "In, one two—out, one two."

Janice imagined loping across the finish line, slowing to a walk, still erect and strong. She looked at her imaginary watch and saw that she had accomplished her goal of finishing in under four hours. She told herself, "I can do it."

The thing about serious running that Janice disliked most was doing regular wind sprints. She knew that they were important for building endurance, but she found them boring—running around the high-school track four times at full speed, then two times at a jog, then full speed again, then jogging, and so on, keeping track of her times and trying to run faster and faster miles. Running like a wild animal along forest trails was more her style. Janice visualized herself driving out to the track every Wednesday and Saturday. She saw herself smiling, looking good, enjoying the challenge of racing against her own time. She repeated to herself, "I'm paying the price. I'm going to get it all back with interest at mile twenty."

In actual practice, Janice imagined that she was a greyhound or a thoroughbred horse, tireless and fleet. Sometimes she imagined that another dog or horse ran at her side, setting the pace, keeping her company, and setting a good example.

On the day of the marathon, Janice felt nervous. She had to tell herself repeatedly, "I've trained for this. I'm at the top of my form." She kept her spirits up by visualizing the end of the race, crossing the finish line, with the spectators clapping and her dad snapping her picture with his old Minolta, a giant grin on his face.

For miles at a time, she felt like she was floating. Later she couldn't even remember huge stretches of the course. She would pick a strong runner near her and match his or her pace for as long as it felt comfortable. Sometimes she imagined that she was in a herd of wild horses, running freely over the plains.

At the big hill, she slowed down but never stopped. She felt that she had run up this hill a hundred times before: "I've done this before, I can do it again."

Janice's time at the finish was three hours, fifty-two minutes, twelve seconds. She still has the picture her dad took of her, prancing across the finish line with a huge grin on her face.

IV

Applications for Therapy

13

Stress Reduction

"A crust eaten in peace is better than a banquet partaken in anxiety"

—Aesop

Visualization is particularly good for stress reduction because of the way relaxation and visualization naturally go together. In order to visualize vividly, you need to be relaxed; and visualization in itself is very relaxing. The longer you visualize, the more relaxed you will become; and the more relaxed you become, the more effective your visualizations will be.

But how do you get started, assuming you are under a lot of stress and haven't done much visualization yet? The first step is to reach a clear understanding of all that is meant by that much overworked word, "stress."

The Nature of Stress

You hear people talk about stress in many ways:

"I'm under a lot of stress."

"I don't handle stress well."

"I feel stressed-out."

"This is a stressful situation."

"Stress" is a confusing term because it means different things to different people. This is partly due to the origin of the word itself. Up until the 1950s, "stress" was a term used only in engineering and physics. It meant a force, usually the force of gravity, operating in a certain direction, on an object or a structure which resisted the force. This is the metaphorical connotation involved in a statement such as "I'm under a lot of stress." It means *I feel like I've* got sixteen tons of concrete on top of me."

Fight or Flight

The groundwork for the modern meaning of "stress" as a psychological problem was laid by Walter B. Cannon, a physiologist at Harvard around the turn of the century. He didn't use the term "stress," but he was the first to describe the "fight or flight" response. The fight or flight response is a four-step process:

1. The conscious level of your brain perceives a situation as dangerous.

2. A message is sent from your higher brain levels to your brain stem.

3. Your brain stem excites the sympathetic half of your visceral autonomic nervous system. These are the nerves that operate your digestion, heartbeat, glands, and the dilation of your blood vessels.

4. Your sympathetic nervous system speeds your breathing and heart rate. Your liver releases stored sugar to nourish your muscles. Your blood pressure rises. Your blood leaves your extremities and your digestive system to concentrate in your heart and the vessels serving your large, striped muscles and your central nervous system. Your adrenal glands secrete adrenalin, plus epinephrine and norepinephrin (messenger hormones that make your body ready to move fast). Your pituitary gland releases endorphins (brain drugs that block pain signals and have a slightly depressing effect on your immune system).

In other words, when you perceive danger, an automatic, complicated, and speedy reaction takes place to prepare you to fight or run away. As soon as you see the bear or the mugger or the forest fire, your body flips into overdrive to save you.

Examining the four steps of the fight or flight response gives a strong clue to the way to fight stress: the whole response depends on your conscious assessment of danger. As soon as you decide that a situation is not dangerous, your higher brain levels stop sending panic messages to your brain stem, which in turn stops sending panic messages to your nervous system. The adrenalin and other hormones and chemicals that keep your body aroused are metabolized quickly. Three minutes after you stop sending your body danger messages, the fight or flight response burns out and you return to normal.

Stressful Events

In the 1950s Hans Selye first used the word "stress" to describe what happens when you confront events that are not exactly dangerous, but which evoke the fight or flight response anyway: giving a speech, meeting strangers, being criticized, driving in heavy traffic, and so on. In these situations, neither fight nor flight is appropriate.

Later, Thomas Holmes, a medical doctor at the University of Washington School of Medicine in Seattle, showed that positive as well as negative events are stressful. Falling in love can demand just as much change, and thus be as stressful for you, as falling out of love and breaking up.

Holmes devised the "Schedule of Recent Experience," a checklist of stressful events, both positive and negative, that he used to predict your chances of getting sick from a stress-related illness. On his Schedule, major changes like getting married, losing your job, getting a divorce, or the death of a loved one are scored very high. Less stressful events like a change in the amount of exercise you get or going on vacation earn you a lower score. You add up the scores for all the items on the list that have happened to you during the last two years. The higher your score, the more stress you are under, and the more likely you are to get sick.

In the last few years, researchers such as Richard Lazarus at the University of California at Berkeley have turned to studying the lesser, smaller disruptions of life. They have shown that the cumulative effects of all the minor, everyday stresses are more harmful than the major life changes on the Holmes Schedule. The unscientific but very descriptive term commonly used for these minor irritations is "hassles." Hassles are the snubs, rebukes, bad weather, car problems, disappointments, tight schedules, red lights, spilled milk, and broken fingernails that everyone encounters and no one can entirely escape, however healthy, wealthy, or wise.

Whatever its source, stress causes illness in two ways. First, stress taxes nerves, muscles, and organs directly. For example, constant muscular tension from over-activation of the fight or flight response results in a sore back and shoulders. Or constant elevation of blood pressure overworks your heart. Second, stress causes illness by suppressing your immune system, making you more susceptible to infection and disease.

Relaxation Techniques

There are several ways to go about fighting stress. The first to try are the techniques whose primary purpose is relaxation: progressive relaxation, body awareness, and deep breathing are introduced in the relaxation chapter of this book. Other primary techniques are biofeedback, in which you are hooked up to machines that tell you how your relaxation is progressing, and autogenics, a simple but effective program of imagery and suggestion similar to self-hypnosis.

Visualization, self-hypnosis, and meditation could be described as secondary relaxation techniques. They don't have relaxation as their primary purpose, but they are very helpful in fighting stress.

Then there are techniques that you could call tertiary relaxation techniques. They are intended for various kinds of self-improvement, but they also can have relaxation as a side effect. Cognitive therapy, in which your habitual irrational assumptions are uncovered and refuted, can help if you tend to overestimate the dangers and hassles of your life. Coping skills or assertiveness training can help if the major source of stress for you is your dealings with other people. Systematic desensitization or stress inoculation might help if your stress comes from certain kinds of objects, events, or experiences. Time management can help if an impossible schedule is the source of stress for you. Improving your nutrition or getting more exercise can help by making you more healthy and fit to handle stress.

For more information on relaxation techniques, see *The Relaxation & Stress Reduction Workbook* by Davis, Eshelman, and McKay. The exact mix of techniques you choose will depend on your personality, beliefs, and the common sources of stress in your life. Whatever techniques you choose, combine them with visualization to get the most out of them.

Stress Reduction Visualizations

The visualization scenes and affirmations that follow take advantage of all the proven relaxation techniques. Some will appeal to you more than others. Take what works best for you and build on it.

Preparing Images of Stress and Relaxation

The best images of stress and relaxation are the ones that arise spontaneously from your unconscious. Take a moment to do a short receptive visualization right now and see what comes to mind.

Don't lie down. Just close your eyes at the end of this paragraph, right where you are, and scan your body for tension. What parts of your body are necessarily tense to hold you in position? Probably you are holding yourself up with your back muscles? Perhaps your arm and hand muscles are flexed just a little to hold the book. Close your eyes now and check it out.

Next, close your eyes for a moment and look for unnecessary, chronic tension. Is your neck stiff, have you been unconsciously clenching your teeth and putting tension in your jaw muscles? What other muscles are tense for no reason?

Now, having identified some muscular tension, close your eyes and empty your mind. Focus on the tension. Zoom in on it and see what images come up for you. What represents muscular tension for you? Is it a visual image? A color? Hot or cold? Rough or smooth? Is there a sound? A smell? A taste? A texture on your palate or skin?

Ideally, you should get at least one impression from each of your senses to represent tension: sight, hearing, taste, smell, and the various senses of touch. For example, a medical doctor associated muscular tension with twisted and knotted white cotton sheets, the color blue-green, steel-toed workshoes, resounding Chinese gongs, a high whistling sound, a metallic taste like tinfoil on silver dental fillings, the smell of ether, the feel of a wire brush, and cold wind on wet skin. You may not get so many impressions. That's OK. The important thing is to get a few images or sensations that you associate strongly with muscular tension in your body.

If you have trouble identifying any spontaneous images, just pick a couple from this list to practice with:

Tightly twisted ropes

Hard, cold wax

Sound of jackhammers

Creaking hinges

Taste of lemon

Smell of hot metal

Feel of sandpaper

Feel of cold wind

Red muscles

Next, close your eyes and imagine that you are completely relaxed. What images come to mind? They may be logical extensions or transformations of your images of tension, or they may be new, unrelated images.

For example, the doctor saw the twisted sheets untwisting and becoming soft and smooth. The blue-green color faded to a pale, peachy yellow. The workshoes changed into fleecy bedroom slippers. The Chinese gong modulated into a soft piano sonata. The whistling sound faded to silence. The metallic taste and the smell of ether were replaced by the taste and smell of jasmine tea. The feel of the wire brush and the cold wind went away, to be replaced by warm sand and sun on the skin. He also associated relaxation with the sight of lions sleeping, the sound of distant calliope music, and the sensations of getting a massage.

If you don't get any spontaneous sensations to represent relaxation, use the logical transformations of your choices from the tension list:

Twisted ropes untwist

Wax softens and melts

Jackhammers become distant woodpeckers

Hinges get oiled and become silent and smooth

Taste of lemon becomes your favorite dessert

Smell of hot metal becomes smell of freshly baked bread

Sandpaper becomes silk

Cold wind becomes warm sun

Red muscles turn blue

The images you choose for your first stress reduction visualization aren't too crucial. As you perform the visualization, you will be attracted to the right images for you, and new images will present themselves the more you practice.

Affirmations

Just as the best images are the ones you create yourself, so the best affirmations are the ones you compose for yourself. Remember that an affirmation is a short, positive, feeling-rich statement that a desired change is already so. In this case, you want to make up three or four short affirmations about how well you can handle stress, how easily you can relax at will, how you don't dwell on hassles or overestimate danger, and so on. Take into consideration the places, people, times, situations, and circumstances that are stressful for you, and tailor your affirmations accordingly. Make up a couple of affirmations to use while doing extended relaxation visualizations, and some to use at any time you feel tense.

To get you started, here are some relaxation affirmations that have worked well for others. You can tell from their variety that there are many good approaches to stress reduction:

Relax.

Breathe deeply and slowly.

I am calm and relaxed, ready for anything.

Let the tension float away.

I can relax at will.

I can handle this.

I am safe, free from danger.

I am peaceful, calm, serene.

Other people are just as nervous as I am.

I just smile and breathe easy.

This is just time pressure.

I have all the time in the world.

Ten years from now, what will it matter?

I will survive this.

I concentrate on being here, now.

I can retreat for a moment to my special place.

Alpha waves are flooding my mind.

I can just think of the ocean and become calm.

Relax the jaw, lower the shoulders.

Aaaahhhh (a slow, luxurious yawn and stretch).

This is perfectly normal.

My body is just preparing to fight or flee.

In three minutes this discomfort will pass.

Wait it out.

Calm in mind, calm in heart, calm in body.

Let the anger dissipate and flow away.

Making your own relaxation tape is a great help. Record this basic scene as a start, and rerecord it as you discover the images that work best for you. The last chapter of this book has more suggestions for making effective visualization tapes.

Basic Scene

Lie down and relax. Spend some extra time on your breathing and progressive muscle relaxation.

Go to your indoor special place. Lie down there too, and close your imaginary eyes. This will deepen and intensify your relaxation.

Bring your images of tension and relaxation to mind and concentrate on the details. If you see a taut steel cable being slackened, then really notice every strand of wire. Feel the cable vibrate and hear it hum with tension. Imagine how your muscles are strung up just as tight, about to snap. Then release the tension. See the vibrations damp down and stop. See the individual wires slackening and the whole cable slumping into a graceful curve as all tension leaves it.

Whatever your images of tension and relaxation, run over them one after another. Constantly relate the images to parts of your body. If you use colored lights, then see the tense red light flooding every nook and cranny of your body. See every muscle fiber flaming with fiery red light. Then transform the light into white or blue or whatever color means relaxation to you. Concentrate on every muscle fiber turning slack as it's bathed in pure, relaxing light. Repeat, sending the light just to areas of special tension, like your shoulders, neck, and jaw.

Each time you switch or repeat images, say one of your affirmations to yourself.

When you have become very relaxed, visualize yourself in some future stressful time. See yourself smiling and relaxed. Watch yourself taking deep, slow breaths and subvocalizing your affirmations. Get up in your special place, still very relaxed, and turn on your TV, movie projector, crystal ball, or whatever device you have. Watch yourself in the same stressful situation as if it were a movie. Notice how well you handle it. See yourself having some difficulty at first, getting hot and bothered. Then see yourself pausing and making use of some brief relaxation technique like deep breathing or reciting an affirmation. Watch yourself return to the stressful situation renewed, refreshed, and able to cope.

Next go outside your special place and walk into the stressful scene you have just viewed. Take some time to create and intensify the details of the scene. Include all the people and things that would normally be there. Act out the scene and experience everything as if it were really happening to you. Allow yourself to feel tense and panicky, then regain control and use your affirmations and brief relaxation techniques.

Leave the stressful scene and continue on until you come to your outdoor special place. Lie down there and repeat your images of tension and relaxation. This time you're going for an even deeper level of relaxation. Continue with the scene as above, viewing yourself in the stressful scene, then leaving your special place and experiencing the scene as if it were really happening to you.

You can continue this basic scene as long as you want, switching from one special place to another, repeating pure imagery, viewed scenes, and experienced scenes.

If you wish, have your inner guide visit you in your special places and recite your affirmations to you or with you. Give your inner guide a chance to comment on your reaction to stress and your blocks to relaxation. You might learn something that will change the way you look at stress, lead you to alter your relaxation techniques, or give you good ideas for revising your affirmations.

Special Applications

Assertiveness and coping skills. If social encounters or asking for what you want are very frightening for you, you need to compose lots of special affirmations to reinforce and remind yourself of your social coping skills. Pay special attention to any catastrophic predictions that you habitually make to yourself and compose your affirmations to specifically refute the predictions.

When you visualize stressful scenes, the first one should be hardly stressful at all—a situation in which you feel just slightly tense, like asking where the pimentos are in a strange supermarket or telling a shoe salesperson to show you a different pair. Continue with this scene until you can really feel relaxed throughout the scene. Then go on to a slightly more stressful scene and practice it until you can feel fairly relaxed from beginning to end.

It helps to sit down and write out descriptions of all the stressful situations you can think of, then rank them in a hierarchy from the least to the most stressful. For instance, hailing a cab might be least stressful, talking about your medical history to a doctor might be somewhere in the middle, and calling up a stranger to make a blind date might be at the top of the list.

Making a stressful scene hierarch and working through them with visualization is a common feature of such cognitive stress interventions as systematic desensitization and stress inoculation. For detailed instructions in these techniques, see *Thoughts and Feelings*, a book I co-authored with Matthew McKay and Martha Davis.

Daily quickies. When you do the basic relaxation scene, notice which images and affirmations seem the most powerful. Use these through the day whenever you feel tense. Just close your eyes for a second, see the wax melting or feel the rays of the sun at the beach, and say, "Relax. I'm calm and at peace," or whatever affirmation works best for you.

What to Expect

Stress is not a problem you can solve once and for all. When you first seriously try visualization and stress reduction techniques, you'll probably experience some success right away. You may even feel that your life is totally changed. But stress will be back. So time spent now mastering visualization for stress reduction will be well spent indeed. You'll need these skills all your life.

The only real way to beat stress once and for all is to change your beliefs and your lifestyle: Stop obsessing about unfairness, failure, catastrophe, being perfect, and so on. Change your job and relationships so that you no longer have punishing schedules and don't have to meet the demands of unreasonable people. Get off tobacco, alcohol, drugs, sugar, and so on to maximize your health.

Unfortunately, few people have the ability or opportunity to make all these changes. They can't eliminate stress, so they have to cope with it. That's why stress-coping skills like visualization are so important.

As circumstances and your visualization experiences change, you may have to create fresh new images of relaxation. You will periodically have to compose new affirmations that fit your changing beliefs and lifestyle.

Contraindications

If you have any serious stress-related physical problems such as high blood pressure, chronic headaches or backaches, ulcers, irritable bowel, muscle spasms, or extreme weakness or fatigue, see a doctor. Remember that visualization works best as a *supplement* to other, more traditional resources. Visualization will not *replace* hypertensive medications, sensible diet, biofeedback, physical therapy, or competent medical care.

Likewise, visualization will not replace the assistance of a trained counselor or therapist. If your stress-related psychological problems such as anxiety, depression, hostility, phobias, or obsessions are severe, get help.

Example

Jan was an air traffic controller at a medium-size airport on the East Coast. Her job entailed considerable stress, since she was responsible for the safety of hundreds of air passengers every day. Sometimes after a long shift she would have trouble unwinding at home. She drank lots of coffee on the job, which increased her tension and kept her awake at night after she finished a swing shift and went home at eleven.

Jan's husband and daughter were very supportive, so her home life was not a source of stress. The only relative who caused her any anxiety was her sister Patrice, who was married to an alcoholic. Patrice often called or visited Jan and complained for hours under the guise of asking her advice, which Patrice never followed.

After a routine checkup, Jan learned that she had borderline high blood pressure. Her physician strongly recommended that she learn relaxation techniques and cut down on salt, animal fats, and caffeine. She went to a local biofeedback clinic where she was taught progressive muscle relaxation, deep breathing, body awareness, and visualization.

In her first visualizations, Jan concentrated on imagining a beach scene. She had a lot of fun trying to find images for tension and relaxation that appealed to her and didn't contradict the basic beach setting, with its restricted set of ingredients: the ocean, the sand, rocks, wind, sun, seagulls, and so on. These are the sense impressions she worked with:

	Tension	*Relaxation*
Sight	Dark clouds	Bright sunlight
	Waves & whitecaps	Smooth swells and ripples
	Jagged rocks	Smooth sand
Sound	Crashing surf	Lapping ripples
	Howling wind	Seagulls
Taste	Gritty sand	Ice cream
Smell	Rotten seaweed	Salt air and campfire smoke
Touch/Feelings	Cold wind	Warm sunlight
	Rocks underfoot	Warm sand
	Jumping over big waves	Floating on gentle swells

Jan would lie down and close her eyes. She'd spend several minutes getting into the beach scene. First, she'd imagine walking on a harsh, rocky, stormy beach. Then she'd come to a protected cove and the sun would come out. She'd lie down and let the warm sand and sun soak into her tense muscles. Sometimes she would go swimming, first in heavy surf, then out past the breakers and relaxing on the bosom of the gentle swells.

Affirmations were an important part of Jan's visualizations and her daily life. During her beach scenes, she would say to herself, "I am getting more and more relaxed.... I am safe and secure here.... Let go, let it all go." When she got uptight at work or after one of her sister's marathon phone calls, she would pause for a moment and say, "Take it easy.... I always do my best.... One step at a time."

When she got very relaxed, Jan would imagine herself at work. She would pretend that several flights were stacked up, that the weather was foggy, and that one of the runways was out of operation. She'd see herself begin to tense up, then take a moment to breathe deeply. She watched herself shifting quickly and decisively from the radio, the radar, the various fuel, schedule, and weather status readouts. Jan heard herself issuing clear, simple directions that sorted out the tangle and got flights onto the ground with generous safety margins. She watched herself go to the ladies room during a break and do her relaxation exercises instead of heading for a cup of coffee in the tower lounge.

Jan imagined getting up and going to a tide pool. She was looking into it and saw the same stressful scene take place in miniature on the bottom of the pool. Then she walked up a path to the top of a cliff, and into a control tower, where she acted out the scene as if it was really happening to her.

When she knew she might have to work overtime, or when traffic was very heavy at the airport during the holidays, Jan got up a little early to do a long relaxation visualization before going to work. She imagined her coming shift and reinforced her images of calm and efficiency.

After a few weeks, Jan began to get bored with her beach scene. It was too limiting to stick with only images that might appear on a beach. She began experimenting with other ways to represent her tension and deepen her relaxation. Here are some of the other sense impressions she ultimately used:

Tension	Relaxation
Jagged ice	Melting
Red light and reggae music	Blue light and the blues
Guy wires with turnbuckles	Slackening the turnbuckles
Out-of-tune guitar	In-tune guitar
Guitar strings under tension	Guitar without strings

In an article about children with learning disabilities, Jan read about a technique that helped her relax during her "coffeeless" breaks. She would imagine that she could take the top of her head off like the lid of a box and remove her brain. She would then imagine washing her brain off under a faucet, rinsing out all the accumulated dirt and grime, all the little negative thoughts and anxieties. Then she'd pop her shining clean brain back into her head and close the lid, ready to go back to work with a "clean mind."

With diet, exercise, visualization, and biofeedback, Jan was able to keep her blood pressure under control and survive her stressful job as an air traffic controller. She still had "bad days," but they weren't as bad as before and she would get over them quicker.

Jan's stress levels finally fell when she retired from active traffic controlling in favor of a training position and her sister moved to Montana.

14

Self-Esteem

"What other dungeon is so dark as one's own heart! What jailer so inexorable as one's self!"

— *Nathaniel Hawthorne*

Self-esteem is such an important and complicated topic that it requires a long book to cover it properly. If you're interested in covering the subject in greater depth, I recommend reading *Self-Esteem*, a book I co-authored with Matthew McKay.

In this chapter, I'll do my best to condense everything you need to know about self-esteem, with special emphasis on using visualization to improve your self-image.

First, let's consider the effects of low self-esteem. When your self-esteem is low, you are your own harshest critic. You feel unworthy and incompetent. You're blind to your good points. You are haunted by your past mistakes and the possibility of making future errors. You can't handle criticism. You're reluctant to ask for what you want from others.

Low self-esteem takes an enormous toll on the quality of your life. Judging and rejecting yourself is so painful that you avoid anything that might aggravate that pain. You take fewer social, academic, or career risks. You find it more difficult to meet people, interview for a job, or strive for success in the face of possible failure.

There are two primary sources of low self-esteem: how you were reared up to age four or five, and *your own thoughts and images since then.*

There's nothing you can do that will give you different parents and change the way you were reared. But there's a lot you can do about the current thoughts and images that keep you locked into low self-esteem.

Thoughts create low self-esteem like this: something happens to you, you have a negative thought about it, and you feel lousy. For instance, you get a report card with mostly C's, have the thought, "Boy, am I stupid," and feel like a failure.

The way to fight this pattern is not just to study hard and raise the grades, but rather to *change the thought.* Better grades by themselves won't do the trick. If you suffer from low self-esteem, it won't matter if the next report card is all B's. You'll still think, "Boy, am I stupid," because you didn't get any A's. The solution is to change your thinking to something like, "I didn't do so well this time, but I'm still a good person" or "I did my best" or "I guess I'd better start getting my homework in on time."

If you're thinking that it's impossible to change your negative thoughts, you're almost right. It's very difficult to change them. Over the years your negative self-appraisals take on a life of their own. They become a carping voice inside your head that I call the "pathological critic."

Your pathological critic doesn't have to wait for the report card. He predicts failure from the beginning. He ignores your strong points and harps on your weaknesses. He never misses the slightest mistake or imperfection, slyly whispering in your ear, "Stupid ... lame ... what a jerk ... why can't you get it right?"

The critic blames you for everything and compares you unfavorably to everybody. He sets up perfectionistic, impossible standards and castigates you for failing to measure up. He reads your friends' minds and convinces you that they are bored, turned off, disappointed, or disgusted by you. The critic exaggerates your weaknesses by insisting that you "*always* screw up a relationship," "*never* finish anything on time," or "*always* say the wrong thing."

The pathological critic uses your powers of visualization against you by showing highly edited home movies of your past mistakes and embarrassments. He projects a slide show of future disasters that obscures any vision of yourself as good or worthy in the present.

How To Raise Your Self-Esteem

The key to raising your self-esteem is to tune into your pathological critic until you can identify the damaging messages. You'll do this in the receptive visualization below by imagining a time when you were down on yourself and by reliving it in slow motion so that you can follow the negative thoughts that flowed through your mind. In another visualization, you'll remember times when you felt OK and make a list of your strengths and good qualities.

Once you have identified the recurring negative messages and images from your internal critic, you'll compose positive affirmations of self-worth. You'll use these affirmations to refute your critic's negative messages and replace them with reminders of your good points. With practice you'll be able to turn down the volume of your critical voice, and sometimes cut it off entirely.

Once you have gained some control over your internal critical voice, you can begin to develop the attitudes and coping skills that bolster self-esteem.

Practicing compassion for yourself and others. Compassion is composed of understanding, acceptance, and forgiveness. You understand yourself—how you operate, why you do the things you do—without negative judgments. You accept yourself—the good, the bad, and the indifferent—again without judging and condemning the "bad" parts. And you forgive yourself—when you make a mistake, appear "stupid," or fall into old habits—without approving, condoning, or defending your behavior. You give others the same breaks you give yourself. You acknowledge that everyone, yourself included, has intrinsic worth as a human being, regardless of accomplishments, virtues, looks, talents, or any other criteria.

Knowing you always do your best. You're hurrying to finish washing the dishes and a glass slips out of your soapy hands and breaks. You tell yourself, "clumsy ass," and feel irritated and depressed by your mistake. But you didn't plan to break the glass. Up to the point where the glass slipped, you were doing your best to finish the dishes efficiently. You always do what seems right at the time. It's only later, when you view the results, that you decide you made a mistake. The high self-esteem way to handle mistakes is to tell yourself, "I made a mistake, but it's all I was capable of doing at the moment. I always do the best I can, given my awareness at the time."

Handling criticism assertively. You don't take criticism personally, since you know that others can't really know the real you, can't judge who you really are, and are operating out of a limited awareness of their own. You respond appropriately to different kinds of criticism: acknowledging constructive remarks with which you agree; asking for clarification when you aren't sure of the critic's motive or meaning; and avoiding unfair or unwanted criticism by changing the subject or refusing to respond at all. You avoid argument, apology, and dwelling on the negative opinions of others.

Knowing what you want and asking for it. You stay in touch with your legitimate needs and wants. You know that you deserve attention, love, respect, peace, fair compensation for your work, a chance to learn and grow, and so on. You can ask others for what you want in a clear, honest way without apologizing or trying to manipulate them.

Each of these strategies could fill a chapter of its own. But the programmed visualizations in this chapter will help reinforce the image of yourself as compassionate, able to handle mistakes and criticism well, and able to ask for what you want.

Receptive Visualization

Lie down, close your eyes, and relax. Go to your special place and get comfortable. It's important to remain relaxed during this visualization.

Get out your TV or movie screen. Begin running the tape or film of an experience that made you feel embarrassed, self-critical, unworthy, or dumb—losing a job, flunking a test, being criticized for sloppy work, or whatever. Relive the experience, re-creating the sights, sounds, and textures of the moment until you begin to feel some of the same emotions.

Now listen to your thoughts, coming like a voice-over as you watch the action. Does a word or phrase or image repeatedly come into your mind?

Rerun the worst part of the experience over and over. Slow the action or freeze the frame at various points. Listen for your pathological critic: "Oh no, blew it again. . . . This is the story of my life, one mistake after another. . . . They all think I'm an imbecile. . . . He's secretly laughing at me." Your internal critic may interrupt your experience of the moment with flashbacks to previous failures or split-second images of you looking like a jerk or a clown or a villain.

Continue viewing the painful scene until you can hear and see what your critic is up to. If you just get vague feelings and no words or images, go on to the next scene.

Move from one painful scene to another, looking for the negative messages from your pathological critic. Keep this up until your critic starts to repeat himself.

End the visualization when you're ready. Get up and immediately write down the messages from your critic. For example:

Jerk, asshole.

What a stupid thing to say.

Screw up.

She hates me.

I always stick my foot in my mouth.

Failed again.

I'll never learn.

Not this again.

I'm so dumb.

I'm homely and awkward.

I'll never figure this out.

I'm fat.

I'm lazy.

Save this list for later. Right now, lie down and close your eyes again. Relax and go to your special place. Now you will again recall scenes from your past, but this time look for pleasant ones. Remember times when you succeeded, when you received praise, when you felt reasonably content, when you enjoyed doing something. Within these times, look for your strengths and good qualities.

You don't have to come up with grand accomplishments and noble virtues. If you have low self-esteem, you'll probably have trouble thinking of even the smallest successes, of even a single area of contentment. But everyone has them. Here are some areas to explore: pleasant aspects of your appearance, ways in which you relate well to others, your friendships, positive personality traits like kindness or patience, parts of your job or schoolwork or chores that you do well, the good parts of your sex life, plus hobbies, sports, or artistic endeavors in which you enjoy some success.

Go from scene to scene, looking for good qualities in yourself. Find at least a dozen good qualities. When you can't find any more, stop the visualization and get up. Immediately write down your list of good points. Here are some examples:

Large brown eyes

Clear skin

Shapely ears

Warm and open

Good listener

Protective of friends

Can keep a secret

Responsible about money

Love to be busy

Hard working

Good at organizing details

Intuitive

Like to learn new things

Conscientious about caring for baby

Usually turned on, interested in sex

Use these good qualities to compose refutations to your internal critic's common complaints. For example, every time you tell yourself, "I'm fat," plan to counter with, "I have clear skin and lovely brown eyes." When you catch yourself repeating, "I'll never figure this out," come back with, "I'm hard working and good at organizing details."

In addition to these reminders of your strong points, you'll need a few affirmations about self-esteem in general. Here are some examples that you can alter to suit yourself:

I love myself.

I am OK just the way I am.

I always do my best, considering the circumstances.

I can handle criticism.

I can get past mistakes.

I have compassion for myself and others.

I can ask for what I want.

Programmed Visualizations

Here are some guidelines that will help you form effective self-esteem visualizations:

Visualize overt behavior. Find images of yourself doing something, rather than just looking a certain way, possessing certain abstract qualities, or having certain things. Keep asking yourself, "What does higher self-esteem mean to me in terms of behavior? What would I be doing if I had it? What would my behavior look like, sound like, feel like?" For example, if you want to create an image of yourself feeling good about your abilities, you need more than an image of yourself smiling. That image could mean anything. Instead, see and hear yourself volunteering for a difficult but rewarding assignment. Hear someone complimenting you on a job well done, and hear yourself calmly acknowledging the compliment without any self-depreciation.

See yourself making small, positive steps each day toward your goal. Include the process as well as the product. If you want to stop being a wallflower, you can visualize yourself leading the band or doing a standup comedy routine at a big party. That's OK, but you should also include some other, smaller steps: Hear yourself asking a familiar-looking stranger where you have met before. See yourself walking up to someone and asking for a dance. Hear yourself offering to pass out hors d'oeuvres at a party as a way to mingle and meet others.

Include the positive consequences of higher self-esteem. See yourself successful at work, enjoying closer and more satisfying relationships, achieving goals.

Include assertive, high self-esteem body language in your visualization: erect posture, leaning forward to people, smiling, arms and legs uncrossed, close to people rather than keeping your distance, nodding as someone else speaks, and touching others when appropriate.

See yourself struggling a bit at first, and then succeeding. This approach has been shown to be more effective than seeing yourself as successful from the very first try.

See yourself liking you more, not just other people liking you more. Imagine congratulating yourself for a job well done, or treating yourself to a hot tub or a good dinner, just because you deserve it. People like you because you like yourself, not the other way around.

Tell yourself, "I'm basically OK right now," just as you are. Don't restrict your "OK-ness" to the future, after you're all fixed up.

Think of self-esteem as something you already have, but are out of touch with. See yourself discovering your self-esteem like a treasure lost and found again. See dark clouds clearing away to reveal the sun that was always there. Hear beautiful music emerging from static as you tune into your self-love. Feel warmth and softness as you pull on a cashmere sweater you misplaced and have just found again.

Use affirmations religiously. Your pathological critic has been bombarding you for years with negative messages. Affirmations are essential to counter that propaganda. Use your affirmations during visualizations and as you are walking around in your daily life. Your affirmations will act like hypnotic suggestions, reinforcing the positive images of your visualizations with a verbal message straight to your unconscious.

Self-Image Visualization

This is the first type of self-esteem visualization you should create for yourself. It is a general purpose session designed to correct the way you see yourself. You create scenes in which your behavior shows that you are worthy instead of unworthy, confident instead of doubtful, secure instead of anxious, cheerful instead of depressed, self-loving instead of self-hating, outgoing instead of shy, attractive instead of ugly, capable instead of helpless, good instead of bad, proud instead of guilty, and self-accepting instead of self-critical. Record the following instructions and play them back.

Lie down, close your eyes, and relax. Imagine that you are taking a shower. Feel the warm, wet water hitting your back and running all over your body. Hear the sound of the running water. Smell the soap and shampoo.

You feel great: invigorated, warm, and loose. Luxuriate in the pure sensual pleasure. Tell yourself, "I deserve to enjoy this." Enjoy the sensation of getting clean all over, feeling new and refreshed.

Now you're out of the shower and dried off. You're getting dressed in your favorite clothes. See the colors of the clothes. Feel the textures as you slowly draw each article of clothing on over your clean, warm body. Tell yourself, "I deserve nice things. I deserve to feel good."

Go to the mirror. Admire your clothes. See how nice you look in them. Stand up straight. Notice with pleasant surprise that your usual aches and pains are gone at this moment. Tell yourself, "I look fine."

Fix your hair the way you like it. Adjust your collar. Smile at yourself in the mirror. Actually feel the muscles in your face form the smile. Gaze at yourself smiling and notice how much more open and relaxed you look when you smile.

When you see the parts of your appearance that you usually don't like, notice that they seem less dominant, less important. If a self-critical thought comes to mind, shrug your shoulders and let it pass. Tell yourself, "I'm actually OK just as I am."

Now go into the kitchen. See the kitchen in detail: the stove, the cupboards, and the sink, just the way they are. Go to the refrigerator and open it. See it full of nutritious, appealing food: fresh fruits and vegetables, milk and juices, lean meats—whatever healthy foods you would like to eat. Look in the cupboards and see nutritious whole grains and beans, wholesome ingredients for the kinds of good food you'd like to prepare for yourself. Tell yourself, "I've got what I need."

Prepare a simple dish for yourself, something delicious and good for you. It could be a salad, some soup, or a nutritious sandwich. Take your time and enjoy the process of getting out the ingredients, slicing bread or vegetables, warming up the soup, arranging things attractively on the plate. Tell yourself, "I deserve to eat well."

See the colors, feel the temperatures and textures, smell the enticing aromas. Admire the dish you have made for yourself. Tell yourself, "I'm good at this."

Eat the dish, sitting quietly at the table and taking your time. Linger over each bite, really tasting and savoring each bite of the delicious food you have made for yourself. When you're finished, experience how full and comfortable you feel, how nourished and at peace with life. Let a feeling of languorous contentment and well-being steal over you. Tell yourself, "I love myself, I take care of myself."

Clean up after yourself. As you are cleaning, drop a cup or a plate and break it. Tell yourself, "Oh well, it's no big deal." If derogatory labels pop into your mind like "stupid" or "clumsy" or "bad," cut them off and shrug your shoulders. Tell yourself, "I allow myself to make mistakes. I'm OK just as I am, mistakes and all. I always do the best I can."

Now get ready to leave your home. You are going for a leisurely walk. Go outside and stroll down the street. It's a sunny day, warm and pleasant. Enjoy the feel of your muscles moving, your lungs breathing the fresh, pure air, the warmth of the sun on your shoulders. Notice how your usual aches and pains seem to have disappeared at this moment. Notice how bright and crisp and clear everything looks. Hear the sounds of birds, a dog barking in the distance, cars going by, music playing on a radio somewhere. Tell yourself, "I can enjoy the simple things of life."

See someone walking toward you, a stranger or a neighbor you recognize but don't actually know. The stranger catches your eye and smiles at you. You nod and flick your gaze downward, breaking eye contact. Feel the little flutter in your chest, the little sinking feeling or chilling jolt of adrenalin that you usually feel and call shyness or reserve.

Now see another stranger approach. Again the stranger meets your eye and smiles. This time, maintain eye contact and give a small smile in return. Tell yourself, "I am willing to take risks."

Once more, see another stranger approach and smile at you. This time, maintain eye contact, smile widely, and say loudly and clearly, "Hi, how are you?" Continue walking down the sidewalk, smiling slightly to yourself. Tell yourself, "I am outgoing and confident."

Now get ready to end this session. Recall your surroundings. When you are ready, open your eyes and get up. As you go about your daily routine, recall this visualization and repeat your affirmations to yourself:

I deserve nice things.

I deserve to feel good.

I look fine.

I am actually OK just the way I am.

I've got what I need.

I deserve to eat well.

I'm good at doing things.

I love myself.

I take care of myself.

I allow myself to make mistakes.

I'm OK just as I am, mistakes and all.

I always do the best I can.

I can enjoy the simple things of life.

I am willing to take risks.

I am outgoing and confident.

Here are some further suggestions for self-image scenes: making a doctor's appointment for a checkup, receiving a compliment gracefully, shopping for new clothes or furnishings, buying vitamins or cosmetics or exercise equipment, enjoying physical exercise or cultural activities, spending enjoyable quiet time alone, being successful at a sports activity, enjoying your favorite recreation. Choose these or other situations in which you tend to be hard on yourself or which would constitute evidence of higher self-esteem for you if you did them.

Make sure that you follow the rules about visualizing overt behavior, including positive body language, stressing self-acceptance first, and seeing yourself as basically OK in the present.

Interpersonal Skills Visualization

This series of scenes focuses on how you feel about your dealings with others. The important issues include feeling comfortable in the company of others, expressing yourself adequately, asking for what you want, responding to criticism, and in general feeling that you can hold your own as an equal, worthy participant in your interactions with others.

The following visualization is just a guideline. Use it as a model for designing your own scenes that are appropriate to your personality and situation in life. Again, tape recording these instructions and playing them back will help keep the sequence straight.

Lie down, close your eyes, and relax. You can view these scenes as if they were in a movie, or live through them as if you were really there. First imagine that you're having dinner in a good restaurant with someone you like. It can be someone you actually know now, someone you would like to know better, or someone you just make up. See the candlelight, smell the food, taste what you are eating, hear the muted clink of cutlery and hum of conversation. Look across the small, intimate table and see your friend. Smile and laugh at a witty remark. Hear your friend laughing with you. Say to your friend, "You know, this is fun. I really enjoy being with you." Your friend replies, "Thanks, what a nice thing to say. I always have a good time with you too." Tell yourself, "I enjoy being with friends. My friends enjoy being with me."

Now imagine that you are at home talking with another person. You have planned to spend the evening together, and this other person is suggesting that you try a new French restaurant and then go to see a foreign film in the next town. See the other person clearly. Hear the tones of voice as he or she tries to persuade you.

Imagine that the other person is someone you want to please, someone with whom you would usually agree automatically. But this time, notice that you are tired and that your feet hurt. You'd really rather order a pizza and stay home and watch TV.

Watch yourself square your shoulders, take a deep breath, and admit, "Well, I'm real tired tonight, and what I'd rather do is order a pizza and stay home. We could watch TV and just relax. I don't feel up to a lot of driving and staying out late."

Listen as your friend expresses sympathy and agrees to stay home with you. Tell yourself, "I can ask for what I want."

Now imagine that you are in a classroom, a business meeting, a committee meeting, or some kind of discussion group. See the room, hear the voices of the other people, notice what you are wearing, the decor of the room, the clock on the wall. Take some time to make the scene real for yourself.

As you listen to the discussion, you realize that the group is trying to come to a unanimous agreement, and that they will never all agree. You realize that you should all vote and accept the decision of the majority.

Watch and listen to yourself as you sit up straighter in your chair, clear your throat, take a deep breath, and interrupt the squabbling by saying, "Wait a minute." When you have everyone's attention, say, "I think we could discuss this forever and still not agree. I suggest that we put it to a vote and abide by majority rule. There are other, more important issues we need to talk about."

See the other people smile and nod their heads. Listen as the leader of the group thanks you and proceeds to take a vote. Tell yourself, "I have valuable opinions. I can speak up in a group."

For the next scene, imagine that you are talking to your mother or father or someone else who knows you well and has strong opinions about your life. Scan this person's face and listen carefully to the tone of voice as you hear the critical comment, "I don't know why you don't move out of that neighborhood. It's turning into a slum. Surely you could do better."

As this criticism registers with you, notice how you lean back from the attack just slightly. Notice how your posture becomes more defensive—perhaps you fold your arms or turn your head away.

Then you see yourself rally to respond to the criticism assertively. Actually feel your arms uncrossing, your head lifting, and your gaze meeting your critic's eyes. Hear yourself responding in a calm, reasonable tone, "Yes, my neighborhood is getting pretty run-down." Notice that you don't apologize or defend or explain or argue. You just acknowledge the one part of your critic's message that contains a grain of truth—just enough to get the critic off your back. Tell yourself, "I can acknowledge criticism and keep my self-respect."

Now become aware of your surroundings and end the visualization. The rest of today and tomorrow, whenever you encounter other people, recall your affirmations:

I enjoy being with friends.

My friends enjoy being with me.

I can ask for what I want.

I have valuable opinions.

I can speak up in a group.

I can acknowledge criticism and keep my self-respect.

Here are some other situations you could visualize: asking for a date, enjoying new people, successfully handling a complaint or a socially awkward situation, returning some unwanted merchandise, saying "I love you" to someone and meaning it as a compliment, asking for a raise, applying for a job, or saying no to someone who wants you to do something you don't want to do. Pick situations in which you usually feel insecure and one-down.

When creating interpersonal scenes to raise self-esteem, the important rules to remember are to include a certain amount of initial struggle, use assertive body language, include the positive consequences of higher self-esteem, and stress how self-acceptance comes before acceptance by others.

Self-Esteem Goals Visualization

Setting and achieving simple, short-term goals is a good way to start boosting your self-esteem. Start small, with the kind of everyday goals that you tend to beat yourself up about: getting to work on time, exercising a certain amount every week, finishing school assignments or memos, writing important letters, getting your teeth looked at, and so on.

The visualization that follows gives several examples of how to envision simple goals. Use them as models for creating your own images of what you want to accomplish.

Lie down, close your eyes, and relax. Visualize getting to work or class on time. Hear the alarm clock go off. See yourself waking up, shutting off the alarm, and getting right out of bed. Continue with your routine of showering, dressing, eating, and leaving—whatever you usually do. Watch yourself doing all of this with plenty of time to get where you need to go. Add the kind of multisensory details that you've used before to make it all real to you.

Throughout this scene, add details that show you are relaxed, unhurried, and efficient. You find your keys and your papers right where you set them out the night before. You have bus fare or gas in your car or a babysitter who shows up on time—whatever you need to have in place in order to be on time. Say to yourself, "I'm organized and punctual."

Invent a few obstacles, such as the phone ringing just as you walk out the door, or your battery being dead. See yourself calmly cutting the phone call short or getting a jump from your neighbor's car. Tell yourself, "I can stay relaxed and focused on my timetable."

Visualize the positive benefits of arriving on time. You are relaxed and ready to start your day. Your boss or teacher or the other people there are pleased with you. You're off to a good start. Tell yourself, "I am managing my time well."

Before leaving this scene, tell yourself, "Right after dinner tonight, before turning on the TV, I will make sure I have everything I need for the morning."

Now imagine another scene. Imagine that you have been putting off working on your dissertation, your tax forms, or an important application that you have to fill out. The deadline is approaching. See yourself going into your office or the library. Set out all the materials you need: paper, pens, files, books, receipts. Notice how you organize your work into logical steps and calmly, persistently work your way through them. Tell yourself, "One step at a time wins the race."

Include some difficulties. Feel yourself getting tired, impatient, and discouraged. Your eyes are burning, your stomach is sour, your mind wants to switch off. Get up and stretch, take a walk around the room, and then get back to work. See yourself getting a second wind, figuring your way past a confusing part. Tell yourself, "I can handle this."

See and hear and feel what it's like to type the final page of the dissertation, sign the bottom of your tax form, or stuff the application into an envelope and mail it. Say to yourself, "I'm finished in plenty of time."

See the positive results of meeting your deadline: the pleased smile of your chairperson when you deliver your completed dissertation, the new CD player you will buy with your tax refund, the notification that your application has been accepted. Tell yourself, "I deserve this reward."

Before leaving this scene, tell yourself, "I will gather up the material I need first thing in the morning."

Now move on to the next scene. Imagine that you have been wanting to get outdoors more, get some exercise, and grow some of your own food. Imagine and fill out with sensory details each of the logical steps you will have to take.

See yourself getting your landlord's permission to plant a vegetable garden. Imagine the sights, sounds, and smells of going to the nursery to pick out tomato plants, radish and lettuce seeds, onion bulbs, and cucumber plants. Tell yourself, "It's easy when I take just one step at a time."

Really feel the earth in your hands, the hard wooden handle of the borrowed spade, the sun on your bare shoulders as you turn over the soil in your planting beds and rake it smooth. Tell yourself, "I'm good at this."

Imagine the careful planting, the straight rows, the watering, the first sprouts, the weeding and watching. Finally, see yourself harvesting your own vegetables, washing them, and fixing a big, bountiful salad. Tell yourself, "I'm nurturing myself as I nurture my garden."

Include the positive consequences: your tan, your muscle tone, how pleasant and productive the backyard looks. See yourself with several friends at dinner. You tell them, "Everything in the salad is from my garden." Tell yourself, "I take care of myself."

Just before you leave this scene, tell yourself, "I will take the first step and talk to the landlord tomorrow after work."

Now get ready to come out of the scene. Remember where you are, and open your eyes when you're ready. Remind yourself of your final affirmation about performing the first step by a certain time and resolve once more to do it. As you accomplish your goals step by step, recall your affirmations:

I'm organized and punctual.
I can stay relaxed and focused on my timetable.
I am managing my time well.
I make sure I have everything I need.
One step at a time wins the race.
I can handle this.
I finish tasks in plenty of time.
I deserve this reward.
It's easy when I take just one step at a time.
I'm good at this.
I'm nurturing myself.
I take care of myself.

When you create your own visualizations, stick to one goal at a time, not three separate ones as in the above sample session. Remember to keep your goals simple and short-term at first. The self-esteem boost that you get from achieving small goals will give you the confidence you need to set and accomplish bigger, more long-term goals later.

The most important rules for forming effective goal visualizations are to break things down into small steps, concentrate on observable behavior, see yourself struggling at first, include the positive consequences of accomplishing your goal, and end with an affirmation spelling out the first step and when you will perform it.

15

Insomnia

"What if you slept? And what if, in your sleep, you dreamed?
And what if in your dream you went to heaven and plucked
a strange and beautiful flower. And what if when you awoke,
you had the flower in your hand? Ah! What then!"

—*Samuel Taylor Coleridge*

More than half of the adults in the United States have occasional insomnia. For thirty percent of these sufferers, insomnia is a chronic problem that they face nearly every time they climb into bed.

Insomnia takes several forms. You may have trouble falling asleep quickly after retiring, but then sleep well. Or you may fall asleep fairly quickly, but wake up too early and be unable to go back to sleep. Or you may have troubled sleeping all night long, waking often, dozing restlessly, and waking in the morning still feeling tired.

Practical Guidelines

Insomnia can have many causes, both physical and mental. Following these guidelines will probably relieve ninety percent of your sleep difficulties. Then visualization will take care of the remaining ten percent.

Eliminate Medical Problems

If you're dependent on sleeping pills or alcohol, all the visualizations in the world won't help you normalize your sleep patterns. Your insomnia is a secondary symptom of a more serious drug or alcohol problem. See your doctor or go to Alcoholics Anonymous.

Likewise, if you're chronically depressed, your insomnia is a secondary symptom of a deeper problem. Read the chapter in this book on depression, anxiety, and anger. Seriously consider going to see a professional counselor.

If your insomnia is caused by twitching or aching legs, get a checkup to rule out any problems in your muscles or nervous system. If you wake up because of snoring and you are gasping for breath, you should also see a doctor. You may be suffering from *sleep apnea*, a condition in which you actually stop breathing for a moment during sleep. Any physical symptoms that keep you awake or wake you up should be referred to a medical doctor.

No Stimulants

Don't drink coffee, black tea, or soft drinks containing caffeine. Cut way back on your intake of all kinds of sugars. Avoid diet pills and any kind of "uppers." All these can disrupt your sleep.

No Naps or Going to Bed Early

It's an insidious pattern: you have a terrible night in which you get only a few hours of sleep. The next day you're dragging around and by afternoon you've *got to have a nap.*

Don't do it. The nap will disrupt the natural sleep pattern you're trying to establish. You'll get just enough sleep so that you'll probably have another restless night. Force yourself to drag around until your *normal* bedtime.

Never go to bed before your normal bedtime. You risk waking up in the wee small hours and not being able to get back to sleep.

No Stimulating Activity Before Bedtime

This goes for mental as well as physical activity. Jogging, a vigorous workout, or shaking out all the rugs before bed will put your body into an aroused state from which it will be difficult to sleep.

Stimulating mind work just before bed will do the same thing. If you plan an exciting weekend, figure out your taxes, or write a poem, your mind will be cranked up and your body will be in a wakeful state of arousal.

In the hour or two before bedtime, try to keep your body and your mind quiet. The perfect activity is sedentary and boring: folding laundry, watching TV, reading a mediocre book, and so on.

Use Your Bed for Sleeping Only

No eating in bed, reading in bed, talking on the phone in bed, watching TV in bed, writing letters in bed, paying bills in bed, grading papers in bed, knitting in bed, and so on. You get the idea.

By reserving your bed for sleeping only, you will no longer associate it with wakeful activities. The mere act of getting into bed will send a message to your mind and body: "It's time to go to sleep."

The one exception is sex. You can certainly engage in sexual activities in bed without disrupting normal sleep patterns.

Correct Your Sleeping Environment

The room you sleep in should be set at a moderate temperature—not too hot and not too cold. There should be some circulation of fresh air. It should be quiet and dark. Your mattress, pajamas or nightgown, sheets, and blankets should be comfortable. This may seem obvious, but it's important to correct anything in your sleeping environment that may be keeping you awake.

Get Up If Not Asleep in Fifteen Minutes

If you go to bed and lie awake for fifteen minutes without going to sleep, get up. Get out of bed and read or do something quiet and constructive until you feel extremely drowsy, then go back to bed. If you still don't fall asleep within fifteen minutes, get up again. Repeat this until you finally fall asleep within the fifteen minutes.

Many studies have shown that this is the *most effective* method for getting to sleep rapidly. It logically extends the rule about not using your bed for anything else but sleeping: you shouldn't use your bed even for trying unsuccessfully to go to sleep.

Use Thought Stopping and Breath Counting to Silence Worries

If you find yourself going over and over the same worries instead of dropping off to sleep, mentally shout "Stop!" to yourself, give yourself a pinch, and focus intensely on your breathing. Breathe slowly and smoothly, counting each inhale and exhale: "inhale one, exhale two, inhale three, exhale four," and so on.

Each time the worries intrude on your counting, repeat the "Stop!" and the pinch and start counting breaths over again.

Visualization for Sleep

Your homework for sleep visualizations involves identifying the habitual thoughts that keep you awake and composing affirmations to counter and replace them.

What do you think about when you're lying there awake? You probably follow one of three patterns:

1. "It's getting late." The most obvious thing to think about is how late it's getting, how much sleep you can get if you go to sleep right now, how tired you'll be in the morning, how awful it is that you're not asleep yet, and so on. The way to affirm your way out of this one is to stress that you'll do something pleasurable or productive if you can't sleep. Here are some sample affirmations:

I'll sleep when I'm ready.

I'll do something productive until I'm ready to sleep.

I'll enjoy myself till I'm sleepy enough to go back to bed.

2. "This is another bad thing that's happened to me." Negative thinking sees insomnia as another bummer in a life of pain. Your sleeplessness makes your entire life look bleak. Your affirmations should counter this by dwelling on the good things that happened in the past day and the good things to come:

Several good things happened to me today.

Tomorrow I can look forward to . . .

3. "I've got to figure this out." Worrying over your problems or figuring out how to accomplish some future task is a common way to keep yourself awake. Whether you are concerned about some negative situation or excited about some positive prospect, the physical arousal and wakefulness are the same. Compose affirmations that remind you to put such thoughts off until a time when you can do something about them:

I put away my problems and plans at night.

Tomorrow is the time to think about this.

I deal with my problems at the appropriate time.

In addition to these "thought stopping" affirmations, you should have a general affirmation tailored to your sleep problem. If you tend to lie awake for a long time before you go to sleep, compose something like "I go to sleep soon after retiring." If you sleep too lightly, say, "I sleep peacefully through the night." If you wake too early, try something like "I wake when I need to, feeling rested and refreshed."

Visualization Instructions

Relaxation is more than half the battle with insomnia. You should review the relaxation and stress reduction chapters to get proficient at progressive muscle relaxation and deep breathing. Practice them during the day so that you will be ready to use them at night.

As you get ready for bed, use your general affirmations: "I go to sleep soon after retiring. I sleep peacefully through the night. I wake when I need to, refreshed and rested."

Lie down and close your eyes. Let your attention drift around in your body and notice how you feel. If you feel twitchy and jumpy, use progressive muscle relaxation to calm your body. Start at your feet and tense them gently. Hold the tension for the space of one breath, then let go on an exhalation. Then do your calves the same way. Work up your body: thighs, buttocks, stomach and lower back, chest, upper back, hands and arms, shoulders, neck, jaw, and facial muscles. Sometimes when you haven't had much physical exercise, your mind is tired but your body is restless. Flexing your muscles and then relaxing them can draw off that twitchy feeling that keeps you tossing and turning. Tell yourself, "I can relax at will."

If you don't feel particularly twitchy, just scan your body progressively and release tension without flexing your muscles. Concentrate on your breathing. Make it slow, deep, and regular. Pretend that you are already asleep and breathe like a sleeping person. Pretend that you're trying to convince somebody that you're really asleep. Lie motionless and slack, breathing long and slow.

Try counting your breaths. Try to make twenty perfect, sleeping breaths. If you lose count or if your mind wanders, start over with number one. Often this will be enough to send you to sleep. It takes your mind off whatever you've been thinking about and puts it on a precise but boring task. It combines relaxation breathing with the same principal as counting sheep.

If worries or plans start intruding, use your countering affirmations. Imagine that you are sitting on a river bank. The water is deep and swift. Watch the river constantly flowing, flowing away. When a distracting thought surfaces in your mind, observe it for a moment, then let the river carry it away. If it surfaces again, let the river take it again. Keep doing this for any thoughts that come. Don't worry if you get "caught up" in a thought for a while. Keep returning to the river image and let it wash your wakeful thoughts away.

You can try some age regression too. Think back to the earliest time you can remember. Imagine that you are in your childhood bedroom. See your toys and clothes and furniture dimly in the dark. Your mother and father come in to kiss you, hug you, and say, "Goodnight, sleep tight." Imagine this even if your parents didn't do it. Imagine an ideal, loving parent tucking you in and wishing you pleasant dreams. Snuggle down in your little bed and feel safe and warm, with no cares or troubles. Hum a lullaby in your mind. See your night light and hug your teddy bear. Remember what it was like to "sleep like a baby."

Go to your indoor special place and imagine getting ready for a nap there, where you are safe and no outside troubles can intrude. Lie down and get comfortable. Put some music on if you want. Dim the light and make everything just right in your special place.

If obsessive ruminations are keeping you from relaxing, try keeping your mind busy with an elaborate, pleasant visualization. Imagine conducting an orchestra in your favorite piece of music, watching your favorite team or an ideal team of all-stars play a game, choreographing a ballet troupe, building a fancy cabinet, planning and cooking a gourmet meal, restoring a car, sewing a coat—any long, positive, engaging process that will distract you from your other train of thought and relax you so that you can fall asleep.

Finally, if fifteen minutes of visualizing don't do the trick, get up and fold laundry, read a magazine, or dust your owl collection until you're sleepier. Then go back to bed and continue visualizing.

Example

Alice was a mother of three school-age children. She typically dropped into bed around eleven o'clock and fell asleep right away. Then she would wake up between two and three in the morning, still tired but with her mind going "a mile a minute." She'd worry about Suzy needing braces, about David's hatred of his fourth grade teacher, about whether the whole family could get back to visit her parents this summer, about her husband's weight problem, and so on and on. She would drop into a deep sleep around four or five o'clock, and have to force herself out of bed at six thirty. It took two cups of coffee to get her going and more coffee to keep her going until after lunch, when she had some free time and could grab an hour's nap.

The first thing Alice did to fight her insomnia was to practice relaxation exercises before lunch. She used progressive relaxation and deep breathing until she could tell when her body was completely relaxed. The second thing she did was to limit herself to one cup of coffee with breakfast and no sugary treats with lunch. This smoothed out the peaks and valleys of energy she had been experiencing during the day.

The hardest thing for Alice was to give up her post-luncheon nap. She had to go outside in the yard or trudge around the block to keep herself awake between one and two in the afternoon.

Before retiring, Alice wrote down a list of things to do the next day. She found that this saved her from popping awake thinking, "I've got to remember that tomorrow." As she climbed into bed, she told herself, "I sleep deeply through the night."

Even with all these precautions, Alice still woke up sometimes in the early hours of the morning. When she lay awake for more than fifteen minutes, she told herself, "I can do something fun or productive" and got up until she once again felt really sleepy. After returning to bed, she often did her progressive relaxation and breath counting to calm her body, and imagined all of her worries and plans drifting away into the air inside of pink bubbles.

Sometimes Alice played a trick on herself. She would say to herself, "I'll count thirty breaths. If I'm still awake after thirty breaths, I'll get up and polish Grandma's silver." She hated polishing silver. She usually fell asleep before she could get to the thirtieth breath.

16

Depression, Anxiety, and Anger

"The mind is its own place, and in itself, can make heaven of hell or a hell of heaven."

—*John Milton*

This could have been called the "Unpleasant Emotions" chapter, but that title lacked pizzazz. It's called "Depression, Anxiety, and Anger" because these seem to be the primary unpleasant emotions. Just as secondary colors like pink, green, and orange can be created by diluting or mixing the primary colors red, blue, and yellow, so the secondary emotions such as disappointment, guilt, and resentment seem to derive from the primary emotions depression, anxiety, and anger.

Therefore, if you want to use visualization to relieve unpleasant emotions of any kind, you're in the right place. What works for depression will work for the blues, laziness, despair, sadness, grief, discouragement, boredom, and many other similar problems. The techniques suggested for fighting anxiety will also work for panic, fear, worry, agitation, nervousness, and so on. You can apply the visualizations for anger control to conquering emotions such as rage, irritation, and resentment.

Some secondary emotions are combinations of the primary ones. For example, jealousy seems to be composed of part anger and part anxiety, so to combat jealousy you should try the visualization techniques for both anger and anxiety. To cope with guilt feelings, you should use the techniques for both anxiety and depression. For envy, try the techniques suggested for depression and anger.

Dynamics of Depression

Depression is such an overwhelming emotion that depressed people were once thought to be possessed by demons. When you're depressed you can show any or all of these symptoms: (1) your emotional tone is dominated by sadness, (2) your motivation drops and you become passive, with no desire to do anything, (3) your thoughts focus on loss, images of yourself as a loser, and suicide, (4) behaviorally you're at a standstill, motionless, unable to overcome your own inertia and get moving, and (5) psysiologically your body feels "blah," incapable of experiencing pleasure.

Your thoughts power the engine of depression. Thoughts of loss keep the whole syndrome going. They color your perception until everything you see or hear seems like further evidence of loss. Surrounded by loss, nothing seems worth doing, describing, or experiencing.

The basic strategy for fighting depression is to change your underlying self-image from "loser" to "winner." To do this, you can start working on any of the symptoms. When depression is severe, experts such as Aaron Beck recommend starting on the behavioral level. You work on overcoming your inertia and accomplishing just one task that you have been postponing. This starts a therapeutic cycle in which performing the task raises your self-esteem, which in turn increases your motivation, which then leads you to accomplish another task, further raising self-esteem, and so on until you spiral up out of the pit of depression.

How do you know if your depression is severe? If you have frequent thoughts about suicide or become so immobilized that you can't make it to work, classes, or out to visit friends, then your depression is severe. You should immediately put down this book, get the Yellow Pages, and look up your local suicide prevention hotline number and the number of a psychologist or other helping professional. Call them right now. Of all the painful emotions, depression is the one that can be fatal.

When depression is less severe, you can start to work directly on the thoughts of loss and hopelessness. Receptive visualization is a good way to uncover your negative thoughts, and programmed visualization with affirmations is a good way to refute those thoughts and replace them with positive self-statements.

The visualization techniques in this chapter will not only focus on the cognitive aspects of depression, but also work on the emotional, motivational, behavioral, and physiological aspects.

Dynamics of Anxiety

While depression has you looking for loss, anxiety has you looking for danger. Even situations that you know intellectually are safe, such as shopping in a department store, may *feel* somehow dangerous.

The symptoms of anxiety show up in the same areas as the symptoms of depression: (1) your emotions are dominated by fear, (2) your motivations are limited by the desire to avoid everything that seems dangerous, (3) your thoughts focus on danger and all the catastrophic things that could happen to you, (4) behaviorally, you confine yourself to a very circumscribed routine in order to avoid everything that makes you anxious, and (5) the physiological symptoms are much more pronounced than those of depression.

The physiological symptoms of anxiety are pounding heart, dizziness, shortness of breath, weakness in your legs, constriction in your throat, and hot or cold flashes. When anxiety escalates into a full-blown panic attack, these feelings can convince you that you are about to fall down, have a heart attack, or go crazy. Actually, the symptoms of panic are natural components of your body's "fight or flight" response to danger, and they are harmless. Within three minutes of escaping the danger or realizing that there isn't any danger, the symptoms disappear.

The cognitive component of anxiety is the key to control. Anxiety follows an ABC model of arousal: you perceive a person or situation (A) that acts as a stimulus. Your reaction is a thought (B) that interprets the simulus as dangerous. Then you feel the emotion (C) of anxiety. For example, you see a tall stack of lumber in the street (A), you think, "That could fall over on me" (B), and feel anxious (C) as you scurry past the pile or cross the street to avoid it.

The thought between the stimulus and the emotion can be a fleeting word or image, so brief that you're not even consciously aware of it. Visualization can help you reexperience anxious moments in slow motion, so that you can study your catastrophic thoughts and images. Once you know the content of your anxiety-provoking thoughts, you can create affirmations to counter them.

When programmed visualization and affirmations are used to fight anxiety, the process is called systematic desensitization. You start with something you're just a little afraid of and imagine a scene in which you use relaxation techniques and affirmations to overcome your fear. When you're able to stay relaxed throughout the entire scene, you're "desensitized" to it. Then you move "systematically" to another scene that is a little scarier, and visualize yourself coping with it until you're comfortable. And so on through as many as twenty scenes, until you can stay relaxed while contemplating even the most stressful situations.

The difference between treating anxiety and depression is that you do your visualization exercises *before* you feel anxious. Preventive rehearsal works much better than trying to apply visualization techniques in the middle of a panic attack.

Dynamics of Anger

The cognitive theme of anger is blame. Everywhere you look you see people at fault, people who are doing something to you that you don't like.

Chronic anger symptoms are obvious: (1) your emotional tone ranges from irritation to rage; (2) your motivation is to win, to control, to score points against your enemies; (3) your thoughts circle around blame, around all the unfair, mean, and selfish things that people do to you; (4) your behavior may be aggressive, with loud voice and threatening gestures, or passive, with a seething withdrawal; and (5) the physiological arousal is similar to anxiety, but instead of feeling shaky you feel strong and ready to fight.

Again, the key to control is in the cognitive component. The arousal of anger follows the same ABC pattern as anxiety. You see someone doing something or hear someone saying something (A, the stimulus). Then you decide that the person is somehow out to get you (B, the interpretation). Finally, you feel your temper rise and the urge to strike out in some way (C, the emotion). For example, your spouse asks you to move some papers off the table (A), you think your spouse is implying some criticism (B), and you feel angry (C).

To rid yourself of anger, you need to intervene in the "B" step. You need to detect, refute, and replace the negative interpretations you habitually make about other people's behavior.

Anger is difficult to overcome because it often feels good to explode or to nurture a grudge. It literally gets your blood going and gives you a stimulating rush. In terms of learning theory, the pleasant discharge of anger reinforces your angry behavior, making you all the more likely to choose an angry response the next time you're in a similar situation.

Some people even say that it's good for you to express your anger rather than bottle it up. But, in fact, anger is not good for you—neither the bottled-up nor the exploding variety is nearly as good as learning not to get angry in the first place.

The trouble with anger is that the pleasant effect is only short-term. When you cool down, you've got to deal with remorse, guilt, and the need to patch things up. In the long term, anger leads to alienation, ruined relationships, and loneliness. And an angry life is not only tumultuous and lonely, it also tends to be short. Recent studies have shown that anger is the most deadly component of "Type A" behavior, the driving, high-pressure lifestyle long associated with early death from heart disease.

Using visualization to overcome anger is a two-step process. First you use receptive scenes to generate insight about your anger patterns and uncover the blaming statements you make to yourself to fuel your anger. Then you compose affirmations and embark on a series of programmed visualizations including deep relaxation, reparenting, compassionate imagery, and stress inoculation.

Receptive Visualization Techniques
for Exploration

Uncovering Self-Statements

Get a sheet of paper and a pencil. Divide the paper into two columns. Label the left column "self-statements" and label the right column "affirmations." Put the paper and pencil where you can reach them during visualization.

Lie down, close your eyes, and relax. Look back to the last time you were particularly depressed, anxious, or angry. Re-create the scene in detail: where you were, who you were with, what you were wearing, what was going on. Include impressions from all your senses—sight, sound, taste, touch, smell, and the feelings of movement and balance, ease and unease in your body.

Run the scene at normal speed and allow yourself to feel the emotions in your body. If you were depressed, feel slow, tired, unable to move. If you were anxious, feel your clammy palms, pounding heart, nervous stomach, and so on. If you were angry, feel the blood throb in your temples, your fists clench, and your jaw and neck muscles tighten.

Now run the scene in slow motion and focus on your thoughts. Slow down the action until you can follow the stream of almost unconscious words, images, predictions, and comments. When you discover a self-statement, open your eyes, roll over gently, and write it down on your paper. Then lie down again and close your eyes. Continue to run the scene over and over, listening for more self-statements.

If you've been depressed, look for statements about loss, hopelessness, uselessness, and meaninglessness. A single word might be all you can hear: "lost," "gone," "useless," "stupid," "cruel." If you keep slowing down the action, you can begin to fill in the full statements:

I've lost everyone I ever loved.

She's gone forever.

It's useless to try.

I'm so stupid I don't deserve to live.

Life is a cruel joke.

Or you may only get a glimpse of an image at first. Lost loved ones may be represented by a tombstone or the sight of your spouse in a hospital bed. A departed lover may be a closing door. Or the "image" may be the sound of someone laughing at you for a stupid remark you made in the third grade. Keep examining the images until you can extract their negative verbal messages. Whatever you get, remember to roll over and write it down. Sense impressions can come very fast during visualization, and you can forget a lot if you wait until the end of the session to write things down.

If you are visualizing an anxious scene, look for catastrophic predictions, warnings about danger, and thoughts about impending collapse or heart attack.

Single-word clues might be "look out," "silly," "die," "fall," "heart." Keep listening for the full statements:

Look out for that dog, he'll bite.

Everybody thinks I look silly. I've got to get out of here.

This intestinal pain means I'm going to die. It's probably stomach cancer.

I'll fall.

I'm having a heart attack.

The statement about the dog biting may first come across as the sound of snarling and an image of teeth. Looking silly may be represented by a distorted, funhouse mirror image of yourself. Your intestinal pain may bring up an image of your dad in the hospital with tubes going into his body. Falling and a heart attack might first appear as the sight and sound of an ambulance. Whatever the initial hints, keep probing for the fullest statements you can extract. The more you can write down in the self-statements column, the more you'll have to work with when it's time to compose refuting affirmations.

If you're working on anger, look for thoughts that tell you what other people are thinking, attributions for their motives and intentions. Watch for negative appraisals of the situation and statements about how you think things *ought* to be. You might hear only "jerk," "ditch," "greedy," or "on purpose," standing for:

Now what does this jerk want?

They'd like to ditch me.

This greedy son-of-a-bitch wants my money.

She's doing that on purpose. She's driving me crazy.

You might get only sense impressions at first. The smell of hair oil might stand for your cousin, who was a jerk and always got you angry. People abandoning you might be represented by a bicycle in a vacant lot, from the time when you were ten and your friends ditched you on their bikes. The attribution of greed in others could be represented by the image of a dollar bill. The idea of someone taunting you might surface as a critical-sounding mumble. Whatever you see, smell, hear, or feel, look for the words underneath and write them down.

This is not an easy process, but it's important. Uncovering the negative self-statements that inspire and perpetuate your negative emotions is half the battle against them.

When you have milked all the self-statements you can get out of the last time you were depressed, anxious, or angry, go back to the time before that and do it all over. Then the time before that, the time before that, and so on. Keep running earlier and earlier scenes until you start hearing nothing but repeats of the same self-statements.

Besides making sure you get a long list of self-statements, visualizing earlier and earlier scenes is good practice for the technique of age regression, which you'll be using later on.

Insight Generation

These are open-ended visualizations designed to let your unconscious tell you something about your emotional life. You'll probably want to record the following instructions and use the tape to guide you.

Lie down, close your eyes, and get very relaxed. Remind yourself to suspend judgment. You will take what you get, however unclear or unexpected it is. Go to your special place and lie down there. Put on some music if you want. Close your imaginary eyes.

Visualize a door in a wall or leading into a house. The door is closed. Put a sign on it that says "Depression," "Anxiety," or "Anger." Open the door and see what you get. You might see a scene from the past, or someone you know now. Do you see yourself doing something?

Keep closing and opening the door. Each time you open it, you can see a different scene, bringing up more and more of your associations with the word on the sign. This is your private lexicon of images for depression, anxiety, or anger. If you want, you can go through the door and relive or explore some of the scenes.

Now bring in your inner guide. Let your guide become your feeling. Your guide personifies your depression, anxiety, or anger. Your guide will be the voice of your feeling. If it doesn't feel right having your guide do this, imagine another person or even an object like a loudspeaker or an intercom taking the place of the feeling.

Now that you've given your feeling a voice, listen to it. Let it tell you all the aspects of your situation from a purely emotional point of view. You may hear some undiluted statements from your unconscious. Let it rant and rave. Don't worry if it doesn't all make sense. Be supportive, loving, and accepting of your feeling as it talks. Resist the impulse to talk back or argue or agree.

Ask questions: "Why am I depressed? What do I get out of being anxious? What would I have to give up if I didn't get so angry? What do you want from me? What will it take for you to leave me alone?"

Age Regression

Visualize the earliest time you can recall when you felt depressed, anxious, or angry. Try to find a time when you were five years old or younger. If you can't go directly back to that time, try "chaining." Think back to the earliest time you can remember, and relive the scene. Then imagine yourself six months or a year younger, and find another example of feeling depressed, anxious, or angry. Keep reliving scenes and chaining back a year or six months at a time.

When you get to the youngest time you can remember, notice how you looked. Concentrate on your hair color, hair style, and what clothes you're wearing. Include your room, furniture, and special toys.

Relive this early painful experience. If the scene is too abusive or traumatic to recall, imagine it happening to an android or robot that looks and acts just like you, but cannot be hurt. Or imagine seeing the scene farther and farther away until the distance protects you enough to watch it.

As you watch the scene, think of what you would like to say to your younger self. What do you know now that would have helped, if only you knew it then? For example, you could tell your younger self, "This too will pass," "Mom is sick and needs help," "It's not your fault," "You're really all right just as you are," or "You won't die from this—you'll make it."

Keep this important message in mind to be used later in your reparenting visualization. Write it down so you won't forget it.

Before you end this receptive visualization, notice any similarities between your feelings and how you handled them as a child and your feelings and coping strategies now.

Active Visualization Techniques for Change

Affirmations

In your own words, write affirmations to refute and counteract your list of negative self-statements. Here are some examples:

Self-Statement	Affirmation
I've lost everybody I ever loved.	I can love again.
She's gone forever.	I can find another good woman.
It's useless to try.	I succeed by taking one step at a time.
I'm so stupid I don't deserve to live.	I am generous and hard working
Life is a cruel joke.	That's just the depression talking. My life is what I make it.
Look out for that dog, he'll bite.	Most dogs are friendly.
Everybody thinks I look silly. I've got to get out of here.	I assume nothing. No mind reading. I can handle this.
This intestinal pain means I'm going to die. It's probably stomach cancer.	I assume nothing. No "awfulizing." It's probably gas.
I'll fall.	Just breathe deeply and look away for a minute. The railing is safe and I can handle this.
I'm having a heart attack.	This is just anxiety. My heart will stop pounding as soon as I calm down.
Now what does this jerk want?	Let go of preconceptions. Just listen, without judgment.

They'd like to ditch me.	*I can let go of mind reading. I check out my assumptions.*
This greedy son-of-a-bitch wants my money.	*Nobody does anything to me. I can stop making myself angry. I can just let go of anger.*
She's doing that on purpose. She's driving me crazy.	*I assume nothing. I give her the benefit of the doubt. Only I can drive myself crazy.*

Try to make your affirmation believable to you. Look for reasons why it may be true. What life experience do you have that shows you could love again, are generous and hardworking or that gastrointestinal pain is usually gas? You will use your affirmations soon when I explain how to use systematic desensitization and other techniques.

Relaxation

Relaxation is an important part of controlling anxiety and anger. When you are relaxed, it's impossible to feel anxious or angry. Both emotions depend on a set of physical arousal symptoms that are the opposite of relaxation.

Also, you will need to be able to relax completely during visualization in order to get the most out of the positive imagery and other exercises later in this chapter. If you have problems getting and staying relaxed, see the chapters on relaxation and stress reduction for extra help.

Reparenting

If you found that your unpleasant emotions have their roots deep in your past, try this visualization technique. The goal of reparenting is to let you handle past traumas with your present resources. Using visualization, you travel back in time and provide the mature insights, strengths, and skills that you lacked as a child. You become your own supportive parent.

You've prepared for reparenting by doing the age regression visualization. You need a clear picture of yourself at some time before age five, when you were feeling depressed, anxious, or angry.

Lie down, close your eyes, and relax. Go to your outdoor special place. Allow your younger self to enter the scene quietly and stand a few feet from you. Concentrate for a moment on your younger self's clothes, eyes, hair, and posture.

Introduce your "now" self to your younger self. Say, "I am your future self." You can show scars or birthmarks, share secret information, or do anything you have to convince your younger self that you are indeed from the future.

Tell your younger self, "First, I want to say to you that you are doing the best you can in your situation. Even though it's not always enough. I know that you're doing your best. I want you to know that too."

Then give your younger self whatever special, adult information that would have been useful to have back then. Give your younger self the benefit of your experience.

Hug your younger self or hold hands. Say, "You are OK as a person, just the way you are." Ask this question in your own words: "Since you can't get what you want from our parents, will you accept it from me?"

Tell your younger self, "Anytime you need to talk to me, just snap your fingers and close your eyes. You'll come right to this special place and I'll be here."

Say goodbye in a way that feels comfortable. Promise to visit often. Reorient yourself to your surroundings and end the session.

Return to your younger self often in your visualizations. There are other things you can do with your younger self:

Actually go to a park and pretend that you are taking your younger self for an outing. Try to get in touch with the things you loved to do as a child.

Create imaginary, inner parents that exist inside your real parents. These inner parents would have filled you with the love you needed, if only your real parents had had a different history. Let these inner parents take independent form and introduce your younger self to them.

To deal with abusive parents, tell your younger self, "You have a robot that looks and acts just like you. You can send this robot in your place when Daddy and Mommy are angry. The robot feels no pain and cannot be hurt." Introduce humor by making up stories of the Incredible Shrinking Parent who shrinks down to doll size and can be bossed around. Sit in your indoor special place with your younger self and watch your parents on the TV. Let a clown with a slapstick run around and swat your parents. The idea is to break up fearsome images of invincible parents and helpless self.

You'll become closer and closer to your younger self the more you visit together. This is a way of healing old hurts and allowing the more "childish" parts of your personality to mature and unite with the more "grown-up" parts.

The next step in reparenting is to allow your younger self to age. As time goes by, make friends with and support yourself at age five, age seven, age ten, and so on up to your present age. It's as if there are many children inside you, all different ages. Each has its own way of knowing the world and coping with painful emotions. The younger versions of yourself are cut off from and resist the understandings of the older versions. Reparenting visualizations break down these resistances and allow your younger traumas to be healed by your older strengths.

Positive Imagery

Psychologist David Schultz studied severely depressed and hostile patients at Yale and the West Haven, Connecticut, V.A. Hospital. He found that depression and anger both could be reduced by visualizing elaborate, cheerful scenes such as winning a lottery, being complimented, or enjoying a gorgeous natural setting.

The two short visualizations in this section will get you started. Work out your own long, elaborate fantasies in which your every wish comes true. If fantastic or improbable situations don't attract you, then try elaborating a more likely alternative. Instead of winning a million-dollar lottery, win a thousand-dollar raffle—and imagine spending your prize a hundred different ways.

For depression, concentrate on seeing yourself in these positive scenes as happy instead of sad, with strong desires and drives, a winner rather than a loser, active, and experiencing pleasure.

For anger, see yourself as relaxed, tolerant, communicating openly and honestly, enjoying the company of others, and taking responsibility for your own feelings.

Lie down, close your eyes, and relax. Imagine that you are at home and the phone rings. Pick it up and say hello. You hear a voice tell you that you have just won a million dollars, tax free. Hang up the phone and spend a lot of time imagining all the things you will do with the money: houses, cars, travel, gifts, and so on. Really get into it and watch yourself enjoying the spending of a fortune. See your face alight with pleasure, your friends congratulating you and thanking you for your generous gifts. Tell yourself, "I'm a winner. I have strong desires and drives. I'm generous and tolerant."

Now imagine that you are a movie star, famous author, scientist, or other well-known person you admire. Imagine that you have just won an important award like an Oscar, Nobel Prize, or Pulitzer. You're on a talk show, surrounded by celebrities, and they're complimenting you on your genius. Hear them listing your sterling qualities and marveling at your accomplishments. As you humbly bask in their praise, tell yourself, "I'm a master of what I do. I set and accomplish goals. I stay relaxed and cheerful in stressful situations."

Now imagine yourself in the Grand Canyon, Yosemite, the Swiss Alps, Tahiti—any natural setting of great beauty. It can be somewhere you've been or somewhere you'd like to go. See yourself totally relaxed in this scene, enjoying walking, running, or some sports activity. Stand by a big waterfall and breathe in great lungfuls of the cool air, charged with negative ions to chase away the blues and calm frustrations. See a big smile on your face and a healthy glow in your cheeks. Tell yourself, "I'm basically a happy person. I stay active. I enjoy _____ a lot. I notice and savor everyday pleasures."

Next climb into a helium balloon basket. Float up high in the sky and look down on the miniature landscape below. Tell yourself, "I'm floating above all my cares and troubles." In the basket with you is a pencil and a thick pad of paper. Find it and on the first page write down something that has been bothering you. Then tear off the page, crumple it up, and toss it out of the basket. Keep writing things down—"health," "money for car repairs," "Charlie's drinking," "bad grades"—and toss them away. Feel the balloon getting lighter and rising higher as you jettison your weighty problems.

If you've been depressed, imagine that there is a small padlock in your head. It is locking all your creative, intuitive impulses, all your motivation for knowing what you want to do and going after it. Imagine there's a key in your hand. Reach up into your own head and unlock the padlock. Remove the padlock entirely from your head and throw it away. Tell yourself, "I know what I want to do and I do it." For the three hours after this session, assume that your intuitive impulses about what to do are one hundred percent right, and act on them. Don't listen to the automatic thoughts about what's right and proper, what won't work, what's silly, what's useless, and so on. Just do what you feel like doing for three hours. At the end of this period, review what you did and how you felt. Compare it to the way you usually operate. If you liked the experience, extend it next time to half a day, then a whole day.

Symbolic Healing

Symbolic visualization is particularly good for depression when you don't really know *why* you're depressed— you're just depressed. Using symbols to represent depression and its relief eliminates the need for insight and understanding. It communicates your intention to cheer up directly to your unconscious and can bring very quick and dramatic results.

Lie down, close your eyes, and relax. Picture your sadness as a black cloud centered in your chest. As you inhale, imagine pure, white light entering through your nostrils. The light mixes with the black cloud, turning it dark gray. Exhale and imagine some of the gray cloud exiting through your feet. Continue to inhale the white light, dilute the cloud, and exhale it through your toes. The cloud gets lighter and lighter. Soon you have flushed out all the darkness of depression and you are filled with white light. Tell yourself, "I am full of positive, cheerful energy."

Next imagine that you are in a dance hall. Beautiful music is playing, dancers are having a good time, and you feel like joining them. But you can't move. Look down and see that your feet are laced into big, heavy leather boots with lead soles that you can't even lift off the floor. Bend over and unlace the boots. Pull your feet free and join the dance. Tell yourself, "I slip out of the bonds of depression, I keep moving."

In the next scene, imagine that you are strolling down a path in a park. The flowers that line the path are wilted and dying. As you pass, touch the flowers and wave your hands over them. See them spring back up, full of life and vigor. As you continue down the path, notice that there are ten- and twenty-dollar bills scattered all over. Pick up as many as you want and put them in your pockets. Then come to two stone statues of a sad little girl and boy cradling a dead bird. Place your hands on their heads and watch them come to life. The bird comes to life too, and the children smile and thank you. Walk under some big, dark trees, but notice that the sun keeps shining on you. It's like you're in a spotlight of sunshine. Tell yourself, "I'm a winner, I'm full of life."

Finally, imagine your blood as slow and lethargic. See it as thick and dark, like molasses. Then imagine a seltzer bottle full of sparkling water. Find some place in your circulation system—your heart, a vein in an arm or leg—where you can insert the spout of the seltzer water. Then squirt some sparkling water into your blood. It becomes effervescent, bubbly, and tingly. You feel light and fluid instead of "blah." Any time you feel lethargic, give yourself a blast of seltzer.

Systematic Desensitization

Systematic desensitization was created by Joseph Wolpe as a specific antidote to anxiety. It works in three steps: (1) you learn relaxation skills so that you know what your body feels like when it's deeply relaxed, (2) you visualize increasingly frightening scenes and use your relaxation skills to keep yourself calm, and (3) you start using your new coping skills in real-life situations.

To prepare for systematic desensitization, review the chapters on relaxation and stress reduction so that you can calm your fight or flight response and know what your body feels like in a relaxed state.

While you're brushing up on your relaxation training, decide which of your anxieties you will work on first. It might be your fear of rejection, fear of heights, nervousness about public speaking, or fear of flying. Make a list of six to twenty people, places, things, or situations that bring on your fear of rejection, heights, public speaking, or airplanes.

When you have your list of items, rank them in a hierarchy from the least frightening to the most frightening. The first item on your hierarchy should be something that makes you feel just a little nervous. The last item should be the most anxiety-provoking thing you could possibly imagine. And the intervening items should cover the range in between, each a little more intimidating than the one before. Here's an example of a fear of flying hierarchy:

1. Seeing planes on TV take off and land
2. Hearing about a plane crash on the news
3. Making reservations for a flight
4. Packing my bag for a trip
5. Parking the car at the airport
6. Watching jumbo jets take off
7. Checking in at the gate
8. Getting on the commuter flight to D.C.
9. Taking off for a transatlantic flight
10. Turbulence
11. The pilot announcing an emergency landing

On a scale of eleven, number one is the least anxiety-provoking, number eleven is the most terrifying, and items two through ten are progressively more frightening. You can generate a hierarchy based on temporal proximity (getting closer in time), physical proximity (getting physically closer to the feared object or situation) or association (items that seem connected to the feared object or situation—like reading a book on disease when you're afraid of death), or any combination of the above.

Now you are ready to begin systematic desensitization sessions. The idea is that reducing your anxiety reaction to item number one will reduce your fear of all the other items to the same degree. It's like getting into a cold swimming pool a little at a time.

Lie down, close your eyes, and relax. Get completely relaxed, with no tension in any of your muscles. Focus for a minute on what that feels like.

When you're relaxed, allow the first item on your hierarchy to enter your mind. Add details and involve all your senses so that the scene becomes vivid and real to you.

Notice how anxious this scene makes you feel. Keep visualizing the scene, and take several deep breaths. Tell yourself, "I am relaxing, I'm letting the tension drain away with each breath. I can let go of fear as I calm myself." Use the relaxing and anti-anxiety affirmations that work best for you.

Notice how much you were able to relax, then switch off the scene. If you have trouble erasing the anxiety-provoking scene from your imagination, go to your special place and hang out for a while until you calm down.

Keep visualizing the first scene over and over, letting it flood your mind for five to ten seconds, then relaxing. Notice how you are able to relax more and more. When you have visualized the scene twice in a row without any anxiety, go on to the next scene in your hierarchy.

It generally takes three or four visualizations of a scene before you can relax completely. A fifteen-minute session might take you through three or four items on your hierarchy. Keep going until you can face the most terrifying scene with equanimity. Then try it in real life, starting with the less anxiety-provoking situations first.

When you've worked through one complete hierarchy, you will probably want to create another. For example, you could handle fear of flying first, then go on to fear of public speaking, and then work on fear of criticism.

If you run up against a scene in which you can accomplish no relaxation, add some milder items to your hierarchy so that you can work up to the tough scene more gradually.

Stress Inoculation

Stress inoculation was first described as an antidote to anger by Raymond Novaco in 1975. It's similar to systematic desensitization in that you work through a hierarchy of visualized scenes, controlling your anger response by relaxation and affirmations. As with systematic desensitization, you might want to go back to the relaxation and stress reduction chapters so that you can relax your muscles and know what relaxation feels like in your body.

This technique builds on the receptive visualization and affirmation sections you read about earlier in this chapter. If you haven't worked through those parts, go back and develop your list of situations in which you become angry, your list of typical angry self-statements, and a matching list of affirmations tailored to counter the self-statements.

To prepare for stress inoculation properly, you'll also need to know what angry and neutral body language look like. Go stand in front of a mirror. Close your eyes for a moment and visualize one of your anger scenes. Really get into it, speaking your part in the scene out loud in an angry voice. Open your eyes and look at your face and posture. Exaggerate what you see: frowning, narrowed eyes, erect and leaning-over posture, hunched shoulders, clenched fists, raised arms.

Now change your body language step-by-step. Release your forehead muscles and stop frowning. Open your eyes wide and let the focus be soft and gentle. Shift your weight back on to your heels. Relax and lower your shoulders. Open your hands and hold them at your side, palms forward in a gesture of peace. Remember what this neutral body language looks like.

Now you're ready for stress inoculation. Prepare a list of six to twenty situations in which you typically get angry. Put them in order, starting with the most minor annoyance and progressing to the situation in which you get most furious. For example:

1. Tall guy sits in front of me at the movies

2. Somebody swerves in front of me on the freeway

3. George tells the same stupid story for the umpteenth time

4. Somebody I'm interested in breaks a date

5. Mother buys me something I already told her I don't want

6. Drapes I ordered are three weeks late and the wrong style

7. My old boss snubs me at a party

8. Pay $500 to fix car and it still makes funny noise

9. Going over divorce property settlement with lawyer

Reducing your anger response to situation number one will reduce your reactions to all the other items to a similar degree. It's like slipping into a hot bath a little at a time.

Lie down, close your eyes, and relax. Let the relaxation saturate your body and become very aware of your loose, warm, heavy muscles.

When you're totally relaxed, allow the first item on your hierarchy to fill your imagination. Add details and sense impressions until it becomes very real. Allow yourself to start to get angry.

Use your affirmations: "Nobody does anything to me. I can let go of anger as soon as it appears." Take a deep breath and calm yourself. See your body language: Brow smooth and soft, posture laid back, arms down and palms open. Notice how much you are able to relax, then switch off the scene.

If you get very angry and can't calm down, go to your special place and spend some time listening to music. Return to stress inoculation when you're composed.

Repeat the first scene several times, until twice in a row you can watch the scene and dampen your anger response completely. Then go on to the next scene and do the same thing. You might have to go through each scene four or five times before you can consistently turn off the anger and bring on the relaxation.

If you come to a scene in which you just can't turn off the anger, add some milder scenes to your hierarchy to build up to the difficult scene more gradually.

By the time you have worked through your entire hierarchy, you'll be ready to try your coping skills in a real-life situation. If you know that you're headed for a confrontation with someone you often get angry at, prepare by imaging the scene beforehand. Concentrate on maintaining the feeling of relaxation in your muscles, the affirmations you will use, and your neutral body language.

Examples

Depression

Silvia was a hospital social worker who had recently moved to town with her new husband, Bob. He had a new job that kept him busy most nights and weekends. Silvia's new job wasn't as interesting as her old one. She missed her old friends and hadn't made any new ones. Silvia and Bob had been trying to get pregnant for fourteen months with no luck.

Silvia felt friendless, alone, and depressed. She sat in their big house watching TV night after night instead of pursuing any of her varied interests: meditation, visualization, furniture refinishing, bridge, piano, or gardening. She felt that she would never have a baby and would be lonely the rest of her life.

One day at work Silvia was counseling a woman with one leg who was in the hospital to have the other leg removed due to a progressive circulatory disease. The woman said, "I don't see any reason why I shouldn't just end it all now. Why go through all that pain again?" Silvia found herself secretly agreeing with the woman that life wasn't worth living. This bothered her enough to make her do something about her depression.

Silvia talked to her old therapist on the phone, and made two agreements: (1) she would start visualizing again at night and in the morning, and (2) whether she felt like it or not, she would do one pleasurable activity each day. Her therapist helped her make a list of seven activities to get her through the first week.

The first day Silvia did a receptive visualization to uncover her depressive thoughts. She imagined that she was walking through a big, empty, new house very much like her own new house. Each time she entered a room, she would meet someone or see something related to her depression. In the living room, her husband, Bob, said, "I'm too busy to have a baby now." In the kitchen, an old friend looked right through her, like she didn't exist. In the nursery she saw an empty crib. In the basement a bunch of her old college friends were playing cards on top of a coffin. One bedroom was set up like a hospital operating room—her idea of the setting for fertility testing.

In each of these rooms, Silvia listened to her thoughts as if they were the soundtrack of a documentary. At first she heard only fragments:

No baby

Dead

Gone

All over

Worthless

Nobody cares

By repeating her visualization in slow motion. Silvia was able to fill out these fragments and write down the full statements they represented:

No baby for me.

I'm sterile.

Bob doesn't really want a baby.

As far as my friends are concerned, I'm dead and buried.

All my friends are gone forever.

My life is all over.

I'm worthless.

Silvia was surprised at the universally negative tone of her self-statements, since she knew "intellectually" that her life wasn't over, that she could make new friends, and so on.

On the way home from work that first day, Silvia bought some lettuce and radish seeds as her pleasurable activity for the day. After dinner she made a sketch of her new garden layout. Then she got to work composing affirmations to counter her negative self-statements:

Self-Statement	Affirmation
No baby for me.	*I can still have a baby.*
I'm sterile.	*I can take a fertility test.*
Bob doesn't really want a baby.	*I can ask Bob what he wants.*
As far as my friends are concerned, I'm dead and buried.	*It's up to me to stay in touch.*
All my friends are gone forever.	*I have lots of friends.*
My life is all over.	*Anything is possible for me.*
I'm worthless.	*I'm smart, warm, and capable.*
Nobody really cares if I live or die.	*My husband and friends love me.*

That night Silvia repeated her visualization of the empty house. As she entered each room, she spoke one of her affirmations. In the living room, she visualized herself asking Bob if he really did want a child. In the bedroom with the operating table, she imagined lying down on it and asking, "Can I have a baby or not?"

During the next week, Silvia used her affirmations whenever she felt depressed. "Anything is possible for me" got her out of bed in the morning. "I'm smart, capable, and warm" got her to work and helped her open up to her co-workers. "I have lots of friends" got her through the early evening and inspired her to write a letter to her old bridge partner.

The affirmations "I can ask Bob" and "I can take a fertility test" helped her finally ask Bob if he really wanted a child. To her relief, he responded with a hearty yes and apologized for being so distracted by his new job. They made appointments for both of them to get fertility tests.

Silvia kept her agreement with her old therapist by accomplishing one "pleasure task" each day: spading two rows in the garden, planting the seeds she bought, browsing in an antique store, unpacking her sheet music, calling the community center to find out about the bridge club, and calling the piano tuner. She also meditated or did a visualization nearly every day. When she forced herself to visualize when she "didn't feel like it," she inevitably got a little lift and was glad she'd made the effort.

Six months later Silvia's depression was mostly gone. Her doctor told her that her ovarian tubes were slightly blocked, but that with Bob's high sperm count, she would get pregnant sooner or later. She joined the bridge club, played her piano more, and started going out to lunch occasionally with a woman she met at work.

Anxiety

Theresa was married to Ray, a contractor just starting out on his own. They had two boys, age five and three. Lots of things made Theresa anxious, particularly helping Ray with the business. She hated making and receiving phone calls for her husband. She worried about giving and getting the wrong message, resulting in delays or cost overruns. She got very nervous when people came to the house when Ray wasn't there to drop off plans or tools. The worst times were when she had to load the boys in the car and drive downtown to drop something off or pick something up at the building department.

Even though Theresa was smart, knew quite a bit about the construction business, and seldom made mistakes, she was still nervous. She couldn't avoid the phone calls and errands, since Ray had to be out on the job and needed her help. So she decided to try visualization to help her cope with her fears.

The most effective receptive visualization technique for Theresa was age regression. At age twelve she remembered her mother angrily grabbing the potholder she was making her grandmother for Christmas and saying, "Here, let me do that before you ruin it." She imagined she was nine years old, helping her mother make cookies. She could hear her mother saying, "No, not that way," and slapping her hands. "You'll never learn, will you? Why can't you get it right? I've told you a hundred times." When she was eight she remembered her sisters laughing at her attempts to learn to ice skate: "You're such a retard, Theresa." She had a vivid memory of being terrified of the Octopus ride at a carnival when she was five. She thought if she went on it she would throw up and everyone would laugh at her.

The big insight that Theresa came up with was that her anxiety stemmed from an image of herself as weak, helpless, and incapable of doing anything complicated in the "real world," despite the many successes she had had in school, raising a family, and so on.

In her family Theresa had been the timid one, the klutz who couldn't do anything right, the baby who had to be protected and taken care of. She realized that her negative self-statements were the same things that her mother and sisters had been telling her for years. Here are some of her negative self-statements and the affirmations she made up to counter them:

Self-Statement	Affirmation
I never get anything right.	*I'm an expert at many things.*
I'm such a retard.	*I can master what I really want to learn.*
They'll all laugh at me.	*They don't care how I do.*
I can't do it.	*I can do this.*
This is too complicated.	*I can do one step at a time.*
It's a disaster.	*Everything works out in the end.*

Theresa combined these affirmations with systematic desensitization. First she wrote down a hierarchy of situations she found stressful, beginning with the easiest and progressing to the most frightening:

1. Taking a phone message from a carpenter who's sick and can't work tomorrow
2. Calling the building department to schedule an inspection
3. Going to the hardware store to get supplies
4. Strange guy comes by the house to pick up a ladder
5. Paying permit fees at the building department
6. Having to get plan signed off at the building department
7. Trying to get hold of Ray while subcontractor sits idle at a job site, waiting for instructions

Before going to sleep each night, Theresa would relax herself with progressive muscle relaxation, then imagine the first situation. At the first sign of tension, she would tell herself, "I can do this," and will herself to relax. When she could imagine the first scene without any anxiety, she went on to the second scene. It took her three nights to get through the hierarchy. She would have done it quicker but she kept falling asleep.

During the day, she used her affirmations whenever the calls piled up or she had to go on an errand. Quieting her fears in real life proved much harder than doing it in the visualizations, but she gradually became less anxious. "The key to getting less nervous," she said, "was to focus on my past successes instead of future disasters."

Anger

Theresa had such good luck with visualization to control her anxiety that her husband, Ray, decided to use it to curb his temper. He would get furious at subcontractors who didn't show up or finish on time, building inspectors who made him tear out perfectly good work and do it over, clients who approved changes in the middle of a project and then balked at paying for them, and his employees who seemed to slow down and goof off as soon as he left the job site.

Ray tried to keep his temper, but he would seethe inside, full of things he would like to tell his tormentors, wanting to strike out and hit someone. A few times he had caught himself about to hit one of his kids, and that really scared him.

When Ray did let his anger out, it invariably alienated his crew, his clients, and the bureaucrats he had to work with on a daily basis. He knew that he had to get control of his anger if he was to be a success in his business.

In a series of receptive visualizations, Ray visited every construction site and city office he had recently frequented and replayed scenes that had made him angry. This netted him a long list of negative self-statements, which he wrote down as they occurred to him. Then he composed affirmations to contradict the angry statements. Here is his list:

Self-Statement	Affirmation
He's to blame.	*He's doing what he thinks is right.*
Nobody cares about this project but me.	*They're only human.*
He's out to get me.	*I can tune out angry thoughts.*
He's doing that on purpose.	*No assumptions about motives.*
Why do I have to put up with this asshole?	*I can put up with it for the sake of the job.*
Now what's wrong!?	*Just breathe deeply and relax.*

Ray also noticed in his visualization that, although he often held back angry comments, his body language gave him away: leaning forward, frowning, clamped jaw, folded arms, stamping around, brusque gestures, curt answers, and so on. In front of a mirror he practiced holding his weight back on his heels, moderating his gestures, breathing slowly, relaxing his jaw, and keeping his arms uncrossed.

He also noticed how much he used his anger as a source of energy. He often drove around in his pickup truck from job site to lumberyard to architect's office, angry all the way, propelled by rage like a locomotive with a full head of steam. He was afraid that losing his anger might hurt his ability to get a lot of things done. He made up another affirmation and wrote it on the back of the sun visor of his truck: "I can get things done without anger."

When Ray knew that he was heading for an anger-provoking situation—a confrontation with a building inspector, a meeting with an unhappy client, or a talk with a goof-off carpenter—he would rehearse the scene in his mind first. He'd plan what to say without blaming or name-calling. He'd watch himself maintaining his neutral body language and keeping his cool. He'd imagine the inflammatory remarks of the other person, and plan his own diplomatic, peace-keeping responses.

In the anger-provoking situation itself, Ray kept repeating his affirmations: "I can get through this without anger," "Nobody is to blame here," "We're just all trying to do our jobs," and "Just breathe slow and deep."

When anger caught him by surprise, he started saying, "Wait a minute, let me think about that." Then he would turn away, close his eyes, take a deep breath, and tell himself, "I can handle this without blowing my stack. Forget about the other guy's motives—what exactly do I want here?"

When he caught himself fuming about some insult or hassle, he would take his mind off it with a pleasant visualization—fantasizing about the house he would build himself one day or the new truck he planned to buy next year. When he got home from work at night, he spent ten minutes in the recliner on the back porch, visualizing a peaceful beach scene and imagining the pent-up anger of the day bleeding off like air out of a compressor with a leaky hose.

It took a year and a half of on-and-off visualization, support from his wife, and a couple of talks with his parish priest before Ray felt that he really had his anger under control. He knew he had turned the corner when one of his con-tractor friends asked his advice on how to deal with a difficult customer who didn't want to pay the last installment on a big remodeling job. "Tell me how to handle this guy," his friend asked. "You're always Mr. Cool dealing with the dead-beats."

17

Shyness

"The luminous island of the self trembles and waits."

—*Lawrence George Durrell*

Shyness is many things. Shyness is hanging back, being a bystander rather than a participant in your life. Shyness is not asking for what you want, feeling that you don't deserve or can't bear attention. Shyness is suffering criticism in silence and not asserting your rights. Shyness is feeling deprived of love and attention, but feeling incredible embarrassment when you do reach out to someone.

Shyness and low self-esteem go hand in hand. If you haven't read the self-esteem chapter already, be sure to get back to it after this chapter.

If you've been shy all your life, you probably believe in several mistaken assumptions. Look at the list below and see if any of these statements ring a bell. If so, you need to counter them with new affirmations. Some suggested affirmations are in the second column.

Mistaken Assumptions	Affirmations
It's selfish to put my needs before others'.	*I can put myself first sometimes.*
Mistakes are shameful.	*I have a right to make mistakes.*
If others don't agree with my feelings, my feelings must be wrong.	*I am the final judge of my own feelings.*
I should respect the views of others, especially if they're in a position of authority.	*My personal opinions are valid and important.*
I must always be logical and consistent.	*I can change my mind if I want to.*
I'm boring. No one would be interested in me.	*I am worth knowing.*
It's not polite to question the actions of others.	*I have a right to protest any action or criticism that seems wrong to me.*
Interrupting is rude. Asking questions shows how dumb I am.	*I can interrupt when I need clarification.*
Things could get even worse. Don't rock the boat.	*I can negotiate for change.*
I have nothing to say worth listening to.	*I can contribute to the conversation.*
I shouldn't take up others' valuable time with my problems.	*I can ask for help and emotional support when I need it.*
Everyone can see how lame and awkward I am.	*They're worried about their own images, not mine.*
Nobody wants to hear about how bad I feel. I should keep it to myself.	*I have a right to feel and express unhappiness.*
I should take all advice to heart.	*It's OK to ignore others' advice.*
I won't think of anything to say.	*I can always talk about my shyness.*
Knowing I did something well is its own reward. Nobody likes a showoff.	*I celebrate my own successes. I accept compliments graciously.*
I should always accommodate others.	*I have a right to say no.*

I'm unworthy.	*I'm worthwhile just because I exist.*
I must be open and available to people. No one must think I'm antisocial.	*I can choose to be alone, even if others would prefer my company.*
I should always have a good reason for what I do.	*I don't have to justify myself to others.*
They'll reject me.	*No mind reading! No predictions!*
When someone is in trouble, I should always try to help.	*I can decline responsibility for other peoples' problems.*
Anyone I like won't like me.	*I'm willing to take a chance.*
I try to be sensitive to the needs and wishes of other people, even when they can't express them.	*I don't have to anticipate other people's needs and wishes. I reject mind reading.*
It's not nice to put people off.	*I can choose not to respond to a situation.*

Homework

Looking over this list of assumptions probably made you think of several situations in which you were shy and wished you had acted more assertively. Pick one of these situations to work on first in your visualization.

Receptive Visualization

Lie down, close your eyes, and relax. Go to your special place and set up your viewing screen. Run a tape or project a film of the shy scene you have chosen.

See the setting, yourself, and the other people as if it is a movie, with some detachment. Watch and listen as the scene is played out. Notice what you say, how you hold your body, and how the other people respond. Pretend that you're an announcer commenting on the scene. Complete these statements:

That person's being shy because _____.

It's safer to be shy because _____.

The advantages of being shy are _____.

If you can't think of any advantages to being shy, have your inner guide pay you a visit and ask your guide, "What do I get out of being shy?" Wait patiently for an answer.

Now run the shy scene again, but this time change the outcome so that you get what you want out of the situation. How do you speak or move differently? How do you look when you're not acting shy? At this point, you may not be able to see exactly how you bring about the desired outcome. That's all right.

Just get a clear image of what you want out of the situation: a date, you're boss's full attention, someone leaving you alone, appreciation for your ideas, or whatever.

End the visualization when you are ready.

Identify and Outsmart Secondary Gain

Secondary gain is the good you get out of a bad situation. Shyness is not all bad. If you weren't shy, you would have to give up the benefits of shyness. Being shy means that you don't have to take risks. You can stay safe. You're not as likely to fail if you hang back and don't draw attention to yourself. Being shy allows you to view others with a secretly superior detachment. All these are secondary gains—good things you get out of a bad situation.

Think back to your receptive visualization and your imaginary commentary on it. Take a moment to write down the good things you get out of being shy. Then compose an affirmation for each one, showing how you plan to outsmart short-term secondary gain by focusing on the long-term gains of being more outgoing and assertive. Here are some examples:

Love is more important to me than being safe.

Others respect me for stating my opinions.

Nothing ventured, nothing gained.

Self-respect is worth the risk.

Saying no equals a minute of discomfort; saying yes equals hours of resentment.

Compose "I" Messages

Consider the revised scene you visualized in which you got what you wanted. If your unshy tactics were unclear to you, now is the time to clarify them. Composing an "I" message is the place to start.

An "I" message obviously starts with "I." It communicates your thoughts, feelings, and desires, without blaming or putting down the other person. Making statements beginning with "I" is less threatening to others than delivering "you" messages.

Here's a typical "you" message: "You're hogging the discussion. You aren't paying any attention to me, you don't give me a chance to talk." All that blame won't get you what you want.

This "I" message is much easier to deliver and more likely to get results: "I think this discussion is getting too one-sided. I feel frustrated in trying to make my points clear. I want you to listen carefully to what I have to say without interrupting until I've finished."

For your problem scene, compose an "I" message in this format:

I think _____.

I feel _____.

I want _____.

The "I think" portion should give your rational assessment of the situation, coolly and objectively, without judgmental language or blaming.

The "I feel" portion reports your emotions concerning the situation. This is where you can be more subjective. Be honest but tactful. Say how you feel but avoid blaming or judging the other person.

The "I want" statement is a request for action from the other person. The request should be for one particular action or behavior change, not for a change of attitude or mere agreement. Here is an example:

I think we have a lot in common.

I feel attracted to you and I'd like to get to know you better.

I want to ask you over for dinner next Friday.

Practice Confident Body Language

Stand in front of a full-length mirror. Put your feet about a foot apart, with your weight spread evenly between both legs. Let your hands hang naturally at your sides, or put your hands on your hips. Stand facing the mirror foursquare, straight on. Stand straight and lift your chin so that you are looking right into your own eyes. Practice smiling and laughing. Reach out toward the mirror occasionally as if to touch yourself on the arm. Practice saying your "I" message.

At first this exercise will probably feel unnatural, phony, and scary. But keep it up until you feel more comfortable. This kind of confident body language says, "I'm straightforward. I'm open. I'm available to you. I'm interested in you."

For contrast, slouch down, cross your arms in front of your chest, stand at an angle to the mirror with your weight back on your rear leg. Lower your head, and keep glancing away from the mirror and back again. Notice how this body language makes you look shy, nervous, withdrawn, and defensive.

Now get a chair and place it facing straight on to the mirror. Sit erect in the chair, leaning forward slightly. Put your hands on your knees. Keep both feet on the floor, legs slightly apart. Again, practice smiling, laughing, saying your "I" message, and reaching out as if to touch your reflected image on the knee.

This posture and behavior will also feel weird. Keep it up until you relax a little. This is confident sitting. This kind of confident sitting says, "I'm interested in what you have to say. Let's talk. I have something important and interesting to tell you. Let's be friends."

For contrast, scoot your chair back and place it at an angle to the mirror. Lean as far back as you can, fold your arms, and cross your legs. Keep breaking eye contact with yourself and looking away. This shy body language says, "I'm nervous. I'm shy. I have little to say to you. Keep your distance."

Remember what this body language looks like so you can use it in the visualization that follows.

Visualizations for Confidence

In the visualizations that follow, you'll relive your shyness scene using your "I" message and assertive body language to create the outcome you desire. Then you'll visualize coping with difficult people, calling on your inner guide in stressful situations, and handling criticism with aplomb.

Lie down, close your eyes, and relax. Go again to your special place and warm up your viewing screen.

Visualize your shyness scene again. Watch it with interest but some detachment. This time, see yourself acting confidently and assertively. Your carriage is erect and graceful. You show clear body language, leaning forward, looking at the other person directly, arms and hands uncrossed. Your voice is loud and clear, not wavering or quaking. You hear yourself deliver your "I" message clearly and directly. Tell yourself, "I can ask for what I want."

If you still have trouble seeing yourself in an assertive role, another technique is to borrow a friend's personality. See yourself acting in the scene the way your assertive friend would. You can also adopt assertive traits from your favorite movie stars or fictional heroes.

Keep watching the scene as you get what you want. You may want to include some stammers and less-than-perfect performance at first, then see yourself gaining confidence and moving on to success. Be sure to focus on the positive benefits that accrue from conquering your shyness. Repeat your affirmations about the risk being worth the rewards.

Rerun the scene on the screen as many times as you need to get the actions and words clear in your mind and become comfortable with the idea of acting assertively.

When you're ready, surrender your detachment and get involved. Imagine the scene as if it were really happening to you. See and hear and feel everything as if it were going on right now. Include the feelings of anxiety and the mistakes at first. Then gain confidence and successfully state what you think, feel, and want. Use appropriate affirmations: "I can negotiate for change," "I can say no," "I don't have to justify myself," and so on.

Use this basic visualization to prepare for any difficult confrontation. Do your homework and visualize the scene until you know just what you're going to say and how you're going to say it. With work and commitment, you will gradually become desensitized to your social anxiety.

As you practice, the use of "I" messages will become a habit, and your increasing confidence will allow you to say what you think, feel, and want "on the fly," without doing a lot of homework and pre-visualizing.

Difficult People

This is a visualization designed to break up your old image of difficult people in your life. You'll create a less frightening, more human image that will help you cope with difficult people more effectively.

Visualize yourself having fun with difficult people: laughing at jokes, roller skating, dancing, eating together. It doesn't matter if the activity would never actually happen in a million years. Just do it. Also, see yourself working with difficult people: cooperating, doing good work, complimenting each other, and enjoying the collaboration.

Imagine talking with difficult people. Listen to what they have to say. Look into their eyes. Really understand their point of view. Know the nature of their pain, what they fear and hope for. Let all judgment and suspicion slide away for a moment. Reply to them with whatever comes up from your deepest level of empathy, not from the everyday level of annoyance, self-defense, and avoidance.

Do this part of the visualization especially just before you will be seeing a difficult person in real life, and notice how it changes the real interaction.

Finally, try humor for visualizing difficult people. Imagine that Robin Williams or Bette Midler or some other comedian is playing the part of the other person. Imagine pushing a pie into his or her face. Try to see something light and funny about the situation. Put threatening people in their underwear, have them seized by a sneezing fit, or give them clown suits to wear.

Inner Guide

You're in a difficult situation and you're feeling shy. You've run through all your carefully composed affirmations and they sound like a mouse squeaking under the paw of a lion. It's time to call on your inner guide.

Imagine that your guide is invisibly at your side like a guardian angel. Silently explain to your guide what's going on. Make an "I" statement *to your inner guide* as a way of clarifying what you think, feel, and want in the situation.

Imagine that your guide can communicate to you silently and give you advice while you're coping with the situation. Communicating with your guide like this is a great way to calm down, achieve some distance and objectivity, and remember your confidence-building visualizations.

Example

Gus was a lab technician who wanted a raise. He worked in a small medical testing lab where raises weren't automatic. You had to ask, and he felt too shy.

Gus recognized two mistaken assumptions he was making: that he shouldn't ever put his needs before others' and that his occasional mistakes were unforgivable. These two irrational beliefs were keeping him locked into his low wage. He began his plan for getting a raise by adopting two affirmations: "I can put myself first sometimes" and "everyone makes mistakes."

Receptive visualization showed Gus that what he got out of his shyness at work was a low profile: nobody noticed him much. He was afraid that if he asked for a raise, his supervisor would start watching him more closely. This might make him nervous and cause more mistakes. His visualization uncovered a further, secret fear: that his raise would be taken away and he'd be humiliated. Gus knew intellectually that this was very unlikely, and exposing the fear to rational analysis helped to partially dispel it.

When Gus tried to visualize himself asking for a raise, he saw just a fog and heard his supervisor's voice saying, "OK, I'll put you in for another dollar an hour." He was clear on his desired outcome, but he hadn't a clue about how to make it happen.

Composing "I" messages helped Gus to see himself as a forthright person who could ask for a raise. Here is what he wrote down:

I think that I make a real contribution to the lab. I'm dependable and loyal, even if I do make mistakes sometimes.

I feel embarrassed about asking, but I feel I must bring this up, or else my morale will stay low.

I would like a raise. I'd like to be making another dollar an hour.

Gus also practiced his body language in front of a mirror. He pretended that he was sitting across from his supervisor's desk with his spine straight, his hands holding some papers calmly in his lap, and his eyes looking directly at his supervisor's face. He practiced delivering his "I" messages in front of the mirror.

In his daily visualizations, Gus told himself, "I can ask for what I want." He'd see himself drinking coffee with his supervisor, or leaning on his bench as his supervisor approached. He would hear himself ask his supervisor, "Have you got a minute to talk?" Then he would make his points calmly and clearly: that he was making a real contribution, that he felt embarrassed but determined, and that he wanted a raise.

For a positive outcome, Gus always heard, "Ok, I'll put you in for another dollar an hour." Sometimes he saw himself with extra cash in his wallet. Other times he imagined buying a new VCR or getting his car painted. He always saw himself walking straighter and prouder at work, moving with confidence and laughing at the jokes of the other techs.

After a week of daily visualizations, Gus actually asked his supervisor for a raise. He stammered a little, but he stuck to his vision of how the scene should go. His supervisor responded, "Well, I think that's reasonable. I'll talk to Dr. Dix about it." Gus eventually got his dollar-an-hour raise.

Gus felt so encouraged about his raise that he later used the same visualization techniques when he had to complain about some runs and drips on his newly painted car, and when he had to tell his brother-in-law that he wasn't available to help him paint his house.

Gus frequently visualized his brother-in-law as the big bad wolf who tormented the three little pigs. He made the wolf burn his tail in the fireplace, fall off the roof, and run howling into the forest. The humor helped him reduce his fear of a very difficult, angry, manipulative person.

Gus also imagined hearing his brother-in-law talk about his feelings of abandonment and failure. He came to understand that much of this difficult person's anger was pure bluster, covering up for underlying feelings of inadequacy. All these visualizations helped Gus to say no to his brother-in-law and to shrug off the resulting outbursts of anger.

V

Applications for Healing and Pain Control

18

Injuries

"Our emotions and words let the body know what we expect of it, and by visualizing certain changes we can help the body bring them about."

—*Bernie Siegel*

This chapter will show you how to use visualization to speed healing of any injury. By "injury" I mean almost any disruption of your body resulting from some mechanical, outside cause—broken bones, sprains, cuts, bruises, abrasions, surgical incisions, pulled muscles, inflamed tendons, burns, and so on.

This chapter will concentrate on healing your injury, rather than coping with your pain. If your injury has left you with lingering pain, you'll also want to read the chapter on pain control.

There are basically two steps to healing injuries with visualization. The first is the receptive or psychological step. This involves relaxing and getting to know your injury and your attitude toward it. Using receptive visualization, you will explore possible blocks you may have to getting better, and prepare images to use in the second step.

The second step is to do daily programmed visualizations in which you imagine the healing process and see yourself in the future as completely healed.

Receptive Visualization

Before you do your receptive visualization, there are a few things you need to know about the psychological aspects of injury. First of all, if you are blaming yourself for getting injured and feeling guilty about it, your guilt might interfere with your healing. You must be willing to forgive yourself for getting injured.

On the other hand, you may be secretly glad you are injured, or at least be enjoying some of the secondary benefits of being injured. Perhaps you don't have to go to work at an unpleasant job, or finish classes you were failing. Maybe everybody is being extra nice to you, giving you lots of attention and sympathy. Or you may be able to avoid some interpersonal conflict because you're in too poor a shape to deal with it right now. These benefits, which psychologists call "secondary gains," can slow your healing significantly. You need to recognize any secondary gains and resolve to give them up in favor of getting better.

Other psychological consequences of injury are painful emotions like anger, anxiety, and depression. Studies of injured athletes have shown that their reactions were similar to profound grief. Psychologically, a serious injury is like losing a loved one. You have lost your fitness and are mourning for it.

You need to acknowledge and express the emotions triggered by your injury, and realize that they will pass. This is particularly important if you tend to make catastrophic predictions. When you're hurt, it's all too easy to tell yourself, "This is the way it will always be. I'll never walk (or run, or lift, or breathe easy, or whatever) again." Part of your visualization work will be to compose affirmations to counter the irrational self-talk that abounds when you're injured.

If you have trouble asking for help, that's another problem to work on with your visualization. Your rapid recovery depends on your being able to ask for and receive all the help you need.

Also, you must be able to help yourself. You need to keep eating properly, taking your medications, doing your exercises or physical therapy, keeping your affairs in order, showing up for medical appointments, and so on. Taking care of yourself often feels like a monumental task when you're injured.

The final psychological preparation for healing is to ask yourself what literal meaning your injury might have in your life. This approach is based on writings by Louise L. Hay and others who believe that every physical problem is caused by or at least reflects some inner conflict. The connection is often derived from the literal meanings of the words people use to describe physical problems and emotional conflicts. For example, Hay would say that ulcers are the result of fear "eating away at you." She would say that neck problems are likely to be developed when you are being "stiff-necked" about something—stubborn and inflexible. Sometimes the connection is made by examining the function of the injured or diseased body part. For instance, since your back serves as the support for your body, it is seen as the emotional support or foundation of your life. Thus, chronic back trouble might reflect feelings that you lack emotional support or might mean that you have been holding back your love from those around you.

Some writers are even more specific, saying that lower back pain is an expression of suppressed sadness, while upper back pain expresses repressed anger.

Louise Hay's *Heal Your Body* is a long listing of physical problems, their probable psychological causes, and affirmations to change your thought patterns and thereby relieve the physical problems. Some of her correspondences seem plausible, such as linking eye problems with an unwillingness to face reality and see things as they are. Other explanations seem arbitrary or far-fetched, like her claim that athlete's foot results from frustration at not being accepted.

The value of Hay's approach is in the basic idea, not the specific correspondences she advocates. In the receptive visualization below, you will query your inner guide about any meaningful, literal connections between your injury and your thoughts, feelings, beliefs, and attitudes. To make it easier to follow the sequence of this visualization, read the instructions onto a tape.

Get ready to do your receptive visualization now. Lie down, close your eyes, and relax.

Let your attention sink into the part of your body that's injured. Put your awareness into the part that hurts or that doesn't work. Get a feeling for the extent of the damaged area. Imagine how much it weighs. Imagine how much water it would hold. Trace the boundaries between the injured part and the rest of your body.

Address your injury as if it were a person. Ask it what it's feeling. Ask what it wants to tell you. Ask what you need to do to heal yourself. Each time you do a healing visualization, ask these questions first. Keep giving your injury a chance to speak directly to you.

Here are some things your injury might tell you (don't record these comments. Leave a twenty-second silence on the tape):

You are to blame.

Now you will have to rest.

I am what you asked for.

Forgive yourself.

I am your friend.

You'll never be rid of me.

You are making it worse.

You'll never be well again.

Take care of yourself.

It's OK to be sad.

It's all right to be angry.

You are more upset than you know.

It's OK to ask for help.

Or your injury might tell you something very different. Pay attention to whatever it says so you can remember it later.

Don't worry if you get no response from your injury. You'll have other chances to question it.

While your attention is centered on your injury, notice any images that arise spontaneously: any sights, sounds, smells, tastes, or feelings you associate with your injury. You might see a colored light, a broken doll, a broken stick, a shattered cup, and so on. You might hear organ music, groans of pain, or a harsh, grating sound. You might smell corruption or get a metallic taste. You might feel coarse stones or hot metal. Pay attention to these sense impressions so you can use them later in your programmed healing visualization.

Now go to your special place. Look in your mirror or reflecting pond and see yourself with your injury. Is your body exaggerated in any way? Do you look crippled or changed? Do you seem to be in pain?

Invite your inner guide into the scene. Ask your inner guide to take on the role of your injury. Have your inner guide speak to you as your injury, or tell you anything you need to know about your injury. Ask respectfully, "Please tell me what I need to know to be healed."

If you have been feeling angry or sad or nervous about your injury, let your inner guide take the part of your emotion. Ask what your anger or depression or anxiety is trying to tell you.

Whatever you hear from your injury directly or through your inner guide, accept it without judgment. Don't worry if it isn't clear or doesn't seem to make sense at this time. With patience and practice, the meaning will come to you.

If you find yourself very resistant to any of these directions, ask yourself why. Give your resistance a color and a sound. Explore your automatic tendency to turn away from certain information. What are you afraid of? What don't you want to hear or acknowledge about your injury? Perhaps you don't want to face the possibility that you will never regain your previous level of activity and fitness. If this is the case, resolve to spend extra time in later visualizations working on an accurate and accepting vision of the future.

Finally, take a different perspective on your injury. Look upon it as something that you may have created in your life for some purpose. Express your willingness to understand how you may be responsible for your injury. Ask your inner guide to tell you the purpose of your injury. Ask to know the literal meaning your injury has in your life. Look back over the last few days and see what good things your injury has made happen in your life. Admit that there is some secondary gain.

Tell your inner guide that you will be back to talk about this another time. End the visualization when you are ready. Do this visualization once or twice a day until you start to get some answers. Then you can compose some pertinent affirmations and start doing some more programmed visualizations.

Affirmations

The affirmations you compose for your programmed healing visualization should do three things: (1) suggest resolutions to the psychological conflicts that you have uncovered surrounding your injury; (2) reinforce the idea of quick, pain-less, and complete healing; and (3) predict a return to a normal or acceptable level of activity.

Make your affirmations short, positive, and in the present tense. Here is a list of samples to get you started:

I forgive myself for getting hurt.

I am willing to give up my injury.

I can cope by concentrating on each moment.

I am letting my anger and sadness go.

My injury will pass.

I ask for help as soon as I need it.

I take care of myself.

I do my exercises daily.

I am keeping my spirits up.

I am open to discovering the meaning of my injury.

My back (leg, incision, burn, etc.) is my friend.

Healing energy surrounds me.

I am getting better every day.

My strength is coming back.

God's healing power is working within me.

I can heal myself.

I am going to walk (run, dance, lift, etc.) again soon.

I accept the recovery I can achieve.

I can live a full life whatever my limitations.

I am willing to take responsibility for my injury.

How Healing Takes Place

Before you start programmed visualization, it helps to know a little about how your body heals itself:

Cuts and Incisions

When you get cut, blood flows out of the wound to cleanse the area. Blood vessels then contract to conserve blood. Special blood cells called platelets gather at the edges of severed blood vessels to partially plug them. Oxygen from the air stimulates the formation of fibrin. This is a stringy substance that forms webs surrounding and connecting the severed ends of blood vessels. Red and white blood cells are trapped in these webs. All this takes place quickly and is commonly called blood clotting.

In the meantime, there are lots of white blood cells that don't get caught in the fibrin. These cells engulf and carry off any bacteria that have got into the wound, preventing infection.

The webs of fibrin are like a scaffolding or framework within which healing takes place. The cells that make up the blood vessel walls start multiplying and grow back together. Skin, fat, muscle, and nerve cells do the same.

Broken Bones

As soon as a bone is cracked or broken, special bone cells called osteoblasts go into overdrive. These cells multiply rapidly at the edges of the break and start secreting an organic material that forms long collagen fibers. Under a microscope these fibers look like tightly packed mats of shredded wheat between the ends of the break. These fibers are the organic matrix for the formation of new bone.

These fibers make the calcium dissolved in your blood want to precipitate out as crystals. The crystals of calcium form in the nooks and crannies of the collagen fibers, gradually filling in the break and repairing the bone. This happens in a matter of days. Then, over the next few weeks or months, the initial calcium crystal deposits are changed into a stronger, more stable form of calcium.

Bone growth is stimulated by putting stress on bones. Because they put more stress on their bones, athletes usually have heavier, stronger bones than sedentary types. This is why your doctor may give you a walking cast or encourage you to put weight on your broken bones as soon as possible.

The images for visualization are obvious: see your bone cells multiply and secreting the "juice" that hardens into the shredded wheat. Then see shining crystals forming your magical new bone.

Sprains, Pulled Muscles, Bruises, Inflammation

When your muscles or tendons are injured, a substance called necrosin is released by the damaged cells. This increases the permeability of the local capillaries, tiny blood vessels that nourish the cells. Large quantities of lymph fluid, protein, and fibrinogen leak quickly into the area, causing it to swell.

The fibrinogen soon makes much of this extra fluid clot, making the whole area very stiff. The effect is to wall off the injured area from the rest of the body. Blood moves very slowly through the swollen, clotted tissue, preventing the spread of poisons from the damaged cells.

Healing is a matter of white blood cells dissolving or eating up the pieces of damaged muscle cells and mopping up the cell poisons. As the debris is cleared and new muscle cells are produced to replace the damaged ones, the clots break up and more blood gets into the injured area, feeding the cells and speeding a return to full strength and range of motion.

For visualization purposes, watch your white cells eating up or dissolving pieces of broken cells, sucking up poisons and carrying them off to be eliminated. See the clots breaking up and the excess fluid draining out. See bright red blood bathing your new cells.

Burns

If you have a severe burn, most of your visualization will probably be devoted to pain control. However, there are a few healing images you should include: See yourself taking plenty of fluids to replace the plasma you are losing through the burned area. Visualize your white blood cells being particularly vigilant to protect you from infection—extensive burned areas no longer have unbroken skin to serve as a barrier to germs. Concentrate on images of healthy skin cells multiplying to fill in and repair the burned area. This is especially important if you are receiving skin grafts—see them taking root, feeling at home, spreading out like a vigorous ground cover establishing itself in fertile soil.

Programmed Visualization

In this visualization you'll use two kinds of imagery: literal and metaphorical. In literal imagery you visualize the actual healing process at the cellular level, seeing the cells multiplying and joining back together, forming healthy, whole tissue. In metaphorical imagery, you use objects, colors, lights, or sounds to represent your injury and the healing process. For example, you might see your injury as a crack in a wall and heal it by filling it with fresh plaster. You'll also combine these two types of images, for instance, seeing your new cells as pieces of a jigsaw puzzle and putting them together.

As always, the best images are the ones you make up for yourself. But here are some metaphors to get you started:

Plastering over a crack in a wall

A butterfly emerging from a cocoon

Rebuilding a collapsed brick or stone wall

Animals growing larger and stronger

Cementing cells together with superglue

Removing damaged cells like pulling weeds

Crystals forming and multiplying like a kaleidoscope image

Putting a jigsaw puzzle together

A harsh, stormy landscape becoming sunlit and gentle

Knitting tissue back together with needles and yarn

New tissue being built up like the great pyramid, by tiny Egyptians

Removing damaged cells with a vacuum cleaner

Tender shoots growing into vibrant plants

Singing a lullaby to an inflammation

Spreading new skin like lotion over a burn

Laying new skin cells like tile on a floor

Smoothing liniment on an inflamed tendon

Changing red light to blue

Harsh traffic sounds changing into pleasant melody

Raking rocks out of a rough path to smooth it

Kneading damaged muscle fibers like dough to remove the stiffness

Divine healing energy in the form of golden light

Poking holes in a full waterskin to reduce swelling

This visualization has four parts: the literal healing process, reinforcing any treatment you are undergoing, the metaphorical images, and looking to the future. Recording the instructions will help you stay on track.

Lie down, close your eyes, and relax. Let your attention flow to your injury, as if you were looking at it under a microscope. Visualize healthy tissue as rows and columns of even, plump cells, like bricks in a wall or tiles on a floor. In your injured area, see the cells as broken apart, in disarray. See pieces of damaged cells lying around like rubble. Visualize white blood cells picking up the broken pieces and carrying them away to be eliminated. You can see the white cells as irregular blobs with a dot in the middle for a nucleus, as busy little bees, robots, janitors, soldiers, or whatever appeals to you.

See the healthy cells around your injury multiplying—first the nucleus divides in two, then the two nuclei separate further and further apart, pulling the cell apart until it divides into two smaller cells, which quickly grow up to full size. See this happening all around your injury, filling in the missing design and making everything uniform again. Imagine blood vessels bringing oxygen and nutrients to your cells, the gas and food molecules going right into the cells through the cell walls. See this in any way that makes sense to you.

Watch this process for a while, adding color and a musical soundtrack. Feel a sense of warmth, smoothness, and ease. Hear your affirmations like a voice-over narration: "I am healing all the time," or "My body knows how to heal itself," or "Soon I'll be better than ever."

Now visualize any treatment you are currently receiving. If you have a cast, notice how it keeps your bones still so that the collagen matrix is not disturbed and so calcium can be deposited to fix the break at the maximum rate. If you have a dressing, notice how it protects your injury from abrasion and repels bacteria. If you are doing any exercises or physical therapy, watch yourself in action and then shrink down to the cellular level. See how the exercise is stimulating the growth of muscle cells. Create a network of nerve fibers like interlaced tree branches and see how the repetitive exercise is making your neural messages stronger and more precise. If you are taking or applying any medication, create a scene in which you can watch it having the desired effect.

Now let your imagination go. Visualize metaphors of your injury and the healing process. If you have a pins-and-needles sensation in your broken arm, imagine that there really are pins in it. See yourself pulling out and throwing away the pins until the feeling is gone and your arm is whole and strong again. If you have a pulled muscle in your back, see it as really pulled out of shape. Pour warm water over it and shrink it back into shape like a wool sweater. If you overheard your surgeon talking about the "lips" of your incision and the image stuck with you, then see your incision as a magic mouth, singing a song: "I'm getting smaller and smaller, I'm going away." See the mouth getting smaller, hear the voice getting higher and quieter until there is just a tiny peeping hole. Then close it up forever with fresh, pink, new skin. Tell yourself, "I am creating and re-creating the healing process every day," or use another affirmation you like.

End your visualization with a vision of the future. Use the viewing device in your special place if you like. Watch yourself taking care of yourself, eating well, taking your medications, going to doctor's appointments, gradually doing more and more, feeling better, coping with stress well, having enough energy and money and time. Eventually, see yourself as completely healed, going about your usual activities freely, feeling fine.

If you have a serious injury that will not allow you to regain your previous level of activity, see yourself in the future as having adapted to your limitations, living a happy and fulfilling life in spite of any handicaps. See your physical condition as a little *better* than your doctors' most optimistic predictions—visualization can be a stronger healing force than most doctors realize.

End the visualization when you are ready. Practice this visualization three times a day.

What To Expect

As you get better, adjust your images to keep up with your changing condition. At first, you might concentrate on images of preventing infection, reducing swelling, and getting plenty of rest. Later, you will concentrate on scenes of getting stronger, regaining flexibility, and resuming regular activities.

Expect setbacks. It's the nature of healing that it goes in stages. Some stages might seem to take forever, and you think you'll never get better. Other stages go quickly, and you'll get too optimistic, only to be plunged into disappointment when you exert yourself too much and realize you're not all better yet. Be patient and reflect on the truism: "time heals all wounds."

If you have extra time on your hands, read up on your condition. Knowing more about your body and what is going on in it can help make your literal healing visualizations more vivid and interesting.

Example

At age eighteen, Lorraine was in an auto accident that crushed her T-12 vertebra. The bone fragments severely damaged her spinal chord and her legs were almost totally paralyzed. Doctors told her that in the next eighteen months some nerves might heal or regrow, and she might regain some feeling or movement. But she would probably never walk again.

Lorraine's first reaction was denial. She just didn't believe that she wouldn't get all better. But eighteen months passed and she regained only some sensation and no movement. She could barely move her thigh muscles, and everything lower down was dead. She finally admitted that she was crippled for life and gave up all hope of cure.

She spent the next three years learning to live in a wheelchair, hating her legs, and praying to God to heal her. She would wake up crying at night with pains in her feet and pound on them with her fists. She wished she could just cut her legs off and get rid of them.

Lorraine was a talented artist. She often used receptive visualization to guide her in creating prints and paintings, so she was open to messages from her unconscious. Over the next nine years she finished college and went on to pursue a graduate art degree. As she went about her life as an active, well-adjusted handicapped person, a curious thing began to happen. Once in a while, a "window" would open in her head. She would get a glimpse through the window of a limitless expanse of space. She would know for an instant, without a doubt, that there were no limits, that she could walk and run and dance again.

The window experience was tantalizing, but frightening. At first she slammed the window shut as soon as it opened. As time passed, she could hold the window open for longer and longer periods. Twelve years after her accident, the window stayed open.

Lorraine decided to use visualization and exercise to walk again. She went to a gym to work on building the strength of her thigh muscles, the only leg muscles she could move even a little. They were very weak and wasted. She could barely budge the lever of the quadracept machine with no weight on it at all. Other women in the gym could routinely lift one hundred pounds on that machine. But Lorraine did make progress. Soon she could lift five pounds, then ten pounds. And it seemed that her coordination and endurance were slightly better.

At home Lorraine taped a medical illustration of the nervous system on her refrigerator. The system looked like tree branches. She would visualize the nerves in her spinal chord budding and branching out like new shoots. She imagined a golden glow of healing energy bathing her spine and legs. She would see the new nerves breaking through scar tissue and growing out to hook up with the disconnected nerves in her legs.

She met a research physiologist and rehabilitation expert named Roger, who was impressed with her determination and the strength that she had been able to regain on her own. Roger thought that she was probably establishing new neural pathways, making little detours around her damaged nerves to find new ways of sending motor messages to her legs.

Roger hooked Lorraine's foot muscles up to a biofeedback machine and told her to try to flex her foot upward. The machine could detect the slightest contraction of the muscles. Movement was nonexistent at first. Over a period of months Lorraine visualized her nerves reaching down to her foot and carrying motor messages. She breathed healing light into her legs. She created an image of herself as a full body, not the legless creature she had been to herself for twelve years. Finally, on the finest, most sensitive scale setting, the machine recorded a twitch. Weeks passed and the twitch became visible to the eye. Eventually she could move the foot jerkily upward in a semblance of one of the many movements needed for walking.

To get relaxed and focused before her visualization sessions, Lorraine would lie down, close her eyes, and imagine seeing just her feet, from above, descending a spiral staircase. She would come to the end of the staircase, go through a short hall, and into a dim room and up to the back of a couch. She'd climb over the couch and sit down facing a movie screen. Then the film would roll and she'd see whatever she had planned to visualize. Since she was a graphic artist, the visual scene dominated her imagery scene.

Lorraine proceeded like this for a couple of years, concentrating on one muscle group and one movement at a time: feet, knees, thighs, hips; rotation, extension, balance, coordination, and so on. At one point she gave a demonstration and addressed the faculty and students at the medical school where Roger was doing research. They said that her case was unique—nowhere in the literature could they find a similar case of spinal regeneration so long after an injury.

By this time, Lorraine's upper leg muscles were strong enough so that she could stand upright in a doorway for a few moments. She would stand there, get her balance, and close her eyes. Looking inward, she'd find her center of strength—invariably in her well-developed shoulder and upper arm muscles. Then she would concentrate on sending her strength downward, into her legs.

Lorraine added affirmations like "My legs are strong," "My balance is improving," and "My legs are slender" (as opposed to "too skinny").

One of her favorite visualizations was to see her whole body as a giant nerve cell, with the axon as her head and the dendrites as her feet. She would imagine bursts of energy like lightning bolts passing from her head, through her feet, and right into the ground—literally a "grounding" exercise. She would also see herself in the future, running on the beach, smelling the salt, feeling the sand and mist, hearing the waves.

She began to stand and maintain her balance with crutches. Soon she took a few steps on the crutches. She became steadier, graduated to lighter, smaller crutches, then a four-point cane. At each stage, she would visualize herself—first walking in her halting, ungainly style, then smoothing it out and walking with a correct, normal motion. Finally, three years after her resolution to walk again, she took her first unaided steps across her living room.

Lorraine rarely takes her wheelchair anywhere now. She gets around on a lightweight pair of aluminum crutches. She has gone back to school and recently got her teaching credential so that she can teach art to kids. She continues her therapy, looking toward walking routinely with just a cane. But she's pretty busy and isn't as intense about her exercise and visualization as she used to be. She says it's important to take some breaks and come back to the hard work refreshed.

(Follow-up: I left the above paragraph unchanged from the 1988 edition because this is my favorite example in the book. As I write this second edition in 1994, Lorraine has returned again to graduate school and become a therapist. She has her own private practice and edits a professional journal. She has stabilized at a level of fitness that allows her to go anywhere and lead a very active life, with help from her crutches. Lorraine has maintained her physical progress, astounding neurological experts who feared that she might "burn out" the new neural pathways that she forged through visualization and exercise.)

Looking back, Lorraine says that the most important obstacle she had to overcome was her self-image, her attitude about herself. "It all finally came down to me," she says. "As long as I sat around in the wheelchair and waited for God to fix this horrible thing that happened to me, nothing happened. I had to accept responsibility for *my* injury that *I* created in my life. Then I had to learn to love my legs again before I could heal them. Then I had to find out who could help me, ask them for help, and then later let them go when it was time to work alone again. There have been so many lessons to learn, so many high points and low points along the way.

"And I could slide right back down to the bottom again, if I don't constantly work on my self-image. If you see yourself as a seriously handicapped person, then you won't get better, or won't sustain any improvements you do make. You have to change your self-image. You have to see yourself as somebody who is temporarily limited, but getting better."

19

Noninfectious Diseases

"There are no incurable diseases, only incurable people."
—*Bernie Siegel*

This chapter covers diseases such as hypertension, gastritis, colitis, emphysema, and so on. If you don't find what you're looking for here, try also the chapters on infectious diseases, immune system disorders, or pain control.

The visualization techniques in this chapter are things you can do in *addition* to traditional treatments for your condition. Visualization is a powerful healing force, but it is no replacement for accurate diagnosis and professional medical treatment. Many of the diseases discussed in this chapter are readily curable or controllable by drugs and surgery. You'd be foolish to attempt to visualize your way to a cure on your own if modern medicine offers a quick and effective fix.

The chapter is divided into the usual two phases: receptive visualization and programmed visualization.

Receptive Visualization

This process will help you assess your situation and accomplish several goals:

1. Explore any guilt feelings you may have about being sick, being a drain on your family, and so on.

2. Expose and circumvent any secondary gain—good things accruing from a bad condition—that may hinder your recovery.

3. Acknowledge all your feelings about your disease: depression, anxiety, anger, and so on.

4. Uncover and refute any illogical, catastrophic predictions you may be making about your illness.

5. Identify and implement all the practical tasks of coping with your condition day by day.

6. Unearth whatever symbolic or psychological meaning your illness may have for you.

The final step of the receptive visualization is the most difficult and controversial. It involves accepting responsibility for your disease as something that you have created in your life. Underlying this idea is the philosophical notion that you create your entire universe—the bad along with the good. The trick is to be empowered by accepting responsibility and control over your life without blaming yourself for creating something as stupid and destructive as disease in your life.

The paradox of blameless responsibility is hard for many people to embrace. If considering that you might be responsible for your disease makes you feel guilty or depressed instead of empowered, skip that part of the visualization.

Instructions

Lie down, close your eyes, and relax. Remind yourself that relaxation is the first step toward getting better.

When you are completely relaxed, let your awareness move into the area affected by your disease. Feel the size, shape, and extent of the area affected. Give it a color that seems appropriate. Imagine how much water the area would hold, or how much it would weigh.

What images arise spontaneously? Do you see a color or shape, hear a sound, feel any bodily sensations, experience any tastes or smells? Do any memories of previous problems come into your awareness? Tell yourself, "I take whatever I get without judgment."

Ask questions of your disease:

Why are you here?

What do you mean to me?

How can I get better?

How long will you be here?

What do I do to prolong you?

What feelings do you represent?

How do you help me?

Accept any answers you get without judgment. File them away for later analysis. The answers may be penetrating insights, banalities, or nonsequiturs. You may not get any answers at all. Don't worry about it at this point. Tell yourself, "I'm open to all information about myself." Talk to your disease in your mind. Tell it how you feel about being sick? Angry? Depressed? Frightened? Guilty? Ashamed? Let the emotions well up inside your body and flood your being. Tell yourself, "I'm willing to learn about emotions I've been avoiding."

What thoughts come into your mind when you dwell on your disease? You may hear one word like "never" or a full statement like "I'm never going to get better." Make a note of any thoughts that pop up during this visualization.

Now go to your special place and turn on your viewing screen or crystal ball. See and hear yourself moving through an average day. Get up in the morning, eat, talk to those you meet, work, play, and rest as you usually do.

As you watch yourself, think of yourself as a sick person. Notice what you do to fix or compensate for your problem. You may go to the doctor's office, turn down invitations, eat certain foods, lose weight, gain weight, take pills or injections, do exercises, avoid some activities you used to do, ask various people to help you, and so on.

How well do you accomplish these things? Do you do them wholeheartedly in an effort to get better, or do you do them resentfully and sporadically? Does depression keep you from taking care of yourself? Does anger or guilt keep you from asking for the help you need?

Now notice what you do that makes the problem worse: missing doctor's appointments, going off your diet, forgetting to take your medication, overexerting yourself, getting tense in stressful situations, and so on. Don't beat yourself up about these images. Just let them flow and take note.

Now notice the positive things you get from being sick: consideration and sympathy from others, time off from a hateful job, a chance to rest, a means of avoiding unpleasant confrontations or of postponing decisions about your life, and so on. Let go of any guilt feelings that these images may inspire. You're just a curious and interested observer.

Zoom in for a close-up of yourself. Make yourself naked and look at yourself full length, then focus on each part of your body. How do you look? What do you like and dislike about what you see? Of the things you dislike, which do you attribute to your disease? See if you can change the image of yourself to one of health and well-being. Don't worry if you're not ready to visualize yourself as healthy. Tell yourself, "I accept my good and bad points."

Now turn off your viewing device and bring your inner guide into your special place with you. Ask your guide the same questions you asked your disease directly:

Why is my disease here?

What does this disease mean to me?

How can I get better?

How long will I be sick?

What do I do to prolong my disease?

What feelings does my disease represent?

How does my disease help me?

Accept whatever answers you get: silence, words, gestures, or whatever. If you don't understand, say, "What else can you tell me about that?" Invite your guide to speak to you about any aspect of your disease by asking, in your own words, "Please tell me what I need to know about my disease."

Let your guide show you any symbols or objects that relate to your disease. Take anything that your guide offers you as a help or a cure. It could be a magic potion, a crystal, a shield and sword, a prayer book—or absolutely anything that has meaning for you.

If you have been feeling especially depressed, angry, anxious, or guilty, ask your guide about your feelings:

Why are these feelings here?

What do they mean to me?

How can I get rid of these painful emotions?

How long will I feel this way?

What do I do to prolong this feeling?

How do I get out of feeling this way?

Under what conditions would my feelings go away?

When you are finished with your questions, allow your guide to leave. Promise to stay in touch and invite your guide to contact you whenever there is something you need to know.

At any point in this visualization, you may have experienced resistance. You may have decided to skip an instruction, or do it in a different, less threatening way. You may have shied away from certain topics. If this is the case, you can invite your guide back. Have your guide take the part of your resistance. Explore your fears and reservations by asking your guide what they mean. The things about your disease that you are afraid or unwilling to face fully might be major obstacles to your recovery. Tell yourself, "I am willing to face facts. I want to understand."

The final step is to accept your disease and take responsibility for its existence. You can do this by visualizing the things you did or didn't do in the past that may have caused your disease. If you don't know what caused it, you can visualize yourself holding or embracing some symbol of your problem like a heart, a crutch, or a part of your body. Even if your problem is one for which you can find no cause in your own life, try telling yourself:

I accept and take responsibility for my disease. In some way I created my disease, and in some way I can remove or relieve it. However, my disease is not my fault. I don't blame myself for it. But for the sake of feeling more in control of my life, I am willing to take responsibility for my disease.

If this statement makes you feel more guilty or depressed than powerful and in control, omit it from your visualization.

End this receptive visualization when you are ready. You may need several sessions to get through all of these steps. And you may need to go back and repeat certain scenes over and over until you achieve your desired result. Keep in mind that the goal of this process is self-knowledge, not self-recrimination.

Affirmations

Make up an affirmation or two about each of the problem areas you encountered in the receptive visualization. For example, if you tend to feel guilty about being sick, you could say:

This is my time to be taken care of.

I am doing the best I can in the circumstances.

Guilt is a luxury I can do without.

If you find that being sick is providing you with some secondary gains such as relief from responsibilities or a chance to rest, counter with:

I can be healthy and still claim the rest I need.

When I'm better, I can make better decisions.

I can cope with _____ without being sick.

Compose affirmations to help you deal with the painful emotions surrounding your disease:

When I'm depressed, I get up and do something.

When I get angry, I remember that I am responsible.

I have the relaxation skills to cope with anxiety.

If you tend to make negative predictions to yourself about your recovery, compose some affirmations that put matters in a realistic, rational light:

Nobody dies from this.

My chances are better than fifty-fifty.

There are many pleasures I still enjoy.

Help yourself accomplish your daily goals with affirmations that underscore your ability to cope and take care of yourself:

I remember my priorities.

I take good care of myself.

I take one step at a time until things are done.

If you have uncovered some special meaning that your disease has for you, compose affirmations to remind you of those insights:

I'm an adult now. When I was sick before, I was only a child.

I deserve health, not sickness.

My father had his own body, I have mine.

In addition to these affirmations to counter specific problem areas or underscore insight, you'll need some specific self-statements that affirm your healing process and predict your recovery. Note that the predictions of recovery are put into the present tense:

I am getting better every day.
My body is healing itself.
I'm getting back into balance.
I am able to play tennis again.
I am completely well and whole.
I have a renewed zest for life.

Preparing for Programmed Visualization

The first part of your programmed visualization will consist of healing images, both metaphorical and literal.

You create a metaphorical image by assigning a color or shape or symbol to your disease, and then imagine change taking place. For instance, a weak kidney could be visualized as a pale blue triangle. Then you would change the triangle to a white circle, representing a strengthening of the kidney. Another example would be to imagine that your heart is actually a mechanical pump. You could see yourself taking the pump apart, replacing broken parts and damaged seals, then reassembling the pump and watching it work much more efficiently, without leaks.

The beauty of metaphorical images is that you don't have to understand the biological workings of your disease. Your body knows how to heal itself. All it needs is a clear message from your mind. The symbolic images of healing communicate your intention and your body does the rest. Metaphorical images are sometimes the only kind you can devise for diseases whose causes are unknown.

This isn't to say that you shouldn't learn all you can about your disease. By finding out how your disease is caused and how it goes away or stabilizes, you can create *literal* healing images as well as metaphorical ones. The literal images will occupy mostly your left brain, and the symbolic images will bring your right brain into play. For example, a literal image for halting emphysema would involve seeing the tiny sacs in your lungs fill with air, displacing fluid and softening hard tissue. The corresponding metaphorical image could be blowing up one of those long, skinny balloons that clowns twist into poodle dogs and bunnies.

Below is a list of some of the more common diseases, their causes, treatment, and suggestions for literal and metaphorical images. Even if your disease is not listed, you can read through this section and get a feel for the correct approach: (1) Learn about the causes, symptoms, and usual treatment of your disease. (2) Create literal images of natural healing based on the physiology of the disease. (3) Visualize your treatments as effective. (4) Create metaphorical or symbolic images to represent healing.

The more you find out about your disease, the better. Tell your doctor what you are trying to do with visualization and ask him or her to explain the workings of your disease in detail. Go to the library and read up on your disease in encyclopedias and medical texts.

Heart Disease

Hypertension. Normal blood pressure is around 120 over 80. The first number is the *systolic* pressure, the amount of pressure in your blood vessels when your heart is contracting and pumping blood out. The systolic pressure can vary considerably. The second figure is the *diastolic* pressure, the residual amount of pressure in your blood vessels as your heart is expanding and filling up. This is the minimum pressure your system is under all the time, and it doesn't vary as much.

Hypertension—too high pressure—usually results when the smooth muscles around your blood vessels contract slightly, narrowing your blood vessels. About ten percent of the time, hypertension results from a glandular imbalance, which is why correct diagnosis is important.

Chronic hypertension means that your heart has to work harder. The left ventricle enlarges and heart failure becomes a possibility.

Visualizing *anything* will lower your blood pressure, because the best treatment is relaxation. For a literal image, visualize the smooth muscles that encircle your blood vessels becoming larger in diameter. Use metaphorical images like a twisted rope untwisting, ice melting, or lights changing colors. To visualize your treatment working, see yourself taking your medication and imagine it going to your muscles and relaxing them. See yourself at your doctor's office having your pressure checked and it registering low.

Arteriosclerosis. Cholesterol is a substance in the blood that comes mostly from animal fats. Cholesterol forms plaques like small tiles of scar tissue. These stick to the sides of your arteries, especially in sharp forks or around old scar tissue from previous repairs. The plaques narrow and stiffen the arteries. As plaques decay and die, they rupture. Circulating blood tries to repair these ruptures by clotting. The clots can cause kidney degeneration, gangrene, or ulcers in the legs.

The most common area for plaque formation is in the left coronary (heart) artery. A clot here blocks blood flow to the ventricular muscles of your heart. They falter or "infarct." If the muscles don't start up again, death follows quickly. Even if they do start up again, the damaged muscles will be repaired with more scar tissue, which will attract more cholesterol plaques, and further impair function of the heart muscles.

The best treatment is prevention by using a low-fat diet to cut down on cholesterol and by doing aerobic exercises to strengthen your heart. Once an arteriosclerotic condition is diagnosed, you can take some medications that will thin your blood and help prevent clots.

When you visualize, use literal images of thin, clot-free blood moving easily through wide-open arteries. See the cholesterol plaques shrinking and dissolving away. Let the lining of your blood vessels become smooth and clean. For a metaphorical image, you can think of a Roto-Rooter truck driving all over your body, clearing out clogged pipes. Visualize your medication as helping in this process. Reinforce your dietary and exercise regimes by seeing yourself eating the right things and going out for walks.

Lung Disease

Chronic bronchitis and emphysema are the most common lung diseases. Initial symptoms are coughing, excessive mucus, and shortness of breath. Your airways are restricted by the excess mucus, by spasms in the smooth muscles encircling the airways, by fibrous tissue within the airways, or by mechanical blockages. Pneumonia can result because your lungs are especially susceptible to infections.

With emphysema, there is destruction of some of the *aveoli*, the tiny air sacs in which the exchange of carbon dioxide and oxygen in your blood takes place. When the aveoli burst, they form larger air pockets, with less surface area for gas exchange to take place. The lung tissue around these pockets becomes stiff and less compressible. This means that you cannot exhale fully. Your lungs become partly expanded all the time, reducing the amount of air you can get into your lungs with each breath.

Treatment is usually with drugs that dilate your bronchial tubes, such as corticosteroids. Smoking, dust, and polluted air make things much worse.

When visualizing, concentrate on images of less mucus, relaxation of your bronchial tubes, clearing obstructions, and softening of lung tissue. See the air as white, healing light flowing freely into and out of your lungs. The air dries up the mucus. See obstructions come loose and get coughed out. Imagine massaging your lungs, working out the stiff spots with your fingers. Visualize your medications working by enlarging and relaxing your airways. Picture yourself as a nonsmoker, breathing clear, pure air.

Skin Conditions

The most common skin problems are dermatitis, eczema, acne, and psoriasis. Their symptoms are similar, differing in location and severity: swelling, oozing, crusting, scaling, pain, itching, and sometimes secondary bacterial infection. Scratching the itch makes things worse. So does any kind of psychological stress.

Dermatitis and eczema are most likely allergic reactions, so treatment begins with avoiding the allergen. Acne is caused mainly by adolescent hormonal changes, and time is the only sure cure. Some symptom relief is offered by over-the-counter creams, antibiotics to clear up infections, sunlight in moderate amounts, and eliminating chocolate, nuts, and caffeine from your diet. The cause of psoriasis is unclear. Some psoriasis cases have been halted by prescribing the tranquilizer Valium, suggesting either a strong stress connection or an unexpected property of the drug itself. All skin conditions benefit from steroid creams to reduce inflammation and thus interrupt the itch-scratch-itch cycle.

When visualizing, start with images of your skin symptoms shrinking. Use metaphors like puddles drying up, sunlight shriveling up leaves, sandpaper or a plane smoothing wood, and so on. Picture sores drying up like mud puddles. Imagine breaking up crusts like hoeing dry ground. See yourself removing scales like old wood shingles off a barn roof. Watch your skin change colors from red to a healthy, normal color.

Visualize your treatment. Imagine smoothing on soothing cream that puts out the fire of itching. Tell yourself, "I'm healing my skin." Imagine the sunlight bathing and cleansing your skin.

Reinforce good skin-care practices. Tell yourself, "When I start itching, I reach for the steroid cream instead of scratching." See yourself wearing the soft, nonirritating clothes, avoiding stressful situations, and staying away from allergens.

Always end your visualization with a vision of the future: you are free of symptoms, with clear, glowing, vibrantly healthy skin all over your body.

Gastrointestinal Problems

Heartburn, hiatus hernia. Gastric juices reflux, or back up into the esophagus, creating the familiar burning pain. Traditional treatment includes taking antacids, avoiding stress and late evening meals, cutting out alcohol and caffeine, and sleeping with the head of your bed elevated. When visualizing, picture a strong industrial strength valve at the top of your stomach. Imagine yourself shutting off the valve firmly to keep the burning juices down where they belong. Visualize other little valves that dispense acid into your stomach. Close them all off tightly.

Ulcers. These are small, open sores in the lining of your stomach or duodenum, brought on and made worse by stress, irritated by stomach acid. Traditional treatments are about the same as for heartburn: antacids, lifestyle changes to reduce stress, and no alcohol or caffeine. The old regimen of bland diets and lots of milk has been shown to be ineffective. In fact, milk can make an ulcer worse. In severe cases, surgery may be the only way to provide relief.

The key to healing an ulcer with visualization is to perfect your relaxation skills. Stress, particularly the stress of anger, is a major factor in ulcers, and stress reduction is the only long-term solution. After you've learned to relax, spend some time with healing images. Picture your ulcer shrinking in on itself, being covered over with smooth, healthy tissue. Change the color from angry red to a healthy pinkish gray. Turn off all the little faucets in your stomach that can release irritating acid.

Diverticulitis. In this condition, finger-like pouches form off of the intestines—small dead ends. Digestive products usually flow into and out of these pouches, causing no problems. But the pouches can become packed with digestive products and unable to empty, causing swelling, possible infection, and pain. Cramps, nausea, and gas are common symptoms. Treatment includes a high fiber diet, exercise, and in some cases surgery.

To visualize your diverticulitis getting better, start with a literal image of little pouches full of hard, packed material. Imagine the material softening, any plugs loosening and coming out, and the material flowing harmlessly out of the pouches. See any inflammation returning to a pinkish gray. Follow with a metaphorical image of your digestive track as a long, winding dirt road. Off of this road are short *cul-de-sacs* choked with tangled brush. Imagine yourself wading into the brush with a machete and chopping it all out, clearing the *cul-de-sacs*.

Irritable bowel, colitis. In these conditions you have a lot of cramping, gas, and diarrhea. Your bowels tend to go into muscle spasms and are very sensitive to the slightest change in diet or increase in stress. It's important to have an accurate medical diagnosis, because similar symptoms can be caused by life-threatening diseases such as cancer of the colon. Pain killers, smooth muscle relaxers, and anti-diarrhea drugs can help to some extent. Relaxation exercises and avoiding food allergens are also recommended.

Focus your visualizations on literal images of the loops of intestine in your abdomen lying quiet and still. The only movement is the long, slow flex of normal peristalsis as it slowly squeezes digestive materials along. Metaphorical images are particularly effective: harsh colors changing to cool colors, calming an angry animal, rough seas becoming tranquil, or discordant music mellowing into pleasant melodies.

Diarrhea and constipation. Although opposite in effect, both of these symptoms can come from the same causes: stress, foreign bacteria, allergies, parasitic infection, diet changes, changes in the amount of exercise you get, and so on. Drugs can clear up bacterial or parasitic infections, and can offer short-term symptom relief. For long-term solutions, changes in diet and exercise are best. Getting plenty of dietary fiber and going for long walks are often the best medicine.

The images suggested above for irritable bowel and colitis should also work for diarrhea and constipation. The main theme is one of calm, peaceful regularity. Especially important is using visualization to reinforce your commitment to diet changes and exercise.

Kidney Stones

Kidney stones are actually crystals formed from chemicals in your urine. They run in families with a genetic predisposition for acidic urine, and they can also be caused by a kidney infection. You're more likely to develop kidney stones if you also have a thyroid disorder, consume a lot of milk or vitamin D, or have certain bone diseases.

Most kidney stones eventually pass from the kidneys into the bladder and out in the urine, causing incredible pain on the way. Treatment consists of keeping up a high volume of urine and sometimes taking drugs containing phosphorus to interfere with the formation of new crystals.

For visualization, imagine that the crystals in your urine are made of simple sugar or salt. See them dissolving and disappearing. Represent the acidic condition of your urine with a blue color, and change it to pink to represent a more alkaline condition. You should be drinking a big glass of water before going to bed, and getting up at least once in the night to take another glass of water. These are good times to do your visualization exercises as you fall asleep.

Hemorrhoids

Hemorrhoids are swollen veins in the anal region. They can be internal or external. The internal ones show up as blood in the stool. The external ones can be seen and are painful and itchy. Hemorrhoids can be brought on by pregnancy, straining at stool, chronic stress, liver disease, chronic diarrhea, infection, or irritation of the anus.

Traditional treatment is by hot baths, ointments or suppositories, stool softeners, and bed rest. Surgery is sometimes indicated to reduce serious hemorrhoids, especially the internal variety.

For a literal image, visualize the blue bulging veins shrinking back to normal size. See the blood flowing smoothly and evenly. Metaphorical images can include balloons losing air, reducing pressure in a hose, or playfully poking bulges back into your body. Spend extra time on the relaxation phase of your visualizations to counter the stress component of hemorrhoids.

Thyroid Conditions

Hypothyroidism. This means that your thyroid gland produces too little of the hormone thyroxin. Left untreated in infants, hypothyroidism causes the complex pattern of physical and mental retardation known as cretinism. Older children and adults can develop the condition. The symptoms are many, subtle, and open to misdiagnosis: puffy eyelids; rough, dry skin; dry, brittle hair; swollen tongue or throat; constipation; anemia; intolerance to cold; susceptibility to bruising; excessive menstrual bleeding; slow reflexes; fatigue; and trouble coping with stress.

Treatment is simply a matter of taking a drug containing thyroxin to supplement the output of your sluggish thyroid. Visualization can help in two ways. First, you should visualize your medication spreading throughout your body, stimulating and regulating your metabolism. Imagine thyroxin as a fuel additive that gives you more miles to the gallon, or a magic tonic that fills you with energy. Second, visualize your thyroid gland and see it producing and secreting more natural thyroxin. Imagine a tiny pump in your lower throat that pumps out a golder elixir. Create a speed control knob on the pump and turn it to a higher speed. In time you may be able to reduce or eliminate your daily dose of thyroxin. Be sure to have your hormone level checked periodically to make sure you're still at the right dosage.

Hyperthyroidism. This is the opposite problem—a thyroid that produces too much thyroxin hormone. Sometimes the thyroid becomes enlarged and a goiter is formed. Other symptoms are bulging eyes, tremor in fingers and tongue, anxiety, excessive sweating, diarrhea, increased appetite but with loss of weight, heat intolerance, uneven heartbeats, and sometimes nausea and vomiting.

This disease most often strikes people in their thirties or forties, and more women are affected than men. Emotional traumas seem to have a big role in bringing on the condition and making it worse. There are two approaches to treatment. The first is medication which chemically blocks the production of thyroxin. You have to take the medication regularly, and sometimes it doesn't prevent flare-ups of the disease. The second treatment approach is removal of some thyroid tissues, either by surgery or by taking radioactive iodine, which permanently impairs the thyroid's ability to produce thyroxin.

Before undergoing surgery or radioactive iodine treatments, it's worth trying to use visualization to calm your thyroid down. Use literal images of your thyroid gland shrinking and your eyes becoming less wide open and staring. Use metaphorical images of your gland as a pump that you can set to a slower speed. See the flow of thyroxin from the gland as a stream of water from a downspout in a storm. As the rain lightens and the sun comes out, the stream becomes a trickle and the trickle subsides to a slow drip.

Gout

Gout is a largely inherited disease that usually strikes people in their thirties and forties. It affects more men than women. Gout is caused by a metabolism that produces too much uric acid, by kidneys that don't eliminate enough uric acid, or by both. The uric acid forms sodium urate crystals in joints, cartilage, bones, and soft tissue, producing inflammation, deterioration, and lots of pain. The worst pain is often felt in the big toes. This pain is sometimes misdiagnosed as arthritic. A decline in kidney function and kidney stones often accompanies gout. The common belief that gout is caused by overindulgence in wine and rich food is not true, although eating certain fatty foods can make gout symptoms worse.

Traditional treatment is with drugs that stimulate your system to excrete uric acid. Visualization can supplement drug treatment with images of crystals dissolving, swelling going down, and uric acid leaving your body in the urine. Imagine a faucet somewhere in your brain that controls your body's output of uric acid. Turn it down to just a drip. Create a control in your kidneys that affects how much uric acid is excreted. Turn the control to "high." Use a color such as peach to represent a high level of uric acid and change it to another color like aqua to represent a lower acid level.

Epilepsy

Epilepsy is a disorder of the nervous system characterized by seizures: sudden, excessive, disorganized discharges of nerves in the brain. A few hours before a *grand mal* seizure, epileptics often experience apathy, depression, irritability, hyperalertness, elation, flatulence, constipation, headache, or twitching. Seconds before the seizure about half of them experience an "aura." The aura can include a strangling sensation, palpitations, numb fingers or lips, flashing lights, or unpleasant tastes and smells. As the *grand mal* seizure continues, the sufferer loses consciousness, falls down, and undergoes violent, full-body convulsions, often biting the cheeks or tongue. This type of epilepsy can strike anyone at any age, and seizures can come frequently or as seldom as once in a lifetime.

The other kind of epilepsy is *petit mal*. This is more common in children. The seizures last from two to fifteen seconds and cause a dimming of awareness and sometimes slight twitching. But the person experiencing the seizure can often continue walking or even riding a bicycle during the seizure. To observers, the seizure looks like "spacing out" for a moment.

Both kinds of seizures can be brought on by flickering lights, going from light to dark or vice-versa, strong emotions, eating a very large meal, or rubbing or injuring a certain part of the body.

The exact cause of epilepsy isn't known, but in many cases it can be well controlled by medications such as phenobarbital or phenytoin. Many epileptics can avert a seizure when they feel one coming on. Doing some familiar, repetitive mental task or physical activity seems to short-circuit the seizure. This is where visualization comes in.

Since epilepsy is an electrical disturbance in the brain, you might try visualizing a circuit breaker or a lightning rod in your head. Imagine that when the potential energy in your neurons reaches seizure levels, the circuit breaker pops off, cutting the circuit and letting the energy level drop back to normal. Or see the discharge that would normally cause a seizure going through the lightning rod, down through your body, and flowing harmlessly into the ground.

Practice *progressive muscle relaxation* and your images beforehand, so that you can use them immediately when you experience any of your common seizure-triggering situations or when you begin to feel aura sensations.

Instructions for Programmed Visualization

The four steps of this visualization are healing images, reinforcement of treatment, coping images, and images of future recovery.

Lie down, close your eyes, and relax. Let your attention drift to the part of your body affected by your disease. Start with the literal images of healing that you have researched and prepared. See the physiological processes of your disease going away—the chemical changes, the cellular changes, the mechanical alterations of tissue, the return of normal functions. Tell yourself, "My body knows how to heal itself."

Next move on to the metaphorical images you have prepared—the changing lights or colors, the imaginary mechanisms that explain how you are healing, the symbolic objects or persons or situations that represent your disease and its cure. Reinforce with an affirmation such as, "My imagination is a powerful healing force."

Now visualize whatever treatments you are receiving—drugs, surgery, exercises, applications of heat or cold, special foods, and so on. See the treatment having the desired effect. Remind yourself: "I'm getting excellent care. I'm taking care of myself."

Continue your visualization by looking to the future. See yourself as fully recovered. Watch and hear yourself loving your family and friends, playing favorite sports, traveling wherever you want, and accomplishing your goals unhampered by any disease. Remember to phrase your affirmations about the future in the present tense: "I am walking without pain. I can breathe freely again. I am fit and full of energy."

Finish your visualization with reinforcement scenes of yourself coping with the disease on a daily basis: sticking to your diet, remembering to take your medication, keeping your spirits up with meaningful activities, asking for the help you need, getting the shopping and cleaning done, managing responsibilities at work or school, and so on. Use affirmations such as "I take care of business. I can cope one step at a time."

Do your healing visualization once or twice a day. When the same old images and affirmations become "stale," make up some new ones.

What To Expect

Healing takes time. It probably took you years to arrive at a state where you became ill, and getting better may take a long time too. If you don't feel better right away, keep doing your visualization exercises. At the very least, they are relaxing and refreshing. Patience and persistence will bring results when your body is ready to get better.

Example

Harold was a forty-five-year old engineer who designed combustion systems for a furnace company. His doctor had been nagging him for five years to lose some weight and do something about his high blood pressure. But Harold was too busy and too "set in his ways" to make major lifestyle changes—until his heart attack.

It was a mild attack as they go, with little permanent damage to Harold's heart. But it was obviously time to take a look at his life and make some changes.

He started taking his hypertensive medications faithfully every day. He went on a low-fat, low-salt diet and started taking a long walk after dinner. He stopped accepting consulting jobs from other companies and kept strictly to thirty-five hours a week of work, giving him time to relax.

Harold started doing visualization under the guidance of his daughter in-law, who had her master's in social work and had a job teaching Simonton visualization techniques to cancer patients. She had Harold do nothing but relaxation visualizations the first week. He learned quickly to slow his breathing and pulse rate, and it became his favorite way to get to sleep at night.

Next, Harold started receptive visualizations. Very early on he developed a relationship with his inner guide, who took the form of his sister Susan, who had died at age three. In his imagination, she was a grown-up woman of thirty or forty, near the age she would have been if she had lived. Since Harold was a confirmed atheist, he was startled that his guide seemed to come to him "from beyond the grave," but he accepted it and came to enjoy his talks with the sister he never had.

From Susan, Harold learned that he secretly expected to die of a heart attack at age sixty-five, just like his father. He also discovered that he had a self-image as stuck in a rut of habits and unable to change. His affirmations therefore focused on his own individuality and the possibility of change: "I am my own person, not my father," and "I can change, I do change, I am changing right this minute."

Harold's programmed visualizations took the same general form each night before he fell asleep. First he created a literal image of his arteries, veins, and capillaries opening up wide to reduce his blood pressure. Then he would see his heart as a strong, powerful steam engine, steadily pumping away. He would imagine some of the white, cleansing steam coursing through his arteries, cleaning them of any cholesterol deposits. Then he would visualize his heart pills as little droplets of oil. The oil lubricated an elaborate system of pressure gauges, check valves, and feedback loops that kept the steam engine from building up too much pressure. His engineer's mind sometimes got sidetracked by working out ever more elegant pressure control designs.

Next, Harold would work on reinforcing any part of his regimen with which he was having trouble. Sometimes he would tell himself, "I am changing my eating style," and imagine eating a delicious salad for lunch. Other times, when he had been avoiding his nightly walk, he would create enticing sights and sounds of nature and remind himself, "I always love it when I get out in the park for a stroll." If he had a checkup in the near future, he would throw in a scene at the doctor's office: the feel of the pressure cuff as the nurse pumped it up, the silver column of mercury rising, and his doctor's pleased announcement that his pressure was back within the normal range.

Harold usually ended his visualization, if he wasn't too sleepy, by checking in with his inner guide, Susan. Sometimes he would just fall asleep with an image of her smiling face and a distinct sensation of her arm draped lovingly over his shoulder.

Six months after his heart attack, Harold was maintaining his blood pressure well within the normal range for a man his age. He was able to cut back on his medications, felt good, and was lighter and fitter than he had been before his attack. A year later he was on even less medication, still holding his weight down, and enjoying a new-found control over his health.

20

Infectious Diseases

"I would rather know what sort of person has a disease than what sort of disease a person has."

—*Hippocrates*

This chapter applies to any infectious disease or condition caused by a microscopic organism such as a bacteria, virus, fungus, or protozoa.

Microscopic life forms are the most common source of human disease. They cause colds, flu, athlete's foot, yeast infections, pneumonia, abscesses, strep throat, urinary tract infections, earaches, tuberculosis, warts, mononucleosis, dysentary, hepatitis, herpes, cold sores, syphilis, gonorrhea, pinkeye, skin and wound infections, and dozens more.

Infection can produce many varied symptoms: fever, chills, swollen lymph glands, nausea, cramps, vomiting, diarrhea, constipation, congestion, sore throat, cramps, itching, pus, redness, swelling, fatigue, weight loss, and so on. Often blood, urine, or stool samples must be tested to determine exactly what kind of infection you have and how it should be treated.

The only drugs that can halt bacterial infections are sulfa drugs and antibiotics. Other antimicrobial drugs are interferon for viruses, anti-fungal and anti-protagoal medications. These drugs work primarily by interfering with the reproductive cycle of the invading microorganisms. By keeping the invaders from multiplying, the drugs buy time for natural attrition and the action of your white blood cells to do the rest.

All the other drugs commonly used for infectious disorders are symptom-relievers rather than infection-killers. For example, aspirin reduces inflammation, relieves pain, and lowers fever. Decongestants dry up excess mucus. Expectorants and cough suppressants ease coughing. Steroid creams can relieve itching.

The most common non-drug treatment for infections is a surgical incision to drain pus from an abscess. This procedure has been used for centuries and actually works very well.

When you think you have an infection of some kind, your first priority should be accurate diagnosis. See a doctor to find out what you've got and what to do about it. Start whatever treatment is indicated. It's especially important to start antibiotics promptly and take them for the full recommended period, even if symptoms clear up before all the pills are gone.

Once you've identified your problem and started the appropriate treatment, then use visualization as an adjunctive treatment. Don't try to clear up a serious toothache or a bad case of strep throat by visualization alone when simple, safe, effective drugs are available.

The exception to this rule is that it sometimes makes sense to avoid purely symptom-controlling drugs. Give your body a chance to fight infection naturally. For example, the symptoms of a common cold are part of your body's strategy to defeat the cold virus. Suppressing your symptom with twelve-hour cold capsules and continuing a high-stress routine could make a cold last two weeks, when a mere two days of rest, fluids, and enduring the symptoms might have cleared it up.

Learning visualization techniques to fight infectious disease is time well spent. The basic images that work for colds and flu can be used also for hepatitis or removing warts. This is because the causes, courses, and cures of various infectious disorders are remarkably similar.

Receptive Visualization

Starting with a receptive visualization exercise accomplishes several goals:

1. You can explore and acknowledge your feelings about being sick.

2. You will uncover negative, catastrophic thoughts about being sick that can slow your recovery.

3. You'll have a chance to explore the personal meaning that this illness has for you, eliciting personal images of great healing power or suggesting particularly potent affirmations.

4. You can find out about any secondary gain involved in your sickness—the paradoxical, hidden benefits of being sick that make it harder to get well.

5. You will review what you need to get done in order to cope with your illness and cure yourself.

Instructions

You'll probably want to record these instructions.

Lie down, close your eyes, and relax. Let your awareness move quietly to the part of your body most affected by your illness. Imagine the shape and extent of this area. Fill it with your awareness like filling a vase with water or a wine glass with wine.

As you contemplate your illness, what feelings come up? Do you feel angry at the person who probably gave you the infection? Are you depressed because this is the third cold you've had so far this year? Are you worried that your symptoms will get worse, that you'll never get better? Are you afraid of missing too much work or flunking out? Do you feel guilty for taking off too much time or for having to be taken care of? Do you feel ashamed of an illness like mononucleosis or gonorrhea because of the social stigma? Are you embarrassed because you consider getting sick a weakness or a self-indulgence?

What meaning does your illness have for you? Who else in your family gets sick like this? How is being sick now like being sick when you were a child? How is it different? Is there some obvious psychosomatic connection between your symptoms and your emotional life? Did you get laryngitis the night before the school play and not have to go on? Or is your yeast infection preventing you from sleeping with that new boyfriend who doesn't seem quite right for you? Or does your cold mean that your body wants you to slow down, to stop overcommitting and overexerting yourself?

Imagine that your illness has a presence and a voice. You can listen to it and question it. If you want, you can even visualize the tiny bacteria or viruses themselves. Ask your illness:

Why are you here?

What do you mean to me?

How do you help me?

When will I get better?

What feelings do you represent?

How do I hold onto you?

Remain quiet, attentive, and nonjudgmental. Take whatever answers you get and don't think too hard about them right now.

Allow yourself to list all the good things you get out of being sick: a chance to rest, a way to avoid unpleasant people or tasks, a good reason to put off thinking about your life, a way to be taken care of and get lots of attention and sympathy. Don't beat yourself up about all this. Just notice the advantages, the secondary gains, the silver linings in the dark cloud of your illness.

Now let yourself feel the symptoms of your illness. Notice the thoughts that spring to your mind when you feel bad. Do you predict more suffering, even death? Do you think, "I'll be this way forever," or "I can't stand this"? If all you get when you try this is a single brief word or image, slow your mind down and tease out the full statement that lurks behind that word or image.

Next think over all the things you need to do to keep your life going and mobilize yourself to get better: doctor's appointments, babysitters, work, school, papers to write, taxes to figure out. Make a mental list of the important tasks you need to accomplish to cope with your illness.

Now go to your special place and meet with your inner guide. Ask your inner guide:

Why is my illness here?

What does it mean to me?

How does my illness help me?

When will I get better?

What feelings does my illness represent?

How do I hold onto being sick?

Compare the answers you get this time to the answers you got by asking your disease directly. You will probably get a little more information this time.

Your inner guide may have some advice for you, or a symbolic gift like a magic potion or a healing charm. Take whatever your guide has to offer in a spirit of humility and acceptance. Maintain an attitude of calm, accepting expectation.

Stay in your special place and look into a mirror there. Say to your reflection: "I take responsibility for my illness. I can remove it from my life. Although I am not to blame, I am responsible."

If you feel uncomfortable with this or any part of this visualization, explore your resistance. You may be shying away from exactly the information you need to achieve self-knowledge and a more profound degree of control over your health. If you have trouble with any part of this visualization, go back and try it again tomorrow and the next day.

End this visualization when you're ready. Get a pencil and a piece of paper and write down the ideas, negative thoughts, images, and other insights that came to you. Use these notes when composing your affirmations.

Affirmations

Compose several affirmations to use during your daily programmed visualizations. Remember that a good affirmation is short, simple, positive, in the present tense, and emotional rather than abstract in tone.

Here are some examples of affirmations that acknowledge feelings about illness and suggest ways to cope with them:

I can channel my anger toward getting better.

When I'm afraid, I do my relaxation meditation.

When I'm depressed, I play my guitar.

If you uncovered any negative, irrational predictions about your illness, counter them with affirmations like these:

Time heals all wounds. This illness will pass.

My chances are six to nine in favor of recovery.

I got sick by chance. Nobody is to blame.

Remind yourself of the personal meaning of your illness with affirmations such as:

I can rest without having to get sick.

I'm grown up now. I can ask Mom for help directly.

I deserve to treat myself well even when I'm healthy.

If there is some secondary gain that you need to circumvent, compose an affirmation to remind you of your strategy:

I can say no to my boss.

Graduate school can wait until I'm ready.

I can say what I really think and feel.

Reinforce your coping skills with affirmations that remind you to make lists, ask for help, conserve your energy, observe priorities, adopt reasonable expectations, and so on:

I stick to my list without going off on tangents.

It's all right to ask for help when I'm sick.

I accept my limitations and work within them.

I remember to take my medicine on time.

Finally, prepare some affirmations that refer directly to the healing process:

My white blood cells are big and strong.

I'm coming back into balance.

I can stay relaxed and let my body heal itself.

The streptomycin is wiping out bacteria by the millions.

Programmed Visualization

It's helpful to make yourself a tape of these instructions.

Lie down, close your eyes, and relax. Make sure you're deeply relaxed, down to the last fiber of the last little muscle. Your body heals fastest when you are completely relaxed. Tell yourself, "Relax and breathe in healing energy."

Move your attention to the area of your body that is under attack by infection. Form a literal image of the infecting bacteria, virus, protozoa, or whatever. These organisms often look like short sticks or rods. Or you can visualize small black circles, or tiny spheres with little feelers sticking out here and there. It's not necessary to form a perfectly accurate likeness, as long as the image you see is very vivid to you.

Now form an image of your white blood cells. Make them at least ten times larger than the infecting organisms. Imagine each of them as a big blob of gray, translucent jelly with little specks in it. In the larger blood and lymph vessels of your body, the white cells plump out into a spherical shape. But they can go wherever in your body they are needed by elongating to fit through narrow capillary vessels or flattening out and squeezing between individual tissue cells. Tell yourself, "My white blood cells are big and strong and smart."

There are lots of white cells. Visualize a vast army, constantly multiplying and growing even vaster. See many of the cells releasing antibodies—molecules that float around like a cloud of dust particles. Some of the antibodies soak up and neutralize the poisons produced by bacteria. Other antibodies coat bacteria to attract phagocytes—killer white blood cells that wrap themselves around the bacteria, engulf them, and digest them. Visualize this process over and over. Tell yourself, "My body has a vast army on its side. My healing powers are invincible."

Extend the battle metaphor by visualizing the various kinds of white cells: sentries and scouts who find invaders and summon other cells to the attack, spotters who mark victims for attack, destroyers who engulf or break up invaders, referees who call off the attack when it's successful, medics who clean up microbial debris, and remembers who will know the invader again if it returns. Tell yourself, "My immune system is a smoothly operating team."

If you don't like military images, see your white cells as dogs or fish that cruise around your body eating bacterial-like worms or hamburger. Or imagine that your white cells are vacuum cleaners that suck up dirt in all the rooms of your body.

Make up symbolic ways to remove localized infections. For example, hepatitis is a viral infection of the liver. You could visualize your liver as a room with soot-blackened walls. Get in there and wipe them down with a big, soapy sponge. Rinse the sponge in a bucket of clear water. When the water gets dirty, dump it out into your kidneys or out a window. Get clean water. Keep it up until the inside of your liver is shiny red and clean. Tell yourself, "I'm mopping up the infection, I'm cleaning the temple of my body."

Use colors. Imagine your infection as a hot red cloud filling your body. As you breathe in, imagine inhaling white, healing mist that displaces the red cloud. As you exhale, imagine the red cloud leaving, cooling and growing pink. Continue breathing in white and out red until you are filled with pure white vapor, free of any tint of red. Try using a mantra with each breath: say "one" or "peace" or any word you choose as you exhale.

Use sound. Imagine your illness as a loud grumbling coming from deep within you. Turn down the grumbling sound until you can't hear it anymore. Gradually turn up the sound of violins, representing a return to health. Hum softly along with the music.

Next visualize any treatment that you're undergoing. See it working the way it's supposed to. If you're taking antibiotics, see the drug as a glue that hardens around the invading bacteria and prevents them from dividing in half and multiplying. If you had an abscess that was drained, imagine that your white blood cells can now get into the infected area and clean out the bacteria. Remind yourself: "I'm giving myself the best treatment. It's working at every moment."

If you're taking drugs to reduce fever or congestion, create images that show the drugs are working. Imagine aspirin as ice that cools your hot forehead, or decongestants as blotters that soak up excess fluid from your dripping sinuses. Imagine that chicken soup or orange juice is a wonder drug, a panacea that can cure anything. Use affirmations like "The flu bug doesn't stand a chance."

Work on your symptoms directly. Use a big paintbrush to coat your sore throat with a cooling, ice-blue anesthetic that tastes of peppermint. Imagine twisted ropes relaxing as the soreness in your flu-riddled joints dissipates. Relieve your chills by warming yourself before a roaring bonfire and pulling a thick, woolly buffalo robe around your shoulders. Poke holes in an imaginary water balloon to make your swelling go down. Tell yourself, "I can make myself feel better."

Try visualizing your symptoms as your body's way of fighting infection. For example, fever enables your body to produce more interferon, an antiviral substance. Fever also increases white blood cell mobility and activity. Visualize the interferon as a poison cloud smothering the viruses. Watch your white blood cells speed up as the temperature rises.

Almost any symptom you can think of has a role in your recovery. Fatigue is your body's way of telling you to rest so that it can devote energy to healing—imagine shutting off the power supply to your brain and muscles while turning up the power going to your bone marrow and lymph system. Chills tell you to get under the covers—see yourself canceling all appointments and taking to your bed. Sneezing expels invaders—watch them getting the bums' rush. Coughing clears congestion—imagine a bulldozer pushing muck out of your chest. Remind yourself, "I accept and welcome my symptoms."

Homeopathic medicine is a complete, alternative system of healing based largely on the idea that symptoms are your body's way of healing itself. Another principal of homeopathy is that the ideal drug is a very small amount of a substance that will create or intensify the exact symptom you are experiencing. If you are taking homeopathic microdoses, visualize them as intensifying and encouraging your symptoms. See your homeopathic remedies as little pushes to a giant flywheel that is gathering speed within you. The flywheel is part of a biological gyroscope, your body's natural mechanism for throwing off infection and returning to center. Tell yourself, "My body is restoring its balance."

Be sure to spend time on images of yourself in the future, fully recovered and feeling good. See yourself smiling, hugging your loved ones, going off to work with a light step, painting pictures, sailing your boat, bowling at the top of your form, eating linguini at your favorite restaurant, or doing whatever represents the good, healthy life to you. Use a present tense affirmation such as "I'm feeling all better now."

Include scenes in which you are still sick, but coping well: getting the rest you need, taking your medicine, arranging for others to help you, making phone calls and appointments, practicing visualization regularly, accomplishing the absolutely essential tasks of housekeeping, shopping, your job, your studies, childcare, and so on. Tell yourself, "I'm taking good care of myself. I'm keeping my life together."

End the visualization when you're ready. This is a long session, so you won't cover all the bases completely the first time through. Emphasize a different area each time you visualize: literal healing images, metaphorical images, coping skills, refuting negative thoughts, and so on.

Practice your healing visualization at least twice a day. Three or four times is better. If you're very sick, you should have plenty of time to practice while you're resting in bed.

What To Expect

First of all, have patience. An infection often must run its course, getting worse before it can get better. It takes time for your immune system to crank up to high gear, especially if high stress runs you down.

Ask your doctor how your illness works. Ask what the invading microorganism looks like under the microscope, where it concentrates in your body, how it affects your body, and so on. Ask how your prescription works to fight the infection. If you're reluctant to quiz a busy doctor, go to the library and look in medical textbooks or the encyclopedia. The *Physicians' Desk Reference* is the place to look up any drugs you are taking. This kind of information is valuable for forming vivid images of the healing process. Also, you will inevitably get bored with doing the same visualization over and over. Gathering more information is a way to create new, more interesting images. The example in the next section shows how learning more about your disease can heighten the healing power of visualization.

Keep doing your healing visualizations once a day for at least a week *after* you are free of symptoms. Your symptoms may disappear, but there can still be a significant population of bacteria or virus ready to multiply and cause a relapse. This is why it's also important to take the full course of an antibiotic treatment: to make sure all the invaders are eliminated, especially the last survivors that may have a degree of natural immunity to the antibiotic.

As powerful as visualization is for helping cure infections, it is even more powerful as a preventive measure. Use visualization regularly for relaxation and throw in images of high energy, interest in life, good diet, enjoyable exercise, and so on. Reinforce the lifestyle changes you need to make to stay healthy.

Example

Pete was a thirty-year-old English teacher with herpes. He caught it from his wife, Judy, when they were courting. He had a pretty minor case, but recently he had been having a lot more outbreaks of the disease than usual. He was under a lot of stress because he was trying to get tenure at the university where he worked.

Since there is no known cure for herpes, Pete looked to visualization as a way to control the symptoms. First he did a series of receptive visualizations in which he explored his feelings about herpes, analyzed his negative thoughts, considered what herpes really meant to him, examined ways he used herpes to his advantage, and looked honestly at his lifestyle as a possible cause of his recent severe outbreaks.

After each receptive visualization, Pete wrote the results in his journal. Here are some of his entries:

Feelings: I very rarely feel resentful of Judy for giving me this disease. Mostly I rant and rave against fate—"It's not fair! Why me? Why Judy? Why us?"

Irrational thinking: I often feel sad because I automatically assume that I'll never go to bed with any woman but Judy, even if we get divorced or she dies. I know this is not true, but the thought intrudes at odd moments: "Never again . . . not her . . . nobody."

Secret meanings: Silas *(his inner guide, a taciturn old Yankee farmer)* said, "That virus is your friend. It tells you to take things easy. Keeps you humble." I take this to mean that when I start feeling like a herpes sore is developing, it's a fair warning that I'm too stressed out, that it's time to relax.

Secondary gain: I use herpes to avoid telling the truth. Half the time when we can't make love because I have an active sore on my penis, I'm secretly glad. I don't want to make love anyway. If I was turned on and really missed being able to make love, I'd take better care of myself so that the sore would heal faster. Or when it was nearly gone, I'd use a condom.

Another common ploy—staying home from parties or ducking out of chores I've promised to do because I'm "too wiped out by the herpes—gotta take it easy." Truth is, I don't want to go to Peggy's party or fix the backdoor lock.

The truthful, healthy way to handle things would be to use visualization and relaxation to prevent or ameliorate herpes attacks. Then I could communicate honestly and directly about sex and what I really feel like doing.

Coping, lifestyle: I'm good at balancing a hundred projects and accomplishing a lot. But that lifestyle means I'm going to get more herpes attacks. I need to make fewer plans and give myself more time if I'm really serious about living free of herpes symptoms.

In another part of his journal, Pete composed affirmations based on his insights during receptive visualization. Here are some of his favorites:

Life's not fair.
Forget the "F" word.
Life is full of possibilities.

Herpes is my friend.

Herpes gives fair warning.

Tell the truth.

I create my herpes, so I can control it.

It's up to me.

Time to relax.

Keep the virus locked up tight.

Pete's inner guide also told him to "do your homework." Being an academic, Pete took this to heart and went to the med school library on campus to study up on herpes. He found that there are two kinds of herpes virus: herpes zoster and herpes simplex.

Herpes zoster causes shingles, a scaly, itchy skin condition usually on the trunk area. Pete didn't have shingles, so he read on.

Herpes simplex comes in two types. Type one causes cold sores or fever blisters on the mouth or face. This wasn't Pete's problem either, so he skipped ahead to type two. Type two is sexually transmitted and causes lesions, usually on the genitals. This was the kind that Pete had, so he started taking notes.

Type two herpes simplex virus enters the body during sex. There has to be contact between mucus membranes, and the infecting partner has to be in an active stage of the disease—has to be "shedding virus" into his or her bloodstream. The initial or primary infection causes the most severe symptoms. Pete remembered having a fever and large blisters on his penis.

No drug has been found to eradicate herpes virus because of the way it "hides out" in the body. After the initial attack, the virus stops reproducing and migrates along the nerves from the genitals up to the spinal chord. There the virus encapsulates itself in a sort of cyst and becomes inactive. Drugs and your white blood cells can't get at the virus.

Pete read a summary of studies by psychologist Ted Grossbart of Beth Israel Hospital and Harvard Medical School. Grossbart studied the role of stress in herpes outbreaks. He found that stress seems to "wake up" the dormant herpes virus. Stress can take the form of just being very tired, strong emotions, fever, menstruation, sunburn or windburn, excessive friction while making love, and so on. When herpes flares up for no apparent reason, there is probably some stressor that you aren't aware of causing a decline in your immune system.

When the virus wakes up, it starts reproducing and breaks out of the cyst. It migrates back down the nerves from the spinal chord to the genitals. That's why sores tend to appear in the same place time after time. Sometimes the virus takes a slightly different route and shows up somewhere else.

Pete found that his outbreaks were pretty typical. He would get a cluster of tiny, clear blisters, which would break in a day or two, forming little open sores. The sores soon scabbed over and healed like normal abrasions.

Most herpes sufferers experience a *prodrome* several hours or a day before the actual appearance of the lesions. Pete's prodromal symptoms included tenderness and warmth at the tip of his penis, numbness along his inner thigh, an ache in his lower back, and burning when urinating.

As Pete read more, he got very excited. He learned that at any time during the awakening and migration of the virus, it can stop multiplying, reverse direction, return to the spinal chord, and go dormant again. This meant that as soon as he felt the prodrome start, he could begin relaxation exercises, get lots of rest, and visualize the virus reversing direction. He hoped to prevent outbreaks or at least make them less severe—one blister instead of five, or blisters that broke and healed quickly.

Over several months, Pete completed his research and experimented with different images and metaphors for his anti-herpes visualizations. Here are the three that worked the best:

Hobbitland.   He envisioned the middle of his body to be Middle Earth, as in the writings of J. R. R. Tolkien. The cyst where the dormant virus slept was a cave in the hills, sealed with a huge boulder. The nerve pathways from his spine to his groin were dusty country roads. His genitals were a seacoast fortress where Gandalf the Good dwelt.

But Gandalf gets word that the forces of evil are on the way. He puts on his ring of power and strikes the ground with his magic staff. A wave of goodness and peace spreads out over Middle Earth, quelling the fear and warming the countryside like the warm sun. In other words, Pete does his relaxation exercises and stops staying up till two in the morning reading term papers.

The virus dwarfs slow down. They drop their sacks and yawn. The ones who started off first and are farthest down the road just drop in their tracks, fall asleep, and fade away. The fresher viruses, closer to the spine, turn around and trudge back. They all file into the cave, pull the boulder in after them, and go to sleep.

The Windlass.   Pete imagines a huge windlass set on the top of a cliff. It's like a giant fishing reel, with hundreds of fishing lines wound up around the drum. The herpes viruses are little lead sinkers tied to the ends of all the lines. When an outbreak starts, a big cog on the side of the windlass is released and the drum starts to unwind slowly. The lead weights start sinking down the cliff, toward Pete's genitals far below.

Pete imagines walking up to the windlass and knocking the cog back down, so that it engages a ratcheted gear and stops the windlass. Then he flips a switch and a motor starts winding the lines back in. When the weights are all back at the top, the motor will turn off automatically. Sometimes Pete goes back later with chains and padlocks to further immobilize the windlass.

Beepers.   This one is similar to the dwarfs setting off on the dusty road, but the attackers become a lot of smartly dressed men and women equipped with electronic beepers. They jump into their BMW's and Mercedes and set off down the road, going to the genitals for a big meeting.

Before they get to his genitals, Pete makes their beepers go off. They use their car phones to call up the home office at his spinal chord. They are told that the meeting has been cancelled and that they must return to the office at once.

The virus drivers all make U-turns and speed back to the high-rise office. They park in a deep underground garage. As soon as they turn off their engines, they freeze in their seats, as if they were robots and had turned themselves off. Pete closes big garage gates and locks them tight.

These three detailed scenes formed the heart of Pete's healing visualizations. He also used his affirmations in creative ways. He was in the habit of using 3 X 5 cards for bookmarks. He'd write "T.T.T." or "T.T.R." on his bookmarks to remind himself to "Tell the Truth" or that it was "Time to Relax."

Within a year of starting his visualization program, Pete cut the number of his attacks in half. Now that he has won tenure, reduced his crazy workload, and joined a health club, he only has one or two attacks a year. His sores used to hang on for eighteen days. Now he can usually clear up a sore in a week.

21

Immune System Disorders

"Depression is a partial surrender to death, and it seems that cancer is despair experienced at the cellular level."

—*Arnold Hutschnecker*

The major components of your immune system are your bone marrow, spleen, thymus gland, and lymph nodes. They communicate with each other and with your brain by chemical and electrical messages. Together, they are responsible for protecting you from outside threats like bacteria or viruses, and inside threats such as cancer cells.

The active agents of your immune system are various kinds of white blood cells. They travel throughout your body in the blood and lymph systems, looking for anything that doesn't belong. When they find some abnormal cells, for instance, they attack these alien cells, engulf them, break them down, and carry the remains off to be eliminated in the urine and stool. Sometimes instead of killing abnormal cells they wall them off from the rest of the body so that the abnormal cells can't spread. Either way, the white blood cells preserve healthy, normal tissue, and eliminate everything else.

It's a lot more complicated than that, of course. There are helper cells and killer cells and cells that engulf bacteria, and messenger cells, and antigens and antibodies, and all sorts of complex chemical interactions right down to the molecular level. But for the purposes of visualization, you don't have to be an immunologist. You just need to create a few key images ages of the most basic processes.

Your immune system reacts both to stimuli from the outside and to internal conditions in your body. It can get out of balance by either underreacting or overreacting. The chart below shows the four basic ways your immune system can get out of balance and allow you to get sick.

Stimuli	Possible Immune System Reactions		
Outside antigens	*Under-reaction*	*Effective reaction*	*Over-reaction*
Bacteria, viruses	Infection, disease	Health	—
Pollen, mold, dust, chemicals, etc.	—	Health	Allergy
Inside antigens			
Cancer cells	Cancer	Health	—
Normal cells or cell products, e.g., cartilage	—	Health	Arthritis

When your immune system underreacts to bacteria or virus, you get an infection or some kind of infectious disease like measles or the flu. These common kinds of problems are covered in the previous chapter.

When your immune system underreacts to your own abnormal body cells, those cells can grow and spread in the form of cancerous tumors. When your immune system overreacts to relatively harmless substances from the outside like pollen, cat hair, or bee venom, the result is allergies, asthma, or even anaphylactic shock. When your immune system overreacts by attacking your own normal, healthy body cells, you get degenerative conditions like arthritis or lupus.

The immune disorders covered in this chapter are cancer, arthritis, and allergies. These common problems represent the three ways in which your autoimmune system can get out of balance.

CANCER

Cancer starts as a single abnormal cell in your body. It can be almost any type of body cell: in your lungs, skin, colon, stomach, bone, breast, and so on. If your immune system fails to detect and destroy the abnormal cell, the cell divides in half to form two abnormal cells. These each grow and divide to make four cells. Four become eight, and so on. If the abnormal cells aren't destroyed by your immune system, they eventually form a tumor—a mass of abnormal cells. The tumor stimulates the tissue around it to develop new blood vessels. The increased blood supply nourishes the tumor and it grows faster.

The tumor begins to press upon, starve, and impede the function of the normal cells around it, sometimes creating symptoms such as pain, dizziness, shortness of breath, coughing, confusion, fatigue, and so on. Another stage of cancer is *metastasis*, in which the cancer spreads by the tumor growing into other parts of your body or by cancerous cells breaking off from the tumor and being carried in the bloodstream to other parts of your body and "taking root" there.

Actually, abnormal cells often form in your body. Your white blood cells encounter them all the time, recognize them as abnormal, engulf and destroy them, and carry off the pieces to be flushed away in stool and urine. "Spontaneous remission" of cancerous cells and even small tumors takes place routinely, without your conscious awareness. Cancer cells are actually weak and disorganized compared to healthy, normal body cells, and your white blood cells have little trouble keeping the upper hand.

Why then do people get cancer?

Causes of Cancer

Several factors can cause your body to produce more abnormal cells than someone else: radiation, certain viruses, a genetic flaw or predisposition inherited from your ancestors, or carcinogenic substances like asbestos, tars in cigarettes, or chemical pollutants.

You can thoroughly frighten and depress yourself by listing all the known carcinogens in our water, land, food, and air. You might begin to wonder why everybody doesn't get cancer. But in fact, relatively few people develop cancer. Most people's immune systems are healthy enough to prevent the growth of tumors.

Research and observations by Lawrence LeShan, Carl Simonton, Stephanie Matthews-Simonton, Jeanne Achterberg, Lydia Temoshok, and many others have shown repeatedly that a key factor in the cause of cancer is emotional in nature. The immune system apparently weakens due to some combination of the following factors.

Low self-esteem. You're at a greater risk for cancer if you have certain characteristics associated with low self-esteem. An emotionally bleak or abused childhood followed by a life with few meaningful, long-term relationships is an especially deadly combination. Low self-esteem often means that you will lack confidence, cope poorly with stressful situations, tend to blame yourself for every misfortune, and find it difficult to ask others for help—all serious impediments to preventing or recovering from cancer.

Recent personal loss. Most people with cancer report having experienced a major personal loss six to eighteen months prior to their diagnosis. They have lost a spouse or other family member through death or separation. They have lost a job, changed jobs, or retired. They have given up or failed to reach an important life goal. They have suffered a catastrophic financial reversal or a betrayal by someone they trusted.

Negative emotions. Everyone gets angry or sad once in a while. The healthy process is to recognize, express, and let go of negative emotions, putting them behind you. People who get cancer and don't recover from it often have trouble with this process. They want to be in control all the time. They have a lot of unexpressed hostility or repressed sadness. They often appear passive and quite "nice" on the surface, but underneath they are seething with resentment over past wrongs, steeping in self-pity, or broiling on the rack of their own martyrdom as they try to take care of everybody but themselves.

The exact mechanism of how these emotional factors lead to cancer isn't known. It obviously has something to do with stress, since many studies have shown that physical and emotional stress weakens the immune system. Somehow a chronic pattern of high stress and inadequate coping skills, topped off by a major personal loss, creates changes in the limbic system and the function of your hypothalamus and pituitary glands. This leads to a greater susceptibility to carcinogens and suppression of your immune reaction. The number of abnormal cells forming in your body increases, and with insufficient response from your white blood cells, a cancerous tumor is allowed to develop.

Medical Treatments

Standard medical treatments for cancer include surgery, radiation, and chemotherapy.

Surgery often works very well by physically removing tumors before they can metastasize to other parts of the body. The surgeon essentially performs your white blood cells' task by removing the abnormal cells *en masse*.

Radiation therapy is often used instead of or in conjunction with surgery. Radiation is a shower of tiny particles of energy that travel very fast and can penetrate flesh and bone. These particles drill microscopic holes through normal cells and cancer cells alike. The radiation is especially harmful to cells that, like tumor cells, are rapidly dividing. It cross-links the DNA of dividing cells, resulting in the cells' death. Your normal, healthy cells are usually dividing much less rapidly than tumor cells, and so they escape radiation damage. Cancer cells are much weaker, less able to heal themselves, and more likely to be in a vulnerable stage of division, and so they die by the thousands.

Chemotherapy works in a similar way. The drugs are actually poison chemicals that attack normal and cancer cells alike. Rapidly dividing cells are especially vulnerable. Your normal cells are strong and few of them will be dividing at any given time, so they can resist the poisonous effects. The cancer cells are likely to be in a vulnerable stage of division and are too weak to resist, so again they die in far greater numbers.

These traditional treatments have two limitations. First of all, they have many undesirable side effects. Surgery is a shock to your already compromised system. Radiation and chemotherapy can lead to loss of appetite, fatigue, pain, nausea, hair loss, and so on. The second limitation is that traditional treatments work by removing or attacking the cancer, not by enhancing your immune system's natural ability to destroy and remove abnormal cells.

That's where visualization comes in. It can do the other half of the job by stimulating your immune system, counteracting the negative emotional factors in your disease, and ameliorating the side effects of traditional treatments while maximizing their cancer-destroying action.

Note that I said visualization does *half* the job. It's not a replacement for surgery, radiation, or chemotherapy. It's an adjunct, something to use in addition to the treatments suggested by your doctor. When you have cancer, you need all the help you can get from *both* traditional medicine and alternative healing practices.

Use of Imagery by Oncologists

Oncologists are medical doctors who specialize in treating cancer. In the late sixties, O. Carl Simonton was a radiation oncologist working at the Travis Air Force Base Hospital. His wife, Stephanie Matthews-Simonton, was an expert in the motivation of business people. He was trying to figure out why some seriously ill cancer patients died while others with exactly the same kind of cancer, receiving exactly the same treatment, got better against all odds. He rejected the usual explanation of "spontaneous remission" as just a fancy way of saying, "We don't know why they get better."

The Simontons noticed that the survivors shared certain personality traits and attitudes that seemed to make all the difference. In search of ways to foster similar personality traits and attitudes in other patients, they studied techniques from meditation, encounter therapy, imagery, Silva Mind Control, positive thinking, mind dynamics, and biofeedback. The "active ingredient" of all the promising approaches they investigated was visualization.

Their first success was a big one. A sixty-year-old man with a "hopeless" case of throat cancer was coached in imagery techniques. Within two months, he had eliminated not only his cancer, but also his arthritic symptoms and chronic impotence. The Simontons knew they were on to something good.

Eventually the Simontons founded their Cancer Recovery Center in Fort Worth, Texas. They worked with "incurable" cancer patients who had been given a year of less to live. Typically, their patients would come to work with them three or four times a year, for a week at a time. On the first visit, patients would be accompanied by their spouse or closest family member, since the Simontons have determined that family support is crucial to success. Most of their patients lived much longer than their allotted year, and some achieved outright remission of their cancers.

The Simonton's techniques have been adopted and expanded by other cancer experts such as Jeanne Achterberg in the Dallas area and Bernie Segal, a surgeon in Connecticut who founded a group called "Exceptional Cancer Patients."

If you have cancer, look in the last chapter of this book and make a note of the books by the Simontons, Achterberg, and Segal. Reading them should be a part of your treatment program.

Steps to Recovery

This series of steps is based on the experiences of the Simontons and others who have helped thousands of people with cancer. They combine all the proven, effective strategies you should adopt to supplement traditional treatment and speed your recovery.

Identify and Accept Your Stress Triggers

Sit down right now and make out a list of the five most stressful aspects of your life prior to the diagnosis of your cancer. In the eighteen months before you found out you had cancer, what outside events or internal conflicts did you experience? What happened that represented a major loss to you and could have helped trigger you disease?

_____

_____

_____

_____

_____

Once you have identified your stress triggers, think about how you coped or failed to cope with them. Did you ignore your own needs in the struggle to take care of somebody else? If a loved one died, did you bottle up your grief and try not to show your emotions? Did you seek support when you needed it? If you were laid off or retired from a job that gave shape and focus to your life, did you slip into depression and find yourself unable to find meaning in other tasks?

Recovery requires that you begin finding a way to accept your losses. By this I mean several things. First, accept that who or whatever you lost is gone, leaving you to carry on with your life. Second, accept that your loss and your cancer are connected, that your emotional reaction to loss weakened your immune system so that cancer could gain a foothold.

Finally, accept the responsibility for your cancer. This doesn't mean you should _blame_ yourself for getting cancer. It means that you should recognize how you _participated_ in the process that led to your cancer. You should recognize that your mental state—the images and thoughts and feelings that habitually filled your mind—played a part in suppressing your immune system. Because if you understood that, you can recognize that the images and thoughts and feelings you entertain from this moment onward will also be a powerful force for your _recovery_ from cancer.

This can be a very difficult, confusing step if you're not used to thinking about your life in terms of emotional causes and consequences. It may be a good idea to seek assistance from a therapist or other counselor with experience in helping people cope with cancer or other serious illnesses.

Identify, Accept, and Outsmart Secondary Gain

Secondary gain means the good things you get out of a bad situation. Having cancer is a very bad thing indeed, but there are still many possible secondary gains:

Avoidance of a distasteful job or person

Reduction of demands placed on you by others

A chance for a rest

Postponing difficult decisions

You can quit a project that's headed for failure

Attention from others

People consider your needs first for a change

Sympathy

Puts all other, lesser problems in perspective

A good excuse to say no to people

Right now, list at least five secondary benefits that come from being ill:

_____

_____

_____

_____

Now that you have identified your secondary gains, you should work at accepting them as legitimate needs. You have a *right* to some rest, to say no, to get out of unpleasant situations, to avoid people or jobs you don't like. These are legitimate needs, and as long as your cancer helps you meet them, you will find it that much harder to recover from your cancer.

You need to outsmart your secondary gains by finding ways that don't depend on illness to fill your legitimate needs. This can be as simple as making a resolution: "When I get better, I'm not going back to that job." Or you may have to learn and practice some assertive skills like tuning in to your own desires first before you automatically say yes to people. Visualization and affirmations can help here. Right now, make up an affirmation for each of your secondary gains which acknowledges your legitimate need and states how you will get them met. Here are some examples:

I take time for the rest I need.

I can say no to my boss when I'm too busy.

My health is more important than the opinions of others.

Life and health first; details and worries second.

I can ask for what I want.

I love myself and take care of myself.

Set Goals

Doctors and nurses in oncology wards often report that the most remarkable cancer remissions are achieved by people who feel they have important unfinished business to take care of. Many seriously ill people whose doctors offered no hope have survived because they wanted to see their kids get married or finish writing a play or live to meet their great-grandchildren or visit Paris in the springtime.

Studies have also shown that the worst way to recover from cancer is to lie around in a hospital bed or mope around the house. Getting back to normal pursuits as soon as possible, to the fullest degree possible, is a lifesaver.

If you give up your old goals and don't set any new ones, you are silently saying to yourself that you don't expect to live. When you set even the most modest goal, like getting your downspouts cleaned, you imply that you expect to be alive this winter. Goal-setting affirms your ability to meet your needs and bolsters your self-image. It is also a practical way to establish priorities so that you can focus your diminished energy on what is really important to you.

Take a moment right now to list at least five goals that you want to accomplish within the next year. Include a material goal, an educational or job-related goal, a social goal having to do with your relationships, an emotional or health goal, and a spiritual goal.

_____

_____

_____

_____

_____

If you have trouble thinking of specific goals, see the chapter on goal-setting for detailed help. It's full of examples and guidelines to help you every step of the way.

Be sure to make up a couple of affirmations to remind you of your goals and your commitment to them. Here are a few examples:

I have unfinished business on this planet.

I'm getting my M.A. by the end of next year.

I take one step toward my goal every day.
I live to see Janie's child.

Correct Negative Assumptions

In our culture, cancer is often seen as a monster, a sure killer, a death sentence. It just isn't so. In *Getting Well Again*, the Simontons identify three common, incorrect assumptions about cancer, and suggest three positive facts to refute them:

Incorrect Assumption	Fact
1. Cancer equals death.	1. Cancer may or may not be fatal.
2. Cancer strikes from without and there's no hope of controlling it.	2. However caused, cancer's mortal enemy is your body's natural defense system.
3. Medical treatment is drastic and ineffective, with bad side effects.	3. Medical treatment is an important ally in support of your body's defenses.

These facts suggest some important affirmations that you should paraphrase and include in your visualizations:

I am surviving this.
I am getting better.
My natural defenses are getting stronger.
The radiation is my ally, my weapon.
Chemotherapy is a strong helping hand.

Get Support

This is the time to let your family and friends take care of you. Line up all the support you can: somebody to talk to, somebody to go to tests and treatments with you, somebody to have breakfast and lunch and dinner with, somebody to phone at two a.m. when you can't sleep, somebody to help you clean your house or plant the garden, somebody to watch your kids or feed your cat. Resist the temptation to isolate yourself. Carry your address book with you at all times, and have someone in mind that you can call at any time when you need to talk or visit or can go out to breakfast with.

Overcome Resentment

In the visualization that follows you will have an opportunity to relive scenes from the past in which people hurt you, took something from you, or received something you felt you should have received. These sources of resentment are in the past and there's nothing you can do about them. To increase your chances of recovery, you will practice letting go of the past, releasing yourself from the tyranny of resentment and old patterns of anger. This will open up space in your mind for images of healing and recovery that you so vitally need right now, in the present.

You will need an anti-resentment affirmation. For example:

I let go of the past.

I want only good things for all people.

Resentment kills, compassion saves.

_____ *is not to blame.*

I do the best I can, and so does everybody else.

Perfect Your Relaxation Skills

One of the most important uses of visualization when you have cancer is to help you relax. Relaxation eases any pain or discomfort you might be feeling. It is a buffer against worry. Relaxation sends a message to your body that everything is OK and provides the optimum state for the functioning of your immune system. Anxiety and fear trigger your adrenal glands to produce high levels of steroid hormones, which decrease the effectiveness of your immune system by killing white blood cells. When you are relaxed, your brain emits alpha waves and endorphins which activate or enhance your immune system.

Spend extra time before each visualization session getting deeply relaxed. If you have trouble letting go, see the chapter on stress reduction for extra help.

Practice Healing Visualization

You should do your visualizations at least three times a day. Five or six times would be even better, because there are a lot of areas to work on.

Each time you visualize, you will include images of the healing process. You'll see your vast army of white blood cells destroying and removing the weak, disorganized cancer cells. You'll visualize any treatments you're receiving as your allies, as helping your body heal itself. Before you go for a new test or treatment, you'll rehearse the procedure in your mind to prepare yourself and reduce your anxiety.

At different times your daily visualizations will also include images to reinforce the other steps to recovery: asking for and accepting support, overcoming resentment, avoiding stress, achieving goals, changing beliefs about cancer, exercising, drawing in your sketchbook, the positive results of recovery, and being assertive in doctors' offices and hospitals.

Keep a Sketchbook Diary

The Simontons have found that drawing simple pictures of your visualization images is a good way to analyze and improve them. After the visualization below there are guidelines for interpreting your drawings. You can also record your thoughts, list your goals, and organize your schedule in your sketchbook.

Eat Well

To heal your body, you must give it optimum nourishment. Proper nutrition is important for proper functioning of your immune system. Cut out junk food, alcohol, caffeine, tobacco, excess fat and sugar and salt. Eat more vegetables and less red meat. Strive for balance, a little from each food group each day. Some experts place great stress on the role of vitamins in recovering from cancer, so start taking them. It can't hurt and everything you can do to maximize your health will help.

Exercise

Get one hour of exercise three times a week: brisk walking or jogging, swimming, an aerobics class, or riding a bike vigorously. Exercise tones muscles, improves your endurance, relieves stress, gives you a lift out of depression, and stimulates your immune system. To prevent overexertion, don't go so fast that you couldn't carry on a conversation while exercising.

Do whatever your physical limitations allow. Even if you're spending most of your time in bed, you can *visualize* yourself getting exercise.

Remember, as far as your brain is concerned, there is no difference between a real activity and an imagined activity. You won't improve your muscle tone or endurance by imagining yourself jogging, but you will still create and release tension in your muscles, fight depression, and stimulate your immune system.

Anti-Cancer Visualization Instructions

Lie down and close your eyes. Get totally relaxed. Spend as much time as you need to release all the muscles in your body. Go to your special place and surround yourself with your comforting special things. Really settle in and get relaxed.

First you'll build up an image of your cancer. Avoid thinking of your cancer as the astrological sign of the crab. Don't use images of cancer as ants or rocks or rats, either. It's important that you see separate, individual cells, not just a blob labeled "tumor." They should be quite small, and soft like sponges or bits of hamburger. These cells are weak and disorganized. They aren't plump and healthy-looking like your normal cells. They're sort of shrunken and fragile, with thin walls and watery insides. Make them gray or some other light, washed-out color.

Now create an image of your white blood cells. The white blood cells in charge of eliminating cancer are called phagocytes. They are large, irregularly shaped cells that arise in your bone marrow and travel throughout your body in the blood vessels, lymph vessels, and lymph nodes. In a blood vessel, where there is relatively more room to float around, a phagocyte looks like a spherical globule of clear jelly with a nucleus and little flecks inside. But phagocytes aren't confined to blood vessels. They can pass through the vessel walls and into the surrounding tissue. They just insert "fingers" into the cracks between cells, flatten out like pancakes, and ooze right through and between the cells.

A phagocyte destroys a cancer cell by *phagocytosis*—flattening out and wrapping itself around the smaller cell, completely surrounding it, digesting it, and spitting out the parts it has no use for. A phagocyte is like a giant free-form mouth with stomach attached, cruising around your body looking for its next meal.

There are actually many other kinds of white blood cells, similar in appearance, but with different jobs to do. You can visualize different kinds of white blood cells: *sentries* or *scouts* that patrol your body looking for cancer cells and summon other cells to the attack: *spotters* that mark cancer cells for attack; phagocyte *destroyers* that engulf and destroy cancer cells; *referees* that call off the attack when all cancer cells are gone; *housekeepers* that clean up the bits and pieces of cells left lying around; and *rememberers* that will recognize any new cancer cells that form.

The main thing to remember is that there are *billions and billions* of white blood cells. They are considerably bigger, stronger, and more numerous than the cancer cells in your body. A common image for white blood cells is a vast army, swarming over a distant plain and filling the landscape from horizon to horizon. In comparison, a tumor would look like a ragtag band of outlaws cowering in one small foxhole.

Repeatedly imagine your white blood cells overwhelming the cancer cells. The specific images you use will depend on your personality and what appeals to you. It doesn't matter as long as the white blood cells are big, strong, clever, and numerous, while the cancer cells are small, weak, stupid, and outnumbered. Many people prefer the aggressive images developed by the Simontons' patients—white sharks attacking small gray jellyfish, fish eating eggs, or big dogs gobbling raw meat. On the other hand, Bernie Segal has found that equally good results can be obtained using more gentle images such as giant sponges mopping up custard, or big, strong men stuffing cancer cells like dead leaves in white trash bags and hauling them off. A little humor helps too—you can visualize cancer cells as food being chomped up by PacMen white blood cells.

Try *becoming* one of your own white blood cells. You're big, you're tough, and you're hungry. You can gobble up cancer cells like popcorn at the movies. They can't run, they can't hide from you. You search them out wherever they are.

See the cancer cells outfought, outnumbered, outsmarted. Their numbers start to dwindle. Cells are dying right and left; some just give up and die before the white cells even get to them. Your white blood cells can get anywhere, even to the center of a large tumor. Remember that your body is mostly water, which makes up your blood, lymph, and intercellular fluid. The white blood cells can swim to the heart of any mass of cancer cells, filling it up with their overwhelming healing power.

Whatever images you use for white blood cells and cancer cells, be sure to include images of the remains of dead cancer cells being carried off to your liver and kidneys, to be processed and eliminated in the urine and stool. You are literally flushing your cancer away. See the housekeeper cells sweeping and mopping and carrying away the debris in bags and buckets. Only clean, shining, healthy cells are left.

Tell yourself:

My cancer cells are weak and disorganized.

My white cells are strong and cunning.

I am overwhelming the cancer with healing power.

I'm purging my body of all misfit cells, flushing them away.

Starving Your Tumor

Now imagine that there is a control room somewhere in your brain. This room contains the valves that regulate blood flow throughout your body. See the details of the pipes with all their bends and turns and branches, extending throughout your body and ending up in the control room. Find this room and find the large shutoff valve or faucet that controls the flow of blood to your tumor. When you find the correct faucet, notice how big it is, the color and texture, and what kind of wheel or handle it has to turn. Now grasp the handle with both hands and turn it clockwise to shut the blood supply down to a trickle. Don't worry about also shutting off the flow of white blood cells. They can still get at your tumor through the lymph system and the intercellular fluid. They will find the starving, weakened cancer cells even easier to remove now that you've shut down their supply lines.

If you're not satisfied that you did the trick, create another, bigger valve and shut that off. Look around and shut off all the big and little valves that have something to do with the blood supply to your tumor. If you want to trace the pipes from your brain down through your heart and out to the tumor site, do that. Shut off valves all the way along the path.

You might imagine electronic controls with buttons to push and switches to turn off. See them as wired up to automatic flow controls surrounding your tumor, like the automatic sprinkler systems you can control with an electric timer.

You can imagine reaching down into your body with tiny but immensely strong hands. Find the blood vessels that feed your tumor and squeeze them. Feel them like the fat, warm water hose that goes into the radiator of your car. As you squeeze, the hose gets smaller and smaller, until it is a thin little capillary tube, smaller than a drinking straw. You can also imagine the blood vessel as a garden hose, and bend it over so that you form a kink and constrict the flow until it's just a trickle. Wrap strong twine around the shrunken or kinked vessels so they'll stay that way.

Tell yourself:

I am shutting off the blood supply to my tumor.

I'm starving my tumor.

The tumor is dying of starvation.

My cancer is shrinking and shrinking.

Visualize Your Treatments

Next visualize whatever medical treatment you have received or are about to receive. First learn what the procedure is like and rehearse it in your mind. See yourself getting through the treatment without fear or embarrassment or anger: checking in at the hospital admissions desk, filling out the forms without annoyance, finding the correct floor and unit, waiting calmly, smelling those hospital smells, watching the other people without comparing or thinking about how sick they look, reading your magazine, greeting the technician, disrobing, asking whatever questions come to you, using deep breathing to calm yourself, regarding the radiation equipment as an ally, answering questions, hearing the machinery and the other sounds of the hospital, holding still while the radiation zaps your cancer, doing your radiation visualization even during the treatment.

At the end of this visualization, tell yourself, "I can cope with my fears. I can stay calm." During the actual treatment, use some prepared affirmations:

I can just close my eyes and say a short prayer.

Breathe slowly, just breathe.

This is helping me, I have chosen this.

Rehearsing a procedure in your mind beforehand will do a lot to reduce your anxiety and put you in a more relaxed state in which the treatment can have maximum beneficial effect.

Regularly picture your treatments as very, very powerful. See them as having the desired effect and acting as allies to your natural healing process. Develop your own symbolism that feels right.

For example, if you need surgery, you could visualize your surgeon as a giant white blood cell, cutting all of the cancer cells out in one operation and bypassing the usual disposal route via liver and kidneys. Or your surgeon could be a strong knight like Saint George, champion of your cause, an undefeatable hero. See your surgery as pruning a weak, misshapen limb off a vigorous tree, or removing a square peg from a round hole, or cutting a soft spot out of an otherwise perfect peach. Tell yourself things like "My surgeon loves me, God loves me. The surgery is a success. The cancer is gone."

You can visualize radiation therapy like a hailstorm in a forest—the strong trees and brush bounce right back, while the softer, weaker plants are beaten to the ground and perish. Or you could see your cells like little people out on a beach in hot sun. Your normal, healthy cells have straw hats, umbrellas, and paba sunscreen. The cancer cells are naked, albino creatures that shrivel up and die under the sun's rays. Or you can see the radiation as a golden, healing aura from a wizard's wand. Tell yourself, "Healing radiation is flooding my body. My cancer is sizzling and frying away to nothing. I'm zapping my tumor."

You could think of chemotherapy working like the "weed and feed" garden products you can spray on your lawn—the selective herbicide kills leafy weeds while leaving the healthy green grass alone. Likewise, your normal cells are too healthy and smart to absorb much poison, while your cancer cells are weak and stupid, so they drink it up and die. You could imagine that your chemotherapy drugs are the same powerful hallucinogenic drugs used by some South American Shamans. The shamans may become dizzy and nauseated, but they are also filled with glorious visions of healing power. Tell yourself, "I'm weeding out the misfits. This will separate the sheep from the goats."

One woman thought of her body as an imaginary kingdom inhabited by mostly good cells and a few bad cells. She saw the chemotherapy as a magic potion that was being administered by order of the queen to all her subjects. The good and honest people—her normal cells—found the potion bitter but bearable. Evil people with darkness in their hearts—her cancer cells—were poisoned by the magic potion. They melted away like the wicked witch in *The Wizard of Oz*. She used the affirmation, "And they all lived happily ever after."

Visualize the side effects of your treatments as mild, bearable, and worth the cost. Using your visualization skills can actually reduce the severity of side effects, so you will feel nearly normal, still have sufficient energy, hang onto your hair, avoid much of the nausea, keep a decent appetite, maintain your weight, and so on. See yourself in the future, doing what you usually do, moving around freely, smiling, laughing with friends, eating normally, still enjoying the simple pleasures. Tell yourself, "My treatments are my allies. They hurt only to heal."

Overcome Resentment

Go to your indoor special place. Make it dim and quiet. Get very relaxed. Sit at one end of the space and imagine a chair at the other end. There is a figure sitting in the chair. You begin to make out the features and realize that it's someone who has hurt you in the past. Someone you have resented for a long time. The person is just sitting there, not looking at you or doing anything.

On a screen placed so you both can see it, replay a scene from your past. Review a time when the other person hurt you by saying something, doing something, or failing to say or do something. Watch the scene through once with detachment.

Now rewind the scene and play it again, reliving it so that you feel the same anger, hurt, and resentment. Try to recapture the feelings you originally had.

Now reverse roles. Take the other person's part in the next playing of the scene. Try to understand and act out the other person's behavior. What are you feeling? What is your motivation? Try to get a sense of why the other person did or didn't do something, and how it felt to them at the time. Notice whether the other person also felt hurt and resentful. Tell yourself, "Everybody does what seems best at the time. There's no alternative. Nobody can read minds or see into the future."

Now change the scene on the screen. Picture something nice happening to the other person, the person who hurt you. See him or her receiving in money, love, success, satisfaction, acclaim, gratitude. It may be hard, but really concentrate on the sights and sounds of good things coming to the other person.

Now turn the screen off and look the other person in the eyes. Say out loud, "I forgive myself and I forgive you. Our differences are in the past and there's nothing I can do about them now. I let the past go. I forgive you and I forgive myself."

This may seem like a strange and unappealing visualization, but it's a very powerful means of purging yourself of resentment. When you dwell on past injustices, it can divert your attention, poison your mind with angry thoughts, and keep you in a chronic state of arousal. This state of arousal is the opposite of relaxation, and only in a relaxed state can your immune system function at its peak.

Inner Guide

If you haven't done the exercises in the inner guide chapter, now is the time to do them. Even if you have created an inner guide in the past, you may want to create a new one specifically to help you in your fight against cancer.

The inner guide chapter will give you the detailed instructions. Essentially, you should look for an embodiment of your natural healing powers. Create an "internal healer" who knows what's going on in your body and can give you advice about the healing images and health practices that are most important for you. Imagine your internal healer working around the clock, supervising your white blood cells, whispering relaxing and encouraging affirmations in your mind's ear, and keeping you on the road to recovery even during those times when your conscious thoughts are elsewhere.

Reinforce the Other Steps to Recovery

Each day choose a step toward recovery that you are working on and visualize its successful completion. If you're working on achieving secondary gains without having to be sick, see yourself talking assertively to your boss about cutting back and reducing stress in your life. Listen to yourself insist on time alone to pursue a hobby. See and hear yourself saying, "I'm tired of all this indirection and mind reading—here's exactly what I want from you." In your mind, practice stating your feelings in a clear, direct manner. Tell yourself, "I have legitimate needs and I can meet them out in the open."

See yourself setting and achieving your goals: moving into your new place, painting the fence, spending more time with your kids, doing volunteer work, cleaning out the basement, finishing that quilt, going to real estate school, and so on. Concentrate on the positive benefits of steadfastly going after what you want regardless of your cancer diagnosis. Tell yourself, "I intend to live, I intend to prosper. I am too busy to be sick. I've got unfinished business in my life."

Hear yourself setting others straight about cancer: that it can be conquered, that your body's natural defense systems are designed to handle it, that you welcome the necessary treatments as your allies in recovery. Tell yourself, "I know the facts. I ignore superstition and horror stories."

Imagine calling a relative or friend and asking for whatever help and support you need. Hear them agreeing to come over, to help you wax the floors, to pick your cousin up at the airport, to read your visualization instructions to you, and so on. Hear others expressing their love, their concern, and their willingness to help. Tell yourself, "I can always call _____ ."

Frequently visualize yourself avoiding unnecessary stress, staying relaxed and calm in the midst of trying circumstances. See yourself having difficulties sometimes, feeling depressed, crying, feeling alone—but then see yourself gathering your strength, feeling better, moving on to accomplish what you have to do. Tell yourself, "I conserve my energy. I take the less stressful oath. I always emerge on the other side of the blues."

A good time to rehearse upcoming stressful situations is while lying in bed in the morning. Before you get up, see yourself setting and achieving your goals for the day. Hear yourself being calm and assertive while talking to your doctor or other professionals. Watch yourself eating a healthy salad and bowl of soup in the cafeteria for lunch and going for a long walk in the afternoon. Choose the affirmations you will concentrate on today.

Your Sketchbook

Carry your sketchbook around with you. After at least one of your visualization sessions each day, make a quick drawing of your imagery. Use colored pencils or pens or crayons. Show how your cancer cells and your white blood cells look to you. Sometimes try drawing with your left hand if you're right-handed, or your right hand if you're left-handed. Drawing with your unaccustomed hand is a way of getting around your critical, censoring mind and uncorking your creative flow.

This isn't art, it's therapy—so style and beauty don't matter. Just draw freely, without thinking a lot about it. Save the thinking until after you've sketched all the images that you used in your anti-cancer visualization.

Look at your drawings and analyze them in terms of the guidelines for effective anti-cancer images. Are the cancer cells separate, small, few in number, and weak looking? Have you made the mistake of making them look like crabs, insects, rats, or stones. Such images are too strong and tenacious—your mind knows how hard it is to get rid of ants or dissolve away stones. Are their colors properly pale and washed out? Are the white blood cells large, much more numerous, strong, and intelligent looking? Are their colors strong and vivid? Are the white cells actively eating the cancer cells? Do they have easy access to all the cancer cells?

The Simontons offer a couple of tips. Your unconscious mind will assume that the larger image will be the winner. That's why it's so important to make your white blood cells considerably larger than the cancer cells. If your images include a lot of big teeth, that suggests that you might have a lot of anger bottled up, so spend some more time on the resentment exercise. If you want to make your white blood cells look smarter, give them a big eye instead of a nucleus.

If your drawing doesn't match the guidelines, make a new, corrected version. The next time you do your anti-cancer visualization, include the revisions. Anti-cancer visualizations are the exception to the general rule that says your spontaneous image is always the best image. A sufficient number of studies and anecdotal reports have indicated which kinds of images work best in fighting cancer.

ARTHRITIS

The term "arthritis" comes from two Greek words for "inflammation" and "joint." Arthritis can affect any joint, most commonly the shoulders, elbows, hips, wrists, fingers, knees, and ankles. There are several types. *Osteoarthritis* is the form associated with the painful joints and restricted movement of old age. Gout is also a form of arthritis. But by far the most widespread and feared form is *rheumatoid arthritis*. That's the form we will concentrate on in this chapter.

Rheumatoid arthritis can strike at any age, as opposed to osteoarthritis, which hits later in life. Rheumatoid arthritis is an autoimmune disorder in which your immune system becomes overactive and starts attacking normal body cells in your joints.

Arthritis runs in families—some people have a greater genetic predisposition to developing rheumatoid arthritis than others. But a family history of arthritis is not sufficient in itself to cause the disease. Your immune system can stay in balance, until emotional factors tip the scales: low self-esteem, recent personal loss, and chronic negative emotions such as unexpressed hostility or repressed sadness.

The same personality traits and attitudes that can help you recover from cancer will also help you recover from arthritis. Learning to cope with stress and express your feelings can lead to a reduction of symptoms and even remission of the disease entirely.

So it is vital that you read or reread the cancer section. Follow the same steps to recovery:

- Identify and accept your recent stress triggers. Consider how to avoid stress currently.

- Identify, accept, and outsmart the secondary gain process whereby your recovery is impeded because you get some good things out of a bad disease.

- Continue to set and strive after goals.

- Get support, overcome resentment, perfect your relaxation skills, eat well, and get as much exercise as you can.

The new things to learn in this section are the changes that take place in your body, the course of the disease, and thus the kinds of images you should create for your healing visualizations.

Causes and Course of Rheumatoid Arthritis

If you're predisposed to get arthritis, a blood test will show the presence of the *rheumatoid factor* (RA factor) in your blood. This is a "confused" antibody that thinks the lining of your joints is a foreign substance and wants to attack it. Normally, the rheumatoid factor is held in check by the presence of *arthritis autoantibody*. Think of the rheumatoid factor as a big, stupid dog that wants to dig up the flowerbeds, and the arthritis autoantibody as trainer restraining the dog with a leash.

You can have these trainer-and-dog combinations floating around in your blood for a lifetime and never develop arthritis. What sets arthritis going is a message from your brain that stimulates production of "substance P" in your joints. Nobody knows exactly why or how your brain does this. Substance P is a neurotransmitter, a chemical that has the effect of weakening the trainers and making them drop the leashes.

The rheumatoid factor is then free to attack the synovial membrane that lines the inside of each of your joints. The synovial membrane is made up of synovial cells. These cells slowly ooze a fluid that lubricates the moving surfaces of your joints, keeping the cartilage on the ends of your bones from wearing away.

The attack doesn't kill the synovial cells. It seems to panic them. Their response to the threat is to start multiplying much faster than normal. Soon they spread to parts of the joint where they don't belong, packing it and restricting movement.

The rapidly growing synovial cells appear to rob nutrients from the slow-growing cartilage cells. At any rate, the cartilage starts dissolving. After a time, bone is rubbing on bone and the bone actually erodes. The whole joint becomes inflamed, swollen, and painful. It becomes increasingly difficult to move the joint in its full range, and it may finally become completely immobilized.

Dead tissue on the surface of the cartilage often forms granules that further aggravate the situation. Small nodules may also form under the skin, typically around the elbows. Your muscles are often aching and stiff, especially in the morning.

The process is degenerative, but not continuous. Once damage is done, it cannot be fully repaired. But the process doesn't go on all the time. Rheumatoid arthritis may flare up for a few weeks or months, then be inactive for months or years, then flare up again, become inactive, and so on.

Traditional Arthritis Treatments

Drugs can relieve pain and slow down or halt the disease for a while, but there is currently no cure as such.

Aspirin is the drug of choice, since it relieves pain and reduces inflammation with minimal side effects. If aspirin doesn't work, there are other nonsteroid, anti-inflammatory drugs such as Motrin. If the nonsteroids don't work, you can try steroids such as cortisone, an artificial version of cortico steroid, which is secreted by your adrenal glands. Cortisone is a powerful anti-inflammatory with some serious drawbacks. It takes more and more to have the same effect, it makes bones brittle, and can lead to fat deposits, weakness, ulcers, and in rare cases, psychosis. Withdrawal from cortisone can induce significant symptoms of depression.

Some antimalarial drugs and injections of metallic gold powder suspended in water are also used. For some they work very well, while others have adverse reactions.

Exercise is very important to preserve the range of motion in your joints. Stretching, swimming, and walking are good. A physical therapist can suggest specific movements to practice that will focus on your particular limitations. Applying hot compresses, heating pads, or lamps can ease stiffness and make exercise easier and more beneficial.

Relaxation exercises are also very important. You can use the relaxation visualizations in this book, biofeedback, meditation, self-hypnosis, autogenics—whatever works best for you. Relaxation helps in three ways. (1) When you're concentrating on your relaxation exercise, you are distracted from pain. This may seem obvious and trivial, but studies have shown that distraction is a major mechanism for pain control—you can only attend to one thing at a time, be it pain in your joints, a meditation mantra, or a cassette tape of woodland sounds. (2) Relaxation can stimulate your brain to release endorphins, brain chemicals that dampen pain in the same manner as morphine. (3) When muscles are relaxed, your sympathetic nervous system is less active, possibly slowing the production of substance P in arthritic joints.

You should lead as normal a life as possible, given your limitations. Plenty of sleep at night and avoidance of stress make sense, but prolonged bed rest is definitely not recommended. You need to get up and keep moving as much as possible to prevent your joints from stiffening. Use whatever you need to cope with everyday problems: a long-handled shoehorn, clothes with easy fasteners, built-up handles on knives and forks, a seat in the bathtub.

Finally, many people find that their arthritis symptoms are worse in cold, wet weather. Moving to a warm, dry climate may be a serious consideration. If you can't actually move to Arizona or New Mexico, you can at least *visualize* yourself there, soaking up the heat and moving about freely.

Anti-Arthritis Visualization Instructions

Lie down and close your eyes. Get totally relaxed. Spend as much time as you need to release all the muscles in your body. Go to your special place and surround yourself with your comforting special things. Really settle in and get relaxed.

Shrink yourself down and imagine that you are floating around in side your own brain. Find the message center from which your brain sends instructions to your immune system and joints. Enter the message center and look around. It might look like a telephone switchboard, computer room, boiler room, or electrical power panel. Scan the switches until you find one labeled "SUBSTANCE P." This control might look like an ordinary light switch, a push-pull knob on the dash of a car, or a big gate switch with open contacts from a *Frankenstein* movie. This switch sends a message to your joints to start producing substance P, the neurotransmitter that starts the destructive process of your arthritis.

Notice that the switch can be set to "off" or "on," and that it is in the on position. Reach out with your imaginary hand and turn the switch off. Concentrate on the actual feelings of turning off a switch—the appearance, the feel of the plastic or metal, the sound of the click, the movement.

You have just canceled the substance P messages. Tell yourself, "I am turning off the substance P." To make sure the switch stays off, put some heavy-duty tape over it, or glue it in the off position.

Every time you do a visualization, drop by the message center and make sure the switch is off. If it's been flipped back on by some physical or psychological stress, turn it off again and tape it down more firmly. After a while, you'll find that the switch stays off.

Now trace some of the wires from the message center to one of your arthritic joints. Imagine that you're so small you can get right into the joint itself, between the ends of the two bones. Imagine that you're standing on cartilage-covered bone, in a little depression like a valley. Arcing overhead is more cartilage-covered bone, the other half of the joint. The bone "sky" curves down to meet the bone "ground" at a horizon line in the middle distance. It's like you're in a cavern of bone, lined with tough, slick cartilage.

Visualize substance P as a smokey haze in the air. Visualize your synovial cells as translucent beach balls filled with clear jelly. There are some big shaggy dogs wandering around, gnawing and scratching at the beach balls. These are the rheumatic agents. There are some people in white coats wandering around with leashes in their hands, but they can't see the dogs because of the substance P haze. These white-coated people are the arthritis autoantibodies.

When the dogs bite a synovial beach ball, it doesn't burst. Instead, it swells up and divides down the middle, forming two beach balls. The cavern is almost full of synovial cells. They jam the corners of the cavern and lie about in big piles that reach to the roof. Dried up husks of dead cells litter the ground. The "sky" bone tries to rotate around, and the sound of grating and crunching comes from the horizon. The dead cells are like sand in a ball bearing, scratching the cartilage and ruining the smooth, gliding motion that should be happening where the sky and ground meet.

Set up a fan, a giant vacuum cleaner, or an air conditioning system to clear the air of the substance P. Listen to the hum as the air purifying system sucks the smoke from the air and removes it.

Take some time to fix this scene in your mind and adjust the details to suit yourself. Now that you've been here for a while, you'll notice that the smokey haze of substance P is getting thinner. The visibility is improving and there's more light. The white coats can see the dogs now. They start clipping on the leashes and dragging the dogs away from the beach balls. Soon all the dogs have been led off down a side tunnel. The cavern is a lot more peaceful now. Tell yourself, "All the dogs are gone now. My arthritis is stopped."

With no more dogs to stimulate them, the synovial cells stop dividing entirely. More and more of them spring leaks, deflate, and die. The piles are getting smaller. Soon there are just a few living beach balls lying around—just enough to keep the cartilage floor smeared with lubricant. Tell yourself, "My joints are returning to normal."

From more side tunnels, white blood cells come in. These are housekeeper cells. You can visualize them as cleaning robots, maids with vacuum cleaners, janitors with mops, or big blobs of jello. They roam around mopping and sucking up all the dried husks and granules of the dead synovial cells. Wherever the white cells pass, the cartilage is left smooth and glistening, perfectly clean and slippery. The thin spots and tears in the cartilage begin to thicken and heal. Tell yourself, "I can move freely now, without pain."

You can take an active part in this visualization. Help the white coats catch the dogs. Walk around picking up granules off the floor and giving them to the white cells. Rub synovial fluid onto the dry areas of your cartilage, like rubbing saddle soap on dry leather. Tell yourself, "I am healing myself. I am ready to recover."

When you're satisfied with the job you've done, move on to another joint and check the progress there. Imagine that the healing process has been going on simultaneously in all your joints, and make a tour of inspection. If some joints aren't as clean as others, stick around a while and supervise the process.

Do this visualization at length once a day. You may not feel comfortable with these particular images, so feel free to make up your own. The key steps to symbolize are shutting off production of substance P, restraining the rheumatic agent from attacking the synovial cells, reducing the number of synovial cells that are packing your joints, cleaning granules out of joints, and replacing lost cartilage cells.

Working in a sketchbook will help sharpen and elaborate your images. Draw simple pictures of your images for affected joints, synovial cells, white cells, and so on. Analyze and refine your images. Looking in an anatomy book will help show you what different kinds of joints look like. One helpful exercise is to draw an enlarged picture of a joint in ink. Then pack the spaces of the joint with circles and dots in pencil, representing the overpopulation of synovial cells and irritating granules. Then erase the pencil marks thoroughly, saying to yourself, "I am erasing my arthritis."

At least once a day, visualize yourself recovered from your arthritis. Include all the positive benefits: freedom from pain, resumption of hobbies and sports, freedom of movement, independence from drugs, reduced strain on close relationships, more self-sufficiency, continuing in job or education, improved mood and self-image, and so on.

On alternate days, perform these visualizations from the previous section on cancer: "Overcome Resentment," "Inner Guide," and "Reinforce the Other Steps to Recovery."

ASTHMA AND ALLERGIES

In asthma and allergies, your immune system treats as dangerous invaders such relatively harmless substances as pollen, cat dander, chocolate, preservatives, perfume, and so on. If you're allergic to cottonwood pollen, for example, it means that your immune system has never learned that cottonwood pollen is harmless. You don't have enough normal cottonwood pollen antibodies to neutralize the presence of the pollen grains you breathe in when the trees are blooming. You do have some cottonwood pollen antibodies, but they are of a type called IgE, which cause rather than prevent an allergic reaction in the presence of cottonwood pollen.

An allergic reaction begins with mast cells. These cells are concentrated in your skin, mucous membranes, and lungs. In the presence of an allergen plus IgE antibody molecules, the mast cells start releasing histamine.

Histamine is a chemical with two unfortunate effects. (1) It makes the tiny blood vessels called capillaries leaky, so that they release fluid into the surrounding tissue. You start sneezing, your nose and eyes run with excess fluid, and your sinuses get saturated and swollen. (2) Histamine can also make the smooth muscles around your bronchial tubes contract, producing the asthmatic symptom of not being able to breathe out fully. In anaphylactic shock, a violent allergic reaction such as some people have to bee stings, the pooling of fluid and contraction of muscles are so severe that blood pressure drops and heart failure can result.

Stress makes allergies and asthma worse. An important part of using visualization for relief is to relax fully and deeply. This sends a message to your immune system to slack off because everything is OK.

Anti-Allergy/Asthma Visualization Instructions

The best time to do an anti-allergy/asthma visualization is as soon as you start feeling symptoms. At the first sneeze or wheeze, stop what you're doing and go somewhere to lie down. It's much easier to prevent a reaction before it escalates than it is to end a full-blown attack. Record these instructions if you find it helpful.

Lie down, close your eyes, and relax. Spend extra time in the relaxation phase. Keep telling yourself, "Relax, it's all right. There's no danger, no need to panic." It's as if you were speaking directly to your immune system.

Form an image of the allergens that bother you and give them an alarming, dangerous color. It doesn't matter if you know exactly what you're allergic to. Just imagine little red dust motes or tiny purple burrs floating in the air.

See the colored allergens coming into your mouth and nose with the air you breathe, irritating the mast cells in your mucus membranes. You can imagine the mast cells as bigger than the allergens, and spherical, with little feelers sticking out. When the mast cells are irritated, the feelers twitch and tickle your nose, making you sneeze. The cells sweat a clear liquid that represents histamine.

Keep watching the allergens coming into your body and coating your mucus membranes until your sinuses, nasal passages, and throat are full of the allergen color.

Now change the color. Pick a contrasting color that means safety or harmlessness to you. For example, change the red motes to a cool green color. Change the purple burrs to a soft peach hue. Your mast cells like this color. They trust this color. They stop twitching and sweating. Tell yourself, "My body recognizes the allergens as harmless."

If you take antihistamines, visualize them working. See the medication as millions of little blotters that soak up the histamine released by your mast cells. See your mast cells firming up, drying up on the surface, no longer sweating little drops of histamine.

Now try a more metaphorical scene. Imagine that your immune system has called out a SWAT team of crack police troops. The team has combat boots, machine guns, bulletproof vests, sniper rifles, and all the gear you see on TV. Your body is like the streets of a big city. The cops are roving the sidewalks and rooftops, looking for anything that looks suspicious. The whole city crackles with tension. Everything is suspect. Weapons are set on hair trigger. The cops think that every innocent allergen is a murderer or terrorist. They're paranoid and apt to shoot at shadows.

Now imagine that the bomb threats and rumors of terrorists taking hostages are all a false alarm. The order comes from headquarters to recall the SWAT team. All danger is past. The tough young cops put their weapons on safety and head for the central square of the city. A big bus comes from headquarters and they all file into it. They take off their boots and their flak jackets and slump down in their seats to snooze on their way back to headquarters. They will all go home to sleep and eat. They're on call in case a real invasion of virus or bacteria come to town, but they're not needed for routine patrol duty. Tell yourself, "It's only a false alarm. I can relax."

The city is quiet. It's now a normal, sleepy summer afternoon. There are just a few rent-a-cops on duty. They're old, slow, and fat. They don't even have guns—just walkie-talkies. They doze in their squad cars, lean on the lampposts, and sit in the donut shops drinking coffee. If anything really dangerous happens, they'll sound the alarm. But they're not going to be panicked by a few harmless allergens floating around. Tell yourself, "Everything's normal. No sweat, no hassle."

Now that you're relaxed and have calmed your allergic reaction, you can spend some time relieving any leftover symptoms. Imagine that your stuffy nose and swollen sinuses are a big sponge in your head. Imagine removing that sponge through a magic trapdoor in your forehead. You can wring it out thoroughly and stuff it back in, much reduced in size and more comfortable. Do this several times.

If you prefer, imagine the sponge remaining in place, and pretend you are a tiny person floating around in your own head. Squeeze and push the spongy lining of your sinuses and nasal passages. The fluid released drains down your throat. Tell yourself, "Let it drain, let it dry out."

If you have asthmatic symptoms, form an image of the bronchial tubes leading like a branching tree into your lungs. Imagine that the tubes are being grasped by a big hand, clenching in panic. Let the hand relax and fall away. See and feel the tubes opening up and letting the air flow freely out. If you use an inhaler, imagine it working. See and feel the cool mist flowing down every branch, widening the passages as if it were air blowing up a balloon or a leg slipping into panty hose. Tell yourself, "I can relax and breathe easy."

Before ending your visualization, tell yourself, "I am on an even keel. I can stay relaxed and clam. I am in balance." Reinforce this affirmation with an image of a gyroscope. You probably played with one of these flywheels in a spherical framework when you were a kid. You wrap a string around the shaft and give the flywheel a spin. No matter how you try to tip it over, the gyroscope always returns to an upright position, even on a tightrope or balanced on the tip of a pencil.

Imaginge that there is a big gyroscope in the center of your chest. It represents your immune system and the homeostatic balance of your entire body. Imagine that every breath you take, every move you make, every sight you see, and every thought you think, gives the gyroscope another spin. It keeps you balanced and upright inside. No matter what the stress, you can't be pushed far off center. If your mast cells start to go crazy over some pollen or house dust, you will quickly calm them down and get your immune system back in balance.

When you are ready, end the visualization. As you go about your daily routine, remind yourself, "I am staying relaxed and calm. I can cope with allergies by relaxation and visualization." During allergy season, try to avoid stressful activities. Get plenty of sleep, exercise moderately, and eat well. Avoid the foods and drink that you're allergic to or that make your other allergies worse.

Make an absolute rule that you will stop and visualize as soon as you feel an attack coming on. Ten minutes taken out of your routine right away can save you hours of misery.

Special Considerations for Immune Disorders

Continue Traditional Treatments

This point needs reemphasis. Visualization works best when it is used to supplement and maximize other treatments. It won't take the place of surgery, radiation, chemotherapy, or even aspirin. But it will make all these things work better.

Along this line, let your doctors know that you are using visualization. Find out from them what your test results mean and use them as feedback to guide your visualizations. For example, if your white count is low, it means you need more white blood cells. You can visualize a speed up in the rate of white blood cell division in your bone marrow.

Don't visualize any extremely theoretical immune system changes that you may read about. If you do get interested in the finer points of immune system functioning and want to try to make specific changes with visualization, do so under the guidance of a medical expert. Unguided, you could actually throw your immune system out of balance. For example, Jeanne Achterberg once coached a man with an autoimmune problem in how to increase the number of B cells in his blood and decrease the number of T cells. He went on a trip, continued his visualization exercises, and overdid it. He created so many B cells and got rid of so many T cells that he laid himself open to a serious viral infection. It was an impressive show of the power of visualization to affect the immune system, and clear warning not to do so without periodic feedback.

Pain

Little has been said about pain in this chapter. For a full treatment of pain management, see the chapter on pain control.

Relapses

Your immune system follows a curve like a roller coaster, not a straight-line progression. When you're under stress and getting sick, your immune system declines a little, rallies for a while, declines a little further, rallies some, declines still further, and so on. The road to recovery has the same shape: you get better, then suffer a setback, then get even better, then feel a little worse, then finally recover.

After treatments and visualization, you may start to feel a little better. Lab results confirm that you're on the mend. You go home from the hospital or start back to work, feeling better and better. You figure you've beaten your cancer or arthritis once and for all. Then one day your symptoms return, or routine retesting shows that you are having a relapse.

Relapses don't mean that all your work was in vain. Relapses may be expected, given the roller coaster manner in which your immune system recovers its balance.

This can teach you two important lessons. First, keep up your visualizations, dietary changes, exercises, support network, and so on—don't stop taking care of yourself just because you feel like your old self again. Remember that it was your old self and your old lifestyle that helped make you sick in the first place.

Second, if you do have a relapse, take it not as a failure, but as a message from your immune system. The message is that you still have work to do. You still need to help your immune system get back in balance. Get to work by asking others for support. See a therapist if you're seriously depressed. Find even more alternative ways to meet the needs that being sick is filling for you. Slow down. Reinstate the healthy practices that you have let slide. If you have drifted back into emotionally unhealthy relationships and situations, face the fact that this time you've got to get out of them.

Statistics

Beware of statistics. Beware especially of "six months to live" kinds of predictions. Beware of trying to quantify your odds by studying medical literature.

The trouble with statistics, especially cancer statistics, is that most self-induced cures don't get into the medical literature. People who cure themselves don't usually go back to their doctors. The doctors assume that they went on to die under some other doctor's care, when in fact they are walking around in good health.

Even when self-cured people do go back to their doctors, their remission is often seen to be a case of wrong diagnosis in the first place. Or if the doctors believe in the cures, they may think that the cases are too mystical or religious to write up for the traditional medical journals. Also, it's hard for most doctors to see how a self-induced cure is applicable to their other cases. The cures are marveled at, but rarely reported, collected, collated, and analyzed.

You can't really blame most doctors or medical researchers for not studying the healing powers of visualization. Even though they know or think that visualization works, they can't explain how it works. They can't even get a handle on how to study the phenomenon. Because it's a subjective, inner experience, visualization is almost impossible to replicate in a controlled, laboratory environment. How do you know that two different subjects are doing the same thing when you tell them to "visualize a red apple?"

The biochemistry of the immune system is much more accessible to researchers, so they study that. And the immune system is so complex that studying it is a life's work and then some. That leaves no time for mere mortals to also devote themselves to the study of visualization.

How Do I Know If It's Working?

You don't. Not right away. That's the trouble with using visualization for reversing immune system disorders, as opposed to using it for something like relaxation.

It's relatively easy to understand, accept, and successfully utilize visualization for relaxation. You can see through a biofeedback machine or simple introspection that your body is responding to your imagery: your heart rate and respiration slow, your hands warm up, your muscular tension decreases, and so on. These immediate and obvious results have made techniques like biofeedback and autogenics widespread and acceptable to even the most conservative practitioners and patients.

It's much more difficult to understand, accept, or succeed in using images to cure cancer or arthritis because you can't see an immediate bodily reaction to your images. Introspection yields no information, and there aren't any biofeedback machines that can show you changes taking place in your immune system right this minute. The lag time between doing your visualization exercises and getting the results of blood tests or X-rays is too long.

I believe that the effects of visualization on the immune system are just as immediate and dramatic as the effects of relaxation imagery. I predict that this will be borne out if and when biofeedback machines for the immune system are invented. If we ever get such biofeedback machines, healing imagery will become the treatment of choice for immune disorders, preempting radiation, chemotherapy, and surgery in many cases.

For now, you don't really know for sure when it's working. The best you can do is to sharpen your powers of introspection. Train yourself to recognize the slightest improvement in your sense of well-being. Tune into your body and become an expert in all the ways you can feel.

Invent an imaginary sense or cue that will tell you that your healing visualization is working. For example, train yourself to focus on your heartbeat so that you can actually feel it in your throat or wrists or chest. After a healing visualization, feel your heart beating strongly and slowly. Let that be the sign that your healing is working. Tell yourself, "My heart is strong and regular. I am getting well again.

22

Pain Control

"Pain—has an element of Blank—
It cannot recollect
When it begun—or if there were
A time when it was not"

—*Emily Dickinson*

This chapter applies to all sorts of pain, including pain resulting from injury or disease, migraines, back and neck pain, arthritis, irritable bowel syndrome, cancer, gall and kidney stones, neuralgias, jaw problems, and so on. Visualization is an important strategy in pain control, particularly control of chronic, nagging pain from a permanent or long-term condition.

The visualization techniques in this chapter work in addition to traditional medicine, not in place of it. Make sure you have an accurate diagnosis of your problem and avail yourself of all the relief possible from traditional treatments for pain.

The treatment that immediately comes to mind for pain is drugs. There are many powerful painkillers that work. For acute, temporary conditions, drugs may be just what you need. But for chronic pain, drugs are not as effective to begin with. They do less and less for you in the same dosages as time goes on. And they cause many undesirable side effects. Another drastic solution is to surgically cut nerves transmitting chronic pain. Unfortunately, the pain often returns after a short period of relief.

Other treatments are less drastic and often more effective over the long term: heat and cold therapy, massage, biofeedback, physical therapy, acupuncture, trigger-point injections of anesthetics, and TENS—transcutaneous (across the skin) electrical nerve stimulators. Special exercises and physical therapy are often necessary to prevent or reverse muscular problems that often accompany chronic pain: muscle weakness and atrophy, tendon and ligament shortening, and joint immobility.

Besides physical symptoms, there are many emotional and practical problems often associated with chronic pain: depression, anxiety, anger, isolation, strained relationships, job loss, financial reverses, and loss of mobility. Visualization can reinforce your efforts to cope with these problems.

For a more detailed explanation of the full range of chronic pain problems, see *The Chronic Pain Control Workbook* by Ellen Mohr Catalano.

The Nature of Pain

Four aspects of pain make it susceptible to control by visualization: (1) pain makes you tense your muscles, (2) pain requires your full attention, (3) pain is in your brain, and (4) pain is modulated by meaning.

Pain makes you tense your muscles. When one part of your body hurts, you tense muscles all over your body in an attempt to favor the sore spot. You try to hold the painful area immobile while walking, sitting down, or getting up. You make other, unaccustomed muscles do the work usually done by the muscles around the painful spot. Your posture gets crooked and gravity itself becomes your enemy. All this extra muscular tension actually makes the pain worse. What started as a small muscle spasm in your lower back can become complete lockup of your upper body.

The relaxation phase of your visualization reverses this process and gives your muscles some rest. As your overall level of muscular tension declines, your sensation of pain from the primary site also declines.

Pain requires your full attention. You can only concentrate on one thing at a time. If you divert your attention away from your pain, you literally can't feel it. At the most basic level, visualization functions as a distraction from your pain. You will probably find yourself looking forward to your visualization sessions not only because they help you in long-term pain control, but also because you just feel better *while* you're visualizing.

Pain is in your brain. When your foot hurts, the pain isn't just in your foot. For you to feel pain, the pain messages must travel up your leg nerves to your spinal cord and up your spinal cord to your brain. Then how much pain you feel, or how long you feel it, depends on your brain's reaction.

Your brain produces chemicals such as serotonin, endorphins, and en-kephalins. These chemicals are neurotransmitters that travel to your spinal cord and brain, where they can stop pain messages from being transmitted to your brain or received by your brain.

When you're engaged in any kind of vivid visualization, your brain is emit-ting alpha waves, a condition that increases your chances of producing pain-blocking neurotransmitters. You further encourage their formation by visualizing the chemicals and how their pain-blocking action works.

Pain is modulated by meaning. Pain is not an automatic, mechanical phenomenon. It fluctuates according to the *meaning* you assign to it each moment. In a classic study, Beecher compared pain ratings made by wounded soldiers and civilian patients in postoperative hospital wards. He found that soldiers consis-tently reported less pain than civilians with nearly identical physical problems. The deciding variable was *meaning*: for the civilians, being hurt and operated on was a frightening disruption of their normally peaceful lives. For the soldiers, being wounded and in the hospital meant that they would soon be going home—they had escaped the horrors of war and their pain was modulated by this posi-tive meaning.

Visualization takes advantage of this by examining the negative meanings you have given your pain, refuting them, and replacing them with more positive meanings. For example, if chronic back pain means to you that you will never ski again, you can counter that negative thought by thinking that now you will have time to write a novel, something you've always wanted to try.

Receptive Visualization

Because pain has such a strong psychological effect, the self-knowledge offered by receptive visualization is particularly important. This is what you should ac-complish in your receptive visualization:

- Explore emotions surrounding your pain.
- Clarify the unique meaning your pain has for you.
- Find your personal images for pain and pain relief.
- Find out if your pain is conferring any benefits upon you, and find ways to get the benefits without the pain.
- Uncover any negative thoughts that might interfere with pain control.
- List the practical tasks associated with treating your pain and main-taining as normal a lifestyle as possible.

Instructions

Lie down in a comfortable position. Experiment with lying on your back or side, propping pillows under your knees, or stuffing them between your thighs—find the most comfortable position that will minimize pain and allow you to release the muscles that are protecting your painful area.

Close your eyes and relax. Imagine that you are lying in the sun, very warm and drowsy. Let the sun's heat collect in the area of your body that feels pain. Your pain soaks up the sunlight like a sponge absorbing warm water. See the painful area glowing a warm rose color. Notice the size and shape of the glowing area. As the warmth eases the soreness, see if you can shrink the painful area a little. Feel muscles you weren't even aware of releasing and relaxing around the painful area.

Spend a few moments entertaining relaxing images and see if you feel a reduction in the pain you are feeling right now. As you practice your pain control visualizations, you'll probably find that the pain often begins to subside as soon as you lie down and close your eyes. But don't worry if you get no relief in this first session.

As you lie still, let your pain fill your awareness. Empty your mind of everything except the fact of your pain. Watch and listen and feel what comes to fill this emptiness. What picture or sound or taste or smell or physical sensation do you experience? Whatever images arise, just accept them and contemplate them.

Some people see colors or jagged shapes. Others get a metallic or salty taste in the back of their throats. Some hear harsh sounds or drumming in time with the beat of their hearts. Images of knotted ropes, fire, sharp needles, hard stones, or broken sticks are common.

Whatever spontaneous images you receive, develop them by adding details and impressions from all your senses. When an image is vivid and complete, imagine changing the image into its opposite. Untwist the knotted ropes until they are loose, silken strands. Change a salty taste to sweet. Glue broken sticks together. These symbolic images will form the basis for your later programmed visualizations. At this point, concentrate on developing several pain images, and don't worry if you can't fully reverse them now.

Next go to your special place. Prepare a screen or a curtain or an alcove where someone can stand out of your sight. Imagine that your pain has taken on a life of its own. Imagine that your pain has become a person, standing behind the screen or curtain, ready to answer your questions.

Ask your pain questions such as:

Why are you with me?

What message do you have for me?

When will you go?

How do I prolong you?

What do I need to know about you?

How do you benefit me?

How can I get rid of you?

Take note of the answers to these questions. Accept them without judgment. You can analyze them later. Just listen with a curious, respectful interest. Your pain may respond with gestures instead of words, by giving you something, or by making ideas just "pop into" your mind. Whatever you get, take it as interesting information from your unconscious.

If you wish, you can also ask your inner guide the same set of questions about the pain.

Now let your pain presence leave. Activate your viewing device. Turn on the TV or take the velvet cloth off the crystal ball. Watch some selected scenes: when you first started having your pain, when you went to the doctor, when you were in the hospital, and so on. Concentrate on the emotional scenes: the time your roommate had to drive you to the emergency room and you were so embarrassed, the time you woke up in pain at three in the morning and felt so depressed, the time you had to stay home from the family reunion and were so angry, the time you were waiting for test results and you had the anxiety attack, the time you felt so rotten that you screamed at your child, the time you thought you were getting better and then got worse, all the times you've been irritable or withdrawn or frightened.

Notice which emotions seem to come up for you over and over. Restrain your judgment. Don't call your emotions good or bad. Just let them roll across the screen and watch them with detached interest.

Now add a voice-over soundtrack to the scenes. Listen in to your thoughts, especially the negative comments about your pain that fuel your painful emotions: "I'll never get over this," "I'm just a drain on everybody," "This is awful," "I can't stand it," and so on.

If you have trouble hearing the negative thoughts, watch the scenes in slow motion or enter into them as if they were happening to you right now. Again, don't be judgmental. Just listen and learn.

Next look for scenes of secondary gain. Look for times when you got some advantage from your pain: the time you got an extra week to study for your calculus exam, the time your obnoxious cousin stayed at a motel instead of with you, the time you got to go first because you weren't feeling well, the time your mother brought you soup and cookies, the times when your spouse just left you alone, not pressing about money or housework.

There's no need to beat yourself up. Every bad situation has some good aspects. Just notice what you get from your pain, and begin to consider ways to get the same benefits without having to be in pain.

Finally review the scenes to discover where you need better coping skills. Notice what practical tasks you have had trouble accomplishing: taking the cat to the vet for booster shots, remembering your symptoms so you can tell the doctor, getting the storm windows up, and so on. Include the health-related things that you have been meaning to do but haven't done yet: reading up on your medical problem, blocking up the head of your bed, starting an allergen elimination diet, setting aside time each day for visualization, and so on.

End this visualization when you have tried all the suggestions, when you feel tired, or when you get too distracted to continue. You may have to spend several sessions using these receptive techniques to explore the unique nature and meaning of your pain.

Suggested Imagery

If you had trouble finding clear images for pain and its relief, here are some suggested images, adapted with permission from *The Chronic Pain Control Workbook* by Ellen Mohr Catalano.

Pain Image	Relief Image
For dull tension headache	
Band tightening around head	Band loosening, falling away
Vice gripping head	Vice disintegrating
Muscles in head contracting	Muscles loose, limp
For sharp, throbbing vascular headache	
Pins becoming tiny dots and disappearing	Pins becoming tiny dots and disappearing
Razor melting	Razor melting
Snow-covered ground, cool	Snow-covered ground, cool colors
For dull, muscular aches	
Bricks or heavy stones pressing on muscles	Bricks or stones dissolving, fading, falling away
Knotted ropes	Ropes untying, limp, or becoming flowing water
For ripping, tearing, burning muscular pain	
Ripping fabric	Fabric mended and strong
Flames	Flames dying out or extinguished by water flowing over them; cool wind blowing out flame
Knife cutting	Knife dissolving, cut healing
For gastrointestinal discomfort	
Flames in abdomen and chest	Flames extinguished by cool water
Acid secretions in abdomen and chest	Acid replaced by healing oxygen with each breath
Muscles tight and contracted	Healing blood flowing in to warm and release muscle tension

Affirmations

Take the time to compose effective affirmations based on your receptive visualization experiences. For example, you can reinforce your personal images for pain and its relief like this:

Pain goes as the ropes untwist.
The sun is melting my pain.
My red pain fades into pink cotton candy.

Any unique meanings associated with your pain should be summed up—in a positive, accepting, healing way—by affirmations such as these:

My pain leaves me as I accept myself more.
The pain tells me when it's time to rest.
I accept my pain as a part of getting older.

Include an affirmation acknowledging and accepting your feelings about pain, and suggesting ways to cope with unpleasant emotions:

It's natural to be angry.
I acknowledge and accept my anger.
When I feel anxious, I do my relaxation mantra.
It's OK to feel depressed. It will pass with time.

If you discovered any hidden benefits provided by your pain that might make it hard to let go of, create an affirmation that reminds you of your ability to get your needs met without pain:

I can rest without migraines.
Saying no is easier than backache.
I face up to George with my true feelings, not pain.

Carefully write out affirmations that refute your automatic, irrational thoughts about your pain:

This is unfortunate, not unlivable.
I have at least an even chance of feeling much better.
I carefully check out new symptoms, with no assumptions.

Reinforce your ability to accomplish all the daily tasks required to cope with your pain:

What's the priority here?
I can ask for help.
This is it. This is my life, the good and the pain.

Programmed Visualization

Lie down in the position you find most comfortable. Close your eyes and spend as much time as you need to get completely relaxed. The most profound pain relief from visualization comes from the physical relaxation it affords. Many patients in pain clinics succeed in controlling their pain using relaxation alone.

Try pacing your relaxation and pain reduction with your breathing and voice. As you inhale, clench your fists and focus on your pain. As you exhale, relax your fists, make a humming or sighing sound, and let the pain fade away a little. Continue in a slow, steady rhythm, sinking deeper and deeper into relaxation as your pain fades further and further away. Tell yourself, "I can relax my pain away."

Begin with some straightforward, relatively literal images. Imagine that your brain is oozing endorphin, the morphine-like chemical that blocks pain messages. See clear droplets of the chemical flowing from your brain down your spinal cord. Wherever the chemical goes it coats nerves and interrupts the pain messages from the part of your body that hurts. Your brain isn't getting the message of pain. The pain becomes faint and intermittent, like a voice on a bad transatlantic phone connection. Tell yourself, "My body knows best."

Now shift your attention to the part of your body that hurts. See the surrounding muscles that are often so tense and protectively clenched. Watch as the muscles relax, letting go. As the surrounding areas relax, the painful area itself is free to relax. See an increased flow of blood moving into the painful area, carrying nutrients in and toxic wastes out.

Reverse or correct the cause of your pain in your mind's eye. For example, visualize inflamed muscles and tendons fading from angry red to healthy pink and shrinking to their normal size. If you have a migraine headache, concentrate on images of your distended carotid arteries shrinking and the blood flowing out of your head. If you suffer from irritable bowel syndrome, see the spastic contractions of your colon slow and stop, easing the stretching and distention. If you have back pain caused by a "slipped" or herniated disc, visualize the disc resuming its natural cushion shape, the swelling subsiding, and the pressure on your sciatic nerve easing. Tell yourself, "I'm getting back into balance."

If you don't have a very clear idea of the mechanics or chemistry of your problem, resolve right now to find out more about it. Knowledge of what's damaged or out of balance will inspire you to create effective images of the healing process. The previous chapters in this book can give you some specific information about many injuries and diseases, and you can also ask your doctor or librarian to suggest other sources of information.

Now try moving your pain to another location in your body. Tell yourself, "I created my pain in my knee, I can re-create it in my foot." Think of your pain as heat being conducted through the solid metal of your body, or as a stage light being faded down on one part of the stage and brought up on another. Many people who have trouble *reducing* their pain find that they can *move* it. If you can shift your pain even an inch, you have established your control over it, and will soon be able to reduce it.

Next move on to more symbolic images. Imagine that there is a faucet in your brain that controls the flow of endorphins and other natural painkillers. Wander up and down the corridors of your mind, looking into different rooms and closets until you find the right faucet. Turn it on all the way. See the endorphins canceling pain messages like water washing away dirt or shorting out electrical wires.

Spend a generous amount of time entertaining and elaborating the symbols of pain and relief that you prepared during your receptive visualizations. If you have a muscle spasm in your back, see your muscles as twisted, knotty tree roots that gradually change to loose bundles of elastic shock cords. For irritable bowel syndrome you could envision your lower gastrointestinal tract as a giant snake that curls up and goes to sleep. For a migraine headache you could think of the blood vessels in your head as heavy-duty canvas firehoses, swelled stiff and rigid with water, and then find the fire hydrant and turn down the valve so that the hoses become loose and flexible again. Use affirmations to reinforce your metaphorical images.

Now visualize your treatments—drugs, exercise, acupuncture, or whatever. See the treatments as powerful and effective. If you have arthritis, see the aspirin reducing inflammation like a fire extinguisher putting out a fire. Watch yourself doing finger and hand exercises and preserving your flexibility. If you have temporomandibular (jaw) pain, you should visualize your yawning exercises stretching your jaw muscles, your acupuncture popping the balloon of pain, and your muscle relaxants working like meat tenderizer to turn your clenched muscles to mush. Tell yourself, "I'm receiving the best of care."

For back pain, see your spine lengthening and straightening during floor exercises, traction, or wearing a brace. For irritable bowel syndrome, visualize the extra fiber or the Gelusil as lining your gut with relaxing cushions. If you're using heat and cold to treat your sore feet, imagine alternate waves of red and blue light flushing the pain away.

Move on to images of yourself coping with your pain: protecting your back by proper lifting, curtailing your social commitments so you have time to rest, asking for the help you need, doing your physical therapy exercises and visualizations faithfully, making and keeping doctor's appointments, saving a little time for hobbies or reading, thanking your kids for their consideration instead of snapping at them when you're irritable, figuring out your bills, regrouting the bathroom sink, reorganizing the carpool so you can avoid driving in the morning when your back is tight, and so on, and on, and on. Tell yourself, "My health is the first priority. I must take care of myself."

Remind yourself: "I am responsible for coping with my pain. I accept it as part of my current reality. I own it. I handle my pain, it doesn't handle me. It's part of the universe I created and I can control it."

Indulge yourself by creating a fantasy meaning for your pain. Your arm hurts because the dragon bit it when you were rescuing the princess in the tower. You limp because of an old war wound acquired while fighting with the French Resistance. You are Camille or Anna Karenina, suffering for love. Whenever you get a twinge of pain during the day, recall your fantasy with a secret smile.

Always finish your pain control visualizations with a vision of yourself in the future, free of pain or at least in control of pain. Feel your lover's arms around you, hear the laughter of your children at the beach, smell the salt air, taste the roast pheasant, receive your diploma with pride, feel your body moving strong and free, and watch yourself arriving at work, energetic and enthusiastic.

In your vision of the future, see yourself taking preventive measures so you won't have a relapse of your problem. If you have a tricky back, see yourself with good posture, lifting properly, and getting regular exercise that tones your abdominal muscles. If you have an irritable bowel, see and taste the high-fiber food you will be eating. Watch yourself taking afternoon naps and skipping the second cup of coffee to keep your stress level down. If you get migraine headaches, see yourself asking for an extension of a deadline, checking in with your feelings to see if you're suppressing anger, and doing progressive muscle relaxation before lunch every day. If you have jaw problems, see yourself throwing away your last pack of gum, brushing your teeth vigorously, and flossing daily. Use affirmations in the present tense, such as "I am free of pain and preventing its return."

End your pain control visualization when you're ready. Don't expect to give full justice to every part of this visualization every time. As always, this outline is just a suggestion to get you started. You should change the sequence to suit yourself and concentrate on different parts of it at different times. Your most powerful images will be those you discover yourself, and only you can determine the best way to put those images together in a given visualization session.

What To Expect

Living with pain, especially chronic or recurring pain, requires persistence and patience. You may experience significant pain reduction as soon as you start using visualization, then two weeks later suffer a relapse of painful symptoms for no apparent reason. Don't give up. Strive to acquire the *habit* of deliberately relaxing your body and visualizing pain relief. During episodes of more severe pain, remind yourself that you're working toward long-term results.

The emotional ups and downs of chronic pain can be as painful as the physical symptoms. If you suffer from overwhelming anxiety or depression, seriously consider talking with a psychologist or other professional counselor.

As you practice visualization, your original healing images may lose their power as they become overly familiar. Occasionally you'll have to do some receptive visualizations and dream up some new symbols. Here are some additional images that have worked for others:

Tunnel

Imagine that your pain is a tunnel that you can enter and exit. As you enter the tunnel, your pain increases for a moment. Then, as you walk along, you see the end of the tunnel coming nearer. With each step, the light at the end of the tunnel becomes larger and larger and your pain becomes less and less. As you leave the tunnel and walk out into the light, your pain fades away. Every step heals your body and makes it stronger. You own this tunnel: you can enter and go through it any time you want, and doing so always makes you feel better.

Numbness

Focus your attention on one of your hands. Imagine that it is becoming numb. First feel a pleasant tingling in the fingertips and a warmth flowing throughout your hand. Let the tingling spread to your whole hand. Now let the feeling fade. Your hand is becoming numb. All feeling drains out of your hand and it becomes totally numb, like a block of wood.

When your hand is completely numb, completely heavy and wooden, place it over the part of your body that hurts. Let the numbness drain out of your hand into your body. Transfer the numbness into the part that hurts until it also is numb.

This is a powerful hypnotic technique called "glove anesthesia." It has been used to perform surgery on hypnotized patients without any other kind of anesthesia.

If your pain is in a part of your body that you can't easily reach with your hand, create the numbness in the part that hurts and don't use the hand transfer method.

Red ball

Imagine that your pain is a large, red ball of energy, like the sun. Watch this bright red ball become smaller and smaller. As it shrinks, watch it change color to a soft pink. It gets smaller and smaller, changing again to a light blue color. As the ball gets smaller and smaller, you feel less and less pain. Keep watching until the ball is just a tiny blue dot. Make it disappear and feel your pain disappear with it.

Cool water

Imagine that the part that hurts is bathed in cool water. Feel the cool water flowing away, taking your pain with it. The water washes away your pain like water washing away mud or sand. The area feels incredibly soothed and relaxed as the water washes away the last traces of discomfort.

Volume knob

Imagine that your pain is a radio turned up uncomfortably loud. Imagine reaching out and grasping the volume knob on the radio. Turn your pain down slowly, like turning down a radio. Turn it down to the merest whisper of sound.

Sensory substitution

This is a good technique to use if you find it difficult to believe that you can eliminate all your pain. Change your pain to another sensation like itching, tingling, heat, cold, or numbness. The substitute sensation doesn't have to be a pleasant one, just *less unpleasant* than the pain. Another advantage of this technique is that it allows you to know that the pain is still there, in case you need to monitor it for medical treatment

Special place

Go to your special place and get comfortable. Tell yourself, "This is my special place, a haven from the pain." When you are fully settled into your special place and the details are very real to you, slowly open your eyes and sit up. Go about your normal routine as if you were still in your special place, directing the actions of your body and your speech by remote control. The idea is to disassociate yourself from your pain. It's as if you have moved up to a higher level of awareness, putting some distance between your consciousness and your pain.

At any time during the day, you can reinforce this fantasy by closing your eyes briefly and intensifying the details of your special place. Tell yourself, "I'm operating from my special, painless place. I'm not fully in the real world at all."

Another version of this distancing fantasy is to imagine that you are an alien intelligence who has taken control of your mind and body in order to learn more about life on earth. As your own "puppet master," you can feel the pain only dimly. You're aware of it, but it's just a minor annoyance in the background of all the fascinating new experiences you're enjoying.

Lockbox

Put your pain inside a small, strong metal or wooden box. Shut the box and lock it. Put the box into the refrigerator or a closet. Slam the door. Lock it, nail it shut, or put duct tape around the edges to firmly seal the door shut. Tell yourself, "I'm locking my pain away. It can't get out."

Example

Melanie was a ceramist and painter who suffered from migraines. When one of her headaches was coming on, she'd become very sensitive to loud noises and bright lights. Her peripheral vision would sparkle or scintillate, and sometimes dark spots seemed to float before her eyes. These warning symptoms would last a couple of hours, with Melanie getting more and more irritable and depressed.

Then the headache would hit: incredible, throbbing pain starting on one side and spreading to the other. For the next six hours she was nauseated, trembling, and unable to eat. She just pulled the drapes, crawled into bed and waited it out. Aspirin, codeine, percodan, marijuana—nothing touched her pain.

Melanie had been using visualization for years in her artwork. "I felt so dense," she says, "the day I realized I could have been using my imagination on my headaches as well as my paintings and pots."

The first thing she did was to read up on migraines. She found that her warning symptoms were very typical of the prodrome or "aura" reported by many migraine sufferers: flushing, pallor, noise and light sensitivity, anxiety, irritability, flashing lights, zig-zag lines or spots before the eyes, and a scintillating disturbance of vision.

In the aura phase, the carotid arteries in the affected side of the neck and head narrow, restricting blood flow. Then in the pain phase, these same arteries overreact and swell. The arteries on the other side may join in. The increased blood supply contains chemicals that signal pain to nearby nerve endings. Some people can get relief by pressing on their arteries in the early pain phase. Melanie's six-hour headaches were about average in duration, and her symptoms were typical.

When Melanie read a description of the "migraine personality," the label irritated her, but she had to admit that she shared many of the characteristics: perfectionism, ambition, rigidity, orderliness, competitiveness, and an unwillingness to delegate responsibility to others. This sounded like her *modus operandi* whenever she had to set up a new show of her work at a gallery.

The triggering factors of migraine were very interesting: performance anxiety, suppressed hostility, stress in general, certain foods like cheese or alcohol, and some drugs like birth control pills. Melanie didn't take birth control pills or drink alcohol, but she loved cheese, had intense performance anxiety before gallery openings, and had trouble expressing her anger.

Armed with this information, Melanie did a receptive visualization in which she strolled through a new wing of the Louvre in Paris. This was the "Melanie Wing," full of paintings and sculptures of herself as a person who no longer had migraines. Most of the paintings were super realistic, like giant photographs. She saw Melanie meditating night and morning, Melanie venting her feelings freely and honestly, Melanie avoiding cheese, Melanie keeping a sketch diary of her feelings and moods, Melanie responding to her warning symptoms with instant relaxation.

In another receptive visualization, Melanie talked to the visionary artist William Blake, her inner guide, whom she affectionately called "Dippy Bill." Bill told her that migraines were her angels, taking her aside to rest when she needed time out from the world. Melanie knew that this was true. She often drove herself into exhaustion, pushing to meet impossible deadlines that she could only escape by collapsing with a migraine. She printed the affirmation: "I schedule time to rest" on a card and pinned it to her easel. She wrote the word "REST" on every page of her Week-at a-Glance appointment notebook.

Whenever Melanie felt her "aura" coming on, she would stop everything and go into her room or someplace else where she could be alone. She would lie down if possible and do deep breathing exercises to relax. Then she would quickly run through a literal image of her carotid arteries relaxing, ceasing to contract. Then she'd go to her special place and talk to Dippy Bill: "It's happening again, Dippy. Would you take me away?"

William Blake took her by the hand and led her into a large picture hanging on the wall, like Alice passing through the looking glass. The picture was usually one of Blake's creation paintings or etchings, and they would walk together into that luminous, magical landscape where angels sing in every apple tree and eternal truths shine forth like suns through the thin veil of the vegetative world.

Sometimes Blake took Melanie up into the sky to rest on a cloud or talk to the bearded old man who was "not quite God but a good friend of hers." Once they visited the first Impressionist show in prewar Paris. Another time they called on Monet in his garden at Giverny and ate cucumber sandwiches on the bridge over the water lily pond.

These elaborate fantasies took Melanie out of the immediate stressful circumstances that precipitated her migraines. The more she could involve herself in the walks with William Blake, the more she relaxed. Six months after starting to use visualization in this way, she was able to avert her headaches about two times out of five. She found that she was getting fewer headaches and her average headache lasted only four hours instead of six.

During an actual migraine headache, Melanie felt too drained to sustain a prolonged fantasy. She relied on simpler methods of pain control. First she would concentrate on her breathing, counting each inhale and exhale in a steady cadence: one . . . two . . . one . . . two . . . one . . . two . . . This helped calm her and distract her from repetitive negative thoughts such as, "I wish I would just die" or "I can't stand this—I'm going crazy."

Lying in the darkened room, Melanie would pretend that the room was a long tunnel of pain, and that her bed was a train taking her through the tunnel. She would imagine a distant light growing larger and larger until she emerged from the tunnel's mouth into a beautiful valley on a warm spring day.

She also used the numbness technique. She imagined that her hands were in very cold water until they actually felt numb. Then she'd place her palms against her temples, wrap her fingers up over the top of her head, and apply gentle pressure. She visualized the cool numbness flowing from her hands into her head.

A vacation to England and France disrupted Melanie's routines and brought on some "killer" migraines. When she returned to the states, she was discouraged and didn't use her visualizations for several months. But she started up again before a big gallery show in San Francisco, and made it through the opening with two auras but no full-blown headaches. Somewhere in the hiatus, William Blake went away and Monet started showing up as her inner guide.

VI

Resources

23

History and Theory

"Every person who has had the extraordinary experience of having a visualization become reality has their own theory of how visualization works. A psychologist might theorize that fixing an image in the mind stimulates the subconscious to be continuously alert to situations that will further the goal and to signal the conscious mind to assertively act in those situations. A religious person might say that it is God hearing a person's prayer and answering it. An occult mystic might say that the energy surrounding the visualization directly influences the objects and people in the world around it."

—*Mike Samuels*

A thousand words *about* visualization cannot substitute for the experience itself. That's why this chapter is at the end of the book instead of the beginning—I wanted you to start doing visualization right away instead of reading about it.

Although it's not strictly necessary to read this chapter in order to learn the skill of visualization, it can be interesting to study the history of visualization and the theories about it. If you tend to be skeptical about "New Age" notions, you'll find it especially helpful to read about the long history and many scientific experiments that underlie the techniques taught in this book.

HISTORY

This is an overview that just hits the high points. If it whets your appetite for a more thorough treatment, read Jean Acherterberg's *Imagery in Healing* or Mike and Nancy Samuels' *Seeing With the Mind's Eye*. The former is neatly organized and focuses on the history of medicine. The latter is wider-ranging, with historical, scientific, and anthropological asides scattered throughout the book.

Primitive Images

Humans have believed from the beginning in the power of the image to affect reality. The earliest human images known to exist are ice-age cave paintings dating from 60,000 to 10,000 B.C. Examples of these found in France, Spain, Africa, and Scandinavia are all remarkably similar. Two common subjects are animals and men wearing animal masks. The animals are undoubtedly objects of a hunt, and the men are probably making magic to ensure a successful hunt.

Later cultures established between the Tigris and Euphrates rivers were more agrarian, growing their food rather than hunting for survival. Images from these cultures show fewer animals and more fertility gods to ensure successful harvests. A culture's most common images obviously arise from its most basic needs.

Shamanism

Shamans are witch doctors who use many visualization techniques to heal their patients or curse their enemies. Shamans can be benevolent healers or violent sorcerers. This supports my contention that visualization can be used for both good and evil.

There are still a few shamans around today in Africa, Lappland, Hawaii, along the Upper Amazon in South America, in aboriginal Australia, and among North American Indians consciously preserving the ancient traditions. Anthropologists and historians of healing study the surviving shamans to learn about the oldest healing methods. Their visualization methods are probably similar to those of prehistoric tribes.

Shamans on separate continents exhibit an amazing number of similarities in their work. They also share an amazing success rate in curing their patients.

Shamans are almost always men. A shaman heals by making an imaginary journey to the underworld on his patient's behalf. He first purifies himself with a fast from all food and alcohol. He sits or lies near his sick patient and closes his eyes, excluding all light. He does relaxation breathing while an assistant keeps up a rapid drumming or rattling sound. The shaman imagines entering the earth through a cave, animal hole, spring, or well. He goes down a ribbed tunnel and comes out in a landscape beneath the earth. He intensifies the experience by involving each of his senses in turn.

While in the underworld, the shaman meets spirits, usually in the form of power animals. They can appear as real animals, as drawings, or as statues. Sometimes only their footprints or droppings are seen. Often the same animal appears in several manifestations during one journey. Each power animal has a human form as well, but rarely shows it. A shaman usually has one or two special power animals that he sees often. His power animals may change from time to time. They may take the form of mythological beasts like dragons or griffins, but they are never insects, reptiles, or fish, which are considered intrusive, harmful spirits.

The shaman asks questions of his power animal, usually simple yes or no questions about himself and his patient. The animal answers by moving toward the shaman in some way or by taking him on an underworld journey. Finally, the shaman returns to the real world by a different route, sometimes bringing a benevolent healing spirit with him. The spirit heals the patient, not the shaman.

The amazing aspects of shamanism are the similarities among widely scattered tribes that have never had contact with one another, the impressive cure rates, and the parallels with other, more "civilized" healing traditions. How do the shaman's underground journeys compare with your receptive visualizations and conversations with your inner guide?

Ancient Traditions

The Greeks

Aesculapius was the first famous healer we know about. He was probably a real person, although we don't know for sure. No written records survive from his time. He was such a legendary healer that he eventually became a demigod in Greek mythology. Over two hundred temples were built in his honor. At temples patients were healed in body, mind, and spirit through the power of dreams.

Hippocrates was a later Greek who originated the Hippocratic oath and is considered the father of modern medicine. He taught that whatever affects the mind affects the body, and that health is a sign of achieving harmony with nature. Greek healers in Hippocrates' time often had a patient dream of being healed by the gods. In that special conscious state (hypnogogic sleep) just before falling fully asleep, the patient would dream of the ancient healer Aesculapius, who would let the snakes around his caduceus slither over the patient's body. The snakes would lick the patient's wounds and eyes, diagnosing the problem and healing it simultaneously.

Galen was a later Greek healer, and the greatest influence on medieval medicine. His contribution to visualization for healing was to stress that the patient's spontaneous images are the key to diagnosis.

Aristotle is also important to the history of visualization because he wrote that all thought is composed of images. His idea influenced such later thinkers as Locke, William James, Francis Galton, and Edward Titchener. Their contention that images are the proper subject of psychology held sway for many years. It went out of fashion when John Watson and the other behaviorists came on the scene in this century. The behaviorists claimed that mental activity is unmeasurable and therefore unsuitable for study—only behavior can be observed and measured, therefore only behavior is appropriate for scientific inquiry. In the last twenty years, introspection has come to be accepted again as a legitimate way of observing mental processes.

Eastern Traditions

Ancient Chinese medical texts speak of "Fu-zheng." This is the natural, self-generated enhancement of your disease-fighting powers—the same phenomenon now being studied so avidly by researchers into the complexities of the immune system.

Another ancient eastern tradition that is still going strong is yoga. Yogis visualized images, projecting different colors and shapes to different areas of their bodies. A similar technique called *dkihr* was used by Sufis and other Moslems. In his book *Seeing With the Mind's Eye*, Mike Samuels says that the Trantic Yoga practiced in the sixth century in India was "the most highly developed system man has achieved for holding images in his mind to achieve an effect."

Also from the east we have the concept of a universal energy that powers the cosmos and everything in it, including human beings. The Chinese call it *chi*, the Indians call it *prana* or *kundaline*, and the Japanese call it *ki*.

The Middle Ages

During the Middle Ages, the visualization techniques and other traditions of the shamans were kept alive by wise women—healers and herbalists who came to be persecuted by the Christian church as witches.

The church claimed that faith alone should be sufficient to cure all that ails you. Shrines and relics abounded. Although there were many negative aspects such as the selling of fake relics and severe mortification of the flesh, doubtless many people were cured or consoled through their own powers of healing. The old Greek idea of a healing temple was revived, with saints Coismas and Damian taking the place of Aesculapius in the healing dreams of pre-sleep.

Alchemy and astrology flourished, despite the church's official disapproval. They both contained elements of visualization. Alchemy was much more than an attempt by early chemists to turn base metals into gold. It was an elaborate system of rituals and symbols intended also to heal illness, purify the soul, and align all human society with God's plan for the universe. Likewise, astrology was an extremely complex system of astronomy, primitive cosmology, and mystical philosophy used for healing and spiritual discipline as well as for predicting the future.

Hermes Trismegistus, supposedly a philosopher of ancient Egypt, was the favorite sage of the medieval alchemists. He posited the primacy of the mind, not matter, in the universe. He said that mental images have energy and vibration levels of their own, that they affect the physical universe, and that they can transmute fear to courage, hate to love, and anger to compassion. Later Hermetic philosophers healed people by having them visualize themselves in perfect health. This is still an important part of healing visualization today.

The Renaissance

The greatest physician and alchemist of the sixteenth century was Paracelsus. He espoused many revolutionary ideas: the use of the vernacular instead of Latin by educated men, the value of direct observation in natural science, the importance of the individual's judgment as opposed to social consensus, the acceptance of women as healers, the value of folk medicines, and the use of opium as a pain killer. He was a great believer in the power of the human mind to heal the body. He wrote, "The power of the imagination is a great factor in medicine. It may produce diseases in man and it may cure them."

As the scientific method was developed, interest in intuitive methods of discovering and changing the world declined. Cartesian dualism forcibly separated the mind from the body. The eighteenth century proudly proclaimed itself the "Age of Reason." The visualization techniques of the wise women, the alchemists, and the astrologers fell into disrepute and went underground. People didn't stop visualizing—the leading thinkers of the day just stopped studying it and writing about it. The study of visualization and other intuitive or mystical practices became the province of secret, cabalistic societies like the Rosicrucians.

The Nineteenth Century

Interest in the occult and the natural powers of the mind revived again in the nineteenth century. Receptive visualization techniques such as automatic writing and crystal gazing became popular. Psychics and seances became more or less respectable.

Anton Mesmer studied "animal magnetism" and used it to calm hysteria, heal psychosomatic illness, and induce anesthesia. Although his theories of the nature of the hypnotic trance were later proved wrong, he was the first practicing hypnotist. He learned that the depth of a trance state and the accomplishment of a desired change both depend on the vividness of the images created in the subject's mind.

In the late 1800s, Mary Baker Eddy founded Christian Science. She took an extreme position regarding the mind's role in creating and curing disease: *all* bodily ills are created by man's mind. The *only* way to cure a disease or heal an injury is through prayer. Prayer is a matter of asking God, who is infinite mind, to restore health.

The first doctor to elicit images to help in curing neurotic patients was Joseph Breuer, a Viennese physician practicing in the late nineteenth century. Freud credited Breuer with the creation of psychoanalysis. Breuer found that he could reduce hysteria by letting patients relate their "fancies and daydreams."

Freud later adapted many of Breuer's techniques for use in free association and dream analysis.

1900-1950

In *Modern Man in Search of a Soul*, C. G. Jung says that images come to your awareness from all parts of your psyche. He calls the center of your psyche the "self" or "soul." From this center come images of the greatest regulating power. Images are the homeostatic mechanism of both the individual and the universe.

Another important Jungian concept is that of archetypes—inborn, universal symbols of great energy. For example, a cave is an archetypal image of the womb of mankind. A tree is an archetypal image of life grounded in earth and aspiring to the heavens. According to Jung, archetypes arise in many individuals at once when the universe needs them. Many of the images that arise spontaneously in receptive visualization are archetypes. They are especially useful for achieving growth and change.

Jung said that a ghost is just as real as a robber to the man who fears both. By this he meant that psychic happenings—mental images triggered internally or externally—are the *only* reality you have.

In 1909 Herbert Silberer published his experiments in "auto symbolism." He had experimental subjects try to think through complex problems while in a trance state. They found this difficult to do. However, the answers to the problems would often come into their awareness in symbolic form. Silberer dubbed this "auto symbolism," the process by which your mind automatically transforms disparate verbal data into unifying visual images.

Emil Coue was a French pharmacist who healed people by encouraging them to develop a positive attitude. He was the first to stress the importance of affirmations, coining the famous saying, "Every day, in every way, I am getting better and better."

In the 1920s, Edmund Jacobson performed an experiment demonstrating that when you visualize yourself running, your leg muscles move involuntarily. This was a key experiment showing the link between the conscious mind and the autonomic nervous system. Jacobson created Progressive Muscle Relaxation, a stress reduction technique that relies somewhat on visualization and is still in wide use today.

Another relaxation technique from the 1920s is autogenics. J. H. Schultz exhaustively covered the six basic autogenics techniques in six volumes edited by his colleague Wolfgang Luthe. They presented 2,400 case histories showing that their relaxation imagery was effective in helping patients recover from surgery and in treating asthma, headaches, arthritis, back pain, and diabetes. In addition to the basic autogenic themes of heaviness and warmth in the limbs, Schultz's advanced patients used images such as standing on top of a mountain, being on the moon, flying over the clouds, and watching a sunrise.

Franz Alexander is considered the father of psychosomatic medicine. In 1939 this Chicago physician wrote, "Many chronic disturbances are not caused by external, mechanical, chemical factors or by microorganisms, but by the continuous functional stress arising during the everyday life of the organism in its struggle for existence." These are the kind of "disturbances" that can best be set right with visualization.

An Italian psychiatrist named Roberto Assaglioli was a student and colleague of Freud, Jung, and Maslow. He created a comprehensive psychology called Psychosynthesis. This system sees human beings as tending naturally toward harmony with their inner selves and the outer world. Assaglioli used visualization techniques to diagnose emotional problems and to train the will to accomplish personal growth.

By 1950, the power of mental imagery was being explored and utilized in many disciplines. Grantly Dick-Read used imagery as part of his natural childbirth techniques. The Rorschach test was developed, using the mind's tendency to create images out of random shapes as a diagnostic tool for psychologists. Henry Murray's Thematic Apperception Test used the interpretation of meaningful images diagnostically. Many researchers were studying the placebo effect. In the more far-out reaches of science, Reich was building orgone boxes to concentrate cosmic energy and Kirlian photographers were trying to capture the body's aura on film.

1950 to the Present

One by one the ancient practices of visualization have been validated in the laboratory. Psychologist Erik Peper showed that fifty percent of a group of untrained people will salivate when led through a detailed visualization of a lemon. Paul Eckman, another psychologist at the University of California, found that mimicking an emotion influences your body in exactly the same way as actually experiencing the emotion.

At the Menninger Foundation, Stoya and Budzynski used autogenic phrases and EMG (electromyogram) biofeedback to relax forehead muscles and thereby ease tension headaches. They treated phobias and anxiety by having their patients combine relaxation exercises with visualizing stressful scenes.

The Immune System

Chlomo Breznitz, a psychologist at Hebrew University in Jerusalem, demonstrated that positive and negative expectations have opposite effects on blood levels of cortisol and prolactin, two hormones important in activating the immune system. Soldiers on hard marches were given different information about the length of the coming march. Their stress hormone levels always reflected their *expectations* of difficulty, not the *actual* difficulty.

Nicholas Hall, an M.D. at George Washington Medical Center in Washington, D.C., showed in 1984 that subjects could use their imaginations to increase the number of circulating white blood cells and their levels of thymosin-alpha-1, a hormone used by T helper cells. Both measures indicate the health of your immune system.

Psychologist Robert Ader and immunologist Nicholas Cohen found that suppression of the immune system can be conditioned. They repeatedly gave a group of rats saccharin water containing an immunosuppressant drug. Later they gave these rats plain saccharin water, with no drug. The rats' immune systems were suppressed anyway, just as if they had been given the drugged water. Their immune responses had been conditioned to the sweet taste of saccharin.

In another experiment, Dr. Novera Herbert Spector conditioned mice to increase their immune responses when exposed to the smell of camphor. Other work by George Solomon, Marvin Stein, Gerard Renoux, and Russian researchers shows that changes in the immune system of animals can be generated by selective damage to the brain's neocortex and hypothalamus.

Until this decade, no one could account physiologically for how conscious mental activity could produce changes in your immune system. The accepted wisdom was that your immune system is the most "autonomous" part of your autonomic nervous system—there was no known connection whatsoever between the higher, conscious areas of your brain and your immune functions. Countless dissections showed that the only connections were lower down, in the brain stem and spinal cord.

But new technology has allowed modern physiologists to see and trace finer and finer nerves in the body. They have now shown that nerves do indeed go from the higher brain centers to the thymus gland, spleen, lymph nodes, and bone marrow—all the key areas of your immune system. Your mind is "hardwired" to your immune system, and you can consciously improve your ability to fight disease through visualization.

Not only are there neural connections between your conscious mind and your immune system, there are also chemical connections. Your brain itself can produce chemicals that serve as messengers to the rest of your body, telling it to feel good, to disregard pain, or to mobilize to fight off disease.

A new specialty has emerged at the frontier of medical research. It's called psychoneuroimmunology, the study of how thoughts and feelings (psycho) interact with your nervous system (neuro) to promote healing (immunology).

Special Populations

Some of the most interesting research has been done with populations whose problems make them obvious choices for studying the mind-body connection.

Jeanne Achterberg's statistical research shows that mentally retarded and emotionally disturbed people have a significantly lower incidence of death due to cancer. Her theory is that these individuals can't understand the images of fear and death that surround cancer in our society. They can't visualize cancer as a sure killer. So they either don't get cancer as frequently, or if they do get it, have a better chance of survival.

In another study, demented elderly patients were repeatedly led through a series of multisensory images. This process decreased their disassociation from their emotions and helped to normalize their brain waves.

Dr. Bennett Braun found in a dramatic way that personality affects disease and allergies. One of his multiple-personality clients had diabetes, but only when a particular personality was in charge. Another man was allergic to citrus only when one of his multiple personalities was in charge.

Popularizers and New Agers

Visualization techniques have been taught and used by many popularizing professionals, evangelists, self-help authors, utopia builders, and new age gurus. For the religiously inclined, there is Norman Vincent Peale's 1952 book, *The Power of Positive Thinking*. The social and business applications of visualization are promoted by Dale Carnegie's *How To Win Friends and Influence People* and the confidence-boosting rallies of Zig Zigler and the like.

The pragmatic tinkerer's approach was taken by Robert McKim at Stanford in the 60s. He created the "Imaginarium," a geodesic dome equipped with light show projectors, loud speakers, smells introduced through the air conditioning, vibrators to shake the floor, and so on. All this gear was used to create totally controlled sensory experiences such as "Become an Apple."

The 70s and 80s brought a bewildering number of new age disciplines and courses, created by a new breed of new age gurus: Werner Erhardt's est, Whin Wenger's publications and courses, Silva Mind Control, Science of Mind, Lifespring, Esalen workshops, Neuro Linguistic Programming, Rebirthing, Reparenting, Transcendental Meditation, and many kinds of bodywork—all of which involved visualization to some extent.

Certain books stand out along the way as major signposts of the growing knowledge and acceptance of visualization as a powerful technique for change and growth: Samuels 1974 *Seeing With the Mind's Eye*, Benson's 1976 *The Relaxation Response*, Oyle's 1976 *The Healing Mind*, Pelletier's 1977 *Mind as Healer, Mind as Slayer*, Gawain's 1978 *Creative Visualization*, Cousins' 1979 *The Anatomy of an Illness*, Simonton's 1980 *Getting Well Again*, Hay's 1982 *Heal Your Body*, Achterberg's 1985 *Imagery in Healing*, Locke's 1986 *The Healer Within*, Siegel's 1986 *Love, Medicine, and Miracles*, and Dossey's 1991 *Meaning & Medicine*.

The Visualization Establishment

From the titles of the books above, you can see that it is the *healing* powers of visualization that create the most interest. This is understandable, since for people with serious physical problems, visualization can tip the scales from death back to life.

The visualization "establishment" today has a strong medical orientation. It is largely composed of respectable M.D.'s and Ph.D.'s who run cancer and pain clinics and do research that validates and expands the ideas of theorists and less-credentialed practitioners. For example, Jeanne Achterberg works with cancer and other patients in Texas, while her husband, Frank Lawlis, runs a pain clinic. Stephanie Matthews-Simonton and O. Carl Simonton founded the famous Cancer Counseling and Research Center, also in Texas. Bernie S. Siegel is a surgeon working with cancer patients in Connecticut and is teaching at Yale. Many influential authors like Larry Dossey and Mike Samuels are M.D.'s. Irving Oyle is an osteo-path.

In 1991, the U.S. Congress appropriated funds to create the Office of Alter-native Medicine, a new department of the National Institutes of Health that will serve as a clearinghouse for information and give grants to study unconventional medical treatments, including the use of visualization techniques.

Another part of the establishment has a more theoretical orientation. Many members of this group can be found in the International Imagery Association. Their guiding light is Akhter Ahsen, a Pakistani psychologist who developed the Eidetic parent test and formulated the ISM model of imagery, discussed later in the theory section of this chapter.

Some visualization techniques have been institutionalized as part of estab-lished treatment procedures. Visualization plays a big role in biofeedback, now a recognized and widely used tool. Paramedics and trauma center workers are be-ing taught PAMFA—Psychological Assist to Medical First-Aid. This procedure was developed at Iowa State University by D. H. Schuster. Injured patients are encouraged to visualize their experience for the five seconds prior and ten sec-onds after their injury, reliving it in detail. This practice reduces fear and counters the automatic avoidance of the memory. Shock is reduced and blood flow in-creases to the injured area to speed healing.

Visualization first sneaked into the established medical care delivery system by way of the nursing profession. For example, Sensory Information is a technique devised by Jean Johnson for use by nurses. A nurse guides a patient through a detailed visualization of an impending treatment, surgery, or test procedure. Knowing all the details of what is to come greatly reduces fear. It's as if the patient has already "experienced" the stressful event and coped with it successfully. An-other more controversial technique used by some nurses is Therapeutic Touch, developed by Dolores Krieger, professor of nursing at New York University, and Dora Kunz, a gifted healer. In Therapeutic Touch, a nurse or other practitioner passes his or her hands over a sick person with the intent to heal by balancing the flow of the body's energy field. Patients can also learn to do Therapeutic Touch on themselves. Although similar to the Biblical "laying on of hands," this technique is not based on any religious system, and carefully controlled studies have repeatedly shown that it does speed healing.

THEORY

What is visualization? How does it work? What can it be used for? Why is it such a powerful, yet mysterious force for change?

I wish I could give a brief, clear account of the official theory of visualiza-tion, but I can't. No one has yet spoken the last word on visualization. Different experts have put in place different pieces of the puzzle.

The best I can do is explain the various approaches to the question of visu-alization, and summarize the more interesting findings and theories.

The Scientific Approach

Science has hardly touched the "how" and "why" aspects of visualization, since there is so much "what" to study. The most promising areas are brain physiology and the immune system.

Brain Physiology

A look at how the human embryo develops shows why the visual sense is so dominant in waking life and in the imagination. The eyes develop in the embryo from buds on the brain. Your eyes are more part of your brain than any other sense, and are your brain's most direct link to reality.

There are only about two billion brain cells devoted to running your consciousness and speech centers. But there are a *hundred* billion brain cells devoted to your unconscious, to handling patterns and shapes, and to keeping track of your history. Thus, by mere numbers of brain cells, the unconscious is more important than the conscious mind. Visualization operates in an area that is larger in scope and richer in resources than the area allocated to mere conscious thought. No wonder it works so well for solving problems, recovering lost memories, suggesting creative alternatives, and so on.

Left brain/right brain. Your brain is divided in half. It's really two brains in one, with little connection between the halves. Assuming you're right-handed, your left brain controls your logical, verbal processes, while your right brain handles your intuitive, spatial processes. Here is a list of the tasks, qualities, and attributes that are divided up between the two halves of your brain. Again, this list supposes a right-handed person. Lefties are vice-versa.

Left Brain	Right Brain
Rational	Intuitive
Intellectual	Emotional
Linear	Random
Scientific	Artistic
Analytical	Creative
Verbal	Musical
Sequential	Simultaneous
Bound by time	Timeless
Masculine	Feminine
Yang	Yin

Visualization is mostly a right-brain activity—intuitive, emotional, and non-linear. That's why a good visualization doesn't necessarily have to make rational, sequential sense.

This division of the brain suggests that you could improve your powers of visualization by improving other right-brain skills such as doing craft work, studying dreams, dancing, playing musical instruments, and so on.

Computational theories. How does your mind form images? The computational theory is that it works like a computer, with three basic functions:

FIND looks for basic details of an object in memory

PICTURE forms an image of the object

PUT adds details

These three functions supposedly occur over and over again with lightning speed, building up complex scenes. This kind of theory is often called a *digital* theory, based on the way digital computers handle computations: shuffling linear strings of numbers around. The digital theories arc pretty good models for how your brain solves math or logic problems, the same problems for which computers were invented.

However, digital theories are not very satisfactory in explaining either perception or imagination. Your brain sees much faster, catches much finer details and distinctions, and perceives over a much broader range than any computer ever built. There is really no comparison. The digital models appear inadequate to explain the visualization process.

Studies of mental rotation are particularly damaging to digital theory. These studies involve a sensitive machine that measures your eye movement while you are imagining a rotating object in your mind. The machine shows that your eyes move smoothly, not in tiny little jumps, as they would if you were creating a series of separate images. These studies suggest that images are handled in an *analog* manner in your mind.

Analog theories propose that your brain creates and manipulates imaginary scenes in some way that is exactly "analogous" to the way you perceive and examine images of the real world. There are many ways in which visualization is similar to actual perception. For instance, visualization has the same narrow depth of field as perception. If you imagine holding a pencil up two feet from your eyes and focusing on it, the horizon in your imaginary scene will be out of focus. Then if you imagine shifting your attention to the horizon, the imaginary pencil will go out of focus or become double, just as you would experience a real pencil and a real horizon.

Scientists don't really know why, but it's clear that *in the brain* there is no difference between an image of reality and a visualized image. The neurological phenomena are exactly the same. This is the key fact, if not the explanation, behind the power of visualization.

The holographic model of brain function. Some theorists say that you must consider the entire electrical field around the body when studying how you sense reality, store memories, or visualize an image. They say that the electrical activity of the brain, spinal cord, and entire nervous system set up criss-crossing electrical waves, forming repeated, meaningful patterns of wave interference lines that are unique to each individual. The patterns are compared to holograms—three dimensional images created by criss-crossing beams of laser light.

This model of brain function could explain the incredibly rapid and dramatic changes that some people have created in their bodies through visualization alone. It certainly supports theories about the existence and importance of energy flows in the body.

However, at this point holographic brain function is more an interesting theory than a demonstrated fact. Researchers are still trying to figure out how to design experiments to test the theory.

The Philosophical Approach

Philosophy has some interesting things to say about visualization. As usual with philosophy, its conclusions are enormous in their cosmic implications, can be fun to play around with, don't lead to any particular action, and can't be absolutely proven to be true or false.

A big topic in philosophy is the nature of thought—whether it is primarily composed of images or words. Many, after considering the records left by primitive man and observing the development of infants, have decided that images are primary. They point out that images come before language both historically and developmentally. Therefore, images must be the actual stuff of cognition, with words serving as a code or shorthand to describe images. This certainly explains the success of a visualization composed only of images and actions, from which you get the solution to a complex problem.

Another contribution of philosophy is to point out the fallacy of the "mind's eye" concept. In *Eye and Brain*, R. L. Gregory points out that "the notion of brain pictures is conceptually dangerous. It is apt to suggest that these supposed pictures are themselves seen with a kind of inner eye—involving another picture, and another eye, and so on." This *reductio ad infinitum* reminds us that, although it's a convenient metaphor to think of visualization as seeing with the mind's eye, the process is much more complicated and mysterious than that.

Contemplation of visualization plunges you into an old philosophical game of categories. What is the mind? Is it the process of thinking? Is it the seat of personality and memory? What is the body? How do the mind and the body interact to let us know the world? There are four distinct "isms" that philosophers have come up with:

> *Idealism:* The mind is all, the body is an illusion.
>
> *Materialism:* The body is all, the mind is an illusion.
>
> *Parallelism:* The body and the mind both exist, but separately.
>
> *Interactionism:* The body and mind both exist, and they interact.

To explain the power of visualization, the most helpful philosophic stances are Idealism and Interactionism. Most people are Interactionists, using visualization to enhance how their minds interact with their bodies.

Some people are Idealists. They see the mind as the primary or only force in the universe. The body and the rest of physical reality are seen as malleable, secondary phenomena, created and maintained in existence by universal mind power. Taken too far, this proposition can become absurd or lead to delusions of grandeur or paranoia. However, it is an empowering notion in one regard: if you do indeed create your universe entirely in your mind, you can create it any way you like.

The Psychological Approach

Psychologists have contributed the most to our understanding of visualization. Psychology explores visualization in many of its endeavors: the study of real perception and experience, psychosomatic illness, insight into unconscious processes, the nature and relationship of thoughts and feelings, and how behavioral change may be accomplished.

Visualization, Experience, and "Real" Perception

In 1964 two American psychologists named Segal and Nathan asked subjects to visualize a number of images on a blank screen and report what they saw. Sometimes a very faint image was back-projected onto the screen at the same time, without the subjects' knowledge. Some of the projected images were similar to the visualized images and some were dissimilar. It turned out that the subjects were unable to tell the difference between the real projected images and their visualized ones. Some subjects even combined real and visualized images into hybrid versions.

You have undoubtedly experienced somatic imaging: you see, hear, read, or visualize about something happening to another person, and feel it in your own body. You see a movie of a boat in a storm and feel queasy.

Practitioners of Neuro Linguistic Programming, a kind of therapeutic hypnosis, use a technique called "anchoring." A client's feelings of confidence are paired with some positive memory. They have found that when a real memory of an actual event is not available, a fantasy scene works just as well.

When you visualize a relaxing beach scene, your body relaxes in exactly the same way as it would in a real beach scene. When you imagine a prowler breaking into your apartment, your body tenses in just the way it would if there were a real prowler. Although you consciously know the difference between imagination and reality, your unconscious, autonomic systems don't make that distinction. The applications of this phenomenon in psychology include various relaxation techniques, treating anxiety and phobias by systematic desensitization, and teaching clients to cope with difficult people or situations by rehearsing them in fantasy scenes.

Psychosomatic Illness

It's pretty widely known these days that illnesses such as high blood pressure, migraine, and asthma have strong psychosomatic components. These complaints occur more frequently among people who share certain personality traits or habitual behavior patterns, and they can be effectively treated by psychological means such as relaxation training, biofeedback, meditation, self-hypnosis, autogenics, and so on.

Insight Generation

Many methods of psychotherapy depend on clients reaching insights about their childhood, relationships, fears, habitual behavior patterns, emotional responses, and so on. Receptive visualization and guided fantasies have long been a primary method of generating insight. By relaxing your body and letting go of conscious control of your thoughts, you open your mind to messages from your unconscious—long-forgotten memories, beliefs, and feelings can pop to the surface of your awareness in the form of enlightening images.

Fantasies and daydreams are more accessible to analysis than night dreams, and they can be deliberately re-created and altered for therapeutic reasons. Jerome Singer and other researchers claim that daydreams are a richer source of information about personality than night dreams. More psychologists are turning away from the analysis of dreams and concentrating on daydreams, guided fantasies, and receptive visualization.

The ISM Model

The ISM model is one of the most useful theories of how visualization works. It was developed by Akhter Ahsen, a Pakistani psychologist who is the guiding light of the International Imagery Association. According to Ahsen, the mechanics of imagery follow a triple code model:

I—Image

S—Somatic response

M—Meaning

An image usually occurs first in your mind. It is immediately associated with a somatic response—an emotion. This in turn brings up a meaning—some thought associated with or commenting on the image and the emotion. All mental activity involves imagery, and all imagery consists of these three components. When you are remembering painful memories, the somatic (emotional) aspects might be stronger. If you are choosing drapes to go with your new sofa, the image element will probably predominate. If you are computing your car's mileage, the meaning component will be foremost in your mind.

The most vivid and powerful images are called *eidetic* images. In *Psycheye*, Ahsen presents an elaborate diagnostic and insight-generating process called the Eidetic Parent Test. You form an image of both your parents and manipulate the images according to a long list of instructions. The size, position, appearance, and behavior of your parents' images are analysed to tell you about your own personality traits and emotional problems.

Ahsen says that you use abbreviated eidetic images to organize memory. Images tend to be repetitive, constantly reinforcing themselves.

You learn and grow by a series of positive, repeated images that move toward unification and resolution of conflict. Your earliest such images center around your parents, and even in later life, important conflicts that are not directly related to your parents are nevertheless represented by parental images. Actively bringing parental images to bear on a current problem is a good way to solve or resolve it. An Eidetic Parent can even be formed in your mind to substitute for an absent or abusive real parent.

Ahsen comes from a psychoanalytic background, and his eidetic parent image techniques appeal most to traditional psychiatrists who are disenchanted with dream analysis and free association. However, Ahsen's active use of imagery is much more directive and goal-oriented than a Freudian analyst's would be. Behaviorists like Joseph Wolpe have adapted and used his techniques freely. Visualization is thus a unifying force among various schools of therapy.

Cognitive Therapy and Behavioral Change

Cognitive therapists explain painful emotions and undesired behavior by altering the sequence of the ISM model to IMS:

Image—either perceived reality or a memory, appears in your mind and is immediately given a

Meaning—in the form of a statement to yourself about the image. If the statement is negative, it gives rise to a painful

Somatic response—a feeling such as depression, anger, or anxiety.

For example, you see an acquaintance on the other side of the street, walking toward you. His eyes sweep right over you and he continues on without waving or calling out to you. This perception is the image. You say to yourself, "He's ignoring me." This is the *meaning* you assign to the image. Then you feel rejected, hurt, annoyed, and a little depressed. This is the somatic response resulting from your assigned meaning. You dismiss the possibility that your acquaintance might have not seen you, and you don't wave or call out yourself.

This brief encounter can start a negative feedback loop. The feeling of being ignored can call up a new image—the memory of somebody else who ignored you. This new image prompts a new meaning—you say to yourself, "Everybody ignores me, nobody cares about me." This new meaning deepens your somatic response—you feel more depressed. Which brings up more negative images, more negative self-statements, more painful emotions. The cycle continues as you work yourself into a massive depression or a smoldering rage. The next time you see your acquaintance, you snub him and lose a possible friend.

Visualization helps by breaking up the negative feedback loop. You deliberately practice forming images of times when you were accepted and loved by others. You compose and practice affirmations like "I'm a likeable person" and "People respond to me when I share my feelings." You visualize yourself as an open, spontaneous person. The next time you see someone on the street and you start to think, "He's ignoring me," you remember your affirmations and flash back to your pleasant visualizations. The negative feedback loop is weakened and broken up. You wave and call to your friend, cross over and have a nice chat instead of continuing down your side of the street under a cloud.

Often a negative feedback loop is not merely prevented, but changed into a positive loop. You replace the negative image with a positive one, replace the negative meaning with a positive affirmation, and thereby avert the bad feeling and bring about a good feeling. The good feeling allows room for more positive images, more positive meanings, and more good feelings. Undesired behavior declines, replaced by more adaptive behavior.

The deautomatization effect. Visualization affects more than just the problems you apply it to directly. It has a generalized deautomatization effect. After doing visualization, you have an increased awareness. You tend to see more of what is around you, and see it more clearly. There is a decline in your automatic tendency to select, filter, and screen out reality. Another way of putting it is that you gain more control of your thoughts. It is easier to focus sharply on one thing at a time, without distraction. You can think more clearly about your problems and come up with better solutions.

The Religious Approach

Visualization can be practiced as a purely secular, pragmatic technique that maximizes your human potential, with no reference to God or the supernatural. Or it can be integrated comfortably with beliefs in Christian, Moslem, Hindu, Buddhist, or other religious systems. Visualization is the way your mind works, regardless of beliefs. It works whether the first mind was created in Adam by Yaweh four thousand years ago, or whether the mind evolved from slime molds entirely by accident millions of years ago.

In many ways, visualization resembles traditional Christian prayer. Receptive visualization is like asking God for enlightenment. Visualizing what you want in life and getting it is like having your prayers answered by God. There is a reliance on powers beyond your full comprehension. Many people's inner guides seem like divine beings. Your special place could be likened to a church, a place of quiet contemplation and repose, away from the hustle of the world, where you can regain contact with your true nature, your best self. Accentuating the positive and being nonjudgmental about your visualizations are reminiscent of religious faith. Affirmations are often an exercise in hope and charity. Visualizations of a successful future are similar to a religious person's hope for a holy death and life everlasting in heaven. The hyper-aware condition of keen perception that often follows visualization feels like a state of grace.

The New Age Approach

Shakti Gawain's two best-selling books, *Creative Visualization* and *Living in the Light,* set forth very well the current New Age theory of visualization:

The physical universe is energy. Everything is some form of energy. Thought is a light, easily changed form of energy, while matter is a dense, less changeable form. This idea is borne out somewhat by modern physics, which is discovering that everything can indeed be considered some form of energy.

Visualization is positively and consciously aligning yourself with the natural harmony of the universe. What you create in your mind by imagination somehow polarizes or organizes loose energy in the universe, causing your heart's desires to eventually be manifested in objective reality. You can visualize and attain goals on any level—material, emotional, spiritual, or mental. Through visualization you make yourself a channel for the energy of the universe. It flows from you to others, enriching their lives, and from others to you, enriching your life.

According to Gawain, it is not necessary to have faith. The universe is run by visualization, whether you believe in it or not. You always visualize, whether you're conscious of it or not. If you visualize lack, pain, and difficulty, that's what you get. If you visualize riches, pleasure, and ease, you get that.

The ultimate goal of visualization is to live in constant touch with your highest self. This term is used in a way similar to the way I use "the unconscious." Your higher self is a source of creative energy, power, well-being, wisdom, and answers to questions. Metaphors or other terms for the higher self are divine light, divine love, God, a golden sun, warmth, spirit, higher power, guidance, and Christ consciousness.

When you are in touch with your higher self, you experience yourself as Source. You see that you are responsible, in a noncausal and nonlinear way, for everything in the universe. There are invisible, unexplainable, but real connections between every person, place, and event.

Jean Bolen also talks about this self eloquently in *The Tao of Psychology.* She says that you can use the universe as your mirror. You look in it and see yourself. You see all the good things and people in your life and know that you created them. You see all the evil in the world and know that you are not yet perfect.

Louise Hay presents a popular New Age theory to explain the healing power of visualization. Her theory might be called "metaphorical symptomology." By means of a kind of acted-out Freudian slip, your mind translates an emotion into a statement that is then taken literally and expressed as a physical symptom. For example, if you feel tired and hassled, your mind might translate that feeling to "The weight of the world is upon me," and express it as back pain. Or if you feel cut off from your emotions, your mind might say, "I need to tune into my inner voice," and cause you to develop hearing problems that force you to shut out exterior noises.

Your Personal Approach

Ultimately, you will develop your own theory of why and how visualization works—the theory that best fits your world view and explains how visualization works for you.

Don't study other people's theories hoping for some blinding enlightenment or total conversion experience. The value of studying other people's theories lies in what you can borrow for your own theory. You don't have to take everything as gospel. Take what seems reasonable and let the rest go. There's plenty for everyone.

For example, the New Agers bandy the word "energy" around until it means nearly everything or nothing. But it's a valuable concept nonetheless. It's like the term "electricity" in the eighteenth century, when the term was applied to every experiment with static, magnetism, glow worms, phosphorescence, lightning, hypnotism, batteries, and so on. It took decades to settle on the exact meaning of "electricity." Likewise with "energy." You can be sure there's some kind of energy involved in visualization, and you can use energy images to your advantage. But you don't have to believe that you personally created the Milky Way to make visualization work for you.

24

Books, Tapes, and Other Aids

"A man's own observation, what he finds good of and what he finds hurt of, is the best physic to preserve health"

—Francis Bacon

Into this chapter I've thrown the bibliography, names and addresses, and a few "good ideas" that didn't quite fit anywhere else in the book.

Books

The heart of this chapter is the bibliography. It doesn't contain everything ever written about visualization, but it includes the most important and accessible sources.

One book I'd like to mention here is Cirlot's *A Dictionary of Symbols*. This is a good book to consult if very mysterious images pop up during your receptive visualizations and you have trouble figuring out what the symbols might mean. This dictionary is a fascinating listing of images and the meanings that have historically been associated with them in art, literature, and mythology.

For example, let's say you visualize yourself walking through the mountains. You encounter a bear who growls at you. You're scared at first, but then you notice that the bear has no teeth and is stuck in the mud. What could this possibly mean?

Consulting Cirlot's *Dictionary*, you would find these suggestions to spark your imagination:

> *Mountain*—Loftiness of spirit, place of meeting the divine, center of the world
>
> *Bear*—Instinct, cruelty, crudeness, strength, power
>
> *Teeth*—Attack, power. No teeth = emasculation, loss of power
>
> *Mud*—Medium of birth, emergence

So you could interpret your vision as your instinctive power being thwarted and hampered. It's stuck, but perhaps ready for rebirth.

On the other hand, maybe your personal history defines mountains as boring, bears as your father, teeth as anxiety about dental work, and quicksand as a reminder of your childhood sandbox. You still have to be the final judge. Do several visualizations to check your book-aided interpretations.

Other treatments of common symbology are Jung's *Man and His Symbols* and Mike Samuels' *Seeing With the Mind's Eye*, especially the chart on pages 96 and 97.

There's one class of literature that isn't included in the bibliography, but reading it might help you experience more creative visualizations. This might be called "right brain" literature, because it relies on an intuitive rather than logical understanding and deals with the creative, magical, and nonrational side of human experience. Examples are Zen koans, Greek myths, *Aesop's Fables*, *Don Quixote*, *The Arabian Nights*, American Indian tales about Coyote, and Idries Shah's collections of Sufi tales about Nasrudin.

Audio Tapes

Leaving music aside for the moment, there are many guided visualization tapes available that rely mostly on the spoken word. They can be helpful in several ways. (1) They can focus your attention if your mind tends to wander during visualization. (2) The more imaginative tapes can supply new, powerful images you might not be able to create on your own. (3) Putting your tape into the machine and donning your headphones can become part of a relaxing, reassuring ritual. (4) If tapes have been created by knowledgeable practitioners with feedback from their clients and their own experience, you can be assured that the techniques have worked for others, boosting your own confidence and expectation of success.

However, using tapes has some drawbacks. (1) By focusing your attention for you, they can delay the development of your natural powers of concentration. (2) They can stifle your creativity by presenting canned, ready-made images. (3) You may become so dependent on the tape machine and headphones that you can't visualize effectively without them. (4) A lot of tapes are of poor quality, and they might put you off visualization entirely.

Do the advantages outweigh the drawbacks? Only you can tell for yourself. Try several different tapes before you finally make up your mind.

I have produced six tapes so far to go with this book:

Visualization for Stress Reduction

Visualization for Allergies and Asthma

Visualization for Treating Cancer

Visualization for Healing Injuries

Visualization for Curing Infectious Diseases

Visualization for Shyness

These tapes are $11.95 each and can be found in some bookstores or ordered direct from:

New Harbinger Publications
5674 Shattuck Ave.
Oakland, CA 94609
1-800-748-6273

Making Your Own Tape

If your mind tends to wander, it may help to make your own personalized tape to keep yourself on track. A personalized tape can also be a big help if you are using visualization for relaxation. You can compose your tape like a work of art, with exactly the timing, tone, and images that help you relax most. You might also want to make a tape to preserve an especially vivid and appealing visualization that you'd like to experience again.

Since it's just for you, your own tape doesn't have to be as slick as a commercial studio product. But you will want a clear, effective recording. Here are a few guidelines to help you make the best possible tape:

1. Work from a script. Write down exactly what you want to say. This is the best way to avoid hesitations, poor organization, and awkward phrasing. If reading from a word-for-word script sounds too mechanical, try working from a detailed outline that reminds you of each point in sequence but allows you to improvise the exact phrasing.

2. Address yourself as "you" on the tape, as if you were hypnotizing yourself.

3. Include all the steps of an effective visualization. You don't want to have to turn your machine on and off during a visualization, so include all the steps: lying down, closing eyes, breathing, progressive muscle relaxation, going to your special place, consulting with your inner guide, deepening relaxation, intensifying images, affirmations, and so on to the end of the session, concluding with "Now open your eyes, get up, and turn off the tape player." If you don't want to record detailed instructions for a part of the visualization, just leave a long period of silence in which to do that part.

4. Maximize technical quality. Use the best machine available to you. Get a decent microphone, not the condenser mike built into most machines. Clean the heads with alcohol on a cotton swab. Buy a new, high quality tape. Record in the quietest room of the house or in the dead of night to eliminate background noise. Experiment with different heights and distances from the microphone.

5. Rehearse to warm up your voice and smooth the rough spots of your delivery. Stand or sit up straight, get relaxed, and speak in a clear, normal tone. Speak slowly and leave longer pauses than it seems you need to—when you're using the tape to guide your visualization, you will be more relaxed, with your time sense stretched out to a more leisurely pace. Don't record when you're tired, jittery, or after a heavy meal.

6. Revise and revise. Use your tape a couple of times, then rerecord it slower, with different words, or in a different sequence. Add and subtract parts until it's just the way you want it.

If you want to combine music with your tape, there are two techniques you can use. If you have rehearsed well and have a good microphone, you can just play music on your stereo in the background while recording your tape. Experiment with microphone placement until the relative levels of voice and music are the way you want them. The problem with this approach is that you have to do the whole tape in one "take," otherwise there will be glitches in the music background where you stopped and rerecorded part of your script. Also, a poor quality microphone or bad acoustics in the room can make the music sound tinny or like it's playing in an echo chamber.

The other way to combine music with your tape is to simply make the tape with voice alone. Then when you listen to your tape, just have your stereo playing in the background. If you use lightweight earphones for the tape and turn the background music up loud, it will come through the earphones at about the right level.

Music

Music, whether "New Age," classical, popular, or primitive shamanistic drums and rattles, can be a valuable aid to visualization. Listening to music is relaxing. It engages your emotional, nonverbal processes. It helps focus your mind. And it often seems to elicit richer images than you can create unaided.

There is a whole school of visualization using music called G.I.M.—Guided Imagery and Music. Helen Bonny is the founder of the Institute for Music and Imagery, which provides workshops and a three-phase training program for practitioners. In a G.I.M. session, you relax and freely visualize while listening to quality recordings of carefully selected classical music. During and after the visualization, you discuss your experience with a trained guide who is there to encourage you, comfort you, and ask questions that can lead you into deeper self-awareness.

Interactive Guided Imagery

I learned this technique from my friend John Argue, who used it as the core of an "affirmation group" in Berkeley, California. This support group gets together every week or so—not to work on particular problems, but to "get good feelings, open up and make more of ourselves available, explore fears, experience wholeness, and do good art."

Here's how it works: you lie down, close your eyes, and relax, focusing on your breathing. Your partner or guide sits nearby, observing your breathing, talking to you, and listening to your story.

You tell your guide what you are experiencing in your visualization. It's your guide's job to get you started and encourage you by such statements as:

Follow your breath inward.

To begin, report your awareness of feelings, sensations.

I give you my support and my permission to _____
(see or do whatever you are seeing or doing in your visualization).

Your guide listens carefully to your description of your vision, and occasionally interrupts if you seem stuck, saying something like:

Can you make that more intense? Less intense? Which do you prefer?

Is there a color (or sound or smell or taste) associated with it?

Would you like to lighten it?

Put that part in charge and see what happens.

Let that image (or person or beast or color) be your ally.

Your guide uses a quiet voice and may sometimes touch you. You can ask your guide for permission not to report on what you're seeing for a while if you want to. If there are others from your group present, they might make some quiet comments. Most people find themselves making hand gestures to describe their visualizations, sculpting images in the air.

The day I tried this with John's group, I found the experience exciting. At first, I thought that describing my visualization and listening to my guide would get in the way of the images, making them fragmented and dim. But the opposite was true. I found that the interaction made my images more vivid, my relaxation deeper, and the "plot" of the experience that I was creating more intricate and satisfying.

I later theorized that the interaction with a guide is like being hypnotized by a hypnotist who uses "fractionation." Fractionation is taking a subject in and out of a trance several times in succession. Each time, the reinstated trance is deepened.

If you have a friend who is also interested in visualization, by all means try this kind of interactive guided imagery.

Other Aids

If you have trouble keeping your eyes closed, try a sleep mask. You can buy them at large drugstores. Consider ear plugs if outside noises distract you. The logical extension of these kinds of aids is the flotation tank. You float on your back in a tank of saline solution heated to a temperature that feels neither hot nor cold. All light, sound, and smells are excluded. The air is warm, moist, and still.

In the 60s subjects spent hours in crude "sensory deprivation" tanks, often after taking hallucinogenic drugs. There was speculation at the time that sensory deprivation could induce psychosis and that it would end up being used for brainwashing by secret police. This furor has died down and researchers now use flotation tanks to enhance relaxation and study its healing powers.

For most people, shutting off outside stimuli is profoundly relaxing and enhances visualization with vivid, exciting, spontaneous images. If you get a chance to float for an hour in a tank, try it.

Another aid to visualization is a diary or journal. Regularly recording your visualizations serves several purposes. You can remember more of your fantasies by getting them down on paper. You have an historical record of your insights and images to consult and enjoy. The act of writing makes you think about your images and helps you to elicit their full meaning.

Bibliography

Achterberg, Jeanne. *Imagery in Healing: Shamanism and Modern Medicine*. Boston: Shambhala Publications, 1985.

Ahsen, Akhter. *Psycheye*. New York: Brandon House, 1977.

Alexander, Franz. *Psychosomatic Medicine*. New York: W.W. Norton, 1950.

Arnheim, Rudolf. *Visual Thinking*. Berkeley: University of California Press, 1972.

Assaglioli, Roberto. *The Act of Will*. New York: Viking, 1973.

Assaglioli, Roberto. *Psychosynthesis*. New York: Hobbs, Dorman & Co., 1965.

Beck, Aaron T. *Cognitive Therapy and the Emotional Disorders*. New York: New American Library, 1976.

Benson, Herbert. *The Relaxation Response*. New York: Avon, 1976.

Bolen, Jean Shinoda. *The Tao of Psychology*. New York: Harper & Row, 1979.

Bourne, Edmund J. *The Anxiety & Phobia Workbook*. Oakland, CA: New Harbinger Publications, 1990

Bry, Adelaide. *Visualization: Directing the Movies of Your Mind*. New York: Barnes & Noble, 1978.

Brown, Barbara. *New Mind, New Body*. New York: Harper & Row, 1974.

Cannon, Walter B. *The Wisdom of the Body*. New York: Norton, 1967.

Carty, Amy O. *Postitive Visualizations. For People with Cancer & Those Who Love Them*. Lee, MA: Birchard Books, 1993

Catalano, Ellen Mohr. *Getting to Sleep*. Oakland, CA: New Harbinger Publications, 1990.

Catalano, Ellen Mohr. *The Chronic Pain Control Workbook*. Oakland, CA: New Harbinger Publications, 1987.

Cirlot, J. E. *A Dictionary of Symbols*. New York: Philosophical Library, 1962.

Copeland, Mary Ellen. *The Depression Workbook*. Oakland, CA: New Harbinger Publications, 1992.

Coué, Emil. *Self-Mastery Through Conscious Auto-Suggestion*. London: Allen & Unwin, 1922.

Cousins, Norman. *Anatomy of an Illness as Perceived by the Patient*. New York: Bantam Books, 1979.

Cousins, Norman. *Head First: The Biology of Hope*. New York: E.P. Dutton, 1989.

Csikszentmihalyi, Mihaly. *Flow: The Psychology of Optimal Experience*. New York: Harper & Row, 1990.

Davis, Martha, Eshelman, Elizabeth Robbins, and McKay, Matthew. *The Relaxation and Stress Reduction Workbook* 4th ed: Oakland, CA: New Harbinger Publications, 1994.

DeMille, Richard. *Put Your Mother on the Ceiling: Children's Imagination Games*. New York: Viking Press, 1973.

Dossey, Larry. *Recovering the Soul*. New York: Bantam Books, 1989.

Dossey, Larry. *Space, Time & Medicine*. Boston: Shambhala, 1982.

Fanning, Patrick. *Lifetime Weight Control*. Oakland, CA: New Harbinger Publications, 1990.

Friedman, Meyer, and Rosenman, Ray H. *Type A Behavior and Your Heart*. New York: Fawcett World, 1976.

Gagne, Robert M. *The Conditions of Learning*. New York: Holt, Rinehart, and Winston, 1965.

Gallwey, W. Timothy. *The Inner Game of Tennis.* New York: Random House, 1974.

Garfield, P. *Creative Daydreaming.* New York: Simon & Schuster, 1975.

Gardner, Howard. *Art, Mind, & Brain.* New York: Basic Books, 1982.

Gawain, Shakti. *Creative Visualization.* Mill Valley, CA: Whatever Publishing, 1978.

Gawain, Shakti. *The Creative Visualization Workbook.* Berkeley, CA: New World Library, 1992.

Gawain, Shakti, with Grimshaw, Denise, ed. *Reflections in the Light: Daily Thoughts and Affirmations.* Mill Valley, CA: Whatever Publishing, 1988.

Gawain, Shakti, with King, Laurel. *Living in the Light.* Mill Valley, CA: Whatever Publishing, 1986.

Ghiselin, Brewster. *The Creative Process.* New York: New American Library, 1952.

Gregory, R. L. *Eye and Brain.* New York: McGraw Hill, 1973.

Hadley, Josie, and Staudacher, Carol. *Hypnosis for Change.* Oakland, California: New Harbinger Publications, 1985.

Hall, John F. *Psychology of Motivation.* New York: Lippincott, 1961.

Harner, Michael. *The Way of the Shaman.* New York: Harper & Row, 1980.

Harp, David. *The New Three Minute Meditator.* Oakland, CA: New Harbinger Publications, 1990.

Hay, Louise L. *You Can Heal Your Life.* Santa Monica, CA: Hay House, 1988.

Hilgard, Ernest R. *Divided Consciousness: Multiple Controls in Human Thought and Action.* New York: John Wiley & Sons, 1977.

Holmes, Thomas H. and Ella H. David, eds. *Life Change, Life Events, and Illness: Selected Papers.* New York: Praeger, 1989.

Horowitz, M. *Image Formation and Cognition.* New York: Appleton-Century-Crofts, 1970.

Hutschnecker, Arnold. *The Will to Live.* New York: Simon & Schuster, 1966.

Huxley, Aldous. *The Art of Seeing.* New York: Harper & Row, 1942.

Jacobson, Edmund. *Progressive Relaxation.* Chicago: University of Chicago Press, 1942.

Jung, C. G. *Man and His Symbols.* New York: Doubleday, 1968.

Jung, C. G. *Memories, Dreams, Reflections.* New York: Vintage Books, 1963.

Justice, Blair. *Who Gets Sick: Thinking and Health.* Houston: Peak Press, 1987.

Kane, Jeff. *Be Sick Well: A Healthy Approach to Chronic Illness.* Oakland, CA: New Harbinger Publications, 1991.

Kanfur, F. K., and Goldstein, A. P., eds. *Helping People Change.* New York: Pergamon Press, 1974.

Kano, Susan. *Making Peace With Food: A Step-By-Step Guide to Freedom from Diet/Weight Conflict.* Boston: Amity, 1985.

Klinger, E. *Structure and Functions of Fantasy.* New York: Wiley, 1971.

Korn, E. R., and Johnson, K. *Visualization: The Use of Imagery in the Health Professions.* Homewood, IL: Dow Jones-Irwin, 1983.

Kosslyn. *Visual Cognition.* Boston: M.I.T. Press, 1986.

Krieger, Dolores. *Foundations of Holistic Health: Nursing Practices.* Philadelphia: J. P. Lippincott, 1981.

Krieger, Dolores. *The Therapeutic Touch.* Engelwood Cliffs, NJ: Prentice-Hall, 1979.

Lazarus, Richard S. *Stress, Appraisal, and Coping.* New York: Springer, 1984.

Lewis, Howard R., and Lewis, Martha E. *Psychosomatics.* New York: Pinnacle Books, 1975.

LeShan, Lawrence. *The Dilemma of Psychology.* New York: E.P. Dutton, 1990.

Locke, Steven, and Colligen, Douglas. *The Healer Within.* New York: E.P. Dutton, 1986.

Luria, A. *The Mind of a Mnemonist.* New York: Basic Books, 1968.

Luthe, Wolfgang, ed. *Autogenic Therapy. Six vols.* New York: Grune & Stratton, 1969. *See also* Schultz, J. H.

McKay, Judith, and Nancee Hirano. *The Chemotherapy Survival Guide.* Oakland, CA: New Harbinger Publications, 1993.

McKay, Matthew, Davis, Martha, and Fanning, Patrick. *Messages: The Communication Skills Book.* Oakland, CA: New Harbinger Publications, 1983.

McKay, Matthew, Davis, Martha, and Fanning, Patrick. *Thoughts & Feelings: The Art of Cognitive Stress Intervention.* Oakland, CA: New Harbinger Publications, 1981.

McKay, Matthew, and Fanning, Patrick. *Self-Esteem,* 2nd ed. Oakland, CA: New Harbinger Publications, 1993.

McKellar, Peter. *Imagination and Thinking.* London: Cohen & West, 1957.

McKim, Robert. *Experiences in Visual Thinking.* Monterey, CA: Brooks Cole Publishing, 1972.

Maltz, Maxwell. *Psycho-Cybernetics.* New York: Pocket Books, 1966.

Marks, David F., ed. *Theories of Image Formation.* New York: Brandon House, 1986.

Markway, Barbara G., et al. *Dying of Embarrassment: Help for Social Anxiety and Social Phobia.* Oakland, CA: New Harbinger Publications, 1992.

Masters, Robert, and Houston, Jean. Mind Games. NewYork: Dell, 1972.

May, Rollo. *The Courage to Create.* New York: W.W. Norton, 1975.

Mednick, Sarnoff A. *Learning.* Englewood Cliffs, NJ: Prentice-Hall, 1964.

Moen, Larry. *Guided Imagery, vols 1 & 2.* Maple, FL: United States Publisher, 1992.

Murray, Edward J. *Motivation and Emotion.* Englewood Cliffs, NJ: Prentice-Hall, 1964.

Naranjo, Claudio, and Ornstein, Robert. *On the Psychology of Meditation*. New York: Viking Press, 1971.

Novaco, Raymond W. *Anger Control*. Lexington, MA: Lexington Books, 1975.

Olson, Robert W. *The Art of Creative Thinking*. New York: Harper & Row, 1986.

Ornstein, Robert. *The Psychology of Consciousness*. San Francisco: W.H. Freeman & Co., 1972.

Ornstein, Robert, and Sobel, David. *The Healing Brain: Breakthrough Discoveries About How the Brain Keeps Us Healthy*. New York: Simon & Schuster, 1987.

Osborn, A. F. *Applied Imagination: Principles and Procedures of Creative Problem Solving*. 3rd ed. New York: Scribner's, 1963.

Oyle, Irving. *The Healing Mind*. New York: Pocket Books, 1976.

Oyle, Irving. *Time, Space and the Mind*. Millbrae, CA: Celestial Arts, 1976.

Patrick, C. *What is Creative Thinking?* New York: Philosophical Library, 1955.

Pavio, A. *Imagery and Verbal Processes*. New York: Holt and Rinehart, 1971.

Pelletier, Kenneth. *Mind as Healer, Mind as Slayer*. New York: Dell, 1977.

Quick, Thomas L. *The Quick Motivation Method*. New York: St. Martin's Press, 1980.

Richardson, A. *Mental Imagery*. New York: Springer Publishing Co., 1969.

Rossman, Martin L. *Healing Yourself: A Step By Step Process for Better Health Through Imagery*. New York: Walker, 1987.

Rugg, H. *Imagination*. New York: Harper & Row, 1963.

Samuels, Mike, and Samuels, Nancy. *Seeing With the Mind's Eye: The History, Techniques and Uses of Visualization*. New York: Random House, 1975.

Satir, Virginia. *People Making*. Palo Alto, CA: Science and Behavior Books, 1975.

Schachtel, E. *Metamorphosis*. New York: Basic Books, 1959.

Schultz, J. H., and Luthe, Wolfgang. *Autogenic Training: A Psychophysiological Approach to Psychotherapy*. New York: Gruen & Stratton, 1959.

Scientific American. *Altered States of Awareness*. San Francisco: W.H. Freeman & Co., 1972.

Segal, S. J. *The Adaptive Functions of Imagery*. New York: Academic Press, 1971.

Selye, Hans. *The Stress of Life*. New York: McGraw-Hill, 1956.

Selye, Hans. *Stress Without Distress*. New York: New American Library, 1974.

Shealy, C. Norman. *90 Days to Self-Health*. New York: The Dial Press, 1977.

Sheehan, P., ed. *The Function and Nature of Imagery*. New York: Academic Press, 1972.

Siegel, Bernie S. *Love, Medicine, and Miracles*. New York: Harper & Row, 1986.

Simonton, O. C., Matthews-Simonton, S., and Creighton, J. L. *Getting Well Again*. New York: Bantam Books, 1980.

Singer, Jerome L. *Daydreaming*. New York: Random House, 1966.

Singer, Jerome L. *Imagery and Daydream Methods in Psychotherapy and Behavior Modification*. New York: Academic Press, 1974.

Singer, Jerome, and Switzer, Ellen. *Mind-Play: The Creative Uses of Fantasy*. Englewood Cliffs, NJ: Prentice-Hall, 1980.

Sontag, Susan. *Illness as Metaphor*. New York: Farrar, Straus and Giroux, 1977.

Stevens, John O. *Awareness*. Real People Press, 1971.

Tart, Charles, ed. *Altered States of Consciousness*. New York: Doubleday Anchor, 1972.

Taylor, Shelley E. *Postivie Illusions: Creative Self-Deception and the Healthy Mind*. New York: E.P. Dutton, 1989.

Thomas, Lewis. *The Youngest Science*. New York: Viking Press, 1983.

Toben, Bob, Sarfatti, Jack, and Wolf, Fred. *Space-Time and Beyond*. New York: E.P. Dutton, 1975.

Tutko, Thomas, and Sosi, Umberto. *Sports Psyching*. Los Angeles: Westwood Publishing, 1976.

Vernon, Phillip E. *Creativity: Selected Readings*. New York: Penguin Books, 1970.

Watzlawick, P., Weakland, J., and Fisch, R. *Change*. New York W.W. Norton, 1974.

Wells, Valerie. *The Joy of Visualization: 75 Creative Ways to Enhance Your Life*. San Francisco: Chronical Books, 1990.

Winger, Wen. *Voyages of Discovery*. Gaithersburg, MD: Psychegenics Press, 1977.

Wolpe, Joseph, with Wolpe, David. *Life Without Fear*. Oakland, CA: New Harbinger Publications, 1988.

Other New Harbinger Self-Help Titles